Julia Kristeva

SUNY series in Gender Theory

Tina Chanter, editor

JULIA KRISTEVA

Psychoanalysis and Modernity

Sara Beardsworth

STATE UNIVERSITY OF NEW YORK PRESS

Published by
State University of New York Press, Albany

© 2004 State University of New York

All rights reserved

Printed in the United States of America

No part of this book may be used or reproduced in any manner whatsoever without written permission. No part of this book may be stored in a retrieval system or transmitted in any form or by any means including electronic, electrostatic, magnetic tape, mechanical, photocopying, recording, or otherwise without the prior permission in writing of the publisher.

For information, address State University of New York Press,
90 State Street, Suite 700, Albany, NY 12207

Production by Judith Block
Marketing by Michael Campochiaro

Library of Congress Cataloging in Publication Data

Beardsworth, Sara.
Julia Kristeva : psychoanalysis and modernity / Sara Beardsworth.
p. cm. — (SUNY series in gender theory)
Includes bibliographical references and index.
ISBN 0–7914–6189–0 (alk. paper) — ISBN 0–7914–6190–4 (pbk. : alk. paper)
1. Kristeva, Julia, 1941– I. Title. II. Series

B2430.K7544B43 2004
194—dc22

2004041628

10 9 8 7 6 5 4 3 2 1

To my family

CONTENTS

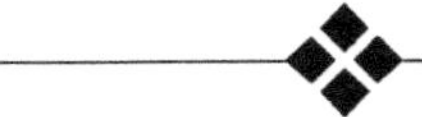

Part II. Religion and Art: Kristeva's Minor Histories of Modernity

Part III. The Social and Political Implications of Kristeva's Thought

ACKNOWLEDGMENTS

This book has taken some while to come to fruition. Its planning and writing covers a period that includes my move from England to America. During the early stages I spent an enlivening two semesters in 1996–1997 as Visiting Assistant Professor in the Philosophy Department at Vanderbilt University. My thanks to David Wood for making this possible, and for his enthusiastic encouragement of my plans to seek a position in America. While doing this, I received support in 1997–1998 as Visiting Research Fellow in the School of Historical and Cultural Studies at Goldsmith's College, University of London. At the University of Memphis a New Faculty Research Initiation Award gave generous financial support for the summer of 2000, which enabled me to make strides in completing the first draft of the book.

More specific intellectual and personal debts are owed to others, including those who, for different reasons, have not been close by as the project was brought to completion. My earliest philosophical debt is to Gillian Rose, the director of my doctoral thesis undertaken at the University of Warwick. Gillian gave me, and others I believe, an initiation into European philosophical thought of such intellectual vigor and spiritual strength that it will last a lifetime. I like to think that she would have appreciated some of the directions taken in this book. The development of my thinking was greatly encouraged and stimulated by Richard Beardsworth and Howard Caygill. Their support for my chosen path of philosophy, as well as their appreciation of and critical responses to my attempts to bring together divergent aspects of European thought, have been invaluable.

There is one person who has seen this project through from start to finish, and who has given unflagging support in the whole task. I owe my deepest debt to Jay Bernstein, not only in these respects, but for a friendship which, thanks to his personal warmth and the generous communication of a genuine philosophical vision, has long been a mainstay of my life and a provocation to thinking. During recent years in America, Gregg Horowitz has also given unstinting support for this project. He has been a vital interlocutor, especially with respect to the rigors and rewards of pursuing psychoanalytic thoughts in a philosophical context. I am grateful to Gregg and Ellen for their friendship. I am indebted, too, in order of appearance, to Tori McGeer and Ron Sundstrom for conversations and friendship in which the gap between the analytic and continental traditions of philosophy narrowed to insignificance, without our losing sight of the values that different trainings have brought us.

I owe a very profound debt to Tina Chanter for the quite concrete support that she has given me in the North American philosophical world, and, no less, for the example of courage and commitment that she shows in the pursuit of her own intellectual paths. More recently, Mary Beth Mader has also broadened my vision of what it is to take on, struggle with, and take departures from the tradition known as French feminism. I am grateful to her for this, for her collegiality, her unique gifts of recognition, her sense of futurity, and her friendship. My thanks to Robert Bernasconi for his encouraging comments on an initial draft and continuing support. I owe a debt of gratitude to many students who have made graduate seminars a genuine forum of learning and exchange, and would like to thank Athena Colman, Stacy Keltner, and Valentine Moulard, especially, for their intellectual curiosity and philosophical acumen, their ideas, and for building their own paths.

I owe a special debt to Jane Bunker at the State University of New York Press for taking on this project, and working with me at the various stages of getting it to press; and to Judith Block for guiding me through the production process.

Finally, I am grateful to my family for their support over the years, in relation to some false starts as well as the propitious beginnings. My parents' energy and excitement in encouraging their children to discover and experience the languages, cultures, and histories of the diverse terrain known as Europe was an invaluable gift. More recently my family has provided sensitive support in my transition from Europe to America. I thank Pat, Neville, Jane, Richard, Valerie, and Brian (*in memoriam*), for having forged new families, and for continuing to teach me—often from afar—what I miss about them, as well as many things about living away from and revisiting one's land of origin, something in which they all had experience long before I did. This book is dedicated to them.

INTRODUCTION

What moves the argument of this book is the thought that unacknowledged suffering is the remnant of freedom in conditions of late modernity. This is Kristeva's thought. . . . Let me begin again by outlining this project's three major objectives. The first is to explicate the central psychoanalytic, aesthetic, ethical, and political concepts in Kristeva's writings from the mid-1970s to the early 1990s, with a special emphasis on her 1980s thought. The second is to develop an interpretation of her thought as a philosophy of modernity sensitive to the problem of modern nihilism, arguing that this interpretation best captures her vision and project and best enables the assessment of that project, especially Kristeva's choice of psychoanalysis and the aesthetic to structure her thought, but also her relationship to religion. Third, I revisit the most troubled questions in the reception of her writings on the basis of this interpretation, in order to clarify why so many are intrigued by them, and then all but the few move on. This book introduces and readdresses the problems but also works to illuminate and reinforce the intrigue by clarifying the reasons for it.

It needs to be acknowledged that, at first sight, the classification of her *oeuvre* as a philosophy of modernity might strike readers of Kristeva as unconvincing. Given her turn to psychoanalysis and art, it would seem to be necessary to recognize that the *oeuvre* is best characterized as a philosophy of culture rooted in the psychoanalytic view of subjectivity. However, it is the very way in which psychoanalysis structures her thought which justifies the claim that it is a philosophy of modernity. I argue that the central texts of Kristeva's writings of the 1980s contain a self-consciousness of the emergence and significance of psychoanalysis as a discourse embedded in conditions of modern nihilism. Moreover, these writings unfold a specific conception of the aesthetic that is only fully intelligible in respect of that self-consciousness. This view of her thought is supported by the structure and content of what will be called the trilogy of the 1980s: *Powers of Horror* (1980), *Tales of Love* (1983), and *Black Sun* (1987). The overarching claim is that Kristeva's sensitivity to the problem of modern nihilism needs to be recognized if the reception of her thought is not to break off in puzzlement over such issues as the apparent ambiguities or ambivalences in her estimation of psychoanalysis, her view of religion, and the meaning of the Kristevan aesthetic. This is the central message of this book, but one that is relatively submerged at moments of close explication of textual passages, since, as is known by readers of Kristeva, her writings tend to lack the kind of critical self-reflection that would thematize for the reader what she is up to. Although such thematization is one of the challenges this book must meet, a more extensive discussion of the meaning of nihilism than appears anywhere in the chapters of this book is merited, indeed required, here. What is attempted as part of this introduction is an account of the meanings of nihilism that have appeared in the history of modern philosophy, and how they have appeared, so that the sensitivity to modern nihilism that I claim is present in Kristeva's writings can be clarified. The following account is designed both to explain the term *nihilism* for those unfamiliar with that philosophical tradition and to allow me to show how Kristeva's thought differs from it.

Suffering: A Piece of the Reality that has Come to Grief

The presence of the nihilism problematic in modern philosophy has a complex and nuanced history. Heidegger declares that the word nihilism apparently first appears in Jacobi's criticism of modern philosophical idealism (1982, 3). In the "Open Letter to Fichte," published in 1799, Jacobi responds to German idealism in the consummated shape it appears to take on in Fichte's philosophy, given the latter's attempt at a reunification of reason after Kant's critical project. The critique of reason undertaken by Kant determined the limits of theoretical reason—of human knowledge—according to a restriction of its object-domain, which becomes the realm of necessity. That is to say, the critical project aimed to overcome the illusions of thought that takes flight from the limits that experience imposes on knowledge. Knowledge is constrained above all by the forms of time and space and by the necessity that concepts cannot be divorced from the manifold given in sensory awareness—what Kant calls intuition—without voiding themselves of all cognitive power. Knowledge in Kant is the organization of the raw material of sensibility by the synthesizing activity of categories such as existence or nonexistence, causality, and so on. The categories have "objective validity": they are a priori universals or antecedent conditions for the possibility of experience, and so for the possibility of objects of experience. Not only are sensible individuals, or intuitions, without concepts "blind," but concepts without intuitions are "empty."[1] When conceptualization attempts to overreach these limits, reason itself becomes entangled in self-conflict on questions such as the origin of the world, the causality of freedom, and the existence of God and the soul. Kant's critical project recovered the realm of freedom only by reserving it for practical reason, that is to say, for unknowable but intelligible pure practical reason as the foundation of the moral law that finite rational creatures give to themselves.[2] The result of the critical philosophy is that the human spirit is henceforth internally divided between freedom and necessity, whose reciprocal communication must remain impossible if both knowledge and morality are to be saved.

Fichte was a great admirer of Kant's achievement in safeguarding actual knowledge and practical reason by dissolving the threat brought to them by metaphysical illusions. However, he was equally sensitive to the blow to knowledge that the critique inflicted, and to the self-alienation it set up at the heart of the human spirit, eternally divided between heteronomy in knowledge and experience (determination from without) and autonomy in morality (self-legislating reason). His attempt to reunify theoretical and practical reason grounds philosophy in a foundational act of the transcendental—that is to say, impersonal—subject from which all knowledge and practice flows. Fichte develops this thought out of Kant's idea of a pure act of spontaneity—the transcendental unity of apperception—which cannot belong to sensibility. In Kant this is the "I think" that must accompany all my representations, without which nothing can become an object for me. Fichte's *Wissenschaftslehre* or doctrine of scientific knowledge (1797) introduces the self-positing "I" as an act that embraces the theoretical and practical aspects of reason, and which is the absolute principle of philosophy as science.

Jacobi does not object to the Fichtean affirmation of the concept of science as the autonomous production of its object in thought, a "free action" of mind. For without this reflection would be a futile activity. What he objects to in the "Open Letter to Fichte" is the desire and belief that this free action of the mind reveals the basis of all truth *to be* the absolutely self-positing I out of which all objects, worldhood, and practical agency develop (1799, 124–125). He finds that Fichte's thought is the philosophizing of pure understanding in which everything is dissolved into the concept. In other words, Fichte's ambition for philosophy as science implies the dissolution of all "essences"—including all beings and productions of unreason (the "not-I" in Fichte's language)—into knowledge that develops on the basis of a thoroughgoing abstraction. The result of this, for Jacobi, is nihilism, a self-destruction of the human spirit whose confinement to the realm of concepts deprives it of everything that would give those concepts meaning and value. Subjected to idealism, the human spirit "must destroy itself in essence in order to arise, to have itself solely in concept; in the concept of a pure absolute emerging from and entering into, originally—from nothing, to nothing, for nothing, into nothing" (1799, 127). Fichte's idealization of philosophy as science does not remedy but intensifies the loss inflicted upon the human spirit by the critical philosophy. It is a purification of spirit so absolute that spirit cannot *exist* in its purity but "can only be present, contemplated" in a pure identity-drive (126, 135). Jacobi opposes this fate of reason and the human spirit with an insistence upon something prior to knowing, which he calls "the true," that gives knowing and the capacity for reason *a value* (131). Although he does not recommend a return to precritical philosophy, he would be content to be understood as affirming "chimera" over the nihilism that Fichte's consummation of transcendental idealism enforces (136).

Jacobi's *naming* of idealism as nihilism, his *discontent* with idealism, and his affirmation of the *privilegium aggratiandi*—"the law [of reason] is made for the sake of the human being, not the human being for the sake of the law" (1799, 133)—can themselves be located as an event of nihilism in a much wider and almost all-embracing sense of the term that arises in a later philosophy: Nietzsche's. This is the most influential thought on nihilism. "When it comes to our understanding of nihilism, we are almost all Nietzscheans" (Gillespie 1995, xii). It is the Nietzschean thought on nihilism that I must carefully, but not overly, distinguish my claim about Kristeva from. There are two major interpretations of Nietzsche's thought on nihilism, the Heideggerian one and the one that captures a major aspect of Weber's and Adorno's debt to Nietzsche. It is worth contrasting these two interpretations since this best clarifies Kristeva's difference from the most familiar thought of nihilism as turning on *the loss of transcendence.* Both interpretations concur that there are a variety of meanings of nihilism in Nietzsche and that their connection is historical, and both agree that the idea of European nihilism in his writings presents a catastrophe with a progressive aspect. However, for one the historicality of nihilism is predominantly metaphysical and for the other it is predominantly political and cultural.

Heidegger reads Nietzsche as a metaphysician whose thought on nihilism presents a metanarrative of the formation and collapse of Western metaphysics and the opening up or chance of a "new beginning." Nihilism means, above all, the collapse of the transcendent that reigns from Plato's forms, to Christian-moral culture, to the apotheosis of the self-reflexive subject of knowledge in Kant and Fichte. This last is what Jacobi grasped as nihilism. So the important point about the Jacobi interpretation of transcendental idealism is that he, like Nietzsche, finds that Kant's reliance on the a priori and the universal makes him the last avatar of Platonic-Christian moral thought. With Nietzsche, nihilism means above all the collapse of "the ideal" that sprang from the reign of the transcendent; that is to say, the end of the Christian God. On this reading, Nietzsche's attack on Platonism, Christianity, and Kant sets out different but interconnected versions of a negation that institutes the domination of transcendent elements over life. Life as the infinite growth of the this-worldly being is what is negated. Western metaphysics is the formulation of ideals, norms, principles, rules, ends, and values that, in Heidegger's words, are "set 'above' the being [*das Seiende*], in order to give being as a whole a purpose, an order, and—as it is succinctly expressed—'meaning'" (1982, 4). The Christian God is a condensation of and guarantee for all the transcendent elements, an ideal enabled only by the pure thought of God as the *truth* of being as a whole. This very ideal of truth—the grounding and redemption of all being "beyond" the whole of being—contains its own undoing, and so the undoing of all the transcendent elements it condenses, as this "truth" shows itself to be untruth. "Nihilism is that historical process whereby the dominance of the 'transcendent' becomes null and void so that all being loses its worth and meaning. Nihilism is the history of the being itself, through which the death of the Christian God comes slowly but inexorably to light" (4).[3]

This predominantly metaphysical interpretation of Nietzsche reads the two most famous of his statements on nihilism in an immanent manner. The first statement, from *Will to Power*, says: "What does nihilism mean? That the highest values devalue themselves. The aim is lacking; the 'why' receives no answer" (1967, 9). Heidegger's interpretation of this historical process turns on his reading of the second statement, from *The Gay Science*, which says: "God is dead." With Heidegger, nihilism is "that event of long duration in which the truth of being as a whole is essentially transformed and driven toward an end that such truth has determined" (1982, 4–5). If there appears to be a *deus ex machina* in this transformation, to seek an external cause for the transformation would leave thinking within the metaphysics whose crisis Nietzsche has diagnosed. Any apparent *deus ex machina* is overcome by Heidegger's view that the thought of nihilism must be co-comprehended with four other rubrics of Nietzsche's thought: the revaluation of all values hitherto, will to power, eternal recurrence of the same, and the Overman (*Übermensch*) (1982, chapter 1). These four rubrics express the possibility that arises with the loss of transcendence, once "only the 'earth' remains" (8).

However, it must first be noted that Nietzsche's thought on nihilism develops out of his attention to its psychological aspect, or his discovery of nihilism in subjectivity. In Nietzsche's psychology we find nihilism in the sense of the *critical condition* that emerges with the loss of transcendence. The critical condition is the experience of the exhaustion of meaning that comes with the collapse of all transcendent elements, a pervasive experience of gloom and terror, a nihilistic attitude that affirms nothingness.[4] It needs to be said right off that this is the nihilism that Kristeva repudiates at various moments in her writings. She is not a nihilist. Nietzsche's own comment on this aspect of nihilism brings us to his idea of will to power. For the famous final statement of *The Genealogy of Morals* says of the nihilistic "will to nothingness" that the will prefers to will nothingness than to cease willing (1989, 163). However, the will in Nietzsche does not point to a volitional subject underlying and surviving the exhaustion of all meaning and values. The co-comprehension of nihilism and will to power in Heidegger underlines this. Haar's valuable essay "Nietzsche and Metaphysical Language" is particularly clear on this aspect of the Heideggerian reading. Nietzsche may find a variant of will to power in the nihilistic attitude but will to power is not a psychological phenomenon. The expression will to power cannot be divided into two parts expressing a cause or foundation (will) and its aim or object (power). Rather, the German, *Wille "zur" Macht* conveys the sense of "movement toward," and the question is: "What, then, is this Power?"

> It is precisely the intimate law of the will and of all force, the law that to will is to will its own growth. The will that is Will to Power responds at its origins to its own internal imperative: *to be more*. This imperative brings it before the alternatives: either it is to augment itself, to surpass itself, or it is to decline, to degenerate. According to the direction that the force takes (progression or regression), and according to the response (yes or no) one makes to the conditions imposed upon life or imposed on life by life itself (as Zarathustra says: "I am the one who is ever forced to overcome himself"), there appear, *right at the origin*, at the very heart of the Will to Power, two types of force, two types of life: the active force and the *reactive* force, the *ascending* life and the *decadent* life. (Haar in Allison 1977, 11)

Will to power is therefore fundamentally reflexive, always overcoming itself through one of the two alternatives. This clears up any appearance of a *deus ex machina* in the historical process Heidegger speaks of. For what appears in Nietzsche's thought on the death of God is the culmination of forces or types of life that the highest idea gathered into itself. This unification strengthened the most reactive of types of life by placing meaning and values in a "*beyond*," in denial of life. When Heidegger makes nihilism the history of being itself ("through which the death of the Christian God comes slowly but inexorably to light") the co-comprehension of nihilism and will to power also takes in another of the five rubrics: the revaluation of all values hitherto. For the nihilistic attitude—the critical condition of the experience of the exhaustion of meaning, that doom and gloom of the will to nothingness—is but a simple negation of "truth" that only reactively repeats the death of God and fundamentally preserves the history of Western metaphysics and the Christian ideal as the only—lost—truth, meaning, and value.

The dominance of the transcendent "become null and void" has another aspect, however: that of *self-perfected nihilism.* For the consummation of nihilism opens up the transvaluation of all values. It both uproots values from their place in transcendence and "breeds" a new need of values, says Heidegger. Will to power is then understood as a nontranscendent grounding which permits a new interpretation of beings, without which the recognition of the new need of values would be a merely unanchored intuition, likely to become reattached to the foundations of the old humanism. The revaluation of values would not be a radical one. On this new interpretation of beings, all being is incessant self-overpowering: being "must be a *continual* '*becoming*'" that has no reference to an end outside itself; hence being "must itself always recur again and bring back the same." Heidegger's co-comprehension of nihilism, will to power, the revaluation of all values hitherto, and the eternal recurrence of the same leads to his definition of the Overman. The Overman is neither the augmentation of any prior humanity nor an "overhumanity." It is, rather, "the most unequivocally singular form of human existence that, as absolute will to power, is brought to power in every man to some degree and that thereby grants him membership in being as a whole—that is, in will to power—and that shows him to be a true 'being,' close to reality and 'life.'" This co-comprehension of the five rubrics shows that nihilism for Nietzsche is not a simple linear unfolding of the construction of ideals and their demise, but a bivalent history of the destructiveness and creativity of Western metaphysics whose "collapse" gives on to knowledge of a specific kind: one of standing "within the moment that the history of Being has opened up for our age" (Heidegger 1982, 5–10).

This interpretation of Nietzsche's thought on nihilism in terms of Heidegger's own philosophy of Being has not met without criticism, however. For some, Nietzsche's account of nihilism as a historical process does not begin and end with the formation, deformation, and crisis of Western metaphysics. Rather, as Warren (1988) has argued, nihilism itself presupposes a prior negation, a social and political one, and must be grasped in its cultural dimension. On this reading, European nihilism in Nietzsche is not only a crisis of rationality but a crisis of legitimacy (an important element in Weber's debt to Nietzsche, as will be seen).

One way of approaching the difference between the two interpretations is through the divergence between Warren's reading of "original nihilism," the nihilism of the ancient Greek world, and Haar's reading of it, which is Heideggerian in inspiration. For Haar the negation that nihilism enacts in its formation of transcendent ideals (the turn against life) is latent in the original form—Plato and Socrates. The negation is manifest in the modern form. For Warren, latency applies most importantly to the manner in which a negation that original nihilism *presupposes* persists in European culture. Better, European culture is the latency of a *prior* negation. On this view, original nihilism—the formation of transcendent ideals in the Greek world—is not some free-floating response of the will to its own internal imperative *to be more.* It rests on the prior negation in social and political relations: violence and oppression or, in a word, slavery. Original nihilism means the escape from the conditions of life through a flight into thought that tries to make sense of suffering. The escape internalizes political violence in the form of a self-enslavement that inhabits every transcendent element.[5] For Nietzsche it is the creation of nihilistic values. With respect to this untruth and unfreedom of transcendence, *the conditions of life—unacknowledged suffering—persist as the remnant of freedom.* This paradoxical truth—one central to Adorno's thought—is expressed in a phrase of Nietzsche's from the *The Anti-christ* that Warren introduces into his interpretation (1988, 28): "to suffer from reality is to be a piece of the reality that has come to grief" (Nietzsche 1895, 137–138).[6] This interpretation permits a stronger reading of Nietzsche's psychology and his attention to subjectivity. The widely discussed ideas from *The Genealogy of Morals* of bad conscience and *ressentiment,* which at times explicate the slave mentality, do not simply capture the reactive response to the imperative of will to power, or the decadent tendency. They are reflections of a piece of reality that has come to grief and must themselves become creative elements, even though the creations are nihilistic values.

This interpretation opposes Nietzsche the philosopher of culture to Nietzsche the metaphysician. For what Warren finds is that European nihilism is the refraction of political experience into culture. The first or original nihilism turns on powerlessness against men, which bequeaths to the slave the choice of either suicidal nihilism or a revaluation of the experience of suffering, a creative recoil against particular social relations. The moments of nihilism amongst the oppressed often lead to "new ways of giving 'meaning' to suffering" (1988, 25).

Without the prior negation in political oppression there are no residues destined to become creative elements. In other words, Warren finds in Nietzsche the idea that the capacities of humans to organize their powers as agency is tied to the constant constitution of subjectivity out of otherness: a background of culture, language, and experience. Without the prior negation that nihilism rests on, which is to say, without the political frustration of those capacities, the creative aspect of nihilism—the attempt to give meaning to suffering—is impossible.

Warren proposes that the moments of nihilism among the oppressed finally lead to "the deification of cruelty in Christian-moral culture" (25). The Christian-moral worldview is thereby connected to the attempt made by victims of political violence to make sense of their suffering. In sum, the structure of nihilistic values has a political content that explains how that structure comes to be. The deification of cruelty in Christian-moral culture rests on the thoroughgoing divorce of interpretation (meaning-giving) from experience. The Christian interpretation inherits the political content of the structure of nihilism but formulates values that lack any contact with actuality. The deification of cruelty is the creation of a world of pure fiction, substituted for the world that presents itself in everyday life, and so enforces a distrust of any meaning *in* suffering and existence. In the salvation religion "such values undermine the conditions for willing in the process of 'saving' the will" (31). Actions are impossible.

On this reading, specifically modern nihilism stems from an internal crisis of interpretation that becomes inappropriate to experience. This crisis is twofold, however. The Heideggerian interpretation of the thought that the highest values devalue themselves only gives us one aspect of the crisis: the crisis of rationality. Recognizing the other aspect, the crisis of legitimacy, requires that the political content of the structure of nihilistic values not be forgotten. For what is crucial on this reading of Nietzsche is nihilism as the loss of self-reflexive identity that is necessary for the experience of transforming the past into the future (Warren 1988, 9). To the Heideggerian view that Nietzsche's five rubrics, co-comprehended, issue in *knowledge* of a specific kind, which comes down to standing historically in the history of Being, Warren opposes the question: "supposing that human subjectivity (selfhood, agency) is intrinsically valuable, how can we conceive of it as a *worldly* (social and historical) phenomenon?" (7). The question asks what human agency might be in a world unsupported by transcendent phenomena. In other words, for Warren, the demise of the Christian-moral worldview *brings out* the question of self-reflexive practices.

His question, unlike Heidegger's on how to interpret Nietzsche's thought that the highest values devalue themselves, guides his reading toward the problem of the crisis of legitimacy, rather than to a thought on standing historically in the history of Being, which allows the death of God to mean only a crisis of rationality. With Warren, the disjuncture between interpretation and experience in the Christian-moral worldview brings Christian culture to the point where the *absence* of experiences supporting the notions of sin, guilt, judgment, and God *imposes* itself (1988, 42). The manifest crisis is the one in which the Christian deification of cruelty—its rejection of any meaning *in* suffering and existence—brings about the experience that what is known or recognized to be part of experience cannot be affirmed. The death of God is above all the problem of the inadequacy of our value system to *practice*. With Nietzsche, we cannot believe the values and therefore cannot have the motivations for agency. In other words, because the values are transcendent the value system undermines the necessary minimum conditions for agency. This is what Warren calls the crisis of legitimacy. Morality's cultivation of truthfulness turns against morality and, as Nietzsche puts it, we discover long-implanted needs for untruth, needs that the value which makes life endurable hinges on. "This antagonism—*not* to esteem what we know [*erkennen*], and not to be *allowed* any longer to esteem the lies we should like to tell ourselves—results in a process of dissolution [*Auflösungsprocess*]" (Nietzsche 1967, 10; cited in Warren 1988, 37).

The first antagonism, the inability to esteem what we know, corresponds to the emergence of the claims of experience in the scientifically oriented acceptance of the testimony of the senses. Knowledge and science become values. This is the crisis of rationalist metaphysics or "the crisis of rationality." In the second antagonism, what Warren calls the crisis of legitimacy, values become unbelievable. This is the deeper process of the "increasing *inadequacy* to the world of everyday practice" (1988, 37). It is the conditions of agency that are undermined. This is equally a premise of Kristeva's thought on the self, the other, and the world, but, as we will see below, her thought is also marked off from the Nietzschean one in a way that doubles the distance from Heidegger on the meaning of the death of God.

To complete Warren's interpretation of Nietzsche, the process of dissolution also opens up the possibility of a practice-oriented culture. The possibility of self-constituting practice therefore depends on the consciousness of its loss, which is to say, on European nihilism as a psychological condition. This means that the consciousness of the loss of the ability to orient oneself in the world must prevail in a way that is not that of demoralization or the nihilistic attitude. The distance from the nihilistic attitude has its only source in the remnants of freedom in suffering *agency*.

I leave these two interpretations of Nietzsche's thought on nihilism at this point. The Heideggerian one, predominantly metaphysical, has allowed the event of Jacobi's naming of idealism as nihilism to be situated in Nietzsche's account of nihilism as a historical process. Jacobi's self-consciousness of the damage that transcendental idealism inflicts on the human spirit would belong to the moment in which the negation that is nihilism becomes manifest. Put otherwise, the Heideggerian inspiration has allowed the history of philosophy to be suspended in the philosophy of history. Warren's account, on the other hand, which understands Nietzsche predominantly as a philosopher of culture, clarifies Nietzsche's position in a tradition of thinking on the problem of "nihilistic modernity," a problem known to political philosophers from Nietzsche, Weber, and Adorno.

For Weber and Adorno, Nietzsche's attention to modern nihilism is a non-nostalgic investigation of the collapse of the rational appeal of values and ideals in the context of scientific methodology's undermining of the claims of religion to be the discourse of truth. Weber extends the analyses of the crisis of rationality and the crisis of legitimacy that scientific methodology cannot thematize or answer to but only intensifies in a specific direction. He extends the analysis in a sociological account of rationalization processes in modern social life. The dominion of bureaucratic organization depersonalizes everyday practices, making them unintelligible and insubstantial. This extension of the idea of the crisis of legitimacy corresponds to how the scientific advancement of knowledge restricts reason to formal calculative procedures, a further dimension of the crisis of rationality. The modern fate of practice and theory voids the world of cultural and spiritual values. The world is "disenchanted."

Adorno and Horkheimer's collaborative work, *Dialectic of Enlightenment* (1969), also engages with the thought of the disenchantment of the world. For them, the separation of philosophy and sociology is itself a feature of modern nihilism. The fields of study of these disciplines have been split by forces of fragmentation.[7] When Horkheimer and Adorno thematically combine the traditional disciplines of epistemology, sociology, and psychology for their critique, they do so in "fragmentary writing" as a means of offsetting the danger of reinscribing the illusory authority of those separate disciplines in their own work, whose subtitle is "Philosophical Fragments." Horkheimer and Adorno analyze nihilistic modernity in terms of the "self-destruction" of enlightenment. The failure of enlightenment ideals, which turn on the idea of free human social life, is inscribed and even accepted within the supposedly progressive kinds of thought and practice that the Enlightenment opened up. The failure is related to the way in which the Enlightenment turned its back on discourses and practices that were deemed irrational, notably magic, myth, and religion. In turning against not only the form but the content of these practices, the discourses and practices stemming from the Enlightenment themselves become irrational.

Horkheimer and Adorno are not nostalgic about the premodern, however. Their continuity with Nietzsche shows up in the investigation of the different forms of the entanglement of rationality and domination in both modern and premodern thought and practices (in myth and enlightenment). However, in *Dialectic of Enlightenment* the thought of the twofold crisis of rationality and legitimacy, which Warren finds in Nietzsche, is focused especially upon the self-reversal of enlightenment in, not only the self-understanding of modern rationality, but modern economic processes and politics. The examination of nihilistic modernity in both modern liberal states and fascism is central to the project.

Dialectic of Enlightenment also shares in the early Frankfurt School's recognition that psychoanalysis illuminates many of the features and trends of nihilistic modernity thanks to its investigations of the structures of subjectivity. However, Adorno is also at times a critic of the perceived tendency in psychoanalysis to repeat the isolation of the "psyche" from social and historical questions, an isolation which reflects the same forces of fragmentation that sustain the split between philosophy and sociology. In this way, psychoanalysis loses its critical power. This brings us to the question of the nihilism problematic in Kristeva's thought.

The Tendential Severance of the Semiotic and Symbolic

The present book shows that Kristeva's thought cannot be counted as representative of the tendency to isolate the psyche from social and historical questions, and that she is a social and political thinker in her own right. It establishes that the problem of modern nihilism is precisely what connects the various dimensions of her thought: the strictly psychoanalytic level of her writings, her thought on religion, her analyses of artworks, and her own view of the social and political implications of her thought, including her feminist thought. It is the presence of the problem of nihilism in her psychoanalytic thought, especially, that links her so strongly to the distance taken from Heidegger in the second view of Nietzsche. Heidegger's story loses everything about Nietzsche being a great moral psychologist. Indeed, if one reads Nietzsche as a philosophical psychologist in the manner of Warren, letting *The Genealogy of Morals* be the central text, then it should be unsurprising to find psychoanalysis encountering the same set of issues. First and foremost, the apparent ambiguities and ambivalences in Kristeva's psychoanalytic thought belong to her discovery of the structure of nihilism—the collapse of meaning, value, and authority—in the structures of the psyche. She is especially attentive to the narcissistic crisis and its implications in late modern societies, and she is aware that the narcissistic constriction is a problem of suffering agency. Yet she equally finds that psychoanalytic experience encounters the remnants of freedom in subjectivity: broken-off pieces of suffering that, to recall Nietzsche's phrase, present a piece of the reality that has come to grief. The 1980s trilogy investigates these broken-off pieces of suffering: our crises in love (*Tales of Love*), the upsurge of "abjection" (*Powers of Horror*), and melancholic depression (*Black Sun*). Even so, Kristeva's writings cannot be related directly to Nietzsche's philosophy. She does not situate her thought in relation to any philosophical tradition as such, repeatedly claiming that she takes the psychoanalytic and literary standpoint. Nonetheless, this standpoint depends on her sensitivity to modern nihilism.

The presence of the nihilism problematic in her thought must be distinguished from how it appears in the philosophical tradition. Neither her psychoanalytic thought nor her conception of the aesthetic turn on the premise of *a wholesale loss of transcendence.* The movement of transcendence, rescued from its placement in the beyond, is a central feature of her thinking. The way it appears in the figures and artworks she discusses is crucial to her demonstration of their, and her own, distance from suicidal nihilism or despair. There is no metanarrative of collapse in Kristeva. Nor does she situate her investigations of problems in subjectivity within overarching analyses of the crises of rationality and legitimacy. These expressions are not found in her writings. We do, however, find constant references to and discussions of crises in meaning, value, and authority, especially the first. It might seem more appropriate to take the nihilism problematic as one symptom of the crises of meaning she discusses, others being secularism, the collapse of authority, and suffering subjectivity. This would appear to be consistent with the absence of any metanarrative of collapse in her writings and with the fact that she never explicitly presents her thought as an analysis of modernity. Kristeva investigates the formation, deformation, and transformation of meaning and the subject in different moments of Western culture, doing so in ways that refuse to place them within an all-encompassing philosophy of history. Nevertheless, making the presence of the nihilism problematic in her thought the most embracing aspect of her analyses of our crises is necessary for grasping that Kristeva's attention to suffering subjectivity is a thought on unacknowledged suffering as the remnant of freedom. More specifically, it is important, possibly vital, for the following four reasons.

First, the centrality of the problem of modern nihilism illuminates the foundational categorial distinction of her thought between the "semiotic" and the "symbolic" by moving beyond the merely typological view of it, according to which the semiotic and symbolic refer to two irreducible dimensions of subjectivity and meaning: the nonverbal (sometimes presymbolic) and symbolic (especially verbal) dimensions. This view has allowed the distinction to be taken up and repeated in unreflective ways in the reception of her thought. Acknowledgment of Kristeva's sensitivity to modern nihilism permits us to see what is necessary for this distinction *to be made at all* as one that has a fundamental categorial status. The semiotic and symbolic in Kristeva are two dimensions of meaning and subjectivity that need to be connected if self-relation, the other, and world-relation are to be possible. The claim made here is that the distinction between the two can itself be made only in conditions of the tendential severance of the semiotic and symbolic, and that Kristeva relates psychoanalytic experience of suffering subjectivity to this tendency. I use the term *tendential severance* in order to underline that Kristeva does not present a metanarrative of the collapse of what is needed for adequate separateness, connections with others, and the social bond. Nonetheless, the sufferings and crises she discusses do coexist in modern, Western cultures, and she does refer them to failings in modern discourses and institutions. The categorial distinction can appear only in conditions where modern institutions and discourses have failed to provide everyday social and symbolic sites or practices for the adequate connection of the semiotic and symbolic. Psychoanalytic insights into suffering subjectivity discover these conditions. When the semiotic and symbolic are inadequately connected, the linguistic universe, symbolic bonds with others (communication), and social bonds are felt to be meaningless and without value. Like Nietzsche, Kristeva discovers the conditions for agency undermined, since the motivations for it cannot be affirmed. Indeed, there is a tendential severance in Nietzsche, too, because of the break between desire and values (what it is not to be able to esteem our lives). With Kristeva, the failings of modern institutions and discourses have left the burden of connecting the semiotic and symbolic on the individual, and the suffering subjectivity that psychoanalytic practice encounters is the suffering of this burden. What I mean by the presence of the problem of modern nihilism in Kristeva, then, is her discovery of the tendential severance of the semiotic and symbolic.

Second, Kristeva's extensions of psychoanalytic thought on the structure of narcissism—which work, especially, to clarify the significance of the "semiotic"—are explorations of a dimension of subjectivity and meaning that is socially and symbolically abandoned. Narcissus, in Kristeva, is an intricate array of nonverbal capacities—corporeal responsiveness and affective relations—open to combinations that support and renew social and symbolic life. The 1980s trilogy explores three moments of the narcissistic structure: prehistorical identifications (love), "abjection" (a primitive moment of separateness), and primal melancholy (a nonverbal parting sadness in respect of loss). However, psychoanalysis has discovered Narcissus—and so the capacity to idealize and the capacity for loss—in a state of neglect. The modern Narcissus shows up in his or her infantile, that is to say, regressive form because of this neglect. Contemporary psychoanalysis, responding to what appears on the couch, is witness less to the struggles with paternal law that Freud tracked in his confrontation with the neuroses (Oedipus) than to complaints about lacks of love, meaning, and self-orientation, as Kristeva frequently avers. These are the sufferings of a "borderline" subjectivity, that is to say, of a subject sent to and abandoned at its borders, at the limit of the ties between the individual and society. The borderline subject shows up where a society does not accompany the subject to those limits, which are also the society's own limits.

Third, this is the thought that illuminates Kristeva's relationship to religion. For she finds that in the formation of the sacred and in the historical religions there are practices—notably rituals—that do accompany the subject on the journey to the limits of the ties between the individual and society. However, religion equally appears as a failure in Kristeva's thought. Its attempt to meet this need of the subject and society either falls short of the need of separateness (in the sacred) or salvages separateness through a God-relation that forgets its rootedness in affective relations (monotheism's suppression of corporeal responsiveness). However, Kristeva's thought on nihilism is primarily an investigation of the nihilism emerging in the aftermath of secularization. For the narcissistic crisis is a central feature of the failure of modern institutions and discourses to accompany the subject to its borders, at the limits of society. Psychoanalysis is witness to the burden this puts on individuals, and tracks what they come up with. It is a "limit discourse" of modernity.

Psychoanalysis is the method of Kristeva's thought, then, because it is an adequate means of approach to a problem of which it forms a part. This means that if the presence of the nihilism problematic in Kristeva's thought is missed, there is no possibility of grasping psychoanalytic self-reflection on its own emergence, significance, and development as a discourse. That Kristeva's thought, especially the 1980s trilogy, contains this reflection has been insufficiently acknowledged in the reception of her writings, even where it is fully recognized that she is concerned with the crisis of meaning and value (for example, by Lechte 1990 and Oliver 1993a).

Fourth, what Kristeva means by the "aesthetic," and her claims for the magnitude of its importance, will be completely missed if the nihilism problematic is overlooked. Her concrete and fine-grained analyses of artworks make up an extensive and vital part of her writings. Kristeva conducts these analyses in order to demonstrate and emphasize the work of *art* as the work of reconnecting the semiotic and symbolic. Works of art, in specific instances, are distinguished from strictly symbolic discourses—the realm of language as communication—insofar as they give a kind of symbolic form to the semiotic, and so to the traces of the reality that has come to grief. That is why, in the 1980s trilogy, the various works of art and literature she discusses are called *tales of* love, *the literature of* abjection, or works *of mourning*. For, in each case, they restore a living history to the broken-off pieces of suffering. This is not an achievement that can be fulfilled once and for all by any work of art. Rather, in each case, the artwork is related to the surrounding social conditions, or to the fate of the semiotic and the symbolic in the cultural environs of the work's production. Kristeva's 1980s trilogy presents "minor histories" of artistic practices in Western cultures. As will be seen, in the discussion of *Black Sun* especially, the need of this work and the difficulties in fulfilling it are particularly pressing in modernity. The important point, for now, is that what the aesthetic means in Kristeva is the way in which the semiotic takes on—is given—symbolic form in conditions of the wider social and symbolic abandonment of this need. Indeed, this is how the "aesthetic" can come to have a wider reach than artistic and literary practices in the strict sense. Any practice that undertakes this form-giving belongs to the aesthetic. This, too, is easily missed or simply puzzling if Kristeva's sensitivity to modern nihilism is not discerned.

The most important points about Kristeva's relationship to and difference from the meanings of nihilism in the philosophical tradition are the following. When we understand Nietzsche as a great moral psychologist, there is a convergence between the philosophical conception of nihilism and Kristeva's thought on the self, other, and the world at the level of *the psychological problems of modernity*. However, she does not embed the crisis in a metanarrative. Rather, she thinks that only the testimony of suffering subjectivity in art and psychoanalysis allow a series of minor histories of modernity to be told. She binds her telling, in each case, to suffering subjectivity. Avoidance of genealogy and philosophy of history in the big sense allows the historical features of the minor histories to bind themselves to the remnant of freedom: to particular sites of suffering and the movement of its overcoming. This doubles the distance from Heidegger. It is why psychoanalysis is the method of her thought.

It must be said that Kristeva's minor histories leave out the moment of high bourgeois confidence that the political state can mediate all the ties between the individual and society. Kristeva—like Nietzsche, as Warren notes (1988, 12)—never specifically discusses the problem of modern institutions in a political theory addressed to their formation and limitations. She does, however, develop both an ethical and a political thought on the basis of her psychoanalytic and literary position. *Strangers to Ourselves* (1988) is a crucial text for understanding what an ethics of psychoanalysis becomes in Kristeva's project. *Nations Without Nationalism* (1993) presents a political thought on a "new" cosmopolitanism for the members of contemporary nation states. Even here, Kristeva does not tell us how to read her. Since she does not give indications *about* the fact that she is a writer of minor histories, many have plunged into *Strangers to Ourselves,* the political essays, or her more specifically feminist writings in order to shore up the desire that Kristeva contributes to the development of a feminist ethics or politics, or provides a theory of contemporary social and political relations. However, the post-Maoist Kristeva not only sees things in a nontotalizing way but refuses to make totalizing gestures, even about the fragmentary.[8] She has the modernist temperament of refusing to totalize even the critical perspective (something that links her with Adorno and Horkheimer, as I will suggest at some length in the final part of the book). Everything goes back to unacknowledged suffering because this is the remnant of freedom.

The development of the chapters in this book therefore works to press the claim that the structure and content of the 1980s trilogy brings out the presence of the nihilism problematic in Kristeva's writings. Each text of the trilogy contains an analysis of the structure of nihilism discovered in the structures of subjectivity known to psychoanalysis, an argument for the remnant of freedom found in suffering subjectivity, and a minor history of the fate of one dimension of the semiotic—one aspect of unacknowledged suffering—in religion and art. The breakdown of this book into three parts reflects the three levels at which the nihilism problematic is embraced in Kristeva's thought of this period: in psychoanalysis, in religion and art, and, finally, with the posttrilogy books of the same period, in contemporary social and political relations.

Part 1 shows that her sensitivity to nihilistic modernity can be accessed only by demonstrating that there are significant differences between her early thought in *Revolution in Poetic Language* (1974) and her later thought of the 1980s, where the problem of nihilism appears. The differences are found above all in the changing implications of her categorial distinction between the semiotic and the symbolic.[9] In the revolutionary standpoint the import of the distinction for Kristeva lies in showing the destructive return of semiotic elements into extant symbolic discourses, transforming meaning and the subject. At this point she attempts to connect psychoanalytic insights and aesthetic practices to political movements. For in this phase of her writing, when she is a prominent member of the *Tel Quel* group in Paris, she is an advocate of Mao's cultural revolution.[10] It is the significance of the disruptive potential of the semiotic for cultural and political practices that interests her. In the 1980s writings she is more attentive to how the semiotic and symbolic fall apart, what I call their tendential severance. Implicit in this development is a changed view of the relationship between psychoanalysis and the aesthetic. The apparent transition from the more political, revolutionary standpoint to the avowed psychoanalytic and literary standpoint, which disappointed and frustrated some of her readers (for example, Smith 1988, and Rose in Oliver 1993b), is rooted in the way in which the significance of *psychoanalysis* changes. The development of Kristeva's psychoanalytic thought from the 1970s to the 1980s is tracked in chapters 1–4.

Chapter 1, on Kristeva's early position, includes a discussion of the Lacanian background to her thought at this time. One sees here Kristeva's dissatisfaction with the constraints that the Lacanian symbolic imposes on the force of negativity, but also her high estimation of Lacan's grasp of the role of symbolic functioning—of language—in the formation of the speaking being. Where Kristeva differs from Lacan is in her reformulation of the "imaginary," a second major category in his project. This allows Kristeva to diverge from Lacan on the significance and power of the symbolic function. On this issue, the discussion does not cover new ground. (See, for example, Grosz 1989, Oliver 1993a, Chanter in Oliver 1993b, and Ziarek in Oliver 1993b.) However, it leads into new ground by addressing, at length, the difference between her 1970s and 1980s writings.

The new argument made in chapter 1 is that the change in the 1980s rests above all on a serious drawback of her methodology in *Revolution in Poetic Language*. For this book divides psychoanalysis and art into the theoretical and practical components, respectively, of her analysis of the social and symbolic inflexibility of the modern bourgeois world, which is the political problem she addresses there. The division inherits the classical Marxist arrangement of theory (psychoanalysis), the problem (the bourgeois world), and work (artistic practice). The consequence is that her theory of the transformation of meaning and the subject in signs ("revolution in poetic language") must posit the historical impact of this transformation—social change—but must also leave that historical impact in endless abeyance. This is important because the continuities and discontinuities in her thought in the 1970s and the 1980s can be specified in a way that is missing from the literature on her: as a genuine *transition* resting on the rearrangement of the relationship between psychoanalysis and art, corresponding to a different view of the "problem" as the problem of modern nihilism. Psychoanalysis no longers stands to art as theory to practice. Rather, theory, the problem, and practice are intertwined to a degree missing in the doctoral thesis, so that these moments do not fall apart and thereby leave us with a thought that posits social transformation but remains empty.

Chapters 2 to 4 show that what leads Kristeva out of the revolutionary standpoint is a deeper exploration of the significance of the narcissistic structure of subjectivity discovered in psychoanalysis. This is what brings the nihilism problematic into the center of her thought. The modern Narcissus, encountered in the therapeutic setting, reveals that modern Western cultures lack the kinds of discourses of love, loss, and separateness that are necessary for symbolic life, connections with others, and the social bond. The narcissistic constriction maintains the kind of subject-object/other relationship that recent continental philosophy addresses, for example, in critiques of the structure of consciousness in modern philosophy (Husserl), the forgetting of Being (Heidegger), ontology as a form of ego-narcissism (Levinas), or the repression of the feminine (Irigaray). Kristeva's attention to the weakness of discourses of love, loss, and separateness in late modern societies does not only grasp the formation, deformation, and transformation of the structure of being with others. It also raises the question of what is lost, what loss is, and what mourning might be in these societies.

Part 2 of the book turns to Kristeva's thought on religion and art. First, chapter 5 shows that *Powers of Horror* provides a minor history of how religions took on the task, neglected by modern institutions and discourses, of elaborating the limits of the ties between individual and society. That is to say, the historical religions provide symbolizations of the instabilities and capacities which make up the less visible features of the structure of being with others. These are the instabilities and capacities that turn on a presymbolic—"non-signifying"—exposure to separateness, otherness, loss, and death (investigated by the trilogy as a whole). Religions partially took on the task of providing a site of engagement of the semiotic and symbolic, but did not accomplish the task. Most important, then, the minor history of religions in *Powers of Horror* actually works to show that religion is a failure in respect of the need to give symbolic form to this exposure, since it ties the semiotic to a foundational instance: to God. In Kristeva's language, religion has the symbolic overreach the semiotic by overreaching itself. The significance of religion for Kristeva has not been sufficiently noted, and where it is brought into the foreground, her thought on religion as a failure, or as this kind of failure, is not fully acknowledged (in Crownfield 1992 and Reineke 1997, for example).

Chapter 6 brings out most strongly the relationship between Kristeva's affirmation of art and the strictly psychoanalytic level of her thought. This is an area of dispute. Some specify the continuity and discontinuity between the artwork and subjectivity (for example, Lechte 1990). Others hold the view that Kristeva imposes psychoanalysis as a metadiscourse on other objects (artworks) and thereby reduces their significance to the subjectivity of the artist (for example, Hill 1993). This book does not agree with the latter view. It lets Kristeva's cognizance of the problem of modern crises have a larger place in determining the meaning of the artwork in her thought. The chapter proposes that *Black Sun* is the centerpiece of Kristeva's thought on the "presymbolic" features of the structure of being with others, and the need for these to take on a kind of symbolic form. This is not only because *Black Sun* brings the nihilism problematic fully into view, but also because it reveals the power of Kristeva's recognition and investigation of the fate of *loss* in late modern societies. To recall the second interpretation of Nietzsche discussed above, it raises the question of how the consciousness of *loss* of meaning and values might prevail in a way that is not that of demoralization or the nihilistic attitude. What is remarkable about Kristeva's sensitivity to nihilistic modernity is that, while she does not presuppose a wholesale collapse of transcendence, she discovers that Western cultures are afflicted by the *loss of loss*. Even the consciousness of loss is threatened. This is not to understand her as proposing a further phase in a metanarrative of collapse, however. Rather, Kristeva's investigation of the loss of loss, one developed on the basis of her psychoanalytic thought on the relationship to the early mother, is a singular contribution to the analysis of nihilistic modernity that feminist debates would do well to accommodate. For Kristeva raises the questions of what is lost, what loss is, and what mourning might be in a manner that really brings out the connection between the failings of extant forms of representation (failings that are criticized elsewhere and otherwise in recent continental philosophy and feminism) and the questions of subjectivity and sexual difference. Kristeva's exploration of the loss of loss is also crucial for grasping the strength of her conception of the aesthetic. Chapter 6, especially, shows how, for Kristeva, only the testimony of suffering subjectivity in art and psychoanalysis lets a fragmented minor history of modernity—or, better, a series of fragmented minor histories—be told.

Part 3 approaches Kristeva's ethical and political writings as contenders to the title of providing an ethics or politics capable of accommodating the discoveries of psychoanalysis with respect to the structure of being with others and the possibility of the social bond. Chapter 7 interprets *Strangers to Ourselves* as an argument for how modern secular institutions and discourses can make good on their failings by taking on the ethics of psychoanalysis. *Nations Without Nationalism* is read as a project of working out a social logic of the part that "identification" with an ideal, in the psychoanalytic sense, plays in the social body. Kristeva's affirmation of the world of politics or of political movements is always somewhat gingerly delivered, and is unfailingly turned in the direction of the psychoanalytic and aesthetic standpoint. It is well known that she rejects feminism as a body of thought, and does so on the basis of personal experience in a particular political environment.[11] This remains a puzzling impediment for her reception in the anglophone world, where she is predominantly known and promoted as a "French feminist." However, light is shed on the tricky question of Kristeva's feminism, especially, by recognition of her sensitivity to nihilistic modernity, for this is what clarifies her conception of the "feminine" and her apparent frequent reduction of it to the maternal function.

Chapter 8 turns specifically to the question of Kristeva's feminist thought. The chapter is composed of two discussions. The first stages an encounter between Kristeva's thought and another project attentive to the psychoanalytic investigation into the structures of subjectivity, one which deploys the same psychoanalytic concepts as Kristeva—abjection, idealization, and melancholy—but which also stands as a prominent critical line on her thought. This is Judith Butler's project.[12] The encounter I stage between the two thinkers argues for a deeper agreement between them than is usually discovered in their writings, but also considers what prohibits the respective frameworks of their thought from being receptive to what the other delivers.

The second discussion in chapter 8 focusses on Kristeva's theory of sexual difference. Her close association of "woman" and "nature" has led to charges of both essentialism and heterosexualism in the reception of her *oeuvre* (for example, Coward in Kristeva 1984, Butler 1990, 1993, 1997). The charge of heterosexualism is addressed at various moments in the book. Chapter 8 introduces a thought from the early Frankfurt School in order to show that the charge of essentialism misses the import of Kristeva's thought on sexual difference, which is an effort to confront a process in which "woman" and "nature" come to be associated in the way—often simply tagged as "Western"—that is the target of feminist critique. The arguments I make to clarify and support Kristeva's discussions of "woman" involve a delicate rapprochement between her thought in two famous essays ("Stabat Mater" [1977] and "Women's Time" [1979], whose significance for her is attested to in their republication in later, book-length works) and the analysis of nihilistic modernity that Horkheimer and Adorno deliver in *Dialectic of Enlightenment.* These arguments show both the significance and the scope of Kristeva's thought on "woman."

With Kristeva, the association of "woman" and "nature" belongs to the way in which pieces of reality that have come to grief have been projected onto women, who are made to carry the burden, or at least the distorted image, of unacknowledged suffering. I argue that the connection between Frankfurt School critical theory and Kristeva's thought lies in their respective acknowledgments of the import of interrogating *phantasmatics* for the distorted return of the pieces of the reality that has come to grief in modernity. In both Kristeva and *Dialectic of Enlightenment* the term *nature* must be understood in the context of this fate. The chapter is above all an attempt to bring together the two areas of psychoanalysis and critical theory, on the one hand, and psychoanalysis and feminism, on the other, in order to show that the space where they intersect provides the most substantial articulation of the problem of nihilistic modernity. The emphasis made here on the presence of the nihilism problematic in Kristeva's writings is therefore meant to illuminate, and not supplant, the issues centrally discussed in her project, and to strengthen what is already a fruitfully diverse reception of that project in the anglophone world.

PART I

From the Revolutionary Standpoint to the Nihilism Problematic

CHAPTER 1

The Early View of Psychoanalysis and Art

Introduction

This chapter gives an account of Kristeva's early thought as it appears in her doctoral thesis of 1974.[1] *Revolution in Poetic Language* contains the only lengthy explanation of her fundamental categorial distinction between the semiotic and the symbolic. Many commentators therefore make reference to it when explicating her later thought. This is not inappropriate since it remains the case that what Kristeva means by the semiotic and symbolic is two dimensions of meaning and subjectivity. To be precise, the notion of the symbolic or, better, strictly symbolic functioning, encompasses everything to do with communicative discourse, especially utterances with propositional content which *say* something (*to* someone). The conception of the symbolic therefore covers the field of the meaningful object, that is to say, a representation, idea, or thing. Semiotic functioning, on the other hand, is the nondiscursive aspect of meaning and subjectivity, given an expanded conception of language, that is to say, one not restricted to the idea of language as the signifying medium. Semiotic functioning embraces the less visible role of tone, gesture, and rhythm, for example, in meaning and the innovative capacities of subjects. When Kristeva discusses these she indicates a dimension of subjectivity and meaning, called "semiotic," that exceeds the field of human capacities and limitations determined by the structure of language. The semiotic is in excess of the "symbolic order." In other words, it is not fully captured by the structure of language defined by internal relations of difference. The category of the "symbolic" comes from Lacan's modification of structural linguistics (explained in the next section).

However, this understanding of the semiotic and symbolic only grasps Kristeva's categorial distinction at the typological level. It is necessary to go beyond this, and understand the distinction at what I will call the philosophico-historical level if the full significance of the relationship between the semiotic and symbolic is not to be missed. For what I aim to show is that the significance of this relationship changes in the 1980s. The account of Kristeva's thought in *Revolution in Poetic Language*, developed below, first explicates the philosophicohistorical significance of the semiotic and symbolic in 1974. It then indicates that there is a problem in the methodology of *Revolution in Poetic Language*. Having abandoned this methodology, Kristeva's 1980s writings are based on a fundamental but easily missed change in the significance of the relationship between the semiotic and symbolic. In other words, a genuine and deep-rooted departure from the revolutionary standpoint takes place in the later writings at the level of her fundamental categorial distinction itself. In showing this, we gain access to the presence of the nihilism problematic in the 1980s trilogy. It is Kristeva's later investigation of the semiotic, and its fate in extant symbolic discourses, that develops the thought that unacknowledged suffering is the remnant of freedom in conditions of late modernity.

The project of *Revolution in Poetic Language* is a different one. It is a theory of radical transformations of meaning and the subject that take place when extant symbolic discourses are exposed to the return, in poetic language, of what she calls semiotic functioning. The relationship between the semiotic and symbolic, here, is a matter of "revolution" in meaning and the subject. For Kristeva, it is psychoanalysis that allows the discovery of this revolution to be made, and that permits its specific dynamic and import to be articulated. The 1974 text therefore takes a revolutionary standpoint on the relationship between the semiotic and symbolic. On account of the importance of psychoanalysis for the theoretical articulation of this revolution, Kristeva's thought develops on the ground of a return to Freud. Unsurprisingly, given the intellectual and cultural *milieu* of her thinking and writing, the return to Freud is made in the context of Lacanian psychoanalysis. That is to say, Kristeva's categories of the semiotic and symbolic develop her own reading of Freud but equally contain a debt to and departure from Lacan. *Revolution in Poetic Language*, like other writings of the period, reformulates the Lacanian categories of the imaginary and symbolic.

Kristeva's reformulation undermines the tight connection between the unconscious and the structure of language that many have found in Lacan's thought. In Lacan the centerpiece of Freud's theory of the unconscious—the oedipal structure—contains aspects that reveal the structure of language. Given the symbolic destiny of "man," who is the *speaking* being in Lacan, the oedipal structure becomes the fundamental structure of culture itself. The stroke of genius here is that, when Lacan shows that structures of subjectivity depend on the structuration of the subject in *language,* he demonstrates how finitude (lack), and the acceptance of finitude, found and remain the mainstay of human powers and limitations. However, the identification of the unconscious with the structure of language also appears to tie culture, as such, to a founding, paternal law (the Law). Kristeva's idea of revolution both presupposes her acceptance of the Lacanian insight into language and lack (finitude) and chips away at the dominion of paternal law over subjectivity and culture. The idea was received as an "emancipatory" move in the feminist reception of Kristeva, especially, because of the cultural and political implications of the Lacanian notion of the symbolic order. For the transcendentalization of the oedipal structure sets strict limits to the historical variation of social identities, especially gender identities. If the meaning of "revolution" in Kristeva's 1970s thought is to be understood, then, her use of the concepts of semiotic and symbolic at that time must be set in relation to this psychoanalytic background.

The Lacanian Background

Since Kristeva deploys and responds to the Lacanian categories of the imaginary and symbolic without addressing herself to their clarification for an uninitiated readership, this chapter provides an interpretation of the major features of those categories. The interpretation begins with a central essay from what has been called the second phase of Lacan's thought, "The Agency of the Letter in the Unconscious, Or Reason since Freud" (1957), making reference, also, to other of Lacan's essays which illuminate the thought contained there. Following this, the chapter explicates the seminal essay introducing the imaginary order, "The Mirror Stage" (1949).[2] The objective of this interpretation is limited to illuminating Kristeva's debt to and departure from Lacan, using moments in the explicatory and philosophical literature on Lacan's *Écrits* that are helpful in the task, before turning to Kristeva's revisions of the Lacanian categories.[3]

The Symbolic, or the Elementary Structure of Culture

The view that there is a second phase in Lacan's thinking refers to the moment when his enlistment of structuralist linguistics to present the psychoanalytic theory of subjectivity enacts a break with Hegelian dialectic.[4] According to the psychoanalytic canon the pre-Freudian "subject" is largely identified with self-consciousness, often the *cogito* or Cartesian conscious thinking subject. Lacan's cultural and philosophical milieu was widely influenced by a course of lectures that introduced Hegel's expansion of the conception of self-consciousness (in the *Phenomenology of Spirit*, 1806). As is widely known, the lectures were delivered in Paris in the 1930s by the Russian émigré Alexandre Kojève. As a consequence of these lectures, which anthropologized Hegel's philosophy, the latter generally came to stand for the conception that self-consciousness, constituted in otherness, unfolds a temporally articulated movement whose moments are stages in a historical development. On this view, Hegel's dialectic presents an objective process in which each stage (for example, the Roman legal person) represents a destruction of the specific shape of the previous one (the subject of Sophoclean tragedy). This destruction involves no loss, however, for it is at once a transition to a higher position (Hegel's "determinate negation"), preserving the elements of the previous figure. The dialectic comprehends the movement in which self-consciousness comes closer to itself, which means that it comes closer to grasping the truth of its history and freedom. "I would to heaven it were so," Lacan remarks (1966, 296).

On this view of Hegel's philosophy the dialectic is read as thought's development through an immanent movement. The view leads to one conventional critique of the Hegelian system. The final position of the dialectic, "Absolute Knowledge," cancels the otherness or non-identity that marks and unsettles the consecutive stages of self-consciousness, and this can only be so because the dialectic is guided from the outset by that position. That is to say, the Hegelian—philosophical—subject comes to itself in an interiorizing movement that gathers up the temporally articulated moments of its history, "without remainder." This understanding of Hegel appears without modification in a lecture given by Lacan at a conference on "*La Dialectique*" in 1960. "This dialectic is convergent and attains the conjuncture defined as absolute knowledge. As such it is deduced, it can only be the conjunction of the symbolic [representation] with a real of which there is nothing more to be expected. What is this real, if not a subject fulfilled in his identity to himself? From which, one can conclude that this subject is already perfect in this regard, and is the fundamental hypothesis of this whole process. He is named, in effect, as being the substratum of this process; he is called the *Selbstbewusstsein,* the being conscious of self, the fully conscious self" (1966, 296).

Something of this convergent movement of the dialectic, made explicit by Lacan in 1960, had been retained in the early phase of his presentation of psychoanalytic experience. "Analysis can have for its goal only the advent of a true speech and the realization by the subject of his history in his relation to a future" (1966, 88). What marks the difference from the Hegelian subject, here, is the idea that the realization of a subject's history emerges "in his relation to a future" and not as the fulfilment of identity to self. Lacan's second phase comes to stress the contrast between the temporality pertaining to the experience of psychoanalysis and that pertaining to Hegelian determinate negation. The former presents a retroactive movement rather than a convergent one. This concept of temporality rests on the "turn to language" in psychoanalysis, for Lacan claims that the retroactive movement is *essentially* the movement of the process of signification. The point is clarified in Weber's *Return to Freud* (1978). "As a signifying medium, language *is* the articulation of non-identity and this is what allows the unconscious to be described as the discourse of the Other" (4–5). In Weber's summary, "what it [the signifier] designates and points toward—a configuration of differences—engenders meaning only retroactively, as the result of the 'pointing,' as it were" (1978, 63). *Return to Freud* aims to specify the negativity of *Entstellung*, "dislocation," which animates this retroactive movement. *Entstellung* is "radically distinct" from determinate negation understood as the movement in which a series of positions are engendered. It is a distortion or "transposition" with no determinate place. The articulation of a temporality introducing a non-Hegelian negativity into the "subject," in and through a return to Freud, amounts to a claim that psychoanalysis reintroduces otherness into self-consciousness. *Entstellung* preempts the arrival of a self-identity, dislodging the "whole" temporality of the Hegelian dialectic, taken to be the temporality of self-consciousness, the conscious subject. In the movement of *Entstellung* the positions of self-consciousness cannot converge on the fully conscious subject, for they are set astray in a radicalization of differences, an utter alterity that is "nowhere and everywhere." Rather than presenting a temporality that belongs from the beginning to an achieved self-consciousness, Lacan presents a subject that belongs to the split temporality pertaining to the structure of language, the signifying medium: "the future anterior of what I shall have been for what I am in the process of becoming" (1966, 86). The Freudian unconscious is rendered neither as an object, nor as an identity, nor as a presence, but as a disjunctive immediacy (Weber 1978, 11).

The presentation of the subject of psychoanalysis in terms of this mode of temporality works to support the claim that Lacan's "return to Freud" is at no point the return to and repetition of an origin. Thus, in one move, the radicality of the Freudian unconscious is recovered and the deployment in this recovery of a science unavailable to Freud at the period of his work is justified.

Lacan's modifications of structuralist linguistics engender a return to Freud because they specify the significance of the unconscious retroactively. Its significance lies, not in unconscious contents or agencies, but in its disjunctive immediacy.

The emphasis on structuralist linguistics in this phase of Lacan's thought is explained by the fact that Saussure's thought represents for him the elevation of the study of language to a science permitting the precise study of the structure of the sign. Linguistics becomes modern at the moment when the study of language becomes the study of the system of signs, which is to say, when Saussure finds that signs take on their value from their relations to each other and not from their referent or the relations between referents. The science of linguistics dismisses the logical positivist view of language as the reconstruction of a given world order. Moreover, the discovery that the value of the sign is determined by relations between signs subverts the claim that a meaning is determined within the contextuality of meanings. Instead, Saussure demonstrated that the sign is comprised of the two orders of the signifier and the signified. What Lacan takes from this is that the principle of the linguistic sign is not contextuality but *articulation:* every signification refers to another signification. The Lacanian theory of subjectivity asserts that the "subject" is constituted in this structure. While this stands as a challenge to the idea of the priority of the self-conscious subject in thought and volition, it does not claim that the subject is at the mercy of an external system. Indeed, Lacan regards Saussure as having resubmitted the articulation he discovered at the core of the functioning of the sign to the notion of a closed order of signs, and so as having abandoned the principle that radical difference determines the value of signs. Moreover, this failing is said to be coextensive with structuralist linguistics' incapacity to address the question of the "subject" (Weber 1978, 38). Language is not a closed order from which the subject is omitted but a structure that preexists the being who enters into it. It is the primary element in the constitution of "the speaking subject." The psychoanalytic recovery of the subject modifies structuralist linguistics and generates a *transindividual* conception of language. "The passion of the signifier now becomes a new dimension of the human condition in that it is not only man who speaks, but that in man and through man *it* speaks (*ça parle*), that his nature is woven by effects in which is to be found the structure of language, of which he becomes the material, and that therefore there resounds in him, beyond what could be conceived of by a psychology of ideas, the relation of speech" (Lacan 1966, 284). The relation of speech is said to be at the center of Freud's discovery of the unconscious: "what the psychoanalytic experience discovers in the unconscious is the whole structure of language" (147).

The most radical moment of Lacan's modification of structuralist linguistics appears where he intensifies the investigation into the principle of the linguistic sign—radical difference—by demonstrating that the process of signification follows the path of the *signifier.* Only if the path of the signifier takes precedence is signification a matter of articulation and not representation. The differential order of the signified—of meanings—is secondary in relation to and brought about by the differential order of the signifier. That is to say, meaning issues from the chain of signifiers. "It is by referring to other signifieds, that is by means of the signifier, that the signified first becomes self-identical, that is, a signified. Its identity thus must be conceived as an effect of the signifier, insofar as the signifier embodies the process of signification in terms of the play of differential relations" (Weber 1978, 41). The order of the signified is not an order of meanings that preexists the signifier but an effective field constituted by the process of signification. Thus "the signified" in Lacan is never equivalent to meaning but is instead "the diachronic set of the concretely pronounced discourses" (1966, 126).

In wresting the analysis of the *structure* of the sign from Saussure's conception of language as a *system* of signs, Lacan introduces an inversion of the foundational algorithm of structuralist linguistics: S/*s*, "the signifier over the signified." The inversion is true to the logical and temporal precedence accorded the signifier, for it specifies the relative positions of the orders of signifier and signified in the process of signification: "we can say that it is in the chain of the signifier that the meaning 'insists' but that none of its elements 'consists' in the signification of which it is at the moment capable" (1966, 153). The process of signification issues in a meaning thanks to a chain structure in which the signifier both unfolds before it, and so anticipates, the dimension of meaning ("All the same it is . . ."), and outreaches the signification that the chain structure brings about. The assumption on the part of Saussure that linearity constitutes the chain of discourse ("Peter hits Paul") is therefore overturned by the attention to the polyphony without which the dimension of meaning cannot unfold. Polyphony is rooted in "an incessant sliding of the signified under the signifier," which corresponds to the negativity of *Entstellung* (154).

Lacan drew on resources in the development of structuralist linguistics in order to specify this mechanism. He acknowledges Jakobson and Halle for bringing greater precision into the analysis of the structure of the sign in and through their identification of metaphor and metonymy as two fundamental mechanisms of signification (Lacan 1966, 176–177, n. 6, 20; Weber 1978, 60). In Lacan metonymy and metaphor are distinguished by the relationship they have to the bar separating signifier and signified in the foundational algorithm, *S/s*. The bar, resisting signification, is central to what the algorithm expresses: the principle of radical difference. It denotes infinity. Metonymy, the mechanism of the connection of signifier and signified, maintains the resistance to signification. In metaphor, the mechanism of the substitution of signifier for signifier, the signifier crosses the bar and so transfers to the position of the signified. Thus *S/s* expresses, not two parallel orders, but two stages of the process of signification (1966, 149). In becoming self-identical the signifier produces an effect of meaning. Conventionally, metaphor and metonymy are taken to be figures of style dependent on a prior meaning, a view which preserves the illusion that the ambiguity of meaning in language is secondary. The error derives from prioritizing the concept of language as communication, where it is assumed that the subject can intentionally avail itself of the very *medium* of language as the site of intersubjectivity. The illusion that "the signifier answers to the function of representing the signified" corresponds to the presumption of a "subject of representation" (150). This wrongly situates *the subject* at the point of the emergence of meaning. Once the privilege traditionally assigned to meaning collapses, on account of the evidence that the laws of the signifier guide the process of signification, the view of language as a medium or tool at the disposal of a subject is displaced: "we accede to meaning only through the double twist of metaphor when we have the one and only key: the S and *s* of the Saussurian algorithm are not on the same level, and man only deludes himself when he believes his true place is at their axis, which is nowhere" (166). Metaphor and metonymy together make up the process of localization, or "sense" (*le sens*). It is metaphor, not the subject, which is situated at the point of emergence of meaning. "Metaphor occurs at the precise point at which sense emerges from non-sense" (158).

Metaphor and metonymy are therefore the essential mechanisms of the differential movement (articulation) that constitutes signification. The conventional understanding of metonymy as a figure of style, the substitution "part for whole," is contradicted by the utterly classical example "thirty sails": "for each ship to have just one sail is in fact the least likely possibility. By which we see that the connexion between ship and sail is nowhere but in the signifier, and that it is in the *word-to-word* connexion that metonymy is based" (1966, 156). Metaphor, the other aspect of the properly signifying function of language, is to be found in the production of the "poetic spark." Taking as exemplary a line from Victor Hugo, *His sheaf was neither miserly nor spiteful . . .*, Lacan comments:

> The creative spark of the metaphor does not spring from the presentation of two images, that is, of two signifiers equally actualized. It flashes between two signifiers one of which has taken the place of the other in the

> signifying chain, the occulted signifier remaining present through its (metonymic) connexion with the rest of the chain.
>
> *One word for another:* that is the formula for the metaphor and if you are a poet you will produce for your own delight a continuous stream, a dazzling tissue of metaphors. (157)

No poetic spark emerges from the simultaneous presence of the "sheaf" and the two attributes "miserly" and "spiteful." Rather, metaphor resides in a substitution in which one signifier ("his sheaf") has taken the place of another (the purported owner). "If, however, his sheaf does refer us to Booz, and this is indeed the case, it is because it has replaced him in the signifying chain at the very place where he was to be exalted by the sweeping away of greed and spite. But now Booz himself has been swept away by the sheaf, and hurled into the outer darkness where greed and spite harbour him in the hollow of their negation" (157).

Lacan's passages on Hugo's Booz express the claim that the subject is constituted in the symbolic function. That claim revolves on an interpretation, developed elsewhere, of Freud's renowned formulation of the dialectic of the subject, *Wo es war, soll Ich werden,* and especially the imperfect tense of the first phrase. "There where it was just now, there where it was for a while, between an extinction that is still glowing and a birth that is retarded, 'I' can come into being and disappear from what I say" (1966, 300). The subject is constituted as absent from the signifier. "Being of non-being, that is how *I* as subject comes on the scene, conjugated with the double aporia of a true survival that is abolished by knowledge of itself, and by a discourse in which it is death that sustains existence" (300). Thus the "entrance into language" or entrance into the symbolic order corresponds to the constitution of the subject as absent from the signifier. Lacan therefore makes the thought of human finitude central to the concept of the subject, who is a subject of lack (being of nonbeing).

It is also important to see how the symbolic aspect of lack is tied to the paternal law (and so to castration). Lacan's selection of the Victor Hugo poem for his account of the production of the poetic spark equally works to underline the discovery that the symbolic function is the symbolic, *paternal* function: "It is in this case all the more effective in realizing the signification of paternity in that it reproduces the mythical event in terms of which Freud reconstructed the progress, in the unconscious of all men, of the paternal mystery" (1966, 158). The subject is constituted under the symbolic Law. That is to say, the coming-into-being of the subject as a "being of nonbeing" is owed to the constituting and empowering instance of the *dead* father, absent from the signifier: Lacan's "Name-of-the-Father."

A major concern in Lacan's claim for the centrality of the symbolic function in the psychoanalytic treatment of the subject is the explicit challenge it makes to the development of the psychoanalytic tradition which treats the subject of psychoanalysis as the *ego,* a treatment which corresponds with understanding the Freudian unconscious in terms of unconscious contents or psychic agencies: an object or a presence. For Lacan, ego psychology has lost the *radical* alterity of the unconscious, which is a movement of alterity without origin, just as—in Hugo's poetic line—the subject is an effect of metaphor, produced retroactively in the movement of substitution that pertains to the signifier. The suppression of this radical alterity, which amounts to a suppression of "the discourse of the Other," severs psychoanalytic theory from analytic practice. Freud, in contrast, provides "a dialectical apprehension of experience, the proportion of analysis of language increasing to the extent that the unconscious is directly concerned" (1966, 159) That is to say, Lacan's thesis is that the unconscious is increasingly involved where Freud follows the path of the signifier. Freud does so most evidently and precisely in *The Interpretation of Dreams* (1900), when he comes to disclose the essence of dreaming by interrogating the disparity between the manifest dream-content (what is commonly referred to as the dream) and the latent dream-content, or dream-thoughts (*die Traumgedanke*), uncovered in the dream's interpretation. Given Freud's attention to the disparity between the dream-content and the dream-thoughts, the significance of the dream (*die Traumdeutung*) comes to the fore in Freud's analysis of the dream-work (*die Traumarbeit*). Lacan cites Freud in support of his reminder that the dream-work is "the linguistic structure that *enables us to read dreams,*" and that this is "the very principle of the 'significance of the dream,'" (159, emphasis added). "At bottom, dreams are nothing other than a particular *form* of thinking, made possible by the conditions of the state of sleep. It is the *dream-work* which creates that form, and it alone is the essence of dreaming—the explanation of its peculiar nature" (Freud 1900).

The insistence on the dream-work as the creation of a form of thinking comes, in Lacan, to demonstrate that Freud's thought is primarily guided, not by any conception of unconscious contents or psychic agencies, but by the idea of the primary processes, the laws governing the unconscious. Thus the "analysis of language" intensifies when the analysis of the dream-work approaches a specification of these laws. The dream-work is defined in terms of four operations: the work of condensation (*die Verdichtungsarbeit*), the work of displacement (*die Verschiebungsarbeit*), considerations of representability (*die Rücksicht auf Darstellbarkeit*), and secondary revision (*die sekundäre Bearbeitung*). The center of the discussion for Lacan is the presentation of condensation and displacement. He turns up a correspondence between the laws governing the unconscious and the laws of the signifier (metaphor and metonymy), following how Freud's analysis of the disparity between the dream-content and the dream-thoughts ventures the conclusion that:

> in the dream-work a psychical force is operating which on the one hand strips the elements which have a high psychical value of their intensity, and on the other hand, *by means of overdetermination,* creates from elements of low psychical value new values, which afterwards find their way into the dream-content. If that is so, *a transference and displacement of psychical intensities* occurs in the process of dream-formation, and it is as a result of these that the difference between the text of the dream-content and that of the dream-thoughts comes about. . . . The consequence of the displacement is that the dream-content no longer resembles the core of the dream-thoughts and that the dream gives no more than a distortion of the dream-wish which exists in the unconscious. (Freud 1900, 307–308)

"Displacement" functions like metonymy, word-to-word connection. As a law of the unconscious, it embraces the transfer of psychical intensities from elements which have that intensity to elements which are, in respect of the dream-wish, close to indifferent. Thus displacement gives the dream-wish an outlet by giving censorship the slip. Lacan therefore aligns the laws of the unconscious with those of the signifier.

> *Verdichtung,* or "condensation," is the structure of the superimposition of the signifiers, which metaphor takes as its field, and whose name, condensing in itself the word *Dichtung,* shows how the mechanism is connatural with poetry to the point that it envelops the traditional function proper to poetry.
>
> In the case of *Verschiebung,* "displacement," the German term is closer to the idea of that veering off of signification that we see in metonymy, and which from its first appearance in Freud is represented as the most appropriate means used by the unconscious to foil censorship. (1966, 160)

That such an alignment is warranted is further indicated by Freud's discussion of a dream image, the boat on the roof. Since the latent dream-thoughts have nothing to do with the signification "the boat on the roof" it is evident that the image is a *signifier,* the connections proper to it and hence its value being quite distinct from those presented in the dream content. Turning to Freud's much discussed claim that the dream is a rebus, Lacan derives this character of dreams from "the agency in the dream of the same literal (or phonematic) structure in which the signifier is articulated and analysed in discourse" (1966, 159). In sum, if the dream is a rebus the relationship of the dream-content to the dream-thoughts is not one of representation. There is no direct relationship between the two. That is to say, dream images are not symbols. The dream-thoughts reside in an articulation that is radically other than the organization of the elements that form the dream-content, and cannot be found within that organization. Dream interpretation is comparable to discovering in a picture elements that have another articulation than the one of the picture's apparent composition. Dream interpretation, the analysis of a rebus, is therefore a technique that follows the path of the signifier, which leads Lacan to call it a deciphering as distinct from decoding. Moreover, the technique is not the external application of an analysis, for following the path of the signifier relies on free association, the dreamer's speech.

In sum, however much Freud's publication of the *Interpretation of Dreams* flew in the face of skepticism about dreams having significance, or the nature of the significance they have, the book's argument is not restricted to the argument for latent dream-thoughts. The center of the project is the analysis of the dream-work, which delivers the laws of the unconscious. And these laws are to be recognized as applying beyond the state of dreaming. "For in the analysis of dreams, Freud intends only to give us the laws of the unconscious in their most general extension. One of the reasons why dreams were most propitious for this demonstration is exactly, Freud tells us, that they reveal the same laws whether in the normal person or the neurotic. But in either case, the efficacy of the unconscious does not cease in the waking state. The psychoanalytic experience does nothing other than establish that the unconscious leaves none of our actions outside its field" (Lacan 1966, 163). When Lacan claims, in a further step, that the psychoanalytic experience discovers the whole structure of language, he explicitly makes the unconscious a cultural category and, at the same time, makes the structure of language *transcendental.* His portrayal of "the psychoanalytic experience" is distinguished by the effort to convey the symbolic *fact* of man, which structures the human being's limitations and powers. One consequence of this "symbolic fact" is the modified significance of the more visible features of volition and cognition, such as "choice" or "reflection." They are altered by the "always already there" of language, more specifically by the negativity and temporality pertaining to the field of the signifier, or more properly by "the discourse of the Other." The conception of the symbolic does not, however, exhaust the categorial edifice of Lacan's thought, since the symbolic is erected on the basis of the prior appearance of lack, which involves, in its broadest implication, a failure to take on finitude, and so a moment that must be corrected by the institution of the symbolic if there is to be adequate separation and connections with others. Here we turn to Lacan's discussion of imaginary relations.

The Imaginary: Lacan's Mirror Stage

Since Kristeva's thought, too, must be seen as an enquiry into conditions for adequate human separateness and connectedness, it is important to underline that Lacan's thought places those conditions within the field of the signifier and desire, that is to say, in the symbolic order or order of language. What distinguishes the imaginary order, then, is the absence or inadequate development of conditions for self-relation and otherness. Lacan's imaginary order comprises relations of similarity, mirroring, or homeomorphism. These relations are the fundamental features in the ego's formation and settle at its core the structure of narcissism and its correlate, aggressivity. The specific dyadic form of these imaginary relations appears as a condition for the maturation of the human being, prior to the entrance into language, and provides the oedipal structure with a coherence it would otherwise lack. That is to say, the "mirror stage" elucidates the appearance of spatiality and the potentiation of the subject-object positionality required if oedipal identification is to be intelligible. In imaginary relations no other or object is as yet distinguished. Rather, imaginary relations are played out at the level of an inner/outer matrix. In his essay on "The Mirror Stage" (1949), Lacan states: "I am led, therefore, to regard the function of the mirror-stage as a particular case of the function of the *imago,* which is to establish a relation between the organism and its reality—or, as they say, between the *Innenwelt* and the *Umwelt*" (1966, 4). The distinction between the *Innenwelt* and the *Umwelt* is the appearance of lack. Moreover, the imaginary relations pertaining to the mirror stage are a special case of the function of establishing a relation between them, one that diverges from the acceptance of lack.

In the mirroring *imago* what appears is the "similar," generating the ego homeomorphically, that is to say, through the attraction of a similar morpheology. Before there is an other for the ego, the ego is "the similar," the direct counterpart to, and set up by, the mirror image. Lacan's introduction of the mirror image was central to his polemic with New World ego psychology, for which the analytic treatment is directed to securing and strengthening the ego. In his essay "Aggressivity in Psychoanalysis" (1948) Lacan asserts that "the ego represents the center of all the *resistances* to the treatment of symptoms" (1966, 23). Moreover, his objection to ego psychology aimed broadly at a culture of which the New World represented the most advanced example: "It is clear that the promotion of the ego today culminates, in conformity with the utilitarian conception of man that reinforces it, in an ever more advanced realization of man as individual, that is to say, in an isolation of the soul ever more akin to its original dereliction" (27).[5]

Lacan's polemic with ego psychology insists that "the human ego establishes itself on the basis of the imaginary relation" (cited in Kristeva 1983, 22). Thus in the seminal essay on the mirror stage he claims: "We have only to understand the mirror stage *as an identification*, in the full sense that analysis gives to the term: namely, the transformation that takes place in the subject when he assumes an image" (Lacan 1966, 2). The nucleus of the ego is formed in an identification which presumes no subjective or objective position. Observations of the infant's activity before a mirror at a period roughly between six and eighteen months illuminate this identification, for that activity is exemplary in exhibiting the *structure* of the mirror stage. Identification, here, means the infant's captation by its mirror image, a "total body form" that is at odds with the direct experience of motor incapacity and nursling dependence. The phenomenon of recognition that Lacan locates in this experience is not an epistemological one, not recognition of self, but an ontological one. The infant undergoes an anticipation of its powers, and of the mental permanence of the I, in and through an image. Moreover, the feelings of identity occur only by virtue of their contrast with the immediate experience of corporeal fragmentation (*le corps morcelé*). "What I have called the *mirror stage* is interesting in that it manifests the affective dynamism by which the subject originally identifies himself with the visual *Gestalt* of his own body: in relation to the still very profound lack of co-ordination of his own motility, it represents an ideal unity, a salutary *imago*" (18–19). The *imago* is a captivation of the subject, transforming it. In the case of the mirror image the transformation introduces distorting features which are central to Lacan's polemic against ego psychology. The primordial form of the I is established by an external, inverted, virtual reality which settles a fictional direction and alienating destination at the core of the ego: "the human individual fixes upon himself an image that alienates him from himself" (19). Where it is a matter of identification, the ego—far from accommodating the subject to reality, or having an integrative power in the face of conflictual demands imposed by id, superego, and reality—always involves the subject in the confusion of self and otherness. If imaginary relations based in the mirror stage are fundamental to the ego, the latter's relationship to others and reality is ensnared in self-deception and the aggressivity instituted by the alienating function of the specular I (19).

With Lacan, the modification of the imaginary, mitigating its hazards, appears only with the dialectic of desire and the entrance into language. The entrance into language works against the centrifugal/centripetal force that dominates the ego and introduces the tendency toward absorption of or absorption into otherness, for the discourse of the Other is a fundamental, ineluctable, and permanent exposure to exteriority. The symbolic order, preexisting the subject constituted through entrance into it, imposes on the human being both his or her "lack of being" (*manque-à-être*) and the requirement that the speaking subject take up a relationship to lack, to "castration." Thus, although Lacan endorsed the activation of egoic reactions in psychoanalysis, the *subject* of psychoanalysis is the subject of language, whose "nature is woven by effects in which is to be found the structure of language, of which he becomes the material" (1966, 284). Moreover, a subject shot through by such effects is a subject of *desire*. The meaning of desire in the Lacanian corpus lies in its differentiation from "demand," the demand for complete gratification aimed at the mother's body. Fulfilment of the demand is impossible, an impossibility that is posited when the object *of desire* is posited in the field of the signifier. Desire consists in a transposition of the demand for complete gratification into object-relation. It is marked by the absolute gap between demand and its fulfilment, that is to say, by the impossibility of satisfying the demand for complete gratification. This gap turns into the "infinity" of desire, in the sense that no object satisfies desire. Desire overreaches any object of desire. In Lacan's words, the object of desire is receding, "metonymic." In sum, the Lacanian subject is a subject of desire in the field of symbolic relations. On the one hand, it is the subject divided by desire and language (finite). On the other hand, desiring metonymy (infinite) sustains the subject in object-relation. That is to say, with Lacan, desire sustains symbolic capacities and, thereby, the social dialectic. On this view of the subject of psychoanalysis, analysis is directed to the passion of the signifier.

Revolution in Poetic Language

To briefly recapitulate the two reasons for beginning the discussion of Kristeva's thought with *Revolution in Poetic Language* (1974): first, it is the only place where her fundamental categorial distinction between the semiotic and symbolic, with its debt to and departure from Lacan, is fully elaborated; second, the claim that her thought contains an analysis of modernity is brought out and substantiated by comparing the status of psychoanalysis and literature in those writings with their status in the earlier work. I will consider the debt to and departure from Lacan in the context of a discussion of the philosophicohistorical meaning of Kristeva's psychoanalytic thought in her doctoral thesis.

In 1974 psychoanalysis has a largely theoretical role and literature is a practice. The respective roles of psychoanalysis and literature are framed by a reflection on the emergence and fate of the modern political world in the shape of, first, the bourgeois revolution, and second, Marxism. In respect of the bourgeois revolution, the meaning of literature for Kristeva rests on an argument that the late nineteenth century displays the decline of the "negativity" of the political revolution, and the removal of negativity from social and political practice to avant-garde literature, or more precisely "poetic language." In respect of Marxism, Kristeva attempts a reformulation of historical materialism, arguing that the one-sided, objectivist view of social and historical transformation, which is owed to the emphasis in dialectical materialism on the history of modes of production, represents a loss of the dialectic, which can only be recovered through a reintroduction of the process of the "subject" known to psychoanalysis. The individual and language are only returned to their sociohistorical imbrication by way of a return to Freud's "discovery" of the unconscious. In 1974 the return to Freud provides the *theory* of the process that poetic language performs. "The theory of the unconscious seeks the very thing that poetic language practices within and against the social order: the ultimate means of its transformation or subversion, the precondition for its survival and revolution" (Kristeva 1974, 81).

This ultimate means of transformation, and precondition, of the social order is developed in Kristeva's conception of *"signifiance." Signifiance*, the "signifying process," encompasses the formation of the subject and meaning that symbolic functioning, strictly speaking, depends on and refuses, the refusal being more or less inflexible depending on the rationality of the social symbolic order. In Kristeva's view, the bourgeois social order is particularly inflexible with respect to the suppression of its dependence on *signifiance,* for it dispenses with the social tensions and dissatisfactions that express that dependence, absorbing them into the unity of the subject or the state. Psychoanalytic theory provides a reconstruction of both the nature of the signifying process, for which the theory of the drives is the key, and the process of absorption, thanks to the theory of narcissism. In the latter case, the process of narcissistic fixation stands as the paradigm for the attachment of the signifying process to the unity of the subject (the bourgeois individual), and for its attachment to a position masking as mere legal neutrality (the bourgeois state). At this point in Kristeva's thought, psychoanalysis stands apart from the problem it diagnoses, the rigidity of the modern social order, as well as from the practice that is needed if any subversion of that order is to be possible: poetic language. "Theory" is set apart. Kristeva's reconstruction of the formation and deformation of modern secular discourses and institutions therefore rests on a recapitulation of the Marxist arrangement of theory, the problem, and "work." Psychoanalysis occupies the first position, *theory,* since it permits *the problem,* the inflexibility of the bourgeois world, to be grasped in terms of narcissistic fixation. Moreover, the discovery of the unconscious allows the operations that counter this rigidity to be theoretically articulated, showing how poetic language carries out the transformation of meaning and the subject, the moment of "work" (*practice*). Because the thought of *Revolution in Poetic Language* rests on this classical arrangement of theory, the problem, and work—and not because it is a thought about literature rather than social struggle—the problem of social transformation is conceived in terms of how the negativity of the signifying process is to have a historical impact. The way in which theory, the problem, and work stand in relation to each other equally affects the articulation of social transformation, as I will suggest.

The rest of this chapter clarifies how the revolutionary standpoint of 1974 develops through Kristeva's departure from Lacan, which is a return to the crossroads of idealism and materialism. Kristeva's "return to Freud" argues that the psychoanalytic theory of the drives is the key to elucidating the negativity repressed by the bourgeois social-symbolic system: "those positions of mastery that conceal their violence and pretend to be mere legal neutrality" (1974, 83). Given that elucidation, Kristeva argues that art and literature have the capacity to inscribe this negativity in and through the very process of the production of the artwork, once social dissatisfactions—erupting in the revolutions of the second half of the nineteenth century—can be dispersed or absorbed owing to the connection between the mechanisms of capitalism and the maintenance of modern, secular institutions. "Capitalism leaves the subject the right to revolt, preserving for itself the right to suppress that revolt. The ideological systems capitalism proposes, however, subdue, unify, and consolidate that revolt, bringing it back within the field of unity (that of the subject and the State). When objective conditions were not such that this state of tension could be resolved through revolution, rejection became symbolized in the avant-garde texts of the nineteenth century where the repressed truth of a shattered subject was then confined" (210–211). Insofar as art and literature inscribe negativity in the formation of the artwork they can provide a site of confrontation with the repression through which bourgeois ideology sustains itself. Kristeva's focus on the functioning of repression rather than the specific meanings and values of bourgeois ideology is supported by the argument that a direct attack on the latter is no longer feasible given the ramification of capitalist society. "Revolution in poetic language" refers to the capacity of poetic language to bring strictly symbolic functioning into an encounter with its process of production, *signifiance,* for *signifiance* involves a functioning other than strictly symbolic functioning: semiotic functioning. The key to the "semiotic," and so to Kristeva's clarification of the negativity of poetic language, is the Freudian theory of the drive.

In Freud the drive is a boundary concept of soma and psyche, indicating that the biological dimensions of the human being are always taken up, or at the point of being taken up, into another register. With Kristeva, this register is neither the symbolic one nor is it destined to be encompassed by the latter. This is where she differs from Lacan. The drive, for her, is a corporeal inscription of the symbolic that is not only prior to the appearance of linguistic capacities or object-relation. It is also distinct from the effects of language that, on the Lacanian view, make the subject the *material* of the *structure* of language. Kristeva is attempting to describe the elements of something outside the realm of symbolic functioning, and so outside the realm of given structures of meaning and values. It might be called natural so long as this is understood, not as the Other of the symbolic field, but as the "not yet symbolized." From the developmental perspective, the semiotic is logically and chronologically prior to the symbolic order. Assuming the entrance into language, semiotic functioning is in excess of symbolic functioning, and heterogeneous to it, so that neither the semiotic nor the symbolic can fully overcome or subsume the other.

Kristeva's thought on the drive insists on the biological, corporeal elements in the constitution of the subject, elements that do not make embodiment a mechanical, naturalized dimension of subjectivity, however. For they are dependent on an exposure to otherness that brings about nonsignifying *alterations* in subjectivity at the level of the body. The alterations are constitutive of embodiment itself, so that the speaking subject is, first, a highly altered "human animal." In Kristeva's writings of the 1980s, where these corporeal elements are elaborated in more detail, what happens to them in the symbolic order is highly consequential for possibilities of self-relation, connections with others, and world-relation. More generally, Kristeva's thought on the drive can be seen as a rejection of the Lacanian tendency to make the subject fully a subject "of language." That there is nothing corporeal that does not centrally involve the structure of language appears to be the consequence of Lacan's insistence that there is nothing about the body that is not detached from its natural foundations. Even the Lacanian drive, then, would be noncorporeal, and so subject to representation.[6]

In "The Gift of Love and the Debt of Desire" (1998) Shepherdson has made a compelling argument that Lacan's thought does not submit the corporeality of the subject to the structure of language, *in toto*. As he acknowledges, on the traditional reading, Lacanian theory would be "plagued by an excessively linguistic or disembodied perspective" (46). He rejects this reading, arguing that what the drive means in Lacan is the residue in subjectivity of prelinguistic moments in the constitution of the subject. The residue is the effect of the repression of those moments on the entrance into language. The argument is particularly clear in Shepherdson's discussion of Lacan's reading of Freud on the loss of the real breast and the emergence of the "hallucinated breast." The latter "is the gift of a hallucinated object in which satisfaction can be taken apart from the satisfaction of need—an object that serves, unlike the natural thing, to give a place to lack, a local habitation, thereby providing the tentative beginning of a limit to this lack, a protosymbolic limit, in relation to which the body will be organized" (39). Here we find the detachment of the body from its natural foundations (from the register of need to that of demand, in Lacan's terminology). However, we do not find that this detachment is, immediately, an inscription in the structure of language defined by internal relations of difference. Rather, the object-relation that pertains to the hallucinated breast is "the corporeal registration of loss," "an oral inscription of lack . . . in its concrete bodily localization" (39). This means that, in respect of symbolic lack, the drive is the *residue* of the *mark* of presymbolic loss. The concept of the drive in Lacan therefore indicates that there are different modalities of lack in his theory. The drive itself is an incompleteness in the subject's structuration in language: "the circuit of the drive is established at the place where the symbolic cut is incomplete" (62). Moreover, the circuit of the drive points to, or calls up—in a manner that is different from but still in a sense tied to—a prelinguistic, ineliminably corporeal alteration in subjectivity: a "cut" prior to the symbolic cut that is so often taken to fulfil the meaning of "lack" in Lacan. Finally, the drive lends a certain autonomy to desire in respect of desire's relation to the mediation of the Law.

On Shepherdson's reading, what prevents readers from understanding the complexity of Lacan's thought on lack is insufficient attention to his thought on "object *a*." For it is this thought that follows through the different divisions in the subject that are brought about in different modes of object-relation—where the latter does not imply an outside object that a subject takes up a relationship to, but the exposure to otherness that Kristeva tracks at different levels as well, above all in the 1980s trilogy. In sum, the Lacanian "speaking subject" is one divided by drives as well as by language and desiring metonymy. All this flies quite in the face of traditional readings of Lacan's conception of the unconscious. It brings his thought very close to Kristeva's departure from it. Indeed, it may be that Kristeva's thought on the "semiotic" only presents a significant departure from Lacan once the relationship between the semiotic and symbolic changes in the later writings. We will find that there is such a departure there, even given Shepherdson's underlining of the discovery of embodiment in Lacan.[7] For the present, this chapter continues to elucidate how the concept of the drive appears in Kristeva's thinking in 1974.

In *Revolution in Poetic Language* the psychoanalytic concept of the drive is the key to explicating the nature of semiotic functioning. With Kristeva, the early life of the drive is predominantly an instinctual motion, and the most primitive registering of a confrontation with the symbolic on the part of a preverbal being that is dependent, from the beginning and for a long period, on an other (paradigmatically the mother). The centrality of this dependence in Kristeva's thought is consistent with Lacan's assertion of the "prematurity" of the newborn infant, following Freud's discovery that a "biological" factor is prominent in the causation of neuroses: "the long period of time during which the young of the human species is in a condition of helplessness and dependence" (Freud 1926, 154). Kristeva builds up her conception of the semiotic out of this combination of features: corporeal life before the appearance of linguistic capacities, which, since it is a life dependent on and thereby exposed to the symbolic being of another, is never "mere" corporeal life. Strictly speaking, this combination of features describes Kristeva's "semiotic *chora,*" the term *chora* being adopted from Plato's *Timaeus* and used to denote "an essentially mobile and extremely provisional articulation constituted by movements and their ephemeral stases" that does not lend itself to phenomenological, spatial intuitions (1974, 25–26). For Kristeva, all discourse, that is to say, everything within the field supported by the distinction symbolic/real, depends on and refuses this realm of the "not yet symbolized" in which the inside/outside boundary, and so subject- and object-positions—which is to say "separation"—are not yet established. The semiotic *chora* can be presented either by analogy with vocal or kinetic rhythm or by theoretical description, but never demonstrated. Here we run up against the theoretical status of psychoanalysis in 1974. Kristeva proposes that psychoanalysis has permitted the description of the *chora* to be made thanks to its specification of unconscious processes.

> Discrete quantities of energy move through the body of the subject who is not yet constituted as such and, in the course of his development, they are arranged [*se disposent*] according to the various constraints imposed on this body—always already involved in a semiotic process—by family and social structures. In this way the drives, which are "energy" charges as well as "psychical" marks, articulate what we call a *chora:* a nonexpressive totality formed by the drives and their stases in a motility that is as full of movement as it is regulated. (1974, 25)

From one point of view, then, the semiotic is an ordering of the drives in relation to the mother's body. The mother's body is a mediator of the symbolic, for the whole corporeal exchange between mother and child conveys familial and social imperatives to the body of a subject, where neither the body nor the subject is constituted as such. From this it is clear that insofar as the semiotic centrally concerns the *mother's* body, this is no presymbolic body. Moreover, Kristeva's insistence that the semiotic involves preverbal capacities on the part of the *infans* challenges a tendency in the critical reception of her thought to identify the semiotic *chora* too closely with "the mother's body."[8] The identification can only be made if the theory of the drive at the center of Kristeva's description of the *chora* is ignored. The source of the drive is neither the naturalized mother's body nor the naturalized organs of the infant. Drive theory works to articulate *preverbal capacities* to struggle with an absolutely unmasterable otherness that is not (yet) "outside." These semiotic capacities consist in a struggle with the impact of the symbolic on the part of a being that is not inscribed in the symbolic register. (Chapters 2–4 below, show how they acquire further determination in Kristeva's later thought as specific dimensions of the narcissistic structure.) The aim of *Revolution in Poetic Language* is to show that semiotic capacities rest on a feature of the drive introduced by Freud and repeatedly emphasized by Kristeva: its dominant destructive wave, isolated terminologically as "the death drive." On the one hand, the death drive is necessary if any psychic configuration is to emerge from the bodily exchange between mother and child. On the other hand, the very nature of the *chora* as a motility whose regulation cannot lead to the establishment of positions is owed to the destructive wave of the drive. Finally, the drive's destructive wave makes the mapping of the body through the ordering of the drives ambiguous in a way that is not captured by the thought that primal mapping is, as such, an imposition of imperatives deriving from the social realm and internalized in the constitution of the subject (a common reading in the feminist reception of Kristeva's notion of primal mapping). The following discussion of Kristeva's return to Freud's theory of the drive in *Revolution in Poetic Language* aims to illuminate this claim.

Revolution in Poetic Language presents a minute logic of the drives that attempts to articulate the transitions from the most elementary moment of symbolic impact to the emergence of the sign itself. First, the destructive portion of the drive is central to what makes instinctual motion a wave motion. The repeated wave motion involves a building up of tension—"excitation"—which, owing to nonsatisfaction (frustration), includes a moment of constraint, thanks to which the wave breaks, leaving a *mark*. "Repeated drives or the shocks from energy discharges create a state of [unsatisfied] excitation . . . [that] produces, through a qualitative leap, a repercussion that delays, momentarily absorbs, and posits that excitation" (1974, 171). The "mark" in Kristeva combines those features of delay, momentary absorption, and the positing of nonsatisfied excitation. It makes possible, in turn, a reactivation of the motion, a return of the destructive wave to divide, displace, or consolidate the mark. This most archaic moment in Kristeva's logic of the drives can be captured in an image. The whole movement is like the formation, division, and displacement of wave patterns on a shoreline. The image fails insofar as, although it is the organs where the drives are applied, the mark is not "made" in some distinct matter. Rather, drives and their stases are inextricably corporeal and psychic inscriptions. Kristeva therefore stresses the meaning of the drive as an articulation (*charnière*), in her words a "rhythmic totality," which orients and connects the infant's body to the mother's body. The concept of the drive, then, is the concept of a presymbolic orientation and connection between the *infans* and an "artificial" extension, tied to the condition of infantile helplessness and dependence. Whenever the mother's body, as mediator of familial and social imperatives, is viewed as the very origin of, and not only necessary for, the motility and genesis of the *chora* the *charnière* is abstracted from.

Kristeva's deploys the term "drive re-jection" to designate the motility and genesis of the *chora*. Although the logic of the drives is at once abstract and mysterious, its purpose is to convey a kind of repetition on the border of soma and psyche that is sparked by the symbolic but not equivalent to its modes of operation, the articulated network of differences expounded by Lacan. Nor, on the other hand, is drive re-jection the Other of those modes of operation. It is not "a merely mechanical repetition of an undifferentiated 'identity'" (1974, 171). Semiotic capacities, which are neither symbolic nor merely mechanical, precede symbolic capacities as their necessary precondition. The whole process, from mark to unstable engram to sign, involves a transition from "the agitated body," where drives hold sway, to "the speaking body."

Kristeva is explicit, nonetheless, that this prelinguistic isolation of the semiotic is no more than a "*theoretical supposition* justified by the need for description" (1974, 68). The semiotic only *exists* within the symbolic field where it is articulated as heterogeneous to the sign. Freudian theory, or psychoanalysis as theory, has enabled Kristeva to articulate a motility of the semiotic, a mode of repetition, which implies the potential destruction of any symbolic arrangement the semiotic is submitted to. This conception of repetition is therefore the key to the thought on negativity in *Revolution in Poetic Language,* and so to its view of the possibility of symbolic renewal, the transformation of meaning and the subject.

Kristeva sees her return to Freud's theory of the drives as setting her conception of negativity off from both the negativity presented by idealist thought, centered on consciousness (Hegel), and negativity centered on language

(Lacan). Thanks to the theoretical isolation of the prelinguistic semiotic *chora,* ultimately Freud's "unconscious," a conception of negativity is expounded which belongs neither to the volitional or cognitive abilities of the subject nor to the Lacanian operations of language, which decentered that subject. Even so, semiotic functioning in the symbolic field does not imply some kind of return to the semiotic "as such." Although the rhythmic space of the *chora* is isolated as preliminary it is found only at the symbolic level, presupposing the "break" which posits the signifier/signified articulation, as well as the positions of object (outside) and subject (absent from the signifier). Semiotic functioning in the symbolic field is an activation, in Kristeva's terms, of the heteregeneous contradiction of semiotic and symbolic: her *signifiance* or signifying process. The affirmation of art, more specifically a certain literature, in *Revolution in Poetic Language* rests on the claim that the heterogeneous contradiction of the semiotic and symbolic is recovered when significations—the meanings that compose prevailing discourses—are dismantled and thereby returned to their nonsignifying, drive-invested elements, which are then amenable to a reconfiguration. This thought makes up Kristeva's psychoanalytic version of the project in which modern literature departs from its role as representation (of an outside object) and seeks out the conditions of its own appearance as a work. In her version what is paramount is the thesis that certain material supports—voice, gesture, color, for example—are susceptible to the imprint of semiotic motility (drive re-jection). In the words of *Revolution in Poetic Language*, the semiotic network is "more or less integrated as a *signifier,*" and this is what permits the semiotic combinatorial system to obtain "the complex articulation we associate with it in musical and poetic practices" (1974, 47, 68). Poetic language brings semiotic motility to bear on symbolic functioning that is immobilized in a deracinated and mastering signification. Dismantling the meaningful object (representation, idea, thing), it deprives the object of the unity which obtains in the specular captivation (optical, as in the mirror stage, and/or conceptual), substituting signifying elements for the meaningful object. The signifying elements—"signifiers"—are drive-invested fragments, notably rhythm, tone, color, or words, which tend to return to nonsymbolic negativity, which is to say, semiotic functioning. Although the return to the signifying elements brings the subject and meaning to the threshold of drive re-jection, in poetic language the fragments are equally subject to a combinatory moment—"fitting together, detaching, including, and building up 'parts' into some kind of 'totality'"—which preempts symbolic collapse (102). In sum, with Kristeva, literature is rhythm made intelligible by a symbolic barrier. Moreover, given that the semiotic network is "more or less" integrated in the signifier, non-symbolic functioning is always in excess of intelligible translation, an excess that represents the possibility of the return and renewal of poetic subversion.

On the one hand, then, the heterogeneous contradiction of the semiotic and symbolic never goes so far as the complete loss of symbolic functioning. On the other hand, conversely, symbolic functioning can never fulfill the abstraction from semiotic functioning. Nevertheless, symbolic functioning as such involves a refusal of the semiotic and a social symbolic order may be especially inflexible with respect to that refusal. This is Kristeva's thought when she characterizes the bourgeois social symbolic system as what brings everything back within the field of unity. That is to say, the bourgeois social symbolic system suppresses the recognition that symbolic functioning involves a refusal of the semiotic. In these conditions *poetic language* recovers the relationship of the semiotic and symbolic dimensions of language.

In sum, Kristeva's particular rendering of the thesis that modern literature reaches into the conditions of its own appearance as a work is one that insists that the signifying elements freed from a deracinated signification are themselves trajectories of the agitated body, semiotic-and-symbolic. There are moments in Kristeva's writings where it looks as though this is a transhistorical capacity of the artwork. However, her assertion that the negativity of poetic language becomes self-conscious in nineteenth-century avant-garde literature provides some acknowledgment that what distinguishes modern art is art's autonomy. Only art freed from doing duty to the ritual, religious, or political realms (which thereby define art's meaning) can represent *signifiance,* and so the semiotic-symbolic relationship. Thus the political meaning of Kristeva's thesis on revolution in poetic language is that the bourgeois social symbolic system both divorces aesthetic practice from social relations and may be subject to critique thanks to the autonomous signifying practice of modern literature.

However, the major objective in this account of Kristeva's return to the theory of the drives has been to show that in 1974 psychoanalysis stands to art as theory to practice. Psychoanalysis is of course included with artistic practice amongst the phenomena that manifest both semiotic and symbolic functioning, for it is defined in part by the destabilization of a subject exposed to an other in the transference-relation, a destabilization which centrally involves the reactivation of nonsymbolized drives, Kristeva's "semiotic motility." On this view, psychoanalytic experience reaches the repressed of the dominant ideological system, accessing the shattered subject of that ideology, and putting the subject in process/on trial (*le sujet-en-procès*). If destabilization is not to lead to the collapse of the subject, a boundary moment must be restored to it. This happens through the realization in language of the activation of nonsymbolized drives, so that the subject is not isolated in a process that goes from unity to destabilization, but is, rather, brought into connection with the signifying process.

Despite this view of the power of psychoanalysis, the import of psychoanalytic experience is assessed, in the last instance, in terms of a revolutionary criterion, the potential it has for a historical impact. In other words, psychoanalytic experience is assessed for its potential for subjective and social transformation. How psychoanalytic experience fares in this assessment rests on the view that this potential is lost where a practice confines the signifying process within a "subjective enclosure," following the path of narcissistic fixation in the formation of the ego. In Kristeva's view, psychoanalysis fails the revolutionary criterion by definition, not because of its setting, but because the realization in language of the subject-in-process takes place in and through an identification ultimately defined by prevailing family and social structures. Kristeva here shares the view that the talking cure is normative, not in any independent fashion, but within the bounds of dominant normativity. Her particular rendering of the normativity of the talking cure lies in her claim that the transference-relation is personified: "transference permits the analysand to take over the (power of) discourse the analyst is presumed to hold. Although it thereby reconstructs the signifying process, this renewal of power locks it up within a discourse that tests intrafamilial relations" (1974, 208).

Although Kristeva does not suggest that every recovery of the signifying process in literature is on the way to having a historical impact, poetic language fares better with respect to the revolutionary criterion. For a historical impact to be possible the realization of the signifying process must embrace social forms. The ambiguity of art's autonomy as a critical practice is paramount here, for the failing of artistic representation lies in its tendency to define itself in opposition to social and political practices, thereby becoming complicit with the marginalization through which the bourgeois system accommodates and avails itself of the negativity it abuts against. In short, art becomes complicit with the system's capacities to use dissent for its own continuation. This is the case with the artistic phenomenon that is the object of Kristeva's *doctorat d'état*, the nineteenth-century avant-garde, even though it is this literature in which the inscription of negativity becomes fully self-conscious. "Expending thought through the signifying process, the text inscribes the negativity that (capitalist) society and its official ideology repress. Although it thus dissents from the dominant economic and ideological system, the text also plays into its hands: through the text, the system provides itself with what it lacks—rejection—but keeps it in a domain apart, confining it to the ego, to the 'inner experience' of an elite, and to esoterism. The text becomes the agent of a new religion that is no longer universal but elitist and esoteric" (1974, 186).

Art's confinement to a subjective enclosure amounts to an attachment of the most unstable moments of the signifying process, drive re-jection, to the unity of the subject. Kristeva goes to psychoanalytic thought again for the articulation of the "unity" of the subject, which, in her early view, is to be found in the account of ego formation. The confinement of art to esoterism follows the path that protects an ego in the process of formation against the destructive force of the drives: the path of narcissistic fixation. Thus it appears that psychoanalysis is irredeemably captured by the structure it discovers—narcissism—because of the need of identification in the transference-relation. The restoration of a boundary moment to the subject-in-process is impossible without the personification of that boundary moment, an addressee ultimately caught in familial and social structures. Poetic language, in contrast, can overcome this limitation because of the absence of any addressee in the restoration of the boundary moment. For the always absent "addressee" of poetic language "is the *site of language itself* or, more precisely, its thetic moment, which the text appropriates by introducing within it, as we have said, semiotic motility. In so doing, the text takes up strictly individual experience and invests it directly in a signification (*Bedeutung*), in other words, in an enunciation and denotation that stem from the socio-symbolic whole. In this way, significations (ideologies) that preoccupy the social group—the ones implied in its acts of controlling them—are put into play by the process of the subject they wanted to ignore" (1974, 208–209)

Poetic language is a practice played out in relation to the boundary moment of language in which the symbolic/real distinction is posited along with subject-object positionality. Kristeva calls this the "thetic moment." From the perspective of subjective diachrony the thetic moment is the moment of entrance into the symbolic field in and through which the semiotic network comes to be more or less integrated in the signifier. Kristeva has therefore extended Lacan's "entrance into the order of language" into a thetic *phase* that embraces semiotic capacities giving access to symbolic capacities. Poetic language is a practice played out in relation to this boundary moment of language, which usually appears in the work as a syntactical constraint. The thought is that semiotic motility "bound" by a symbolic barrier, rather than bound in relation to a personified addressee, is withdrawn from attachment to the unity of the subject. If the path of narcissistic fixation is held off, the subject-in-process invades representation. In sum, "revolution in poetic language" means that the negativity of semiotic functioning is sustained within the objective arena and so counters the prevailing organization of negativity, dismantling the significations which preoccupy the social groups. "Poetic language" is the site of transformation of meaning and the subject.

In 1974 this practice comes to define the only mode of intersubjectivity worthy of the name, the only intersubjectivity that remains once social and political relations serve and are reproduced by the mechanisms of capitalism. Poetic language is then equivalent to, if not more than, ethics. "'Ethics' should be understood here to mean the negativizing of narcissism within a *practice;* in other words, a practice is ethical when it dissolves those narcissistic fixations (ones that are narrowly confined to the subject) to which the signifying process succumbs in its sociosymbolic realization. Practice, such as we have defined it, positing and dissolving meaning and the unity of the subject, therefore encompasses the ethical. The text, in its signifying disposition and its signification, is a practice assuming all positivity in order to negativize it and thereby make visible the *process* underlying it. It can thus be considered, precisely, as that which carries the ethical imperative" (1974, 233). Kristeva's argument for the significance of art and literature in *Revolution in Poetic Language* is therefore bound to focus on the realization of semiotic motility in artistic representation.

If a greater emphasis on symbolic functioning is detectable in her writings of the 1980s this is because Kristeva has been led to consider art and literature from a different viewpoint. Her thought on psychoanalysis and art is now situated within a different, broader, problematic: not the repression through which a social-symbolic system maintains itself, but the dearth of a site of engagement of the semiotic and symbolic within the modern social-symbolic system. The background presumption of Kristeva's thought is now the failure of modern secular discourses and institutions to provide a site of engagement of the semiotic and symbolic: the problem of nihilistic modernity. Religions, in contrast, had provided a site of this kind. The question of the demise of historical religions, by which she appears to mean religions constituting social symbolic systems which bind and individuate their members in ways that accommodate the semiotic in a manner specific to each system, is of major import in Kristeva's thought (see chapter 5, below). It provides a crucial point of access to her analysis of the absence of symbolic forms that accommodate the semiotic at the everyday level in secular modernity. Once modern secular institutions and discourses provide no site for the engagement of symbolic and semiotic, the task of engagement gets confined to individual experience, leading to the modern "isolation of the soul." Although religions are a possible recourse for the individual in such conditions, resorting to religion brings on a dispersion of individuals into various temporal and spatial moments. The individual may choose Eastern or Western religiousness, or affiliate him- or herself with a body of beliefs selected from the history of Western monotheism. In an interview she remarks: "Today's religious discourses are remnants or archaeological excavations of a lover's discourse from the past that some individuals still use in our plural, non-homogeneous history, an era in which each person lives in his own time. We may all *be* citizens of the twentieth century, but we do not all *live* in the twentieth century. Some of us live in the thirteenth century, others in the fifteenth, and still others are Buddhists, nihilists, and so on" (Guberman 1996, 69). One may alight on one of the peaks of Western monotheism or abruptly bear oneself away from that tradition. This temporal isolation implies that religions today do not make up for what is lacking to the individual: the possibility of establishing ourselves as *particular*—separate and connected (Kristeva 1983, 7).

This whole change in perspective implies that Kristeva has abandoned the attempt to seek out a logic of social transformation on the grounds of negativity in literature. More precisely, she has abandoned the attempt made in *Revolution in Poetic Language* to elucidate the transition from a transformation of meaning and the subject to social transformation. As has been seen, a major objective of that book was to modify dialectical materialism by exposing it to psychoanalysis and art. The endeavor relied on the possibility of bringing the conception of the Cultural Revolution into connection with her psychoanalytically inspired theory of signifying practices. "While affirming that the *activity of production* determines all practical action, he [Mao Tse-tung] adds class struggle, political life, and scientific and aesthetic activity to the range of possible practices" (1974, 200). What remained to be worked out in the doctoral thesis was the mediation that carries the negativity inscribed in artistic representation into the social realm. Kristeva describes it in one passage as an agency without self-consciousness. "Having joined the course of historical processes—though uniquely within representation—the signifying process gives itself an agent, an ego, that of the revolutionary who has no need of knowing and even less of closely examining the mechanism of rejection that pulverizes or brings him together again, since objectively this misjudging—imaginary or ideological—ego is the module by which the mechanism of rejection in question invades the social realm" (206).

However, this whole undertaking disappeared along with Kristeva's withdrawal from Maoism, a withdrawal which represents an abandonment of the underlying arrangement of the elements of the 1974 thesis. To recall her reiteration of the classical Marxist arrangement, psychoanalysis, in the role of theory, stands apart from the problem it grasps and elucidates—the mechanisms through which the modern bourgeois social order is maintained—but remains impotent with respect to the problem. Equally, psychoanalysis stands indefinitely apart from the artwork whose "work" as practice it can articulate theoretically. *Revolution in Poetic Language*, in line with the difficulties that beset the classical Marxist conceptions of theory and "work," reaches powerlessly for the moment of social transformation, for the three moments of theory, the problem, and practice are insufficiently bound together for the transition to social change to be anything more than a theoretical posit.

CHAPTER 2

Primary Narcissism

The Appearance of the Nihilism Problematic

Kristeva's three works, *Powers of Horror* (1980), *Tales of Love* (1983), and *Black Sun* (1987) compose a trilogy with a vision and project in common. There is a change in mood in these works—a departure from the revolutionary standpoint—that has led some to the view that Kristeva has betrayed the need of social transformation in favor of an allegiance to individual suffering. The accusation that she has lost the political vision of *Revolution in Poetic Language* appears in Smith (1988), for example. Rose (in Oliver 1993b) finds that the trilogy shows Kristeva racing back into the arms of the law. These positions miss the deep significance of the new relationship between the semiotic and symbolic in the trilogy, where Kristeva is less dedicated to the idea of the semiotic as the "excess" over representation that can return to disrupt the symbolic order, and more interested in investigating the fate of semiotic elements in social and symbolic life. For this is what allows her a much deeper reach into the problem she addresses: the crises of meaning, value, and authority in modern Western societies.

What is more, there is a new arrangement of the relationship between theory, the problem, and practice in the later writings. Psychoanalysis is no longer the theory that can articulate the problem, and the kind of practice art is in relation to the problem, while having no important practical implications of its own. Rather, psychoanalysis is the methodology of Kristeva's thought as an adequate means of approach to a problem that it forms a part of, a problem that is, in its furthest reaches, that of nihilistic modernity. It gains its theoretical distinction, not as the insight into the force of change, but as the self-consciousness of modernity's crises as they impact on individual lives, where the burden is shouldered. Moreover, psychoanalysis provides access and responds to the problem as a practice, and not solely as theory. Psychoanalysis and the aesthetic are, in different ways, what allow minor histories of modernity to be told, because they bear testimony to suffering subjectivity and the movement of its overcoming. In this way, the moments of theory, the problem, and work are so intertwined that the question of social transformation does not appear as the pinnacle of the project, one that threatens to topple off. It is ever present and has to be read through the central issues that the trilogy discusses. Kristeva, then, has not *restricted* the scope of her project to an allegiance to individual suffering. She has *expanded* it, going beyond the standpoint embedded in an ultimately powerless methodology, by finding in unacknowledged suffering the remnant of freedom in conditions of late modernity. This is why she binds the telling of her minor histories of religion and artworks to the psychoanalytic experience of suffering subjectivity.

To take another tack, the keystone of the discontinuities between the 1974 thesis and the 1980s trilogy lies in Kristeva's return to and more profound exploration of the structure of narcissism in psychoanalysis. This structure is no longer absorbed by the idea of the path of narcissistic fixation in the formation of the ego, which, in *Revolution in Poetic Language*, delimited the role of therapy to being a handmaiden to prevailing social structures. Kristeva's later exploration of the triadic structure of primary narcissism is an x ray on unacknowledged suffering, which is not a merely private and individual affair, but has a social and historical significance. Moreover, her discussions of the narcissistic structure substantiate the meaning of the "semiotic" in her writings. For what is important, now, is not only the negativity of the drive, but the presymbolic moments of subjectivity where Kristeva thinks the life of the drives is most emphatic. Her psychoanalytic accounts of the structure of narcissism in the trials of individuation reveal a level of corporeal responsiveness and affective relations that turn on a prelinguistic exposure to otherness, separateness, and loss. This is the "semiotic," or, roughly, embodied experience that needs to be accommodated in social and symbolic life if there is to be adequate self-relation, connections with others, and social bonding. For her, the fact that contemporary psychoanalysis is witness, less to oedipal struggles with paternal law, and more to experiences of failings in love, lacks of meaning and self-orientation, and depression, reveals that modern Western societies neglect this constitutive dimension of separateness, connectedness, and the social bond. That is to say, for Kristeva, psychoanalysis discovers the tendential severance of the semiotic and symbolic: the problem of modern nihilism. This is why the figure of Narcissus is apparently so ambiguous in her thought. For Narcissus shows up today in his or her infantile, regressive form, socially and symbolically abandoned. On the other hand, unacknowledged suffering is the remnant of freedom because the suffering subjectivity that Kristeva attends to—the abandoned Narcissus—is where the semiotic is lodged. In sum, it could be said that narcissism is the complication which opens up Kristeva's analysis of modernity.

The trilogy of the 1980s therefore focuses on the need, and failure, of the semiotic to take on symbolic form in prevailing institutions and discourses; on what happens in this failure and in the moments that do provide the semiotic with a symbolic life (psychoanalysis and artworks). What the failure means, above all, is that Western cultures are deprived, especially, of the discourses of love, loss, and separateness that are necessary for being *with* others and for discourses to have meaning and value. From a different perspective, psychoanalysis reveals the weaknesses of the maturational processes typically available for subject-formation in Western cultures. This is not only a matter of how we are to understand, or assess, the value of the symbolic, paternal function. It is just as much, if not more, a question of the fate of object-relations whose paradigms turn on the relation to the early mother prior to the sway of symbolic law, that is to say, the "pre-oedipal" relations that make up primary narcissism.

At the strictly psychoanalytic level of Kristeva's thought, we find the tendential severance of the semiotic and symbolic in the dissociation of representation from embodied experience. In slightly more technical terms, drives and affects—the registrations of nonsymbolized exposure to otherness, separateness, and loss—are cut off from the life of signs. The psychoanalytic thought conveys and reflects on what appears on the couch. That is to say, psychoanalysis is witness to *unacknowledged* suffering, in one sense of the term. At this level of her thought, then, the more "narrowly" individual or subjective the object of her analysis appears to be, the more it represents the wider cultural and societal conditions. The narcissistic constriction is the foremost psychological symptom of the failings of modern institutions and discourses to accommodate the corporeal, affective, and mimetic dimension of separateness and connections with others. As a result, the trilogy is neither a focus on the self in abstraction from the social and political—except insofar as it encounters the worldless self as a symptom of abstractedness—nor is it an emphasis on the law (the symbolic) in abandonment of the semiotic. It is, rather, an investigation of the pervious border between the individual and society where psychoanalysis found Narcissus, abandoned—found the problem of nihilistic modernity. When Kristeva diagnoses the weakness or absence of values, meaning, and the "other" in suffering subjectivity, she discovers the society's failure to represent its own limits—the limit of the ties between the individual and society. She therefore finds a world deprived of psychic life, where psychic life *means* the possibilities available to subjects in a society that reflects on its own borders, as well as those of subjects.

An important implication of this is what follows for Kristeva's difference from Lacan. When Lacan's account begins with the mirror stage (lack), and the symbolic as the acceptance of lack, the symbolic is hooked on to the oedipal structure. As a result, he, like Freud, cannot cope with the new maladies of the soul that start earlier in the developmental account. Put otherwise, we might say that Kristeva allows us to see that, if subjectivity is tied to the oedipal, and only this is investigated, then, like Heidegger, there is only a crisis in rationality. Although this exists it does not *get at* the structure of suffering, since it is not law we lack but adequate relations to ourselves, and so on. From this point of view, Lacan is antipsychological. There's only one message—accept your lack! live with mediation!—even if it takes a lot of work to accept it. This fails to get at the nature of suffering at a fundamental level. Lacan goes for exorbitant cases—explorations of psychotic disorders—because the suffering is not fine-grained in relationships to self and others.

The thought I am presenting is contentious, but it's hard to see any other way around the question, because it is a question of a fine-grained account of subjectivity that is going to do the work of getting at the structure of suffering. This is why Kristeva's trilogy stays riveted to the presymbolic (largely pre-imaginary) moments. Once again, doing more on the difference between Kristeva and Lacan on the drives will not shift the story. An exorbitant way of stating the difference between them is this. Lacan's stroke of genius is also the source of his inadequacy. He saw that the deepest existential truth about the subject—lack, finitude—is equally what is at stake in the resolution of the Oedipus complex: the acceptance of finitude. So his thought harbors an explicit philosophical claim: *life* is meaningless to the family romance. It is a stroke of genius, but if it becomes the only thought, then it turns out to be an antipsychological one, in the deep sense, so that everything happens at the level of the existential and symbolic, and the psychological is a derivative. Kristeva inherits the Lacanian stroke of genius. Because she overly accepts the story about language and lack (for her, finitude, so that the feminist protest against the Phallus is an unnecessary fuss), she forces everything else that's important psychologically—that Lacan finds unimportant—into the pre-imaginary level where the life of the drives is most emphatic (other than the imaginary father, as we will see). This disbars her at moments from an adequate engagement with cultural materials (to this extent I am in agreement with Hill 1993). However, for the sake of *this* book, I am going to have to suffer this inadequacy with her. For the aim is to draw out as far as I am able the scope of Kristeva's attention to the structure of suffering subjectivity, by relating it to the presence of the nihilism problematic in her thought.

Kristeva's vision and project are reflected in the structure of each book of the trilogy. Each one begins with chapters on the strictly psychoanalytic level of her thought, which are then followed by a "minor history" of the ways in which the semiotic *has* taken on symbolic form in Western cultures. The discussion of various levels of Kristeva's thought in the trilogy—the psychoanalytic theory, the thought on religion, and the analyses of artworks—takes us to the end of Part 2 of this book. The rest of Part 1 is dedicated to the strictly psychoanalytic level of Kristeva's thought, not only on the premise that the complication of the narcissistic structure opens up her analysis of modernity, but because the minor histories of art and religion must remain tied to suffering subjectivity, for reasons that have been addressed.

A simplified, and far from exhaustive, history of psychoanalytic thought on narcissism, and its extension into other fields, is helpful at this point. Attention to phenomena of ego instability in the therapeutic setting led to the development of a body of thought on narcissism that displaced the genetic centrality of the Oedipus complex in Freud's account of subject formation.[1] Nonetheless, psychoanalytic thought on narcissism is usually traced to Freud's "On Narcissism: An Introduction" (1914), an essay which foreshadows the major modifications of his theory of the unconscious in later works.[2] The narcissistic structure is a function in the formation of the ego. Freud's essay illuminates the most familiar connotations of narcissism: self-love and "illusory omnipotence." He proposes that the deflection from autoeroticism that begins psychic life occurs through a libidinal *self*-investment. More precisely, the narcissistic position is an organization of the libido prior to libidinal investment in objects. In other words, self-love precedes object-love. Narcissism therefore underlies and informs the self known in terms of its symbolic capacities and its relations to others. It shows up where those capacities and relations are weakened or have collapsed. The extensions of Freud's thought on narcissism appear in a body of thought that has become known as, or is attentive to, object-relations theory, a development first motivated by the prevalence of narcissism on the couch.[3] Klein, Winnicott, Kohut, and Abraham are central figures in this tradition.

The psychoanalytic view of narcissism has entered into social and political theory, where it is used, for example, to illuminate the collapse of social being. In *The Culture of Narcissism* (1979) Christopher Lasch lines up the problems in ego stability attended to by psychoanalysis with developments in capitalist society. Lasch writes of the "new Narcissus" as a figure who belongs to the waning of a historical sense of time, the abdication of authority, and the trivialization of personal relations. More recently, Joel Whitebook (1995) has drawn psychoanalytic thought on narcissism into a review of the role of rationality as a source of social and political transformation. His book *Perversion and Utopia* is committed to the traditional ability of Frankfurt School critical theory to embrace the discoveries of psychoanalysis in the critique of modern reason without abandoning reason to its debased forms. It reconsiders the significance of the ego once two divergent uses of psychoanalysis in social theory have proved inadequate to the task of assessing possible sources of social and political change. These uses are, first, the idea of the transgressive potential of the id (Marcuse 1955) and, second, the endorsement of the social function of the superego, which makes all divergence from the paternal universe a failure in differentiation and an attack on social reality as such (Chasseguet-Smirgel 1986, Whitebook 1995, 56f). For Whitebook, the psychoanalytic account of ego formation provides a way of presenting the capacity for modern rationality to accommodate rather than repress its others. The ego and reason are both synthetic functions, subject, certainly, to an array of aberrations (those critiqued by postmodernist thought) but they cannot be identified with those aberrations. There are pathological and nonpathological forms of synthesis.

Kristeva's reinterrogation of narcissism complicates the situation. She does not situate her thought in terms of the repressive hypothesis on which the theses of Marcuse and Lasch both rely. Nor would she follow through Whitebook's revaluation of modern rationality without considering the structure of suffering that weakens the ego's synthetic function.

The objective of this and the following two chapters is to clarify Kristeva's thought on the triadic structure of narcissism, whose three dimensions are primary idealization (discussed in *Tales of Love*), abjection (*Powers of Horror*), and primal melancholy (*Black Sun*). I begin with the discussion of primary idealization, rather than following the order of publication of the three texts, because, although each of Kristeva's psychic structures is an aspect of the narcissistic structure, *Tales of Love* shows most clearly that the new direction Kristeva's thought takes in the trilogy turns on a reinterrogation of narcissism.

Primary Idealization

In its clearest theoretical ambition the project of *Tales of Love* is to argue the need for a fully secular articulation of both the human being's constitutive exposure to exteriority and the guarantee or support for taking up a relationship to it. In other words, the book seeks out an articulation of a "groundless ground" that sustains a self by fulfilling the conditions for adequate separateness and connectedness. Kristeva repeatedly emphasizes the psychoanalytic discovery—Freud's discovery—that to assume the balance of individuals is to overreach the complexities of subjectivity that stem from the constitution of the subject in exposure to exteriority. There are difficulties and failings of subjectivity that must be related to the way in which the subject is constituted, and if a theory of human intersubjectivity is grounded on the assumed balance of individuals, those failings are only intensified. Psychoanalysis is a discourse that explicates the difficulties of subjectivity and what is required to avoid the collapse of the subject. It turns, then, on the question of the constitutive exposure to exteriority and what is required to take up a relationship to it.

Lacan's thought on the constitutive exposure to exteriority is developed in his idea of "the discourse of the Other." As we have seen, the Lacanian symbolic stands for both the exposure to exteriority and the guarantee for taking up a relationship to it. The notion that the speaking subject is a "subject of lack" means that to sustain a self is to accept and negotiate that one's self is not a unity, that the subject is divided by language and desire. To sustain a self is to accept the paths of desire and the fact of language, both of which cut us off from any ultimate fulfillment of desire. In Lacanian terms, the fulfillment of desire would be the negation of language. For language conclusively separates the subject from the thing, paradigmatically the maternal container. The conversion of the maternal container into the *object,* paradigmatically the mother as object of desire, is necessary for the emergence of a *subject* now set on the path of social and symbolic being. The negation of language is often thought of in terms of a merger with the maternal container. With Lacan, it is a collapse into the "real." In Kristeva's terms, the fulfillment of desire is an impossible return to a pleasure fused with nature. Nonetheless, her return to the question of exteriority in psychoanalysis argues that the relationship to lack ("castration"), which is an acceptance that the subject is divided by desire and language, is a necessary but not sufficient condition for adequate individuation and connectedness. On the one hand, she stresses that:

> certain texts written by Freud (*The Interpretation of Dreams,* but especially those of the second topology, in particular the *Metapsychology*) and their

> recent extensions (notably by Lacan), imply that castration is, in sum, the imaginary construction of a radical operation which constitutes the symbolic field and all beings inscribed therein. This operation constitutes signs and syntax; that is, language, as a *separation* from a presumed state of nature, of pleasure fused with nature so that the introduction of an articulated network of differences, which refers to objects henceforth and only in this way separated from a subject, may constitute *meaning.* (1979, 198).[4]

Thus "castration" is taken to be the imaginary construction of the symbolic function, which is the principle of the symbolic order and the condition for entrance into it. The symbolic function is indispensable to social and symbolic being. On the other hand, with Kristeva, what is also required for social and symbolic being is a symbolic accommodation of the semiotic. Her theoretical isolation of presymbolic psychic structures giving access to the symbolic function aims to show what needs to *take on, be given symbolic form* if there is to be value and meaning. Her psychoanalytic thought details this requirement and provides an approach to its wider implications. At the level of strictly psychoanalytic accounting, the dispositions giving access to the symbolic function configure an exposure to exteriority that is logically and chronologically prior to lack. In short, the struggle with the impact of the symbolic on the preverbal child turns around *loss/emptiness.*[5] Kristeva's account of the advent of and struggle with loss/emptiness presents foundations of the imaginary that precede the mirror stage. Her psychoanalytic thought amounts, then, to a reevaluation of the imaginary and its relation to the symbolic. The reevaluation is clearest in *Tales of Love,* which expands on the imaginary relations at the basis of the ego.[6] Considered as a reformulation of the Lacanian imaginary, Kristeva's reinterrogation of primary narcissism begins with the question: "Does the 'mirror stage' emerge out of nowhere?" (1983, 22).

Conventionally, psychoanalytic accounts of narcissism set out from its classical dyadic structure: an ego in love with itself or, in more precise terms, an ego taking itself as the object of libido that has been *withdrawn from* an object (an other). However, the detection of problems in ego stability provoked a turn to the investigation of an archaic—"pre-objectal" and correspondingly obscure—position of narcissism known as primary narcissism. Kristeva is extending this investigation when she expands on the most general psychoanalytic thought on narcissism, present since Freud. This is the thought that the love-relationship is *attached* to narcissism.

> Freud seems to suggest that it is not Eros but narcissistic primacy that sparks and perhaps dominates psychic life; he thus sets up self-deception at the basis of one's relationship to reality. Such a perpetuation of illusion,

> however, finds itself rehabilitated, neutralized, normalized, at the bosom of my loving reality. For Freud, as we know, binds the state of loving to narcissism; the choice of the love object, be it "narcissistic" or "anaclitic," proves satisfying in any case if and only if that object relates to the subject's narcissism in one of two ways: either through personal narcissistic reward (where Narcissus is the subject), or narcissistic delegation (Narcissus is the other; for Freud, the woman). A narcissistic destiny would in some way underlie all our object choices, but this is a destiny that society on the one hand, and the moral rigor of Freud on the other, tend to thrust aside in favor of a "true" object choice. (1983, 21)[7]

Two claims come to the fore in this redescription. First, the primacy of eros in psychic life, which becomes the primacy of desire in Lacan, gives way to narcissism as the beginning of psychic life, if not what rules it. To substantiate this claim requires the details of Kristeva's account of the most primitive moments in the formation of the ego. Second, certain implications drawn from the discovery that narcissism underlies the relation of the desiring ego and the object of desire must be reviewed. Kristeva turns up new features of the narcissistic structure that put into question the valorization of true object choice, governed by societal or moral demands, over narcissistic destiny. Thus the second claim takes issue with the view that to find narcissistic primacy at the heart of the love relationship, and Narcissus at the basis of the relationship to reality, is necessarily to discover that self-deception is the core of the ego. The latter view was strengthened by Lacan's conception of the mirror stage, where narcissistic primacy is explained by the function of the *imago* in the formation of the ego. The transformation of the subject through the assumption of an image comprises features that establish the connections between primary narcissism, love, and self-deception, for it shows how these features settle at the basis of the ego the tendency to assimilate or be absorbed in the other. The deflection of this tendency, that is to say, the modification of narcissistic primacy in psychic life, requires the impact of language—the symbolic function—which establishes the subject as a subject of desire. In Lacan the path of "desire" is precisely what overreaches any given object, so desire is the very dynamic of going beyond the assimilation of or absorption in the other. He therefore distinguishes the subject of desire from the ego. What is important for our purposes is that the features of the mirror stage exhaust the connection between the structure of primary narcissism and the love relationship. This means that the illusion intrinsic to narcissism is above all that of Ovid's Narcissus, an ego in love with itself, mistaking its image for an essential reality, and caught up in its Ovidian destiny—the death of the subject rather than its realization. In the essay on "Aggressivity in Psychoanalysis" (1948), Lacan states: "We call ego that nucleus given to consciousness, but opaque to reflexion, marked by all the ambiguities which, from self-satisfaction to 'bad faith' (*mauvaise foi*), structure the experience of the passions in the human subject; this 'I' who, in order to admit its facticity to existential criticism, opposes its irreducible inertia of pretences and *méconnaissances* to the concrete problematic of the realization of the subject" (1966, 15).

For Kristeva, this confirmation of the tendency to see the illusion of love in terms of self-deception—Lacan's *méconnaissances* of the ego—aggravated a lack of attention to the nuances of the transference relation in psychoanalytic experience. In Lacan narcissism prevails in the activation of the so-called negative transference, which comprises the resistances to the transference "proper" required for the realization of the *subject* in departure from the inertia of the ego. He viewed the hostile reaction to the analyst as evidence for the resistance based in *amour-propre*: "I can't bear the thought of being freed by anyone other than myself" (1966, 13). Idealization of the person of the analyst, the other pole in the pendulum motion that informs the narcissistic structure, will equally act as a resistance to the treatment. This view supports the claim that activation of the transference "proper" depends on the activation of the prohibiting, separating, judging function, that is to say, the symbolic function, for this is what deflects the subject onto the path of desire. The acceptance of the symbolic function is the acknowledgment that one is separated, which is to say, divided. This is how the Lacanian symbolic function stands for both the encounter with exteriority or otherness and the guarantee for taking up a relationship to it. The negation of language is the source of madness because it is the collapse of exteriority or otherness. Lacan gives us the Other *as* language (see Fink 1995, 5). Thus the transference proper follows the path of desire in the field of the signifier. When Kristeva insists that renewed attention to the transference relation in psychoanalysis indicates spoors in the unconscious of nonsymbolic dispositions of the symbolic, giving access to the symbolic function, she is not merely arguing for stages on the way to the discovery and acceptance of lack. She is concerned with the *value* of certain psychic structures that correspond to those dispositions of the symbolic in the structure of narcissism.[8]

In line with this, her objection to the Lacanian view of the transference focuses on its attribution of any manifestation of *love* in the therapeutic setting to *resistance*. The objection is supported by the argument that the meaning of narcissism is not fulfilled by the ego in love with itself, lined by aggression. There is more to the illusion or "seeming" of narcissism than self-deception and "the fake." If Kristeva is to argue for further attention to loving idealization in the transference-relation, she must undermine the impression that narcissism is an inert structure stuck in a dyadic relationship. That is to say, she must counter Lacan with a *ternary conception* of primary narcissism, showing that the dyadic relationship is modified not from without (the externality of the symbolic function or the appearance of the Father), but from within (within the relation to the early mother). That is to say, she must argue for an absolute otherness that arises within the narcissistic structure itself. Moreover, if her view of transference love is to have the significance she wants for it, she must distinguish the advent of the presymbolic third from any conception of lack, even its protosymbolic modalities. The objective of *Tales of Love,* then, is to reveal an elementary ternary disposition within narcissism, one that bears *and* withstands aggressivity.

Since Kristeva's discussion of the ternary disposition in the narcissistic structure sets out one dimension of the semiotic, we will come to see what it *means* for psychoanalysis to have discovered it. That is to say, we will come to see that her notion of the presymbolic third clarifies the thought that unacknowledged suffering is the remnant of freedom in conditions of late modernity. This will only come to light at the close of our discussion of the psychoanalytic thought of *Tales of Love,* since Kristeva's conceptualization of the clinical experience she emphasizes does not itself contain a reflection on the message about the modern Narcissus that appears at the end of the book. However, I will make reference to the broader issues in the course of my elucidation of Kristeva's concepts.

Kristeva's view is that Lacan's attention to psychoanalytic experience restricted the support for the treatment to the symbolic function and desiring metonymy because he misheard the psychic object of *transference love,* taking idealization to be idealization of the person of the analyst as a stand-in for the dyadic relationship that blocks the path of desire. We can assume that this also works as a criticism of her own position in *Revolution in Poetic Language,* where she took the transference relation to be personified in a way that locks it up within prevailing family and social structures. She now detects a "metaphorical object" in the transference, a fleeting and sustaining *ideal* distinct from both the person of the analyst and the metonymic object of desire. Its peculiar function in the transference relation points to an elementary—prelinguistic—idealization of otherness that is quite different from the mirror *imago,* and therefore distinct from the appearance of lack, for it is not a moment of separation and relation between self and world (*Innenwelt* and *Umwelt* in Lacan).

Primary identification is sparked at the level of the bodily exchange between mother and child, where Freud and Lacan tended to see only the symbiosis of mother and child or autoeroticism. For them, the introduction of a third into the dyadic relationship is fully compacted with the appearance of the prohibiting, separating Father, and so oedipal triangulation. When Lacan translates the oedipal father into the "Name-of-the-Father" he pointedly relieves this role not only of any attachment to an actual father but also of any idea of concrete human agency. What converges on the paternal apex in oedipal triangulation is a function, the symbolic function: separating, prohibiting, judging. This function lies in the *fact* of language as what separates the subject from the thing (from pleasure fused with nature), which henceforth becomes the "real," an impossible domain that the speaking subject is cut off from, so that the negation of language threatens chaos.

Although Kristeva does not, and seemingly cannot, dispense with the conception of the symbolic, "paternal" function, she introduces a third that is not the breakup of the bodily exchange between mother and child but brought about within it, and thanks to it. She returns for the exposition of this third to Freud's rendering of a narcissistic structure prior to object love. This leads her to embed the ego's tendency to self-deception, which becomes fixed in Lacan, in a process that begins earlier. The endeavor to counter Lacan with a ternary conception of narcissism draws attention to a moment in Freud's troubled investigation of narcissism where he remarks that for narcissism to emerge out of autoeroticism there must be "a new psychical action" (1914, 77). Kristeva's detailed elaboration of that remark, that a new psychic action *conditions* the advent of narcissism, seeks out the nature of this action and what triggers it. She turns first to Freud's notion of *Einfühlung,* understood initially as the assimilation of other people's feelings. *Einfühlung* comes up as a problem in Freud's discussion of crowd psychology, for it represents the abdication of the ego and judgment (Freud 1921). Kristeva claims that Freud never followed through on something that appears in his discussion of *Einfühlung,* and that subsequent extensions of his thought then pass over it. Lacan, notably, insists on the absence of any indication of *Einfühlung* in early infancy. "Primary" identification is exhausted by the infant's captation by the *imago* of the human form. For Lacan the child's behavior in the presence of his similars—"the child who strikes another says that he has been struck; the child who sees another fall, cries"—is evidence for transitivism in early infancy and not assimilation of another's feelings (1966, 19). The view underlines further the dominion of the *imago* in the primitive ego. The mother-child relationship is notably absent from these observations on infancy.

Kristeva's elaboration of *Einfühlung* does not turn around some kind of passage of feelings between mother and child, however. Rather, she points first to something at the center of Freud's discussion: the assertion that *Einfühlung* is an *objectless* and immediate identification. The fact that *Einfühlung* is immediate is, for Freud, the problem. It implies the abdication of the ego detected in crowd psychology. Assuming that crowd psychology requires the abdication of judgment *to* something else, an object, it is clear why Kristeva emphasizes Freud's expression "*objectless* and immediate." She takes *Einfühlung* to be Janus-faced: the advent *and* loss of the ego. The claim for a ternary disposition within primary narcissism turns on the elucidation of an immediate and objectless identification that is nonetheless an idealization opening up to, and through, a nonobjectal third. Since primary identification sets up an "opposite" to the third, these are the beginnings of ego-formation. There is a virtual ego or what Kristeva calls a "not-yet-ego" in immediate identification with a "not-yet-object." The ego and its correlate are undifferentiated with respect to subject-object positionality, which arises only with oedipal triangulation, yet some kind of thirdness is present, and it is a condition for "one," and an other for one to be connected to, to emerge.

The precise steps of Kristeva's strictly psychoanalytic account of primary idealization provide, first, an inquiry into the nature of immediate identification with a nonobjectal third, second, a consideration of its advent, and third the conditions required for its advent. Following through these steps will take us to the question of the modern fate of the living and loving father. In other words, we will find that Kristeva makes her argument for a nonsymbolic third (an ego ideal essentially distinct from the superegoic oedipal father) in conditions where it has been *lost* as a support for self-relation and the possibility of the "other." This is a major feature of her analysis of modernity. Modern Western cultures have neglected the specific and necessary value of loving idealization in bonds with others.

In Kristeva's first step, the obvious question to raise is, if primary identification is an identification with something nonobjectal, what is it directed to? Kristeva draws both on Freud's idea of the "father-of-individual-prehistory," who does not share in the prohibiting, separating features of the oedipal father (Freud 1921, 105; 1923, 31), and on the Lacanian notion that metaphor is one of the foremost mechanisms of the unconscious. However, her synthesis of the operation of metaphor and the father of individual *prehistory* challenges the dominion of the linguistic metaphor in the unconscious that appears where Lacan aligns unconscious processes with the process of signification in which there is always the *possibility* of meaning. Her "primary identification" does not belong to the process of signification, for the transference onto a "nonobject" involves no displacement of meaning. Meaning is absent from the semiotic *chora*. The non-object is therefore rendered in such terms as a drawing power, a withdrawing presence or "the actual drifting of a possible metaphoricity" (1983,

37). Kristeva is attempting to bring out something in the workings of transference that is lost when the unconscious is approached in terms of the linguistic signifier. When Lacan aligned the laws of the unconscious, condensation and displacement, with the linguistic operations of metaphor and metonymy, he asserted that nothing was beyond, not only the impact of the signifier, but its *field*. Metaphor and metonymy in Lacan always function in the field of *possible* meaning. In contrast, Kristeva's "drifting of a possible metaphoricity" expresses a dimension of what is introduced when she proposes an impact of the symbolic where no phenomenon of meaning is possible. The linguistic signifier may in the last instance be what sparks primary identification, but its effects cannot be seen in terms of a linguistic operation. The signifier, here, is *enigmatic*: a sound (or silence) on the fringe of my being (1983, 37).

Indeed, Kristeva's elucidation of the process of idealization is more akin to monotheistic treatments of idealization than psychoanalytic discussion of linguistic operations. The process appears at one moment as "the immediate transference toward the imaginary father, who is such a godsend that you have the impression that it is he who is transferred into you" (41). *Transference love* is a loving idealization that is transference onto a nonobject. In other words, primary identification, now primary transference, is directed to a withdrawing presence that acts as a magnet for identification. This is what she calls the "imaginary father."

In a second step, Kristeva considers the emergence of this process of idealization. From the viewpoint of subjective diachrony (the developmental account of the trials of individuation), the imaginary father arises thanks to the impact of the symbolic—of desire and language—on the preverbal child. In more Hegelian than Saussurean fashion, the exposure to exteriority consists in the indispensability in the constitution of the subject of the *unmanageable* symbolic being of *an other*. Given that, in psychoanalytic accounting the other is paradigmatically the mother, the advent of the imaginary father lies in "the mother's gift." When she states that love, if it stems from narcissistic idealization, "has nothing to do with the protective wrapping over skin and sphincters that maternal care provides for the baby," Kristeva stresses that the mother's gift is intrasymbolic, not mere nurturing prior to the advent of the prohibiting and separating symbolic—"paternal"—function (1983, 34). The ternary disposition within the narcissistic structure consists in an elementary separation and potential identity brought about by the mother's diversion to a third, prompting "immediate transference to the site of *maternal desire*" (46).

Before proceeding with my own reading of how Kristeva's thought on primary identification develops from this point, a comparison of two other recent readings—Shepherdson (2000) and Oliver (1998)—is useful for highlighting the stakes of this thought. When Shepherdson discusses maternity and femininity in Kristeva, he puts all the emphasis on the import of maternal desire, so that he can argue that the mother in Kristeva is a symbolic mother. He has understandable reasons for doing this, since he is arguing against the view that Kristeva aligns the imaginary with "femininity" and the symbolic with "masculinity," a view that has encouraged the challenge to her that she leaves the feminine without access to language or culture. Reading Kristeva through some Lacanian schemas, Shepherdson even goes so far as to say that the mother cannot appear in the imaginary. Unfortunately, although Kristeva's mother is (also and necessarily) symbolic, this argument makes it impossible to access how she is imaginary, and not only in the distortions of fantasy. It seems that Shepherdson has missed the extent to which her conception of the imaginary differs from Lacan's, for he equates the imaginary with what appears in Kristeva's discussion of the archaic mother of prehistory, that is to say, with the semiotic *isolated* from the life of signs. If she did make this identification one would, of course, want to make Shepherdson's strict distinction. For, in this case, the mother could only ever have the form she takes on in phantasmatic distortions of primal loss.

Shepherdson seems to have an inkling of Kristeva's difference regarding the imaginary, however, when at the close of his discussion he notes that much of Kristeva's writing on love and desire probably remains to be read. But Oliver (1998) has already given us an excellent reading of the significance of Kristeva's thought on the imaginary father and love, showing just how it is a question, in technical terms, of the maternal function (68–76). Less technically, on Oliver's reading, Kristeva unearths a different story about what makes separateness and connections with others possible. Primary identification, not as identification with the mother's body, which must be given up, but with the mother's love—the "metaphor of love"—is what fills discourse with meaning. On this reading, one can clearly see how a culture in which the symbolic has dominion will not only be a merely linguistic universe that deprives subjects of meaning, value, and nature. It will be shot through with the myth/s of woman that feminism has criticized, for the lost past will *only* be recovered in fantasy (an argument I make at length in chapter 8, below). We see, with Kristeva and Oliver, that such a culture is predicated in part on collapsing maternal love into the maternal body.

Although Shepherdson gestures toward the possibility of a reading like Oliver's, he makes it hard to open it up because the imaginary for him remains the phantasmatic. This is the view of the imaginary that Kristeva has labored so hard to overcome, and it unfortunately makes Shepherdson's thought, on this point, appear quite consistent with the patriarchal failure. Less contentiously, the problem seems to lie in how he has located only one transition in Kristeva's developmental story turning on the mother. He sees the transition from the imaginary (by which he means the semiotic, the archaic) to the symbolic. He misses the second one she gives us: from the semiotic to the symbolic accommodation of the semiotic in the imaginary *register,* one of whose implications is that love is a resource for separateness and connectedness, different from desire, and necessary for bonding, as Oliver has shown.[9]

The reading I will develop, beginning here and fulfilling it in chapter 8 below, is that Kristeva's imaginary is a conception that covers, not only the issue of phantasmatics turning on the maternal body, but the ways in which the "lost past" of the archaic mother, an impossible past as she says, is recovered *within* the symbolic order in the shape of imaginary constructs that do not repeat the infantile form of primary narcissism, but *re*form it. The imaginary constructs are within the symbolic order but, in a certain sense, not *of* it, not grasped within the field of its effects. This is why, for her, love is also other than desire, and loss is also other than lack. My reading differs from Oliver (1998) insofar as I underline Kristeva's stress on the need for the nonsymbolic dimensions of subjectivity—including the imaginary father—to take on some kind of symbolic form (her imaginary constructs). Without this, they remain a neglected semiotic "content," ripe for an outbreak in distorted and destructive forms.

Returning to the details of Kristeva's account of the imaginary father in *Tales of Love,* we do find that Kristeva adopts the Lacanian thought on desire, but not in order to make the symbolic foundational once again as the only protection against the maternal body. Rather, the conception of desire as metonymic, receding, helps her out in showing what it *is* for the mother's desire to prompt primary identification, or to be—as Oliver underlines—the metaphor of love. In taking up the Lacanian thought that no object *is* the site of desire—that desire is receding, always "elsewhere"—Kristeva gives desiring metonymy a further twist.

> The imaginary father would thus be the indication that the mother is not complete but she *wants.* . . . Who? What? The question has no answer other than the one that uncovers narcissistic emptiness; "At any rate, not I." Freud's famous "what does a woman want?" is perhaps only the echo of the more fundamental "What does a mother want?" It runs up against the same impossibility, bordered on one side by the imaginary father, on the other by a "not I." And it is out of this "not I" (see Beckett's play with that title) that an Ego painfully attempts to come into being . . . (41)

The impact of the symbolic on the preverbal child is the impact of "want-loss," an expression that captures the immediate connection of the mother's desire (want) and its impact (loss/emptiness). In Lacanian thought, the rift that breaks up the illusion of the phallic mother (the mOther as the site of the demand for complete gratification), including the illusion that the gap in the mother can be filled by the child, potentiates and gets tied to the desiring subject (Fink 1995, 49). Kristeva takes a different tack. It *is* the mother's desire that imposes and sustains the rift between the mother and the child. Yet, long before the desiring subject is instituted, the rift has another outcome, one that lies within the narcissistic structure, and is necessary for the emergence of the loving and desiring subject. It emerges precisely because desire is metonymic, receding, and without a determinate place. Since the site of the mother's desire is "nowhere," desiring metonymy draws in *a withdrawing presence* that permits a protection against emptiness, not through the illusory and potentially catastrophic wish to fill the gap in the mother, but by *preserving* emptiness.[10] Narcissism itself is a fragile defense against chaos or a collapse into the real. "Within sight of that Third Party I elaborate the narcissistic parry that allows me to block up that emptiness, to calm it and turn it into a producer of signs, representations, and meanings, I elaborate it within sight of the Third Party. I seduce this 'father of individual prehistory' because he has already caught me, for he is simple virtuality, a potential presence, a form to be cathected" (42–43).

Given this indication of a ternary disposition within primary narcissism, Kristeva can argue for an idealizing *distance* in the transference (a withdrawing presence) that is other than the distance upheld by the prohibiting, "paternal" function. "Concentrating, *for a while,* one's thoughts on love within analysis actually leads one to scrutinize, in the treatment, not a narcissistic merger with the maternal container but the emergence of a *metaphorical object*—in other words the very splitting that establishes the psyche and, let us call this splitting 'primal repression,' bends the drive toward the symbolic of an other" (1983, 31). Primary idealization is a fragile defence against the impact of want-loss. Its placement in the narcissistic structure corresponds to the claim that loss/emptiness is prior to lack in the constitution of the speaking being.

The third and final step in Kristeva's account of primary narcissism is the claim that the advent of the imaginary father is nothing merely "given." Indeed, the prevalence of narcissism on the couch, and the predominance of the view of the narcissistic structure that overlooks the centrality and significance of primary idealization, both indicate a problem in respect of the elaboration of the narcissistic "parry." This brings us to the question of what it means for *psychoanalysis* to have discovered the question of the imaginary father, for psychoanalytic discoveries are made in encounters with suffering. The problem comes to the couch from a wider context. First, if the narcissistic parry is aided and supported by transference onto the imaginary father, who gives access to the life of signs, an upsurge of negative narcissism would indicate that this support is absent. The imaginary father, who acts as a consolation for loss/emptiness, is weak or missing. Second, if the imaginary father lies in the mother's gift, the tendential absence of this compensation for loss suggests a fragility in maternal *desire,* and so a fragility in her inscription in the symbolic order. This vision dovetails with the discussion of sexual difference in "Stabat Mater" (1977), republished in *Tales of Love,* where Kristeva proposes that the woman lacks a go-between in order to assimilate the supposedly paternal Law. Now, it seems that the go-between would be the imaginary father. If he is lacking to her (to her mother) he is lacking to her child. One aspect of this problem is the failure of a world defined by symbolic law, and so unable to recognize the real significance and scope of the maternal function. As a result, the mother's desire with respect to the symbolic is compromised—it may not be strong enough to propel the advent of the imaginary father for the child. What is at stake, here, is one dimension of what, in the final analysis, is the problem of modern nihilism.

From a slightly different perspective, the problem of maternal desire reflects modern secular discourses' and institutions' neglect of the task of working out "a secular variant of the loving father" (1983, 374). Here I am pressing the thought that Kristeva's discovery of the imaginary father, on its own, presents no way out of the problem for either the subject or the culture. What is necessary is that the presymbolic affective relations she discovers *take on* some kind of symbolic form. Insofar as secular modernity lacks *signifying ideals,* the subject is left exposed to the impact of want/loss and unsupported in the struggle to elaborate the narcissistic parry that preserves emptiness. The upsurge of negative narcissism therefore indicates a de-structuration of psychic *space.* This is a loss of psychic life, that is to say, of the possibilities for self-relation and connections with others. These require a society that reflects on its own limits, as well as the borders of the subject—on the limit of symbolic law, we might say. In a society that does not, love is devalued, a devaluation that leaves us without discourses to support idealizing constructions. This is not to imply the reduction of social issues to issues of intimacy (which are themselves debased by the devaluation of love and the restriction of its forms). Rather, as will be seen when we come to Kristeva's thought in *Nations Without Nationalism,* in chapter 7 below, the recovery of the possibility of idealizing constructions is also the recovery of the capacity for making identifications that transcend the individual, the family cell, or the groups that reflect one's "own" culture and history.

What *Tales of Love* gives us is Kristeva's fragmentary minor history of love, which is a minor history of the formation and deformation of psychic *space.* Her view is that contemporary psychoanalysis, having inherited the "whole, speculative, Western history of psychic space," encounters, explores, and negotiates the *suffering* of emptiness: a sedimented and deracinated subjectivity (1983, 372f.). The book argues that one line of Western history can be found in discursive elaborations of narcissism that construct psychic space as an *inner* space. Its central chapters compose a minor history of "love stories" that are symbolizations of the presymbolic dynamic of loving idealization. In brief, there is a Western construction of a psychic space in connection with an Other, which supports the confrontation with emptiness. It belongs especially to the history of Christianity and finds its highest moment in the representation "God is love." According to Christian love—*agape*—the foundation of individual and social life is an overflowing divine love. God loved us *first*. The injunction to "love thy neighbor as thyself" can only be fulfilled on the basis of the love through which the *self* comes into being and is upheld.[11] A major moment in the development of this God-relation is articulated in the thought of Bernard de Clairvaux. Kristeva's attention to it is a reminder of the ontological account of the subject in religion, which is overtaken by the epistemological account when philosophy responds to the demise of religion. On the religious view, being is prior to thought, not given by it. The very being of the subject lies in a primacy of affect not of the *cogito*. That is to say, the Cartesian primacy of *cogito, ergo sum* is displaced by the Bernardine *ego affectus est*. In other words, as Kristeva explains it, there is an "I" that is passion before the "I" knows how to *be* because it thinks (1983, 169). Kristeva then finds that the Thomist promotion of the absolute value of singular individuality, which is "access to *one's own good*" without which "there can be no access to God," prepares the way for the advent of the *ego cogito*. "Poverty and greatness of the knowing subject who repressed his advent as a loving subject" (176, 181).

In sum, the three chapters in *Tales of Love* on "God is Love," Bernard de Clairvaux, and Thomas Aquinas present a minor history of Western subjectivity in discourses that sublimate narcissism. I use the term *sublimation,* here, not in reference to Freud's thought on the possible destiny of erotic or aggressive instincts, but as a word for giving form to the semiotic. What Kristeva discovers with respect to the Christian sublimation of narcissism, is that narcissism is no longer dealt with when Christian thought "forgets" that it rumbles over emptiness. Thus the nihilism problematic is present in Kristeva's thought on religion, since she proposes that the deformation of the Christian God-relation arises because the religion of salvation overreaches its deepest source. It founds itself, instead, in the transcendent ideal. This view recalls Nietzsche's thought on nihilism, that the highest values devalue themselves. However, to repeat the argument of my introduction to this book, Kristeva's thought does not inherit the idea of the metanarrative of collapse, the view that the secular aftermath of religion is a wholesale loss of transcendence. For Kristeva's minor history turns to the literary project of elaborating primary narcissism: those "tales of love" that come to unfold a dynamics of *metaphor.* Such a literature, in her view, inscribes the very process of idealization within signs, without personification of the imaginary father. To press the point, art steps in where the social symbolic system fails, for modern secular institutions and discourses have failed to develop something *like* what monotheistic religion provided. Art provides the semiotic with a symbolic articulation of the struggle with the suffering of loss/emptiness that underlies all symbolic capacities, a struggle that contains the moment of transcendence—transference on to the imaginary father—that settles the loving Other at the heart of the self. In brief, with Kristeva, our most powerful discourses of love appear in works of art.

Her minor history of love stories in religion and modern literature also casts light back on psychoanalysis itself, illuminating its appearance and significance as a discourse. Psychoanalysis discovers narcissism at the pervious border between the individual and society. The absence of signifying ideals at the level of social symbolic resources has made of subjectivity a site of imprisoned suffering, the problem that psychoanalysis meets in the consulting room. Psychoanalysis aims to strengthen the confrontation with the suffering of emptiness by increasing the capacity to discern and permit oneself transitory ideals that strengthen the desiring ego, but can, and at times must be, other than the object of desire.

Wherever Kristeva goes over and expands on the disconnection of the affect or drives from language encountered in psychoanalytic experience, she points up the psychoanalytic discovery of nihilism at the pervious border between the social and the individual. Thus, if we assume that psychoanalysis takes subjectivity simply *as* the site of suffering, this leaves the isolation of the individual uninvestigated, and brings with it the danger, condemned by Adorno, of "the psyche that has been abstracted from the social dialectic and investigated as an abstract 'for itself' under the microscope" (1968, 81). Adorno condemns the practice of examining subjectivity in abstraction from history and society, as though the psyche were something autonomous and self-sufficient, as though the individual could be fully mended in a broken world. Kristeva's thought on the *pervious* border between the social and the individual meets Adorno's concern by deepening our understanding of the place of psychoanalysis in modernity. The minor history of *Tales of Love* works to show that there is an absence of signifying ideals in modern discourses and institutions, that psychoanalysis appears as a discourse that responds to the isolation of the soul, which is a *fate,* and that if it is to respond to that isolation it must continue to track this fate.

This leaves the wider question of the absence of signifying ideals, that is to say ideals within the social symbolic field, open to further analysis. It seems to be necessary to draw the conclusion that Kristeva does not only reveal the need of primary idealization and its symbolization in variants of the loving father. She equally shows that these requirements have never been met. Religion is a failure in part because it ultimately fails *this* need. The modern failure can be viewed in the following way, although it has its limitations. If the preservation of emptiness depends on the mother's desire, and the mother's desire must be for the Father's phallus (as she puts it at one point in *Tales of Love*), primary idealization must *always* run into difficulty. In conditions where social reality is founded upon the paternal universe access to the symbolic poses extreme difficulties for women. Maternal desire—the diversion to a third—is undermined from the start and, if this is so, primary idealization is undermined from the start. In other words, the maturational processes typically available in Western cultures are inadequate for subject formation. Here Kristeva shows, precisely, the fundamental failure of the Western arrangement of sexual difference and how the possibility of a just society is bound up with the fate of sexual difference. The possibility of a just society is preempted because there is no loving father without a desiring and loving mother, and no desiring and loving mother without a loving father to mediate women's access to the symbolic. The problem appears circular only if one fails to see that the Western arrangement of sexual difference makes the maturational processes available for subject formation inadequate. Kristeva only appears to have reduced her focus to individual suffering because, if the ideal and the object of desire cannot be combined—if there is no real difference of or in the sexes, no relations between beings of different sexes—the subject must find support in transitory ideals in the form of the cathexis of other passing objects. Kristeva does not herself present such a dim view of the fate of sexual difference in Western cultures as the one I have outlined, however. She knows that the difficulties the symbolic poses for women also permits them to see through its illusory universality. I will defer further discussion of this point to the conclusion.

The fact that primary idealization always runs into difficulty brings us to the intimate connection between *Tales of Love* and *Powers of Horror,* whose topic is "abjection," or more widely, the problem of nondifferentiation—of separation—in Western subject formation. The connection is clearly articulated at a point in *Tales of Love* just where Kristeva shows that psychoanalysis, for Freud, is tightly bound up with the question of religion, and especially the demise of Christianity as a historical religion. Kristeva's insistence on the ternary structure of narcissism argues that Freud *rehabilitates* the Narcissus who is to be found in central tranformations of the dynamic of idealization fundamental to incarnate salvation religions. She points not only to the humanistic culture that "made him heir to Christian spirituality and symbolism" but to his attempt "to take over where the 'religion of salvation' left off" (1983, 124). Far from suggesting that psychoanalysis replaces religion, these indications of Freud's heritage claim that he confronts what brings the salvation religions to be dismantled. "With Freud, rehabilitation of narcissism did not therefore lead to a promise of salvation but to *the discovery of death's work*. A personal fantasy? The echo of a tragic era? The fact remains that the conclusion of the twentieth century, which began with the fulfilment of Freud's work and two world wars, hands down to us an unbearable amorous space. . . . Freud relied on Narcissus, first in order to rehabilitate him by including him in his libidinal apparatus—Eros is initially narcissistic; then to emphasize, in a very biblical fashion this time . . . that *love is no more than a chancy stasis of hatred*" (124, emphasis added).

Kristeva's articulation of the void or emptiness at the core of the speaking subject encompasses an inquiry into the brittleness and fragility of the symbolic matrix built up around it once symbolizations of primary idealization at the everyday level have weakened. Negative narcissism indicates the brittleness of narcissism, which threatens chaos. For the failure to elaborate the narcissistic "parry" that preserves emptiness brings out the proximity of primary narcissism to drives, above all the death drive. We recall the thought that the death drive restores to the subject the destabilizing materiality that is prior to the assumption of "a total body form" (mirror *imago*), and certainly to the emergence of a body as such (*le corps propre*). Kristeva situates the advent of death drive—the material inscription of the most archaic exposure to exteriority—within the bodily exchange between mother and child, making it a condition of the elementary separateness that has shown up in the narcissistic structure. Death drive, then, marks the *violence* of the impact of want-loss. It is the "rebound" of pure aggressivity and destructiveness that contributes to the struggle with that impact.

This aggressivity is fundamental to the second of Kristeva's presymbolic dispositions giving access to the symbolic function: abjection. *Powers of Horror* both proposes that abjection is a presymbolic moment in subject formation, necessary for separation, and shows what an upsurge of abjection means for social and symbolic being. The idea of abjection turns up in a passage in *Tales of Love* that summarizes the whole content of Kristeva's evolutionary postulate.

> The immediate transference toward the imaginary father, who is such a godsend that you have the impression that it is he who is transferred into you, withstands a process of rejection involving what may have been chaos and is about to become an *abject*. The maternal space can come into being as such, before becoming an object correlative to the Ego's desire, only as

> an *abject*. In short, primary identification appears to be a transference to (from) the imaginary father, correlative to the establishment of the mother as "ab-jetted." Narcissism would be that correlation (with the imaginary father and the "ab-jetted" mother) enacted around the central emptiness of that transference. (1983, 41–42)

When Kristeva recovers the connection between Freud's thought on narcissism and his understanding of the dismantling of the salvation religions, she shows that to go further into the narcissistic structure is to discover beneath love both hatred and death. In devoting itself to this question, the psychoanalytic thought in *Powers of Horror* expands on the role of the semiotic in the trials of individuation, and extends the analysis of the fate of the semiotic in modern societies.

CHAPTER 3

Ab-jection

Introduction

I am arguing that Kristeva's profound exploration in the 1980s trilogy of the structure of narcissism in the trials of individuation contains an exploration of the problem of nihilistic modernity. From the perspective of the strictly psychoanalytic level of her writing, we discover that this is a condition in which the less visible features of self-relation and connections with others are neglected in social and symbolic life. In the technical terms of her fundamental categorial distinction, psychoanalysis is witness to the tendential severance of the semiotic and symbolic. We have seen Kristeva substantiate her conception of the semiotic in a developmental account of the constitution of the subject in exposure to otherness, an exposure and an appearance of otherness whose registration gives us the nonsymbolic aspects of the development of selfhood and the capacity for meaning. Those registrations, however, need to take on some kind of symbolic form—for example, the discourses of love that retrieve and re-form primary idealization—if self-relation and connections with others are to be possible. Kristeva's psychoanalytic thought also tracks what happens to selfhood and the "other" if this need is not met. Modern institutions and discourses have failed to meet it.

In *Tales of Love* the problem of nihilistic modernity is the problem of lacks of love, the weakness of discourses of love, and the absence of idealizing constructions to support social bonding. In brief, we can call this the loss of ideals in conditions of late modernity. As we will see in chapter 4, below, Kristeva's investigation of primal melancholy also discovers the loss of the capacity for loss in these conditions. The significance of the discovery of the loss of loss is particularly underlined in this book, and will be returned to in various discussions throughout it. This chapter turns to the other aspect of the triadic structure of narcissism, investigated in *Powers of Horror*: "abjection." Abjection is the most primitive of the three moments of presymbolic subject-formation, and is closest to the function of the destructive wave of the drive in the constitution of the subject. The thought of abjection can be viewed as a further exploration of psychoanalytic thought on aggressivity (Lacan) and as an extension of Freud's discovery of the close tie between love and hatred in object-relation (his discussions of emotional ambivalence in, for example, *Totem and Taboo*). We can see, then, that there is a difficulty in formulating the problematic of abjection in relation to the question of nihilism. For it would be bizarre to characterize the problematic of abjection in terms of a loss of hatred or aggressivity. It might even be more appropriate to consider the question of abjection only in terms of the threat it poses to relations with others and the social bond. Indeed, much of recent critical thought deploying the term *abjection* has gone straight for a theory of the political significance of abjection in order to figure out the deep forces of oppressive social and political relations (Butler 1993 is an obvious case in point). In these kinds of debate, abjection is a scarcely visible dynamic of aggressivity that is used to shore up identities that institute and maintain existing power relations.

A thought on the political implications of abjection *does* appear in Kristeva's writings. However, to proceed immediately to the social and political implications of the theory of abjection would be to divorce her project from the psychoanalytic inquiry, and so, equally, from what makes her a social and political thinker in her own right. That is to say, the abstraction of the term *abjection* from Kristeva's investigation of the trials of individuation collapses the presence of the problem of nihilistic modernity in her writings. The question I must answer is, if Kristeva finds that unacknowledged suffering is the remnant of freedom in conditions of late modernity, how does the discovery of abjection develop this thought?

First, if the essay on abjection forms part of her account of the triadic structure of narcissism, then abjection, like primary idealization and primal loss, must be an important moment in the constitution of the subject for Kristeva, and cannot stand only as the bad news. For we have seen that her exploration of the "semiotic," theoretically isolated in the developmental story of subjectivity, exhibits presymbolic *capacities*—however unstable—in the trials of individuation. These capacities give access to signifying capacities and must themselves be accommodated in the life of signs. What role does abjection play in this story? For Kristeva, the dynamic of abjection reveals, above all, a primitive moment of separateness in the earliest—not only presymbolic but pre-*imaginary*—structure of subjectivity, where the life of the drives is most emphatic. If psychoanalysis encounters the problem of abjection, then, it would seem that this aspect of suffering subjectivity reveals something about the loss of *separateness,* and the weakness of our discourses of separateness, in late modern societies. There is a truth to this, but it is not a straightforward one, since, as we will see, the question of abjection does not only lead to the thought that this is a dimension of the semiotic that needs to take on some kind of symbolic (not social) form. The question of abjection runs up against, and is easily confused with, another problem: that of the weakness of the symbolic—separating—function, or, put otherwise, the collapse of the oedipal structure, often called the demise of paternal law or the crisis in the paternal function. This problem can generally be understood either as a lack of law or, when the thought on the imaginary father is taken in, as a lack of love (see also Oliver 1998, chapter 4, on this). The discussion of Kristeva's thought on abjection in this chapter will address why, at this point of her writings, what she comes across is the weakness of the symbolic function as the separating and *prohibiting* function. This does not mean that she has shifted her vision from the issue of the semiotic, the issue that opens up for her and keeps in sight the thought of unacknowledged suffering and the movement of its overcoming. Yet it would be hazardous to suggest that the overcoming, here, is a matter of a recovery of abjection—similar to the need of a recovery of signifying ideals or of loss. The question of how the psychoanalytic inquiry into abjection relates to the thought on the remnant of freedom must be suspended for the present, until we have a better understanding of what Kristeva is getting at in her focus on this structure of subjectivity.

At the psychoanalytic level of Kristeva's thinking, abjection is the most unstable moment in the maturation of the subject because it is a struggle with the instability of the inside/outside border, that is to say, with spatial ambivalence that turns on the need of a place for the "ego" to come into being. With Lacan, this inside/outside border only appears in the imaginary, that is to say, in the splitting of the subject that corresponds to the *imago.* His essay on the mirror stage shows that the distinction between *Innenwelt* and *Umwelt* turns up in the alteration of the subject through the assumption of an *image.* The function of the *imago* is to establish a *relation* between the organism and its reality. For Lacan, then, the imaginary is the moment of the appearance of lack, and the symbolic will be the acceptance of lack. Where Kristeva differs from this is that, long before the imaginary shows up, the primitive ego is in a struggle with the instability of the inside/outside border in relation to the mother's body, where the latter remains a vital necessity and is not parted from. Ab-jection of the mother's body, the attempt on the part of the *infans* to deal with spatial ambivalence, therefore shares in the instability of the inside/outside border that abjection belongs to and is barely distinguishable from. No wonder, then, that Kristeva claims that abjection is above all ambiguity. For *Powers of Horror* presents the most confusing aspect of the narcissistic structure, one, let us say, that reveals the moment of subjectivity closest to irrationality.

One way of getting at the ambiguity of abjection is as follows. On the one hand, abjection is a psychic differentiation that is necessary for the child's separation from the mother's body, a highly significant moment in the trials of individuation without which access to the life of signs is impossible. Kristeva claims, at the outset of the book, that there is a point where abjection and the abject are "my safeguards," even "the primers of my culture" (1980a, 2). On the other hand—given separation—the upsurge of abjection as a boundary subjectivity reveals the deepest collapse of selfhood, the "other," and the world. Moreover, *Powers of Horror* relates certain twentieth-century phenomena of misogyny and anti-Semitism to the appearance of abjection.

There appears to be nowhere to stand in order to measure this ambiguity. Everywhere, the negative and positive meanings of abjection are tightly held together. Once again, we note that this narrow space has spawned a field of cultural theory on abjection that uses the idea to capture how subjective and social boundaries are established in ways that set up acceptable and impossible paths for desire and identity by excluding the less determinate aspects of subjectivity. It is thought that abjection *is* the dynamic of exclusion that regulates the subject just where its borders are established (Butler 1993). The thought of abjection is now widely, and to some degree fruitfully, used to critique class relations, race relations, gender, and sexuality in Western cultures because it appears to grasp how injustices are upheld at a level much more insidious than that of the organization of the members of society that is imposed from outside (see Chanter and Colman 2001, for example). The injustices are upheld in and through the very formation of the subject who suffers them, and so by the subject who suffers them (Butler 1993). Nonetheless, these uses of the term abjection do not fully capture how it functions in Kristeva's discourse. This is because her attention to the trials of individuation first discovers "abjection" as a fragile defense of the emergent subject undergoing the impact of loss/emptiness where there are no symbolic means to negotiate the impact. The long debate with Butler in chapter 8, below, is an attempt to think through these differences. The debate cannot be launched, however, without attending to what abjection means at the strictly psychoanalytic level of Kristeva's thought.

To begin with a broad definition of the Kristevan meaning of abjection, the topic of *Powers of Horror* is the appearance of a subject that is not quite a subject because it has no determinate relations to objects. There is no object world because objects have no *significance*. Thus the correlation of the desiring ego and the object of desire is lacking. With Lacan, the collapse of the desiring subject is so tightly linked to the fate of the speaking being that the failure of desire threatens the collapse into psychosis. Not so with Kristeva. Objects have no significance, yet they remain signifiable. That is to say, there is language but it does not "speak"—does not produce meaning in the subject for another subject. Kristeva's thought on abjection captures the fact of "lives not sustained by desire," a borderline condition of the subject where there is a collapse of meaning, but the speaking being survives in a certain sense, within the demise of the relation to others. The meaning of this survival is itself highly ambiguous.

"Abjection," then, captures a condition of the subject that is sent to its boundaries, where there is, as such, neither subject nor object, only the abject. In *Powers of Horror* Kristeva proposes that the abject shares but one feature of the object: "that of being opposed to *I*" (1980a, 1). The psychoanalytic account of presymbolic subject formation illuminates this thought by presenting abjection as a structure that composes the *fearsome beginnings of otherness*, where there is as yet no other, and no space for the ego to come into being. What abjection means here is the struggle to set up such a space, a struggle, precisely, with what is not parted from, and which threatens to collapse that space: paradigmatically, the mother's body. "Abjection preserves what existed in the archaism of pre-objectal relationship, in the immemorial violence with which a body becomes separated from another body in order to be—maintaining that night in which the outline of the signified thing vanishes and where only the imponderable affect is carried out" (10).

Abjection is a fragile defense against nondifferentiation, and can be viewed from the perspective of the trials of individuation as the first, and most unstable, attempt to establish an inside/outside boundary. The abject is opposed to "I" in the sense that it is the focus of the attempt to secure a space for the ego. It is what the border of the subject presupposes but is itself only an *unstable* boundary. The phrase "ab-jection of the mother's body" expresses a semiotic capacity for turning the maternal container into a maternal "space" from which the subject-to-be may separate. What prompts the struggle that sets up the "abject" is not an external prohibition on access to the mother's body—not the symbolic, "paternal" law—but something that arises within the connection to the mother's body itself. Abjection can therefore be understood, first, as a response to a presymbolic *imperative* to separate, where the mother's body remains a vital support and is not parted from. Here Kristeva gives further attention to the notion of primal repression, the one that turns the "paternal" prohibition into a secondary repression, which, on her account, overlays the first and is affected by its precariousness. She calls primal repression the "demarcating" imperative in order to underline that it does not and cannot impel separation as such. It bears on the pre-imaginary field of the bodily exchange between mother and child, and is a kind of "mapping" of the body before a body is distinguished from another body. The demarcating imperative founds neither the object nor the subject, nor even the relation of the organism to its reality. It founds the *abject.* In Kristeva, the abject is, first, a margin or border that does not, however, bound a space. It is, moreover, an ineliminably corporeal inscription of the maternal hold on the early infant's development. Finally, it is a corporeal inscription before there is "a body," and this is why, for Kristeva, it is a matter of the unstable boundary of subjectivity. Nonetheless, the abject is, for this reason, the "object" of the infant's attempt to break away from the maternal hold. The abject is the target of the destructive wave of the drive, whose repeated motion works both to solidify the boundary but also tends to displace it. The abject therefore stands between the absence of differentiation (autoeroticism) and the emergence of the *imago* and, later, of the object understood as the correlate that serves to support separateness and autonomy. Where the subject and its object world turn up the abject as unstable boundary "drops out." But where the object world collapses, the abject returns and can absorb all significance. There is an upsurge of abjection, then—of a subject uncertain of its borders—wherever there is a looming of the abject in a breakdown of not only the "other" but the world.

The Phobic Object

On psychoanalytic ground, this admittedly speculative presentation of abjection must be supported by an analysis of a phenomenon that manifests the structure of abjection. Kristeva finds this phenomenon where psychoanalytic thought has turned to the phobic object. This section elucidates how Kristeva discovers the structure of abjection in that of phobic suffering. She finds abjection by sticking closely to the enigma that phobia presents to psychoanalytic knowledge of object-relation (of how a subject takes up a relationship to others).

Kristeva begins her investigation with the available and most well-known case studies of phobia in children: Sigmund Freud on Little Hans (1909) and Anna Freud on Sandy.[1] Her rehearsal of Freud's case study goes over his confrontation with the enigmatic character of the phobic object. Phobia is enigmatic, first, because normal or precocious linguistic activity is present in the child, but symbolic *capacities,* that is to say, the ability to be inscribed in symbolic connections with others, and so object-relation, is weak. Second, there is an incommensurability between the two features that phobia conjoins: the affect *fear* and the *object* of fear. The phobic object is an unlikely one, first, in the sense that there is an excess at the level of visual and auditory experience. It is an "hallucinatory" object. That is to say, it displays excessive features. The phobic object is "unlikely," second, on account of its lability. Freud remarks on the extension of phobia on to new objects and events. In the central document of his inquiry into phobia, little Hans is afraid of horses. His fright sets in at the sound of the animal's beating hooves, but his fear is also displaced onto other objects, situations, and locations. This phenomenon led Freud to conclude that the phobic object is a "secondary" one *substituting for* the primary object of fear: the father in oedipal triangulation. As Kristeva notes, Freud takes the words and experiences of little Hans to confirm the center of his theory. "Long before he was in the world, I went on, I had known that a little Hans would come who would be so fond of his mother that he would be bound to feel afraid of his father because of it" (1909, 42). At the point of publication of this document Freud focuses on object-relation (fondness for the mother and fear of the father) and considers phobia to be a manifestation and elaboration of *castration anxiety.* That is to say, the phobia is taken to be a flight from and disguise for the unresolved Oedipus complex. The interventions that the psychoanalyst makes in the father's analysis of his son encourage the father to bring the child back to the primary object of fear, and so to the oedipal struggle.

Freud's reflections on this childhood phobia belong to a period in which he stood by his early theory of the instincts and maintained a view of anxiety that is reworked at a later date. He insisted throughout this period on the duality of the instincts as a conflict between the object-related *sexual instincts* and the *ego instincts* of self-preservation. The Oedipus complex is a conflict between libidinal investment in the mother and castration anxiety (the imagined force of a paternal prohibition on access to the mother's body and the concomitant fear of losing a highly valued part). The "dissolution" of the Oedipus complex (see

Freud's essay of that title, 1924) is achieved on the part of the little boy through a triumph of narcissistic investment in a highly valued part (a triumph of the ego instincts) over fondness for the mother (over the sexual instincts). In the dissolution of the Oedipus complex castration anxiety is allayed, leading to the latency period.[2]

On Freud's interpretation of the case study, the essence of phobia, with its conjunction "fear-and-object," lies in defense against an affect that has no object: *anxiety*. The precise meaning of this affect is decided at this point of Freud's thought by regarding it as a transformation of unsatisfied libido. On this view, object-relation is achieved across the breach of suppressed anxiety. In Freud's view, if castration anxiety is not allayed in and through the dissolution of the Oedipus complex, there is only one way out of anxiety hysteria. "From the outset in anxiety-hysteria the mind is constantly at work in the direction of once more psychically binding the anxiety which has become liberated; but this work can neither bring about a retransformation of the anxiety into libido, nor can it establish any contact with the complexes which were the source of the libido. Nothing is left for it but to cut off access to every possible occasion that might lead to the development of anxiety, by erecting mental barriers in the nature of precautions, inhibitions, or prohibitions" (1909, 117). The erection of mental barriers is the only option because, at this stage of Freud's thought, "liberated" anxiety is thought to be a conversion of ungratified libido, and so any attempt psychically to bind anxiety would mean returning to the conflicts from which the subject is removed. If this is the essence of phobia, the latter manifests a flight from the conflict that makes up the center of the Oedipus complex. Childhood phobia is, for Freud, "a type or model" of the Oedipus complex.[3] His interventions in the case aim to reinstall the primary (paternal) object of fear, revealing that there is a problem at the level of the triangulating function of the paternal prohibition.

This is the point of focus for Kristeva's reinvestigation of phobia, since it suggests to her, not that the Oedipus complex has not been brought to term, but that there is an insufficient development of it, a problem that must pertain to oedipal triangulation itself, and not simply be related to a flight from the oedipal struggle. For Kristeva makes explicit that what Freud's consideration of the phobic object has discovered is a weakness in oedipal triangulation, revealing that the problem lies *with* the triangulating function. If this is so, the logic of "substitution," according to which the phobic object stands in for the primary object of fear—the father—cannot explain the enigmatic features of phobia. As Kristeva remarks in respect of the case study, "within the symbolic law accruing to the function of the father, something remains blurred in the oedipal triangle constituting the subject" (1980a, 35). The triangle, Ego-object-Other, is not set in place with sufficient strength. That is to say phobia *stages* a frailty or breakdown in object-relation that refers us to the collapse of the oedipal structure.

Since, without the logic of substitution to help us out, the major features of phobia remain enigmatic, another interpretation of the "fear-and-object" conjunction and the lability of the phobic object is required. Paying particular attention to the latter, Kristeva initiates a different account of the essence of phobia by relating it to an engulfment of ego and object that implies a weakness in *the function of the Other* in oedipal triangulation. "Does Hans's father not play a bit too much the role of the mother whom he thrusts into the shadows? Does he not overly seek the surety of the professor? If phobia is a metaphor that has mistaken its place, forsaking language for drive and sight, it is because a father does not hold his own" (1980a, 35). Kristeva elucidates the phenomena of phobic hallucination and the lability of its object by considering the phobic object as a hallucinatory metaphor. What we can conclude from this is that she is aware that the paternal metaphor that would secure the subject in object-relation has gone astray. It has wandered from its place as an apex of oedipal triangulation. But the phobic object as hallucinatory metaphor is not the appearance of its straying. We recall that the phobic object is not a substitution for the primary object of fear. Rather, the hallucinatory metaphor must be linked to the withdrawal of the mother's body, which is to be deemed premature on account of the failure of oedipal triangulation, or the failure of the paternal metaphor to do its job. This means that the drives and impulses turning on the relation to the mother's body are cut off from the investment in objects that would be the outcome of the oedipal struggle, on a Freudian view. When Kristeva calls the phobic object a hallucinatory metaphor she means that it is a representative of the semiotic—here, a drive—deprived of investment in an object, so that the phobic object represents a drive or impulse that cannot *make* sense for the subject. That is why she says that she finds in phobia a condensation of named fear—Little Hans can say, "I am afraid of horses"—and unnameable fear: the anguish of unrepresentable inaugural loss. "The statement, 'to be afraid of horses,' is a hieroglyph having the logic of metaphor and hallucination. By means of the signifier of the phobic object, the 'horse,' it calls attention to a *drive economy in want of an object*" (35).

On Kristeva's view, then, phobia calls up an implication of drive in the symbolic prior to object-relations and to the assumption of the prohibiting function which supports them. In childhood phobia a drive has found the *symbolic* (linguistic activity) but not the *object*: "symbolicity itself is cathected by a drive that is not object-oriented in the classic sense of the term (we are not dealing with an object of *need* or *desire*), nor is it narcissistic (it does not return to collapse upon the subject or to cause its collapse)" (1980a, 45). Phobia is a defense that preserves neither the object nor self-love, but oddly, the subject. "Strangely enough, however, it is the *subject* that is built up, to the extent that it is the correlative of the paternal metaphor, disregarding the failure of its support—the subject, that is, as correlative of the Other" (45). What Kristeva presents as the essence of phobia is the preservation of a subject who "is" no more than an archaic matrix of drives and the symbolic, a subject who is struggling, not in flight from the Oedipus complex, but with the anguish of inaugural loss. The precocious linguistic activity in childhood phobia points to a premature withdrawal of the mother's body. The drive has found language but not the object. Thus Kristeva suggests that, while there is considerable *sense* for little Hans in his affections and experiences, they lack *significance* (34). Hans is aware of and elaborates his suffering but his symptom does not *have* meaning for him, showing that the symbolic function that produces meaning in the subject for another subject is unstable. In sum, Kristeva detects in childhood phobia a position of the subject in relation to the symbolic where the latter is not operating as the separating, judging function. Is the same true of adult phobia? Kristeva finds in the latter the same marked linguistic activity, but here the phenomenon of the *elaboration* of the symptom is missing. "The speech of the phobic adult is also characterized by extreme nimbleness. But that vertiginous skill is as if void of meaning, travelling at top speed over an untouched and untouchable abyss, of which, on occasion, only the affect shows up, giving not a sign but a signal. It happens because language has then become a counterphobic object; it no longer plays the role of an element of miscarried introjection, capable, in the child's phobia, of revealing the anguish of original want" (1980a, 41).

What psychoanalysis encounters in the phobic speech of the adult is a barricaded discourse void of meaning, a discourse commensurate with the brittleness of narcissism and indicating that it has reached a point of crisis. Kristevan "abjection" turns up with the narcissistic crisis. It marks the emergence of the subject from its narcissistic fortress, *before it meets objects*. More precisely, psychoanalysis encounters narcissism converting its walls into a permeable inside/outside limit, and this brings out the archaic arrangement that Kristeva calls abjection. That permeable limit—the abject, paradigmatically the ab-jetted mother—shows up prior to and as a precondition for the object. The narcissistic crisis can therefore issue in the abjection of *self*. The abject is the self. "[The abject] is experienced at the peak of its strength when that subject, weary of fruitless attempts to identify with something on the outside, finds the impossible within; when it finds that the impossible constitutes its very *being*, that it *is* none other than abject" (1980a, 5). In abjection the border of the subject has become an unstable object. It appears as *other* or, better, the subject is "put literally beside itself." Kristeva's most lucid description of the abject appears in an oft-quoted passage on experiencing the corpse (*cadaver*).

> That elsewhere that I imagine beyond the present, or that I hallucinate so that I might, in a present time, speak to you, conceive of you—it is now here, jetted, abjected, into "my" world. Deprived of world, therefore I *fall in a faint* [*cadere*—to fall]. In that compelling, raw, insolent thing in the morgue's full sunlight, in that thing that no longer matches and therefore no longer signifies anything, I behold the breaking down of a world that has erased its borders: fainting away. The corpse, seen without God and outside of science, is the utmost of abjection. It is death infecting life. Abject. *It is something rejected from which one does not part,* from which one does not protect oneself as from an object. Imaginary uncanniness and real threat, it beckons to us and ends up engulfing us. (1980a, 4, emphasis added)[4]

The description of abjection given here points up the status of the abject: something rejected from which one does not part. Kristeva maintains that psychoanalysis witnesses the outburst of abjection but does not have the power to linger over it. Only art has this power. Nonetheless, she pursues an account of abjection on the basis of her evolutionary postulate of an archaic disposition of the symbolic giving access to the function that is to secure the distinction subject/object. On the developmental account, *separation* is nonexistent in the preimaginary. Ab-jection of the mother's body is a primitive mode of separating that struggles to set up an inside/outside border that, however, remains unstable. The maternal "space" that arises in this struggle is neither an object nor a partial object, but "essentially divisible, foldable and catastrophic." We are reminded of Kristeva's logic of drive re-jection. Ab-jection of the mother's body is a separating through which no separate position is established and is, accordingly, multiple or internally repeating: "the ability of the speaking being, always already haunted by the Other, to divide, repeat, reject. Without *one* division, *one* separation, *one* subject/object having been constituted (not yet, or no longer yet)" (1980a, 12). The suffering of phobia shares in this archaic matrix, a multiple separating whose stabilization requires other factors, and which can be called up where separation is presupposed but has run into difficulty. We know from Kristeva's thought on presymbolic subject formation that re-jection will be situated where language does not "speak." She states this clearly in *Black Sun*.

"Never is the ambivalence of drive more fearsome than in this beginning of otherness where, lacking the filter of language, I cannot inscribe my violence in 'no,' nor in any other sign" (1987, 15).

Kristeva acknowledges Freud's indications of the presence of the oedipal problematic in phobia, but equally shows the phobic object to be a hallucinatory metaphor tied to unsymbolized drives. She calls the hallucinatory metaphor a "proto-writing," and little Hans—deprived of others—is stage director of his own drama. This point allows her to assert that there are certain features that writing shares with phobia. In a certain kind of writing—literary writing—there is a language of *fear*. "Not a language of the desiring exchange of messages or objects that are transmitted in a social contract of communication and desire beyond want, but a language of want, of the fear that edges up to it and runs along its edges. . . . The writer is a phobic who succeeds in metaphorizing in order to keep from being frightened to death; instead he comes to life again in signs" (1980a, 38). We see here Kristeva's notion of a writing that accesses and gives form to the semiotic, one distinguished from symbolic discourses that serve to communicate. She believes that there is "a literature of abjection."

"*Where* Am I?"

What we have found is that, for Kristeva, the phobic object is a signal of the descent into semiotic processes, and this is the dimension to which art and literature can give symbolic form. This is why Kristeva calls the "subject" of abjection, whose symptom is the rejection and reconstruction of languages, eminently productive of culture. We see here a relativization of the field of the effects of the symbolic function, but one that arises only in conditions of the collapse of oedipal structure. Thus abjection looms where the symbolic function supporting object-relation, relationship to an other, is absent or unstable. Abjection is a configuration of I/Other where the *distinction* I-Other is not established. What is particularly important for the implications of the demarcating imperative that triggers abjection as a structure of subjectivity, one intimately bound up with that imperative (thus I/Other), is that, here, the founding (the imperative) and the founded (the abject) fold into one another. The emergent ego is both upheld in the Other and caught in its hold. "The ego of primary narcissism is thus uncertain, fragile, threatened, subjected just as much as its non-object to spatial ambivalence (inside/outside uncertainty) and to ambiguity of perception (pleasure/pain)" (1980a, 62). Without the resolution of spatial ambivalence—one beset by abjection asks "*Where* am I?" instead of "*Who* am I?"—the confrontation with unnameable otherness cannot cease (8). The more traditional understanding of this moment in subjectivity, usually called the phallic mother, captures the problem of the overbearing and overinclusive nature of the early mother's power. She is "omnipotent" (some say "phallic") because no space for the ego can arise in this situation. This is the classical reason for emphasizing the appearance of the paternal metaphor as a second authority that is needed to establish separation. Yet this framework also leads to worries that the maternal is only what must be killed off, as well as to the view that misogyny and violence toward women can be explained in terms of this archaic matrix of subjectivity (Reineke 1997). This goes too fast. What is more important, it leaves us stuck with both the structure of infantile abjection and the oedipal structure. Kristeva does not leave us with them, however. If we are to see this, we must tarry with the psychoanalytic theory.

We have already seen that Kristeva's thought on the semiotic introduces a pre-oedipal third into the trials of individuation: the imaginary father. Loving idealization is one of the capacities that calls up a presymbolic moment of subjectivity. We also need to see that the essay on abjection introduces another capacity of the semiotizing *infans,* precisely in relation *to* the problem of omnipotent maternity. The semiotic capacities corresponding to this "place" of unresolved spatial ambivalence are ones of *driving out,* "a violent, clumsy breaking away," but with "the constant risk of falling back under the sway of a power as securing as it is stifling" (1980a, 13). On this view, we can see, on the one hand, that Kristeva has maternal power be a problem, certainly, but she also ties it to certain capacities that serve separation, even if they are insufficient on their own. The archaic mother is not *merely* a baleful power. On the other hand, the ambiguity of this "place" raises the question: how, in this ambiguous relationship, where what supports an ego in the process of taking shape equally counters the attempts to break away, is the release of maternal hold possible? While Kristeva turns, as always, to the prohibiting, separating function, marked as paternal, that would fully come to the aid of the emergent ego, she adds a proviso with respect to her affirmation of the functioning of symbolic law. The symbolic function *can* only aid the emergent ego if it marks itself on articulations that are already active: the semiotic capacity to "demarcate territories." In this way, there would be a kind of synthesis of maternal authority and paternal law that would accommodate the semiotic in the symbolic.

That is not all, however. The imaginary father must of course count as a powerful aid in the infant's attempts to throw off maternal entity without simply moving into a structure of subjectivity that rests on dis-identification with the mother. Nonetheless, Kristeva's discussion of the *chora* in *Powers of Horror* does not stress this source. Rather, the whole discussion emphasizes the demarcating imperative that must be operative in order to make the maternal vessel coalesce with the *abject,* so that a body can separate from another body. This separation is possible only as relation to an entity that is identifiable, here, neither with the mother's body as "nurse" nor with the maternal object (the object of desire, which only becomes possible through abjection). That is to say, in the separation of a body from another body, and as a precondition for the emergence of the object, *something falls out* or, in Kristeva's words "is jettisoned." "It is simply a frontier, a repulsive gift that the Other, having become *alter ego,* drops so that 'I' does not disappear in it but finds, in that sublime alienation, a forfeited existence" (1980a, 9). For that reason, the abject, paradigmatically "jettisoned from" the mother's body, and corresponding to an unnameable otherness, falls out of object-relation. It is always elsewhere than desire, always elsewhere than relationship to another, *literally* beside the subject, its permanent lining. "It lies there, quite close, but it cannot be assimilated. It beseeches, worries, and fascinates desire, which, nevertheless, does not let itself be seduced. Apprehensive, desire turns aside; sickened, it rejects" (1).

To return, finally, to the wider question of what Kristeva discovers in her attention to the presymbolic and pre-imaginary structures of subjectivity, what gives her trilogy its distinction is the thought that social and symbolic capacities are doomed to fathomless frailty unless *the semiotic takes on, is given, symbolic form.* What has been ignored, or has received little attention, in her account of the process of the formation, deformation, and transformation of meaning and the subject, is the *extent* of the social-symbolic dimension of the fragility of the symbolic function. This dimension is, thus far, best elaborated in a thought that sticks closely to Kristeva's discovery of it in subjective structures and her elaborations of them (see Oliver 1993a, 1998). The fragility of the symbolic function is inherent for Kristeva, since if it is to function it must take up, and therefore be modified by, the instability of the demarcating imperative. This is a kind of psychoanalytic imperative, one that belongs especially to the exigencies of the therapeutic setting. However, the appearance—even prevalence—of the instability of the symbolic function is a prominent feature of modern Western societies. The appearance of abjection *as* abjection in conditions of late modernity *corresponds to* the instability of the symbolic function or, we might say, the collapse of the oedipal structure. This is the thought that points to the presence of the nihilism problematic in *Powers of Horror.* Chapter 5, below, shows how Kristeva follows through on this thought in the rest of the book. It stresses that she discovers the outbreak of abjection, *as* abjection, in the secular aftermath of religion. She presents an "archaeology"—a fragmentary minor history—of the moments in which the historical religions took on the task of elaborating this instability, abjection, so that the latter does not appear *as* abjection. It becomes clear that what religion means for Kristeva is the attempt to give symbolic form to the limit of the ties between self and society, where the subject stumbles across its borders. That is to say, the central chapters of *Powers of Horror* are an articulation of how social-symbolic systems have given form to the abject: what she calls "codifications" of abjection. The minor history of religions then works to clarify the significance of the appearance of abjection *itself* in the modern social symbolic system. For the appearance of abjection *as abjection* is a clear indicator of the nihilism problematic. Only given the tendential severance of the semiotic and symbolic *could* abjection come to light as it does in modern Western societies.

Finally, my account of Kristeva's thought on what gives symbolic form to this moment of the semiotic in these conditions—her analysis of the literature of abjection—is reserved for the discussion of Butler and Kristeva in chapter 8. This is because I consider there the differing approaches of these two thinkers to the meaning of abjection, and this is a propitious place for showing how hazardous an adventure the literature of abjection is. A second motive for confronting this aspect of *Powers of Horror* in Part 3 of the book, rather than Part 2 on religion and art, is my intention to launch an argument that the question of abjection has received so much attention in recent years that what is much more *valuable* in Kristeva's thought in the trilogy—the issues of love and loss—has been swamped. To promote this view, I need certain other arguments in place on Kristeva's ethical, political, and feminist writings. The current discussion, on Kristeva's evolutionary postulate of the "semiotic," now turns to the third and final moment of the triadic structure of narcissism: her thought on primal loss in *Black Sun*.

CHAPTER 4

Primal Loss

> Talking about depression will again lead us into the marshy land of the Narcissus myth. This time, however, we shall not encounter the bright and fragile amatory idealization; on the contrary, we shall see the shadow cast on the fragile self, hardly dissociated from the other, precisely by the *loss* of that essential other. The shadow of despair.
>
> —Kristeva, *Black Sun*

Introduction

Black Sun unfolds the third moment of Kristeva's triadic structure of narcissism: primal loss. Further discussion of this topic, in chapters 6 and 8 below, argues that Kristeva's thinking on loss reveals the widest implications of her thought on psychoanalysis, religion, art, and sexual difference. The aim of the present chapter is to see how the question of loss first appears at the strictly psychoanalytic level of her writing, where loss turns up as the third "value" of the presymbolic struggle with an exposure to otherness and separateness. We do not face, here, the difficulties we faced at the opening of the previous chapter, on how to formulate the significance of this moment in the structure of narcissism in relation to the nihilism problematic. For Kristeva, similar to Butler, finds that Western cultures are afflicted by melancholia. In Kristeva's thought this means the loss of the capacity to lose. It is a major objective of this book as a whole to draw out the significance and scope of this thought.

Psychoanalysis encounters the problem of loss in suffering subjectivity. We note from the outset that, in Kristeva, there will be no strict opposition between melancholia (the failure to lose) and mourning (the capacity to let go). This opposition appears in Freud's central text on the subject, *Mourning and Melancholia* (1917), where the enigma of melancholic suffering, for him, lies in how the subject has lost an other but, unlike the one who mourns, does not go through the grief of loss and move beyond it. The melancholic remains tied to the lost object, as though he or she does not know what they have lost *in* the other. A later work of Freud's (*The Ego and the Id* 1923) presents changes in his thought on the ego that implicitly undermines this opposition, but Freud does not draw the conclusions for his theory of mourning and melancholia. In *Black Sun* Kristeva does draw the conclusions, and we will see how she relates her theory to Freud's thought along the way. Let me first underline the major reason why no strict opposition between melancholy and mourning appears in her attention to suffering subjectivity. *Black Sun* shows that psychoanalysis is the method of Kristeva's thought because, in conditions of the tendential severance of the semiotic and symbolic, the forgotten problem of loss turns up in psychoanalytic experience of melancholy/depression as the remnant of freedom.

This discussion will show how the psychoanalytic chapters of *Black Sun* present a thought on primal loss as one of the semiotizing capacities of the preverbal *infans* in relation to the early mother. In other words, it shows what primal loss is as part of the triadic structure of narcissism. We can then see how the narcissistic *constriction* prevalent in Western cultures is a matter, not only of the demise of the imaginary father, but of failings in separateness and connections with others that turn on the loss of loss. *Black Sun* reveals most clearly that recent and contemporary psychoanalysis explores the modern isolation of the soul, for its topic is the suffering subjectivity that struggles with symbolic collapse, once the individual is left to shoulder the burden of connecting the semiotic and symbolic; that is to say, the burden of taking up a relationship to otherness, separateness, loss, and death where the symbolic resources available to aid the subject in the encounter are inadequate.[1] In other words, the problem of nihilistic modernity comes to the surface in the third book of the trilogy. For the psychoanalytic chapters of *Black Sun*, following through the attention psychoanalysis gives to the pervious border between the individual and society, finds nihilism there, at the limit of the ties between the subject and the social.

As we would expect, each new investigation of the narcissistic structure in Kristeva's trilogy introduces a further dimension of an exposure to and struggle with a radical and inassimilable exteriority on the part of the preverbal *infans*. Since this struggle appears prior to the emergence of a "self," the discussion will turn on another corporeal registration of the presymbolic exposure to otherness in primary narcissism. We should not be surprised, then, to find that long passages of the psychoanalytic chapters in *Black Sun* are attempts to convey the meaning of the drive and the affect in psychoanalysis. We recall, first, that these are the registrations, ineliminably corporeal, of the relation to the early mother. It is this semiotic content—drives and affects—that show up in the psychoanalytic encounter with melancholy/depression, where a subject suffers from symbolic collapse: a sense of meaningless and nothingness in which, as Oliver puts it: "The discourse is experienced as empty even though it is full of drives and affect representations" (1998, 70). In other words, the subject is suffering drives and affects cut off from representation and refusing extant modes of representation. The sufferer complains of or insists upon a lack of meaning. The general theme of the absence of significance recalls Kristeva's attention to the case of little Hans in *Powers of Horror,* but here we are on slightly different terrain with respect to the incapacity to bear the loss of the mother. Let me turn to the strictly psychoanalytic thinking on this predicament.

For psychoanalysis, the key to depression/melancholy is the question of *affect*. Affects are the most rudimentary of representations. They record "energy signals." It must be kept in mind that this thought does not posit a presignifying corporeality that is the site of raw energies. Affects are "the most archaic inscription of inner and outer events," the psychic register of energy displacements and inscriptions, terms that indicate the symbolic determinant of bioenergic events (1987, 23).[2] What this means is that they register the exposure to separateness and otherness. Acknowledging the theoretical vagueness of the psychoanalytic conception of affect, Kristeva turns to consider the more accessible phenomenon of mood. Mood, Kristeva says, goes beyond its verbal and semiological expression. In other words, it can be silent, invisible. When variety in mood decreases to the point where despair reigns, it being known that melancholy falls into mutism, one mood remains as the outward sign of that fall: *sadness.* From the psychoanalytic position, sadness indicates the dominion in depression of a buried affect. This perspective leads Kristeva to reiterate and rework the conception of melancholy that detects in it intolerance for object loss: the idea, known from Freud (1917a) that the melancholic is in despair over a rejection or abandonment, for instance. Kristeva comes to present a melancholy/depression in which the subject remains sequestered with what she calls a "nonobject." This thought turns on her insight into the inaugural loss of the mother. The special focus of *Black Sun* is what befalls the primitive self in respect of the archaic and incomplete parting from the mother: the shadow cast on the fragile self by the impact of want-loss. Thus the book investigates the suffering of primal loss considered apart from its consolation, the "imaginary father," which the subject might be deprived of. Moreover, the focus on melancholy/depression brings to light a new dimension of the semiotizing capacities of the *infans*.

The two major parameters of the psychoanalytic thought in *Black Sun* are specified where Kristeva notes, and sets aside, the symptomatological distinction between clinical melancholy, pertaining to psychosis, and depression, pertaining to neurosis. According to that symptomatology, melancholy and depression are distinguished in terms of the intensity and frequency of oscillation between sadness and uplifted spirits, with clinical melancholy denoting the oscillation between asymbolia and manic exultation. Kristeva notes this in order to consider the psychoanalytic view of what the two conditions share, drawing out, once again, a borderline position of the subject. "If temporary sadness or mourning on the one hand, and melancholy stupor on the other, are clinically and nosologically different, they are nevertheless supported by *intolerance for object loss* and *the signifier's failure* to insure a compensating way out of the states of withdrawal in which the subject takes refuge to the point of inaction (pretending to be dead) or even suicide" (1987, 10). The first parameter is the classical one, intolerance for object loss. Kristeva draws out a profound feature of it: *impossible* mourning for the (archaic) maternal object. The second parameter, which assumes Lacanian thought, is the signifier's failure to ensure a compensating way out. This thought refers us to the fragility of the symbolic function known from *Powers of Horror* and to the demise of the imaginary father known from *Tales of Love*. More broadly, however, Kristeva is not relating everything about loss to a lack of love or law understood as the province of paternal functions. She is getting at the fate of the semiotic, turning on the relation to the early mother, in modern Western societies. The rest of this chapter examines the two parameters of object loss and signifying failure in turn, before turning to the wider context of the exploration of loss.

Intolerance For Loss

Black Sun adopts the same procedure as that taken in the reformulation of the "essence" of phobia in *Powers of Horror,* by recalling the classic psychoanalytic conception of the depressive object before formulating the nonobjectal position of melancholy/depression. "According to classic psychoanalytic theory (Abraham, Freud, and Melanie Klein), depression, like mourning, conceals an aggressiveness toward the lost object, thus revealing the ambivalence of the depressed person with respect to the object of mourning. 'I love that object,' is what that person seems to say about the lost object, 'but even more so I hate it; because I love it, and in order not to lose it I imbed it in myself; but because I hate it, that other within myself is a bad self, I am bad, I am non-existent, I shall kill myself'" (1987, 11). Here Kristeva reminds us of psychoanalytic thought on the intolerance for loss that underlies depression in the field of secondary identifications, that is to say, where a subject has taken up a relationship to an object it is distinguished from but that relationship has come to grief. The *intolerance* for loss sustains object-relation, no longer in the form of a relationship with an outside object, an other, but as an ambivalent love-hatred for an object that is *not* lost but preserved within. Kristeva contrasts this with a form of melancholy situated theoretically in the narcissistic structuration of the subject that is prior to object love and the frustration of libido stemming from object loss in this sense.

> Far from being a hidden attack on an other who is thought to be hostile because he is frustrating, sadness would point to a primitive self—wounded, incomplete, empty. Persons thus affected do not consider themselves wronged but afflicted with a fundamental flaw, a congenital deficiency. Their sorrow doesn't conceal the guilt or the sin felt because of having secretly plotted revenge on the ambivalent object. Their sadness would be rather the most archaic expression of an unsymbolizable, unnameable narcissistic wound, so precocious that no outside agent (subject or agent) can be used as referent. (1987, 12)

The depressed *narcissist,* she concludes, "mourns not an Object but the Thing" (13). Kristeva borrows the metaphor "black sun" from the poet Nerval for the title of her book on melancholy. The metaphor suggests an unnameable narcissistic wound where the only consolation, the "godsend" of primary identification with the father of individual prehistory, has dropped away. We recall that, in *Tales of Love,* Kristeva talks of the narcissistic constriction in terms of the effects of a lack of a secular variant of the living and loving father. *Black Sun* suggests that narcissistic depression afflicts a society where the psychic representatives of the impact of loss/emptiness are cut off from the life of signs. The depressed person is not the prisoner and guardian of a lost object, but the prisoner and guardian of an affect recording immemorial loss. This implies that intolerance for loss underlying narcissistic depression cannot be rendered intelligible in terms of existing symbolic connections. More precisely, intolerance for loss indicates the incommensurability between the impact of primal loss and symbolic articulations of loss. No extant discourse captures "this." Kristeva will not suggest that there are words that can capture inaugural loss *as such*. "Let me posit the 'Thing' as the real that does not lend itself to signification" (1987, 13). However, metaphors like Nerval's "black sun" convey primal loss. Psychoanalytic theory, on the other hand, is a reflection on the experience of therapy, which attempts to articulate primal loss as a structure of subjectivity. In line with the strategies of *Tales of Love* and *Powers of Horror,* the theoretical elucidation of the states of withdrawal that show up in narcissistic depression brings out an aspect of the preverbal infant's struggle with the symbolic. "The looming of the Thing summons up the subject's life force as that subject is in the process of being set up; the premature being that we all are can survive only if it clings to an other, perceived as supplement, artificial extension, protective wrapping. Nevertheless, such a life drive is fully one that, *at the same time,* rejects me, isolates me, rejects him (or her). Never is the ambivalence of drive more fearsome than in this beginning of otherness where, lacking the filter of language, *I cannot inscribe my violence in 'no,' nor in any other sign*" (1987, 15, final emphasis added).

As we have seen, Kristeva's attention to the ambivalence of drive in *Powers of Horror* led her to propose a presignifying inscription of violence which primes the constitution of otherness, an ability to expel nonsignifiable things and so to mark out territories that compose a maternal "space," which as yet lacks any delimitation. The thinking on the drive in *Black Sun* draws out the full ambivalence of archaic separating, for the violence of ab-jection is not fully distinguishable from the life force. Not only is the destructive wave of the drive a function in the repulsion of the other, so that a body can separate from another body. It can only be sustained within a clinging to what is in the process of being lost, the vital support. We can see that the "life" drive is at the same time the expropriation of the life-support, enforcing separation: "rejects me, isolates me, rejects him (or her)." Expulsion, clinging, deprivation, splitting—all of these are features of the preverbal infant's struggle with the symbolic within the bodily exchange between mother and child or, more specifically, within the withdrawal of the mother's body. *Narcissistic* depression calls up this struggle for mastery over the nonsignifying, fearsome, otherness that looms in archaic separating, where the other is not parted from.

The issue now is the significance of melancholy in this matrix of primary narcissism. Kristeva finds support for her own working out of this question in Klein's thought on the significance of depression in pre-oedipal separating. There are two moments in Klein's thought on depression, differentiated in accordance with how they are situated in respect of a nonintegration of the primitive self in the early mother-child relationship. The first is Klein's "depressive position," a *parting sadness* which indicates the preverbal child's consent to lose the mother's body. This capacity of the semiotizing *infans,* parting sadness, appears in Kristeva's thought as a fragile integration of energy-displacements and inscriptions into the single but composite affect, *sadness,* which signals an acceptance of loss and preparedness for the life of signs, "when that intrepid wanderer leaves the crib to meet the mother in the realm of representations" (1987, 41). The second moment in Klein relates to the appearance of depression, given separation, where it functions as a protection against schizoid fragmentation for a subject whose signifying system is threatened: a fragile integration of drives and affects that could otherwise destabilize the subject. Depression points to semiotic capacities that mediate between drives and signs by elaborating affect-representation, and this can prepare the way for symbolic capacities.

Having relayed the Kleinian thought on parting sadness, Kristeva also indicates a depression/melancholy other than that which acts as a protection against schizoid fragmentation. For if there is a withdrawal from *symbolic activity,* the value of depression is inverted. This withdrawal indicates the tendency to call up the nonintegration of the self. The subject is absorbed in the buried affect of inaugural loss. Strangely, in this case, dis-integration can become the saving action. The thought is that schizoid "parceling" is not only a threat to the subject but may act as a protection against *primal* melancholy. Kristeva returns, once again, to the concept of the death drive in order to elucidate the nature of this protection, drawing on Freud's speculations in *Beyond the Pleasure Principle* (1920), which postulate a tendency in living beings to "return to an earlier state" in order to illuminate the—newly accepted—existence of a special aggressive instinct. Freud's text unfolds, not a concept of nature, but a speculative idea of a tendency in living matter to return to the non-living state. The idea of "thanatos" is the idea of a portion of the drive (its destructive wave) that can be in conflict with eros, the pull of life. The duality of the instincts is now an opposition between the death drive and the life drive, which comes to embrace the relata of Freud's earlier opposition between the sexual instincts and the instinct for self-preservation. Freudian eros is captured in Kristeva's phrase "lives sustained by desire." What is best known of the death drive, on the other hand, is its outward-directed discharge in the service of life: aggressivity and destructiveness in response to a threat. Freud detects such a discharge in the phenomenon of sado-masochism, a phenomenon which exhibits a dialectic in the field of subject-object relations. Eros and thanatos are cooperative. Nonetheless, Freud also confronts the problem set by the phenomenon of noneroticized suffering. He considers the possibility of a "primary" masochism, anterior to—or given the collapse of—the dialectic that presumes libidinal investment in objects.

Noneroticized suffering points to a retention of the destructive portion of the drive "within," as distinct from its outer-directed discharge. Primary masochism, for Freud, is deprived of eros, and this leads him to posit a state of disunity of eros and thanatos (see Kristeva 1987, 17). Kristeva also considers the possible state of disunity of eros and thanatos. However, she proposes a cooperation of eros and thanatos which is, nonetheless, and *contra* Freud, set apart from their dialectic in the field of object-relations: a pre-objectal composite of the drives that protects against depression. Kristeva is returning to and expanding on the thought of abjection in these passages of *Black Sun*. Since this "protection" is beyond both erotic and symbolic bonds, it is neither desire nor the ego that are preserved here, but *life*. On her account, withdrawal of the mother's body is a real deprivation, immediately bound up with a nonsignifying imprint of loss. The impact of loss/emptiness, with and beyond real deprivation, befalls the infant as a thanatic threat. Infantile struggle with the symbolic is adapted to its impact: "a Thanatic reaction to a threat that is itself Thanatic" (18).[3] The child responds to the advent of things which *are* not, and are not signifiable, by driving them out, thereby creating territories that it strays in. The discussion of ab-jection of the mother's body in *Powers of Horror* now reappears in a way that suggests that abjection can work as a protection against the despair of loss. For the thanatic response to the threat of loss is death-bearing but preserves (inaugurates) life for the subject. Thus abjection is "an ambiguity that, through the violence of a revolt *against*, demarcates a space out of which signs and objects arise" (1980a, 10).

This thought now illuminates how schizoid parcelling, from one point of view a disintegration of the self that sadness protects against, can equally be viewed as a composite of life and death drives that protect against narcissistic depression. Schizoid parcelling calls up the mechanism of abjection. What Klein's idea of parting sadness shows Kristeva is that the elaboration of affect, sadness, appears in and as the *deflection* of the death drive. It is a turning away from the violence of abjection. Parting sadness integrates the representations of energy signals (drive representatives) and—retrospectively—protects against schizoid fragmentation. Kristeva acknowledges the nonverbal integrity of the depressive mood: *"sadness reconstitutes an affective cohesion of the self, which restores its unity within the framework of the affect"* (1987, 19, emphasis added).

However, depression has another significance once attention is given to the *demise of meaning* in depression. There can be a destabilization of the protection of the self through sadness, owing to the signifier's failure to ensure a compensating way out of the states of withdrawal. "The depressive denial that destroys the meaning of the symbolic also destroys the act's meaning and leads the subject to commit suicide without anguish of disintegration, as a reuniting with archaic non-integration, as lethal as it is jubilatory, 'oceanic'" (19). In a sense, then, the anguish of disintegration is a protection against death-dealing sadness. Understood in this way, the most violent and volatile of the three aspects of Kristeva's archaic matrix of the drives (abjection) does not carry the greatest menace—for the self. Perhaps this is why current critical thinking is drawn so much to the explosion of abjection in the culture. It might be that the evasion of depression is a source of this explosion. If this is so, much of the critical attention to abjection is missing the problem of loss and depression that it overlays. Butler (1997) is not susceptible to the temptation to overlook the question of loss. She knows that the culture is afflicted by melancholy. What Kristeva reveals is that depressive suffering that falls short of or refuses the path opened up by ab-jection is, in the absence of eroticization, most laid open to the thanatic threat to the self. Kristeva acknowledges that the concept of the death drive is the outcome of theoretical speculation, but she finds support for the speculation in the notion that mood presents us with the psychic recording of the exposure to exteriority. The alternative, then, to the triumph of the depressive affect is diversity in mood: "variety in sadness, refinement in sorrow or mourning, are the imprint of a humankind that is surely not triumphant but subtle, ready to fight, and creative" (1987, 22). On the other hand, "messengers of Thanatos, melancholy people, are witness/accomplices of the signifier's flimsiness, the living being's precariousness" (20).

What marks narcissistic depression, in contrast with the symptoms that call up abjection, is a slowing down of linguistic activity, a breakdown in the development of syntactical organization. In order to capture the constituents of narcissistic depression, Kristeva offers an account of the development of syntactical organization, consisting in the serial linkage of elements. On the one hand, Freud's primary processes—condensation and displacement—are interpreted as the serial organization of semiotic imprints. On the other hand, the symbolic field rests on the "concatenation" of signifiers, comprising words (verbal sequences) and action (contrasted with states of withdrawal). Entrance into the symbolic order is a transition into spatial and temporal articulation, the life of signs.

As we have seen, Kristeva accepts Klein's depressive position as a precondition for the development of signifying capacities. The emergence of the sign presumes the *absence* of the object, and so the acceptance of loss. We are now approaching Kristeva's thought in *Black Sun* on the need to accommodate the semiotic in the life of signs. First of all: "That critical task of *transposition* consists of two facets: the mourning gone through for the object (and in its shadow the mourning for the archaic Thing), and the subject's acceptance of a set of signs (signifying precisely because of the absence of object) only thus open to serial organization" (1987, 41). The acceptance of a set of signs requires the integration of affect-representations and drive-representatives. With Kristeva, sadness is the *signal* of such an integration. Parting sadness is an elaboration—an "awareness"—of loss. If awareness of loss is missing, signifying capacities are impeded. The beginning of language lies, then, in following up the elaboration of loss with the "negation" of loss. "Signs are arbitrary because language starts with a *negation* (*Verneinung*) of loss, along with the depression occasioned by mourning. 'I have lost an essential object that happens to be, in the final analysis, my mother,' is what the speaking being seems to be saying. 'But no, I have found her again in signs, or rather since I consent to lose her I have not lost her (that is the negation), I can recover her in language'" (43). Kristeva, following Freud in his essay on "Negation" (1925), reminds us that the lost past—what is subject to repression in Freud—turns up in the symbolic in the form of denial ("I have not lost her"). At the same time, however, the loss is accepted insofar as the subject accepts a set of signs ("I can recover her in language").

The Signifying Failure

We have reached the point where the second parameter of Kristeva's psychoanalytic thought on melancholy can be fully brought into view. On her account, a disavowal of *negation* leaves the melancholy person imprisoned in the denial of the signifier. The poverty of linguistic activity that marks depression—gaps, silences, and the inability to complete verbal sequences in dialogue—points to the dominion of semiotic traces that remain unsymbolized. Kristeva's confrontation with narcissistic suffering therefore presses the claim that the negation of loss—necessary for the entrance into language—must encompass a transposition of semiotic imprints that register the impact of loss/emptiness. Accepting a set of signs requires not only the ability to renounce loss ("I have not lost her," the negation), nor the counterindication of this renunciation in the acceptance of a set of signs ("I can recover her in language"), but the *conveyance* of loss. This brings us to the center of the psychoanalytic thought in *Black Sun*: "verbal sequences turn up only if a trans-position is substituted for a more or less symbiotic primal object, this trans-position being a true reconstitution that retroactively *gives form and meaning* to the mirage of the primal Thing" (1987, 41, emphasis added). That is to say, symbolic and social capacities can arise and be sustained only if psychic representatives of archaic or immemorial—objectless—loss take on symbolic form. Oliver recognizes this in her discussion of *Tales of Love*. "Kristeva maintains that the imaginary is the ability to transfer meaning where it is lost" (1998, 70). Kristeva develops this thought furthest when she expands upon the psychoanalytic view of mourning in *Black Sun,* drawing out and articulating immemorial loss. Although it remains the case that the pivotal moment in mourning would be the capacity to shift to the symbolic order in respect of loss, taking on the "break" that opens up the realm of signs (symbolic lack), the special focus and real issue of *Black Sun* remains the need for semiotic traces to be given form within the symbolic. "Would the fate of the speaking being consist in ceaselessly transposing, always further beyond or more to the side, such a transposition of series or sentences testifying to *our ability to work out a fundamental mourning and successive mournings*?" (1987, 42, emphasis added).

It is certainly the case that the transition to the symbolic order—the transition from the semiotic to the symbolic that Shepherdson (2000) emphasizes—presumes the consent to lose the essential "object." But this thought does not get the whole picture. On this view, mourning would be fulfilled by ever renewed, manifold symbolic connections in a merely linguistic universe. The failure of this would show up in narcissistic depression/melancholy, marked by the slowing down of verbalization and the inability to sustain signifying sequences, pointing to the failure to take on the loss of the essential object. This contrast appears to settle the distinction between mourning and melancholy. They remain opposed. Yet, with Kristeva there is an essential moment in what might be called "incomplete" mourning that is indispensable to mourning and upsets any settled dividing-point between it and melancholia. Symbolic capacities dissociated from and providing no conduit for semiotic imprints are themselves on the path of despair, a refusal of sadness and loss. The brilliant but empty and barricaded discourse characterizing the "crisis" of narcissism would be a realization of this tendency. Narcissistic suffering of this nature is, then, akin to depression but takes the opposite path: increased linguistic activity rather than broken speech interspersed by silences.

The strict opposition between mourning and melancholy does not survive Kristeva's account of narcissistic depression, then. She goes beyond the thought of the melancholic preservation of the lost object, embedded "within" *versus* the achievement of "letting go." Incomplete mourning includes a moment of arresting the signifying path and returning to the site of pain. This thought *expresses* her recognition that unacknowledged suffering is the remnant of freedom. For what this "return" means in Kristeva is a discovery of suffering subjectivity where loss and mourning have been locked in. Therapeutically, the return involves bringing the barricaded discourse into connection with the affect from which it is cut off. But Kristeva's claim is much broader than this. The psychoanalytic and literary position holds that the return to the site of pain is made "in order to discover, in the mother tongue, a *'total word, new, foreign to the language'* (Mallarmé), for the purpose of capturing the unnameable" (1987, 42). The import of the innovation indicated here needs to be grasped. When Kristeva comes to present her fine-grained analyses of artworks in the rest of *Black Sun*, she binds the historical features of the fragmentary minor history of modernity it offers to particular sites of suffering and its overcoming. For her, this is to bind them to the remnant of freedom in those sites. "The work of art that insures the rebirth of its author and its reader or viewer is one that succeeds in integrating the artificial language it puts forward (new style, new composition, surprising imagination) and the unnamed agitations of an omnipotent self that ordinary social and linguistic usage always leave somewhat orphaned or plunged into mourning. Hence such a fiction, if it isn't an antidepressant, is at least a survival, a resurrection" (51). Her words "new style, new composition, surprising imagination" can be passed over too quickly. For here she stresses the notion of mourning as fundamental and successive mournings. First, variety in sadness or refinement in sorrow is fundamental to human capacities for meaning and value in separateness and connections with others. Second, we see that what Kristeva means by the aesthetic is unique discourses that are successive symbolizations/experiences of loss (as well as love).

The point at which she finds the loss of loss in subjectivity is where "the weight of the primal Thing prevails, and all translatability becomes impossible" (1987, 42). Kristeva is therefore quite clearly formulating a dimension of intersubjectivity that differs from and underlies the Lacanian one in which it is only in becoming subjects of desire (lack) that we become symbolic and social subjects. The repudiation of desire, "foreclosure" of the Name-of-the-Father, is a downfall that affects the subject's integration in sociality. Let us note Kristeva's alternative, here. "Denial focuses on the *intrapsychic (semiotic and symbolic) inscription of the want*, be it fundamentally an object want or later eroticized as woman's castration. In other words, denial focuses on signifiers liable to inscribe semiotic traces and transpose them in order to produce meaning in the subject for another subject" (44). Denial, here, is a failure to shift to the symbolic order *insofar as* the need in this shift of giving the semiotic symbolic form is failed. "The semiotic foundations (affect and drive representatives of loss and castration) underlying linguistic signs are denied, and the intrapsychic value of the latter for creating sense for the subject is completely annihilated" (46).

Here denial bears as much on a value as it does on lack, and the denial isolates the subject in a different way than repudiation of desire does. Intersubjectivity is failed insofar as the production of meaning in the subject for another subject is failed. The depressive denial of value is a denial of the imaginary, in a certain sense—Oliver's, we note (1998)—since it bears on the signifiers giving form and meaning to the primitive psychic representatives of want-loss and emptiness. This is the transition—from the semiotic to the imaginary—that Shepherdson (2000) misses. My reading of Kristeva concurs, then, with Oliver's insight that the denial of the Kristevan imaginary is a symptom of a culture that is overly linguistic, disembodied, and tied to a repressive and empty law. I take this to be a major argument of her chapter on Kristeva's thought on love in *Subjects Without Subjectivity* (1998, chapter 4). On Kristeva's view, the absence of signifiers of loss leaves the depressive person a prisoner of affect, closed up with a weight of meaning, a painful innerness which *has* no meaning. "Denial of negation deprives the language signifiers of their role of making sense for the subject" (1987, 52). For persons in despair, "a signifying sequence, necessarily an arbitrary one, will appear to them as heavily, violently arbitrary; they will think it absurd, it will have no meaning. No word, no object in reality will be likely to have a coherent concatenation that will also be suitable to a meaning or referent" (51). On Kristeva's account of the intense experience of the arbitrariness of language, "the chasm that settles in between the subject and signifiable objects," when nothing means anything, reveals "a chasm in the very subject." Kristeva is very precise on this point: "On the one hand, objects and signifiers, denied to the extent that they are identified with life, assume the value of non-meaning: language and life have no meaning. On the other hand, on account of splitting, an intense, extravagant value is attributed to the Thing, to Nothing—to the unsignifiable and to death" (51–52).

I have compiled these citations from *Black Sun* in order to underline once more my argument for Kristeva's sensitivity to the problem of nihilistic modernity, in a specific sense. Her recognition and interpretation of attachment to the arbitrariness of language does not lead to any overarching thought of a crisis in rationality, or a metanarrative of the collapse of metaphysics. For she knows that what is lost is values, meaning, and the "other" as conditions for self-orientation and a life. Her discussion of psychic denial has affinities with Nietzsche's grasp of the nihilistic attitude as a critical *condition* of Western cultures. To repeat a point made in the introduction to this book, if we do not bypass Nietzsche the philosophical psychologist, it is unsurprising to find that psychoanalysis is encountering the same set of issues as he did. In Kristeva melancholy is an inability to forget the arbitrariness of signs, or an appropriation of the absurdity of language, that is to say, a symbolic abdication that makes its abode in the absurdity of bonds and beings. Moreover, melancholic lucidity about the arbitrariness of the signifier, when the lucidity is deprived of transience, brings loss of life.

This implies that the production of meaning requires an elaboration of, setting aside, loss and the affect which attends it. This binding of affect underlies and is necessary to the life of representation. Denial of loss works precisely against this, denying not only the signifier but the *affect*: "the depressed subject has remained prisoner of the nonlost object (the Thing)" (1987, 47). If semiotic traces are denied, along with the value of their signifiers, the subject is prisoner of immemorial loss. The particularity of Kristevan melancholy lies, then, in the denial of signifiers that have to do with (consent to) loss, pain, and life.

Having set out the mechanisms of narcissistic depression and the disconnection of language and affect that supports it, Kristeva specifies the function of psychoanalysis as a *counterdepressant*. "By analysing—that is, by dissolving—the denial mechanism wherein depressive persons are stuck, analytic cure can implement a genuine 'graft' of symbolic potential and place at the subject's disposal dual discursive strategies working at the intersection of affective and linguistic inscriptions, at the intersection of the semiotic and the symbolic. Such strategies are real counterdepressant reserves that the optimal interpretation within analysis places at the disposal of the depressive patient" (1987, 52–53). We might say that, as counterdepressant, psychoanalysis is a limit discourse of modernity. Following through Kristeva's understanding of psychoanalytic practice, we find that what therapy means for her is the recovery, not simply of the symbolic, but of the *imaginary*. Moreover, this has implications for the meaning of the transference. Continuing from the previous quote: "At the same time, considerable empathy is required between the analyst and the depressed patient. On that basis, vowels, consonants, or syllables may be extracted from the signifying sequence and put together again in line with the overall meaning of the discourse that identification with the patient has allowed the analyst to discover. This is an infra- and translinguistic level that must often be taken into consideration and linked with the 'secret' and the unnamed affect of the depressive" (53).

As in *Tales of Love* and *Powers of Horror*, Kristeva draws attention here to the importance of the countertransference—empathy, identification with the patient—as a function required in the treatment, alongside or in alternation with the "symbolic" function of anonymous distance. The countertransference is crucial for the discovery of the unnamed affect in the analysand's dead speech, and for its translation: the production of meaning in the subject for another subject. Without the countertransference, the analytic goal will be failed, for even though speech is the key to the analytic experience (Lacan), it is speech that melancholy persons are alienated from: "the speech of the depressed is to them like an alien skin; melancholy persons are foreigners in their maternal tongue. They have lost the meaning—the value—of their mother tongue for want of losing the mother" (1987, 53). On Kristeva's view, consistent with her acceptance of the Lacanian story of language and lack (finitude), one must restore *to language* the foreignness that the subject has appropriated. Nevertheless, the recovery of the imaginary remains crucial. It is necessary if the subject's symbolic system is to be reconstructed against the threat of collapse when facing further separations and losses, and the confrontation with fearsome, nondifferentiated otherness they cast up. The act of translation of the buried, and cherished, affect accomplishes that restoration and, simultaneously, provides the one afflicted with a "graft" of symbolic potential.

The central thesis of Kristeva's account of melancholy is, therefore, the necessity of a symbolic form-giving that integrates the most archaic, or primitive, recording of loss/emptiness within the symbolic field: culture and language. Put otherwise, the imaginary is a necessary component of culture. From a broader perspective, then, this requirement of form-giving can be viewed as one that needs to be met by the social-symbolic system. If failed, it may rebound on the subject, in situations of separation, loss, and their aftermath, in the form of denial of the symbolic. In other words, narcissistic despair—a nihilistic attitude—is a symptom of nihilistic modernity when suffering loss is deemed pathological or, worse, paid no heed to in the culture. Once again, unacknowledged suffering is a *remnant* of freedom in these conditions. With Kristeva, then, the psychoanalytic encounter with the collapse of the subject's signifying system brings into view conditions in which representations once widely taken to be fundamental to social life are deracinated, and despair breaks out. Kristeva's relationship to religion, which is not ambivalent but quite carefully drawn, is not a nostalgic one. She can speak of the need to "go over" the religious and the sacred precisely in relation to the upsurge of a nihilistic attitude—or even in relation to an avowed dedication to the liberal discourse of rights in response to the horror of religious wars—without recommending a return to symbolic systems that fall short of articulating or, in conditions of conflict, maintaining human rights. However, it is not simply the adoption of the nihilistic attitude that threatens the subject. For there remains the wider issue of how the prevailing social and symbolic discourses in Western cultures cut the symbolic field off from the infrasymbolic realm. Her point is that the symbolic field must embrace this realm if it is to support the elaboration of meaning and values.

Kristeva's attentiveness to modern nihilism is accompanied by the perception that modern Western societies are those in which there has been a central belief in the conveyability of what can be called "other than or outside language." They are societies in which melancholia is a cultural feature. Kristeva suggests that philosophy in the West, before it dispenses with the notion that the meaning of life is its own, special and intelligible concern—or when it challenges such a view—recalls the melancholia at the foundation of its conceptual labor. "The melancholia he [Aristotle] evokes is not a philosopher's disease but his very *ethos*" (1987, 7). Philosophical representation knowingly moves beyond melancholia (mourns) and in doing so runs the *risk* of completed mourning, or of lining up with a culture that tends toward the promotion of a merely linguistic universe. It would appear from certain passages in *Black Sun* that this tendency is equivalent to the demise of metaphysics, suggesting that the central and perhaps defining belief of metaphysics is belief in the conveyability of the so-called other of language. Such a belief leads, Kristeva asserts, to the strong individuality and multiple styles characteristic of Western culture, and these lead—in turn—to multiple conveyances. However, once the multiplicity of styles loses sight of its anterior and exterior foundation—the other of language—metaphysics declines. "The Western subject, as potential melancholy being, having become a relentless conveyor, ends up a confirmed gambler or potential atheist. The initial belief in conveyance becomes changed into a belief in stylistic performance for which the near side of the text, its other, primal as it might be, is less important than the success of the text itself" (68).

It needs to be underlined, once again, that Kristeva is not delivering a metanarrative of the collapse of metaphysics, or a proposition about the wholesale loss of transcendence. Rather, the opening chapters of *Black Sun,* like those of the other works of the trilogy, present a sort of psychoanalytic version of a central thought of Kant's. Not only are intuitions without concepts blind—in Kristeva, semiotic content without symbolic form is mute, invisible, and deprived of a history. But concepts without intuitions are empty—in Kristeva, a linguistic, symbolic universe deprived of connections with the infrasymbolic representations of exposure to otherness, separateness, loss, and death, is one without meaning or values.

Finally, the analyses of artworks that make up the rest of *Black Sun* compose one of her fragmentary minor histories of modernity in the trilogy. This one exhibits how she sees these works confronting the nihilistic attitude and the fetishization of the artwork, and overcoming these positions insofar as the works remain bound to the sites of suffering. This is the topic of chapter 6, below. Since Kristeva engages with the question of the aesthetic in terms of the secular aftermath of religion, we first return to *Powers of Horror*, where the significance of religion in her minor histories is perhaps set out most clearly, in part because the value of the literature of abjection is such a tricky question, an issue we have yet to address.

PART II

Religion and Art

Kristeva's Minor Histories of Modernity

CHAPTER 5

The Powers and Limitations of Religion

Introduction

Chapters 2-4 have shown the appearance of the nihilism problematic in the strictly psychoanalytic level of Kristeva's writing in each book of the 1980s trilogy. Her interrogation there of the suffering subjectivity that shows up in psychoanalytic experience suggests that psychoanalysis is witness to a weakening of psychic life. She detects a cultural failing of what is required to uphold social and symbolic existence, in other words, to maintain self-relation, connections with others, and social bonding. If it is to fulfill this requirement, a society must negotiate the nonsymbolized exposure to the beginnings of otherness and separateness or, from a different perspective, the confrontation with separateness, otherness, and loss at the limit of the ties between the individual and the social. These less visible features of selfhood and connections with others are failed in modern Western societies, which tend toward the promotion of a merely linguistic universe cut off from the embodied dimension of bonds with others: the corporeal, affective, and mimetic moments of subjectivity and meaning that are never past in psychic life but require accommodation in the symbolic if there is to be a world of nature and not only a linguistic world.

We have seen that Kristeva's expansion of psychoanalytic thought on primary narcissism is a sustained attention to these less visible features of individuation and bonding composed in the figure of Narcissus. When she unfolds her triadic structure of narcissism in terms of the capacities of the semiotizing *infans* to negotiate the exposure to otherness and separateness with ab-jection and with nonverbal forms of idealization and loss, she presents the content (the "semiotic") whose transition into a form of representation within the life of signs (the "symbolic") provides the culture with possibilities for meaning and values. Each successful transition delivers what Kristeva calls an imaginary construct or imaginary discourse, and this is a vital aspect of her conception of the imaginary, one that is insufficiently considered or frequently misunderstood in the reception of her thought. Western cultures have typically failed the task of providing sites for making these transitions, and psychoanalysis encounters the outcome of this failure: the individual's struggle with the burden of reconnecting the semiotic and symbolic unaided by cultural resources. Psychoanalysis is witness to the narcissistic constriction that shows up in these conditions: crises of love and self-orientation, and the weakening of the capacity for loss. These sites of suffering—deemed pathological or insignificant, or simply overlooked in modern Western societies—make up an unacknowledged suffering that is the remnant of freedom. For each site of suffering, each failing that Narcissus exhibits when he or she shows up in an infantile, regressive form, is the suffering of a piece of the reality that has come to grief (Nietzsche). However, as I have continually stressed, Kristeva's analysis of modernity does not present a metanarrative of collapse. She is persistently focused on the formation, deformation, *and* transformation of meaning and the subject: the sites of suffering and the movement of its overcoming.

The significance of her project is therefore clarified when it is grasped that the psychoanalytic disclosure of the formation and deformation of the subject—what shows up on the couch—*reveals* nihilism. However, given Kristeva's view of what it *is* that the subject suffers, the problem of nihilism is only fully approached through an exploration of the formation and deformation of *the symbolizations of the semiotic*. The trilogy is therefore an exploration of the fate of the semiotic, how it takes on, or fails to take on, symbolic form in discourses of love, loss, and abjection. The major articulations of the semiotic—Kristeva's "imaginary discourses" —belong to art and religion. I will at times refer to these discourses as mediations. They are not mediations of law, but of the corporeal, affective, and mimetic aspects of bonding, which Kristeva tracks in minor histories of the fate of love or loss or abjection in religion and artworks. *Powers of Horror*, *Tales of Love*, and *Black Sun* unfold, in turn, discontinuous and nonoverlapping, fragmentary histories of the fate of their subject matter. Each movement of the minor histories is another fate of abjection, love, or loss, respectively. This is the moment of modernism in Kristeva's thought.

Tales of Love and *Black Sun* work especially to show how art takes over the work of mediation from religion. Each fate of love or loss is given in a major artistic *oeuvre,* from Mozart to Bataille in *Tales of Love,* from Holbein to Duras in *Black Sun*. In marked contrast to this, the minor history in *Powers of Horror* is largely taken up with the historical forms of religion. Although this book discusses a number of modern writers in the opening chapter (for example, Dostoyevsky and Proust are seen as writers of abjection), when it comes to the detailed analysis of the literature of abjection in her final chapters, she confines her attention to one author. In other words she presents, not a minor history of abjection in literature, but just *one* fate of abjection: the literary adventure of Ferdinand Céline. This is because, unlike love and loss, abjection only appears *as this*—as the lack of mediation of abjection—in modernity. *Powers of Horror* does not and cannot present the kind of fragmentary history of the fate of abjection that is possible with respect to the artistic representation of love and loss. The concrete and detailed analysis of the literature of abjection is therefore restricted to a single *oeuvre*. Moreover, the analysis of Céline's writings stresses the highly ambiguous nature of this artistic mediation of abjection, proposing a profound continuity between Céline's fiction and his anti-Semitic political pamphlets. The continuity is proposed in respect of how the literary exploration of abjection displays the near absorption of the *figuring* (Céline's "scription") into what is figured (abjection), threatening the collapse of social and subjective identity. In Céline the imaginary discourse of abjection is a profound exploration of the undoing of religion, morality, and politics that appears in his x ray on, especially, the cataclysms of two world wars. But the discourse is barely set off from what it discovers beneath those systems: abjection.

Kristeva therefore discovers a looming of the "abject" in Céline's whole literary enterprise. We recall that the abject, the unstable boundary of self and society, is the psychic representation of the threat to social and subjective identity. Her analysis of Céline shows that the literature of abjection does not protect against the abject, or nondifferentiated otherness. This consummate writer of abjection is therefore left open to a threat in relation to which he must resort to another defense, a "merely" subjective one this time. The one exposed to the threat of abjection turns the *abject* into an *object of hatred.* A despised other appears, and spreads out as political hatred (Céline's anti-Semitism, but also his misogyny). Kristeva appears to celebrate the writing of abjection—"possible at last"—for its exposure of the "impossible" constituted by nondifferentiation beneath religion, morality, and politics as systems of representation. However, the literary endeavor is never powerful enough to set aside the collapse of meaning and identity. In other words, the literary mediation of abjection is a suspended mediation. "But we are dealing here with a sublimation without consecration. Forfeited" (1980a, 26). It is unclear what the possibilities for the literature of abjection are, for there is a poverty of secular cultural resources for the artistic endeavor. I note, once again, that current uses of the concept of abjection other than Kristeva's focus on the political significance of the defense against the threat to an identity whose illusoriness shows up in modernity. Butler (1993, 1997) is a stringent critic of this defense with respect to the illusory identities of "masculine" and "feminine" that are reimposed as a regime of power—the heterosexual one—works to maintain its dominion. However, we will miss the social and political implications of Kristeva's thought if we do not see the presence of the nihilism problematic in her discussion of abjection, and how it determines her relation to religion and art as the necessary background for her more explicit consideration of ethics and politics later on.

The major objective of this chapter is to show that the analyses of the historical forms of religion in *Powers of Horror* best illuminate the significance of religion in Kristeva's thought, shedding light on the importance to her of the aesthetic in the secular aftermath of religion. Her confrontation with abjection in the historical forms of religion illuminates both her view of the failings of secular modernity and the secular commitments that inform her turn to art. I have indicated that, in Kristeva's attention to the formation of imaginary discourses, her minor histories of art and religion remain bound to sites of suffering. Her thought on art and religion does not leave the psychoanalytic position behind, as though there were a movement to be made from subjectivity as a merely private, individual phenomenon to the public realm. It is no surprise, then, to find that Kristeva opens up her analysis of the historical forms of religion with psychoanalytic attention to the prehistory of religion. It was equally this prehistory—the formation of the sacred—that drew Freud's attention in his attempt to communicate the significance of the structure of subjectivity he discovered in neurosis: the oedipal structure (*Totem and Taboo*, 1912–1913). Kristeva's attention to the prehistory of religion comprehends Freud's thought on the sacred, and goes beyond it in order to open up her analysis of the aspects of the sacred and religion that are mediations of abjection, which is discovered today as one dimension of the triadic structure of narcissism. She therefore substitutes a focus on Narcissus for Freud's focus on Oedipus. This is because the symptoms contemporary psychoanalysis attends to exhibit, not a struggle with paternal law, but crises of love, loss, and self-orientation. It is a question of, not law, but lacks of meaning and values to support selfhood and connections with others. For these are the alterations in subjectivity Kristeva discovers at the level of the relation to the early mother, prior to and distinct from an oedipal struggle.

Kristeva's turn to the prehistory and history of religions discovers in the formation of the sacred and in religious practices—those rituals structured by biblical abomination in the Hebraic religion and by the notion of spoken sin in the Christian one—a specific achievement with respect to the problem of the abject or nondifferentiation at the limit of the ties between the individual and the social. For what these practices accomplish with respect to the abject is *causing it to exist* through an act of exclusion that shifts the abject from the border of the subject. The religious codifications of abjection shore up the subject and society *at their limits*. Thus, while Freud discovered in the formation of the sacred the underpinning of social organization at these limits, the function of authority predicated on the relation to the father, Kristeva discovers there, not the law of the father, but the symbolization of what is beyond its reach: the limit of law.

Consistent with my argument that Kristeva's fundamental categorial distinction between the semiotic and symbolic can only be made in conditions of their tendential severance, it is only once modern secular discourses neglect the task of providing a discourse of abjection that the religious symbolizations appear *as* symbolizations of abjection. Correspondingly, the lack of mediations of abjection in secular modernity appears *as this*. Nihilistic modernity therefore shows up in *Powers of Horror* in her indication that abjection appears *as abjection* in late modern societies.

Psychoanalysis and the Sacred

Let me begin the elucidation of Kristeva's minor history of religion with a moment in her text that throws light on the meaning of abjection at this level of her thought. The analysis she gives of the religious symbolizations of abjection builds on a statement contained in Bataille's sociological essays. Abjection "is merely the inability to assume with sufficient strength the imperative act of excluding abject things (and that act establishes the foundations of collective existence)." With Bataille, this act of exclusion "is precisely located in the domain of things and not, like sovereignty, in the domain of persons" (cited in Kristeva 1980a, 56).[1] Bataille's emphasis on this "imperative act" shows what, on the social level, corresponds to the maternal function that her strictly psychoanalytic thought attends to. The maternal function is discovered in primal repression, as the *demarcating* imperative that sets off the struggle to ab-ject the mother's body. In its social form, the demarcating imperative causes the abject to *exist* by founding abject *things*. In *Powers of Horror* religions take on the task of transposing the semiotic (abject) into the imaginary and, in doing so, provide a *social* symbolic elaboration of the unstable border of self and society. Religion protects the subject and society by shifting the border into the realm of things. This act is fundamental to collective existence. On Kristevan ground, collective existence in the sacred and religion is founded, not only on paternal law, but on the symbolic accommodation of a—forgotten—maternal authority. To cause the abject to exist as an abject *thing* means that this "thing" works to settle the unstable border of the subject and society by removing it from both and presenting itself as something excluded from them: defiled, abominated. Sacred and religious practices uphold this foundation by having the members of society reenact, in relation to the abject thing, the warding off of the unstable boundary. This is the meaning of rituals in this context.

Kristeva's manifold extension of this thought proposes that, if this social-symbolic accomplishment is failed, abjection recoils on the subject and society. In the abjection of self it is "no longer I who expel, 'I' is expelled. The border has become an object" (1980a, 4). Alternatively, the subject evades the downfall of its borders by venting abjection in social existence: "the crushing anarchy or nihilism of discourse topples over and, as if it were the reverse of that negativism, an *object* appears—an object of hatred and desire, of threat and aggressivity, of envy and abomination" (178). *Powers of Horror* tracks the manner in which each form of religion develops a logic of the abject, and founds a different abject. In this way it comes to illuminate the appearance of abjection *as abjection* in conditions of modern nihilism.

Kristeva first approaches the problem of abjection in modern societies by going over Freud's discussion of the father complex in the sacred, religion, and the oedipal structure of subjectivity (*Totem and Taboo,* 1912–1913). With Freud, the demise of traditional (religious) authority in modern societies is not its end. It continues as the oedipal structure of subjectivity. As is well known, Freud finds the conflictual workings of paternal law in the psychosexual development of modern subjects, whose critical moment is the assumption of the separating, judging, prohibiting function that bears the features of the paternal law underpinning the sacred and religion. The authority of the dead, murdered, father is one source—the unknown principle or "unconscious"—of sacred and religious systems. Later works—*The Ego and the Id* (1923), *Civilization and Its Discontents* (1930), and *Moses and Monotheism* (1939)—either suggest or explicitly state that the oedipal structure is the trace of religion in the psyche, and that it acts, not as the propitiation of individuation and social bonding, but as a tyrannical instance of the Other (the unconscious sense of guilt) that undermines possibilities for selfhood and the emergence of an (outside) other. This does not prevent Freud from arguing that the oedipal struggle and the assumption of paternal law brings about the critical alteration in subjectivity that is necessary for entrance into the social dialectic. Nevertheless, as a structure of subjectivity the Oedipus complex reveals that what initiates the social dialectic is also what checks it. If Freud's "discovery" of the unconscious is a discovery of the persistence of traditional authority in internalized form, recognition of the oedipal "destiny" of the subject is equally the recognition that the modern subject founders on this ambiguity. In other words, the father of psychoanalysis is the first to run up against the crisis of the paternal function.

Kristeva acknowledges the dialectic of paternal law and its modern fate as presented in Freud's thought. Yet her development of the psychoanalytic inquiry into primary narcissism insists that Freud skirts around another fate in social existence. This is because Freud analyzed the father and not the mother. We have seen, in chapter 3 above, Kristeva's reading of the case study, "Little Hans," which presents a microcosm of the demise of paternal law. She stresses throughout *Powers of Horror* that the undermining of individuation and connectedness has two aspects, however. If, with Little Hans, it is the moment of separateness that goes this is because *the loss of the mother cannot be borne*. It is not the problem of symbolic lack, tied to the oedipal structure, that is the problem here. It is the loss of *loss*, and so of an other to be connected to. Little Hans's phobia displays a suffering of nondifferentiated otherness, a struggle with abjection, where the drive has not found a place in connection with an other. Under these conditions "I" can only connect narcissistically. In the minor history of religions, Kristeva's development of Bataille's statement on abjection draws out and articulates the imperative that the appearance of the abject turns on, the one that doesn't found separation (ego–object, individual–society) but which maintains the *beginnings* of separation (primitive ego/abject). This means that her expansion of the Bataillean thought of abjection adds a psychoanalytic story on the fate of maternal or "semiotic" authority to the Freudian story on the fate of paternal authority. This is a vital feature of her emphasis on primary narcissism, and *Powers of Horror* aims to establish the ramifications of this thought.

Essential to this objective is a return to the founding myth of psychoanalysis, which is a construction of the formation of the sacred. It is well known that the founding myth of psychoanalysis investigates the function in social existence of incest taboo and the taboo on patricide (*Totem and Taboo*, 1912–1913). As psychoanalysis first envisaged it, the formation of the sacred exhibits the foundation of social existence in the dialectic of paternal law. With

Kristeva, the formation of the sacred also presents a logic of the abject, and so of the workings of the demarcating imperative. That is to say, she finds in this formation a symbolization of semiotic authority. Her analysis of the sacred relates directly to the question of modern nihilism stressed throughout this book. For she shows that to neglect the investigation into the fate of maternal authority is to miss the depth of the problem of modern social existence. A clarification of this claim requires a rehearsal of the meaning of Oedipus in the psychoanalytic tradition.

As we have seen, according to the oedipal dialectic, the prohibition barring access to the mother's body is established through the internalization of paternal authority, a psychic event forming the nucleus of the superego, which then underlies (undermines) the ties of collectivity. To speak of the oedipal dialectic in respect of religion is to speak of the transfer or "inheritance" of paternal authority that upholds social and symbolic existence by establishing separateness and judgment. At the center of this analysis is the mythical event, "endowed with founding properties," which initiates oedipal destiny: the taboo on patricide. Kristeva recalls the founding myth: "the archaic father and master of the primeval horde is killed by the conspiring sons who, later seized with a sense of guilt for an act that was upon the whole inspired by ambivalent feelings, end up restoring paternal authority, no longer as an arbitrary power but as a right; thus renouncing the possession of all women in their turn, they establish at one stroke the sacred, exogamy and society" (1980a, 56). That is to say, the myth indicates the unconscious origin of the two foundational laws of totemic society: the taboo on the murder of the father (represented by the totem) and the taboo on incest.

When Freud has this founding myth establish the centrality of the Oedipus complex in his thought, it is the first taboo that comes into the foreground. With respect to the second taboo, as Anthony Wilden remarks: "Freud's 'myth of origins' paradoxically explains the present, not the past, and accounts not for the prohibition of incest, but rather for the fact that incest is unconsciously desired" (1968, 252). Kristeva returns to *Totem and Taboo* in order to draw out how Freud's rendering of the myth of origins in fact abandons the other taboo, the taboo on incest. She asserts that there is one aspect of the formation of the sacred that is "defensive and socializing" (which absorbs Freud's attention), while the other, underlying incest taboo, "shows fear and indifferentiation." Recovering the second aspect suggests that the formation of the sacred would be "oriented toward those uncertain spaces of unstable identity, toward the fragility—both threatening and fusional—of the archaic dyad, toward the non-separation of subject/object, on which language has no hold but one woven of fright and repulsion" (1980a, 58). Incest taboo, which Freud did not account for, turns on non-differentiation in pre-objectal relationship. The retrieval of the import of incest taboo therefore brings the maternal function into view. It leads Kristeva to outline what religious codings of abjection bear on. "What will concern me here is not the socially productive value of the son-mother incest *prohibition* but the alterations, within subjectivity and within the very symbolic competence, implied by the *confrontation with the feminine* and the way in which societies code themselves in order to accompany as far as possible the speaking subject on that journey. Abjection, or the journey to the end of the night" (58).

Kristeva's effort to think through the "journey" of abjection therefore expands on the alterations within subjectivity that belong to the confrontation with the feminine, rather than paternal law. It should be noted in passing that much of the attention given to "the feminine" in post-Lacanian deployments of psychoanalysis has been absorbed in the thought of *jouissance,* the "pleasure" that exceeds symbolic regulation. In the feminist critique of Lacan, he is found to have *jouissance*—closely bound up with the feminine—be inaccessible to the speaking subject articulated in the symbolic order. The feminist challenge recovered *jouissance* from that relegation, and the development of the conception of *écriture féminine* is a central moment in this tradition ("French feminism"). Although Kristeva acknowledges this thought, and the idea of *jouissance* turns up in many places in her writings, she proposes another aspect of alterations in subjectivity that correspond to confrontation with the feminine: "abjection, or the journey to the end of the night." We have seen her isolate the workings of abjection by means of her postulate of a presymbolic disposition of the symbolic. Nonetheless, just as the feminist challenges to Lacan worked to show that *jouissance* operates in the symbolic field, so Kristeva's point is to show that abjection lies within symbolic competence even as it is not tied to the capacities bound to the symbolic function. The journey beyond these capacities invokes the entanglement of "fear-and-indifferentiation" that also appeared in phobic suffering.

When Kristeva considers the religious codings of abjection, she is fundamentally concerned with how they respond to the alterations in subjectivity that turn up at these limits of selfhood and society. Her focus is therefore on their response to the entanglement of fear and nondifferentiation. In her view, the historical religions have provided symbolizations that aid the subject in warding off what pertains to the passive mood, "where the subject, fluctuating between inside and outside, pleasure and pain, word and deed, would find death" (1980a, 63). In other words, the religious codings of abjection symbolize the struggle to set up the border from which a subject separates in order to come into being and, in doing so, *shifts* the unstable border away from the subject.

We recall that this struggle, called ab-jection of the mother's body, brings about no negation or position, no subject or object, but only the abject: the permeable border that offers a "target" for the destructive wave of the drive, in the service of separation. Kristeva is at pains to emphasize the specific logic of the abject discovered in religions. The codings of abjection do not function in the manner of secondary repression, which sets up the unconscious/conscious opposition constituting the split subject as desiring/speaking being. Instead, they "accompany" the subject on its journey into abjection, which is a logic of exclusion, as will presently be seen.

Kristeva therefore finds within the establishment of the sacred the problem of nondifferentiation which corresponds to the risk of the weakening of symbolic bonds. Her analyses of the variants of religious codings of abjection advance the hypothesis that "a (social) symbolic system *corresponds* to a specific structuration of the speaking subject in the *symbolic order*" (1980a, 67). That is to say, the analysis of forms of religion in *Powers of Horror* brings into view "who" the speaking subject is in respect of the specific coding of abjection that a religion achieves. It equally brings into view what each coding tells of the risk of the weakening of symbolic bonds. Thus the book considers, not the symbolic as the elementary structure of culture (see chapter 1 above), but the formation and deformation of the subject and society. In other words, Kristeva unfolds the moments of a fragmentary minor history in which each formation and deformation of the subject is intimately connected with that of a social symbolic system. The first moment is the establishment of the sacred, the second Hebraic monotheism, and the third Christian monotheism.

Religious Codifications of Abjection

Defilement

Kristeva's analysis of the formation of the sacred turns on the social value of practices that mime the warding off of the abject, the unstable border of subject and society. This analysis, especially, draws out what she means when she differentiates between the religious uptake of maternal authority, on the one hand, and of paternal law, on the other, in terms of a logic of exclusion as distinct from the setting up of an unconscious/conscious opposition. The practices she attends to here are rites of purification turning on the notion of defilement. Defilement, on this reading, is a social symbolic articulation of abjection, raising its dynamic of repulsion to the ritual level. This articulation does not present a symbol of subjective dynamics, however. It is, rather, an act of inscription. That is to say, defilement is not a code that linguistically represents some prior content. It is an *act* that transforms the content and, in doing so, stabilizes a social organism into a specific order of relationships (1980a, 65). Drawing on anthropological attention to purification rituals, Kristeva describes this act as follows.

> It is as if dividing lines were built up between society and a certain nature, as well as within the social aggregate, on the basis of the simple logic of *excluding filth,* which, promoted to the ritual level of *defilement,* founded the "self and clean" of each social group if not each subject. The purification rite appears then as that essential ridge, which, prohibiting the filthy object, extracts it from the secular order and lines it at once with a sacred facet. Because it is excluded as a possible object, asserted to be a non-object of desire, abominated as ab-ject, as abjection, filth becomes defilement and founds on the henceforth released side of the "self and clean" the order that is thus only (and therefore, always already) sacred. (1980a, 65)[2]

In brief, the act of defilement, reiterated in purification rituals, releases a sacred order by extracting an element from within social existence and excluding it as a possible object: *element prohibited as filth (abject)/the "self and clean" (social organization).* The social order is henceforth always "on the other side" of the sacred, which is lined by abjection. In Kristeva's view, the thought of defilement renders the pure/impure opposition intelligible by discovering its basis in a prohibition, the demarcating imperative. Loathing of defilement is the repeated assumption on the part of the members of society of the pure/impure opposition. It is a particular form of assuming the imperative act of excluding abject things, an act which upholds the integrity of subjective and social organization. The "abject," then, is not a content that is repressed, but something that is there only by virtue of being excluded as a possible object.

Kristeva's interpretation of purification rituals conducts a departure from structuralist anthropology (Lévi-Strauss), which argues that social organization is a *classification system.* On this view, the workings and significance of society and its laws are discovered by analyzing them as a system of signs. Once the psychoanalytic question is introduced—where is the subjective dimension?—social organization is no longer seen as a structure corresponding to linguistic structure. For the psychoanalytic question leads to the formulation of the hypothesis that a (social) symbolic system *corresponds* to a specific structuration of the speaking subject in the symbolic order. Kristeva stresses that this hypothesis avoids the chicken-and-egg question of cause and effect: "is the social determined by the subjective, or is it the other way around?" It asks about the ways in which societies *code themselves* such that they accompany the subject to that border, "where the object no longer has, or does not yet have a correlative function bonding the subject," where symbolic bonds are weak or missing (1980a, 67). That is to say, the psychoanalytic hypothesis rests on an exploration of the symbolic resources available within a specific social organization for the journey to the border made up of an I in confrontation with a nonobject (the abject). This is not, to repeat, a matter of generating symbols of some prior subjective dynamic. Rather, those resources are the ways in which a social symbolic system *represents its own limits,* and so the limits of the tie between the individual and the social. The psychoanalytic investigation of this limit does not discover an "individual being" prior to its social organization (Freudian thought is never a metaphysical individualism). Its object of analysis, the psyche, is transindividual, a pervious border between the individual and society. Kristeva discovers in purification rites the repetition of the act through which the borders of self and society are given, but the rites equally exhibit the instability that such a repetition indicates. In brief, defilement is the symbolization of abjection in the formation of the sacred, a particular fate of abjection.

Kristeva pursues the structuralist hypothesis in anthropology because it helps her to draw out a distinction between the effects within social and symbolic life of paternal law and what is neglected where the symbolic function is posited as the one foundation of social and symbolic life, or simply overemphasized. She is investigating the neglected question of the fate of semiotic authority. According to structuralist anthropology: "Basic symbolic institutions, such as *sacrifice* or *myths,* expand on logical processes inherent in the economy of language itself; in doing so they realize for the community what makes up in depth, historically and logically, the speaking being as such. Thus *myth* projects on contents that are vitally important for a given community those binary oppositions discovered at the level of phonematic concatenation of language. As for *sacrifice,* it solemnizes the vertical dimension of the sign: the one that leads from the thing that is left behind, or killed, to the meaning of the word and transcendence" (1980a, 72–73). Societies where myth and sacrifice dominate reveal to structuralist anthropology, first, the laws of language (interchangeable units and their ordering) and, second, a practice which symbolizes access to the order of language itself (the word kills the thing, and symbolic capacities are born in that murder). With Lacan, "the symbol manifests itself first of all as the murder of the thing" (1966, 104). Myth and sacrifice are social representations of symbolic order and its establishment. In contrast to this, Kristeva's focus on purification rites asks after the significance of defilement as, not a symbol of the murdered thing (paradigmatically the mother's body), but an inscription of a prior relationship. She interrogates the objects that purification rites are directed to in order to work out the meaning of their protective function: what defilement amounts to as a social representation.

The investigation draws on the thought of Mary Douglas in order to show what the analysis of defilement brings out that the linguistic focus has led structuralist anthropology to miss. Grosz has argued that "Kristeva's use of Douglas's work on pollution and defilement shifts it from the sociological and anthropological into a psychological register" (1994, 193). Although this is true, she overstates the case. Kristeva's view that the psychoanalytic standpoint brings in the subjective dimension means both to change the way in which social organization is understood (going beyond the structuralist view) and to bring out what social symbolic elaborations of the semiotic (here, of abjection) do for the subject *and* society. In other words, if psychoanalysis goes to the pervious border between the social and the individual, it is not in order to distinguish the psyche from the object-domain of sociology and anthropology, but precisely to show the connections between them. Her deployment of Douglas's thought on pollution and defilement displays this ambition.

Mary Douglas noted that the objects of purification rites center on excrement, menstrual blood, and what gets assimilated to them. These elements suggest what applies to or gets jettisoned from a boundary (Kristeva 1980a, 69). Hence, with Kristeva, "the *defilement* from which ritual protects is neither sign nor matter," for the objects of purification rites are not "mere" matter (73). In a further step, Kristeva notes that not all elements relating to borders of the body become objects of purification rites—"neither tears nor sperm, for instance" (71). She therefore expands on Mary Douglas's insight by considering why the excremental and the menstrual are dominant types for polluting values, and it is this consideration which brings her to the discovery of semiotic (maternal) authority within the formation of the sacred. "Fecal matter signifies, as it were, what never ceases to separate from a body in a state of permanent loss in order to become *autonomous, distinct* from the mixtures, alterations, and decay that run through it" (108). Thus "excrement and its equivalents (decay, infection, disease, corpse, etc.) stand for the danger to identity that comes from without: the ego threatened by the non-ego, society threatened by its outside, life by death" (71). Recollecting the psychoanalytic view of the connection between regulation of fecal loss and separation from the mother, Kristeva suggests an isomorphism between purification rites and a primal mapping of the body that corresponds to an archaic authority. "Through frustrations and prohibitions, this authority shapes the body into a *territory* having areas, orifices, points and lines, surfaces and hollows, where the archaic power of mastery and neglect, of the differentiation of proper-clean and improper-dirty, possible and impossible, is impressed and exerted. It is a 'binary logic,' a primal mapping of the body that I call semiotic to say that, while being the precondition of language, it is dependent upon meaning, but in a way that is not that of *linguistic* signs nor of the *symbolic* order they found. Maternal authority is the trustee of that mapping of the self's clean and proper body; it is distinguished from paternal laws" (1980a, 72).

The symbolic, paternal function conventionally taken to condition socialization amounts to a repression of this archaic authority (possibly corresponding to a triumph over matrilineality). "Secondary" repression is not merely grafted onto primary repression but is a repression of it. On this view, the proliferation of purification rituals in a society is an indicator that paternal law is poorly secured. It reveals that the separation of powers is indistinct, and this is where the second type of polluting value enters in. Menstrual blood "stands for the danger issuing from within the identity (social or sexual); it threatens the relationship between the sexes within a social aggregate and, through internalization, the identity of each sex in the face of sexual difference" (1980a, 71). The appearance of menstrual blood as a type of polluting value reveals an attempt to hold up the fixed relationship between the sexes, and so the separation of powers, where the centralization and hierarchization of authority has not taken hold. What is discernible in purification rites, then, is maternal authority, the primal repression that secondary repression overlays in order to institute the splitting *clean-and-proper body (abject)/speaking being*. When the establishment of paternal law is strong, the "clean-and-proper body," separated from the signifying chain, becomes the abject. Kristeva here presents the transition from primal to secondary repression in terms of the fate of embodiment in respect of two different authorities. The logic of defilement, *filth(abject)/the self and clean*, indicates the workings of an authority that is a more archaic and less decisive imperative than paternal law. The securing of the latter is indicated where a different logic prevails: *speaking being/clean-and-proper body (abject)*. The presence of purification rituals in a society therefore points to the weakness or demise of the symbolic, paternal function. Conversely, where there is an instability in the function that stabilizes the language/body opposition semiotic authority shows up. Purification rituals manifest the effort and failure of symbolic, paternal law to fully regulate the members of society. "It is as if, lacking a central authoritarian power that would settle the definitive supremacy of one sex—or lacking a legal establishment that would balance the prerogatives of both sexes—two powers attempted to share out society. One of them, the masculine, apparently victorious, confesses through its very relentlessness against the other, the feminine, that it is threatened by an asymmetrical, irrational, wily, uncontrollable power" (70). What is significant for Kristeva is that defilement manifests a different functioning in respect of splitting: "rites would not be limited to their signifying dimension, they would also have a material, active, translinguistic, magical impact" (74).

Kristeva's analysis of the logic of defilement does not purport to be a discovery of matriarchal society. For the problem of the separation of powers bears on the fear of generative power where paternal control is trying to establish itself. By extrapolation, and Kristeva offers evidence to support this, where writing and legal order are developed religious prohibitions will not be connected to sexual ones. Thus Kristeva describes the alignment of different powers—written and unwritten law—with naturalized sexual positions relating to production and reproduction. She asserts, not the hierarchization of the powers, but how their differentiation points to the necessity of the speaking being as divided by sex and language. This may be—and has been—taken as support for the heterosexual imperative. But she does not appear to think that differentiation in sex and language prescribes a trajectory for object-desire. Once again, what is at issue in defilement is not desire but the coding of abjection: "one could suggest that rites surrounding defilement, particularly those involving excremential and menstrual variants, shift the *border* (in the psychoanalytic meaning relating to borderline patients) that separates the body's territory from the signifying chain; *they illustrate the boundary between semiotic authority and symbolic law*" (1980a, 73, emphasis added).

When this boundary is elaborated in terms of the opposition pure/impure, it turns on an opposition between feminine and masculine powers, as though the process of setting up the polarities of "feminine" and "masculine" shows up where the feminine is absorbed in an image of a baleful, generative power. Kristeva does not reject the fact of this dimension of maternal authority, although it needs to be borne in mind that she does not reduce the maternal function to the problem of the overbearance and overinclusiveness of maternal power, which shows up in borderline patients whose suffering reveals the sway of an archaic authority. The connection between Kristeva's thought on the borderline subject and the social value of purification rites appears in her suggestion that defilement is an elaboration of the *objective frailty* of the social symbolic order. The pure/impure opposition represents fear of the mother's generative power, but Kristeva does not stop there. "One is then led to conceive of the opposition between pure and impure not as an archetype but as *one* coding of the differentiation of the speaking subject as such, a coding of his repulsion in relation to the other in order to autonomize himself" (1980a, 82).

We recall that the ambiguity of abjection lies in the problem of the unstable inside/outside border: the pervious border both threatens the subject with non-differentiation and gives the emergent ego something to attempt to separate from. We have seen that purification rites cope with the threat by shifting the abject onto the realm of things: not objects, but what parts from the body's borders. The rituals do not represent a merely subjective moment—the border of the subject. They are an instance of how the pervious border of the subject and society is itself inscribed within the society. Purification rituals show that a society *can* represent its own limits, and the benefit that accrues to its members as a result. At the same time, Kristeva draws attention to this act of inscription as a symbolization of maternal authority, emphasizing the boundary between this form of authority and paternal law.

Biblical Abomination

Kristeva's minor history of the religious codings of abjection turns next to Hebraic monotheism, in order to stress the "colossal revolution" that it represents with respect to the fate of maternal authority when the demarcating imperative is successfully used to support the stabilization of paternal law. Although purification rituals persist within biblical abomination, which is where Kristeva finds the logic of abjection in this form of religion, what is basic to social order is not the pure/impure opposition but the particular character of the prohibition that sets up impurity, that is to say, the specific workings of the demarcating imperative in this social-symbolic system. She clearly specifies that what interests her in this whole investigation is the historical features of the fate of abjection. As I have repeatedly stressed, she ties those historical features to sites of suffering subjectivity. This is why in the minor history of religions she consistently asks what *benefit* the specific logic of abjection brings to the subject. For she is showing how the sacred and religion attempted to take on the task of accommodating the semiotic in the symbolic. These motivations are evident in the following passage on different disciplinary approaches to the analysis of ritual.

> the question for the analyst-semiologist is to know how far one can analyze ritual impurity. The historian of religions stops soon: the cultically impure is that which is based on a natural "loathing." The anthropologist goes further: there is nothing "loathsome" in itself; the loathsome is that which disobeys classification rules peculiar to the given social symbolic system. But as far as I am concerned, I keep asking questions. Why that system of classification and not another? What social, subjective, and socio-subjectively interacting needs does it fulfill? Are there no subjective structurations that, within the organization of each speaking being, correspond to this or that

> symbolic-social system and represent, if not stages, at least *types* of subjectivity and society? Types that would be defined, in the last analysis, according to the subject's position in language, that is, by the more or less partial use he can make of his potentialities? (1980a, 92)

Kristeva's reference to language, here, should not be taken to be a retreat to the reassurance of linguistic primacy: the primacy of the symbolic function. Rather, what reappears here is her emphasis, contra structuralism, on the signifying process (*signifiance*): the process of formation and deformation of meaning and the subject. She claims for it the status of the only concrete universality that defines the speaking being. Once again, however, the social-symbolic variant is declared to be embedded in, and crucial to, this process. On religion, the position of the analyst-semiologist draws out, not a unilateral isomorphism between subjective development and various types of religious organization, but an analysis of different forms of the interaction of subjective and social organization. That is to say, this is an analysis of the formation, deformation, *and* transformation of the subject and society, which are considered as "types," in accordance with Kristeva's avoidance of an all-encompassing philosophy of history. The question bearing on the subjective dimension is not that of the "truth" of the subject, but of its capacities, turning on innovation in *Tales of Love,* on separation in *Powers of Horror.* These capacities can only be approached in terms of the correspondence between the organization of the speaking being and specific social-symbolic systems. What Kristeva's step-by-step account of the fate of abjection in the establishment of Judaic monotheism stresses is a "tremendous project of separation." Her attention to the biblical treatment of impurity seeks out the formation of the subject which *corresponds* to the elevation of impurity to *abstraction* and *the moral register.* On this account, the "subject" of Hebraic monotheism is formed in accordance with the development of a system of laws that has the potential to leave behind the pure/impure opposition and carry out, in and of itself, the demarcating imperative. That is to say, the social order itself presents the very *establishment* of the symbolic within a logical and legal order, but one that encompasses a logic of the abject. Put otherwise, Kristeva discovers in what is often viewed as the great religion of law a social and symbolic accommodation of its own limit: what departs from symbolic order.

Kristeva finds, first, that the limits of the domain of law are *related* to divine law in and through a metonymic articulation of the pure/impure opposition: life/death, vegetal/animal, flesh/blood, hale/ill, otherness/incest. For her, this metonymy represents the distance between man and God, that is to say, between man and immortality considered as the power over death. According to their semantic value, the variants of abomination fall under three major categories: food taboos, corporeal change and death, and the feminine body and incest. The principle of distance from God (immortality) is therefore arranged into dietary distinction, what converges on the life/death distinction, and finally sex as a separating value. Kristeva insists that these variants correspond to a topological concern, "one's being allowed to have access or not to a place—the holy place of the Temple," and a logical concern, conformity to the *law* of purity (1980a, 93). The correspondence between access to holiness that is defined by topology and logic, on the one hand, and biblical abomination on the other, shows the dependence of the relation to divinity upon separating values that accommodate matter, body, and sex. Biblical abomination stands for *responses* of symbolic law in the sphere of subjective economy. It represents a series of material separations which relate ultimately to fusion with the mother. Judaism "carries into the private lives of everyone the brunt of the struggle *each subject must wage during the entire length of his personal history* in order to become separate, that is to say, to become a speaking subject and/or subject to Law" (94, emphasis added). Orality, death, and incest are meanings with a separating value, or, conversely, they are separating values that bestow meaning on the struggle of becoming separate.

It is notable—given the and/or of the final sentence in the last quotation—that Kristeva is not equating the constitution of the speaking being *with* subjectivation to Law (the One), but indicating that achieving this complementarity *is* the colossal revolution of Hebraic monotheism with respect to subjective economy. At the same time, Hebraic monotheism does not present dichotomies that would correspond to the conscious/unconscious opposition: logical/corporeal, or divine/material. Alterations in the field of dietary distinctions accommodate what is irreconcilable, keeping what conflicts with holiness in relation to symbolic Law. Notably, the reinscription of dietary distinction negotiates ineliminable destabilizations and, accordingly, the *heterogeneity* of the speaking subject, by giving them access to symbolic functioning. Thus Kristeva attributes a more precise, and thereby more abstract, rendering of the pure/impure distinction to the Yahwist covenant set up between Moses and God.

Powers of Horror therefore tracks the fate of the semiotic in the establishment of what Freud, interrogating it on different terrain, called this great moral and spiritual system (*Moses and Monotheism*). Kristeva notes that the treatment of impurity can break loose of the original governing distinction (life/death) and operate as *a legal order* through which separation and identity are maintained. The impure would no longer be only a fascinating element but "any infraction to a *logical conformity*" (1980a, 98). But the logic of dietary distinctions must first expand into other domains, especially that of the sick body. Kristeva insists that this passage from food to the borders of the body goes via the woman in childbed, or parturition. In respect of her offspring, the girl "shall be unclean two weeks, *as* in her separation" (Lev. 12:5). For the boy, circumcision *duplicates* separation. Circumcision is an act that *institutes* separation from maternal defilement—"a sign of the alliance with God"—but at the same time carves out the other sex, "impure, defiled" on his very flesh. Notwithstanding the alliance with God: "By repeating the natural scar of the umbilical cord at the location of sex, by duplicating and thus displacing through ritual the preeminent separation, which is that from the mother, Judaism seems to insist in symbolic fashion—the very opposite of what is 'natural'—that the identity of the speaking being (with his God) is based on the separation of the son from the mother. Symbolic identity presupposes the violent difference of the sexes" (1980a, 100).

As before, in the discussion of defilement, Kristeva draws out the phantasmatics that attends this symbolic elaboration of nonobjectal relationship. When the symbolization bears directly on the fecund feminine body, it *displays* the haunting of a lost past: the fantasy of an archaic maternal power that threatens nondifferentiation. She is the one "who also constitutes, in the specific history of each person, the abyss that must be established as an autonomous (and not encroaching) *place* and *distinct* object, meaning a *signifiable* one, so that such a person might learn to speak" (1980a, 100). Lev. 12 is therefore read as an inscription in symbolic Law of the phantasmatics that forms in respect of abjection of the mother's body: the fantasy of the mother's overbearing power. What is crucial here is not the fantasy alone but the fate of maternal authority that impels ab-jection of the mother's body. As a condition for access to the realm of signs and objects, abjection is the struggle to set up a space that is distinguished from the abject *through the very formation* of the abject. We recall that the abject is not equivalent to but "jettisoned from" the mother's body. It is a pervious border of the subject, providing on its own no stable "between" for a correlation of subject and object. The maternal imperative and what it founds are so intertwined that the failure and success of the imperative are hard to distinguish. This is why the mother's power is overbearing and overinclusive. Kristeva's attention to the historical religions shows that the abject requires symbolic elaboration in order to have it exist and so shift it *from* subjectivity into the realm of things. The symbolization found in Lev. 12 turns on the very *phantasm* of archaic power that takes shape with respect to primal repression. The abject is shifted into defiled maternality. That is to say, sexual difference is itself made a *limit* for the sake of "the organization that is 'clean and proper,' 'individual,' and, one thing leading to another, signifiable, legislatable, subject to law and morality" (1980a, 100). Kristeva has noted how the violent difference of the sexes is a support for this moment of symbolic identity in the development of the moral and spiritual system of Hebraic monotheism. She does not reduce the latter to this violence, however, for she finds the violence to be, not *the* constitutive moment of the whole, but a moment in its development.

With Kristeva, biblical abomination passes through defiled maternality into what signifies a threat to corporeal integrity. There is abomination of the very *image* of the body and its limits. Only circumcision, ritual symbolic duplication of the scar of parturition, ensuring symbolic difference, is permitted. The abomination of superfluous markings, together with leprosy, disabled bodies, or bodies lacking members, as well as corporeal flow, secretions, and discharges continues to reflect a fantasy of "that non-introjected mother who is incorporated as devouring, and intolerable" (1980a, 102). Thus, for Kristeva, Judaic abomination manifests the haunted imagination of "a nation at war with the surrounding polytheism" (100). It manifests and seeks to control the phantasmatic construction of the archaic power. Biblical abomination is a loop of prohibitions that exhibits and represents the process of establishing *mono*theism and *transmission of the divine word.* At this point in the formation of Judaic discourse, "impurity moves away from the material register and is formulated as profanation of the divine name" (104). This establishes the basis for moral prohibitions concerning justice, honesty, and truth, which themselves reiterate the logic of separation. Nonetheless, the final pages of the essay on biblical abomination return to incest taboo, claiming for it the status of unconscious foundation of the logic of separation, even where rabbinical legislation connects impurity, beyond the material register, with morality. "Far from being *one* of the semantic values of that tremendous project of separation constituted by the biblical text, the taboo of the mother seems to be its originating mytheme" (105–106).

What the psychoanalytic position aims to bring into view is the connection between archaic or nonobjectal relationship, "as undifferentiated power and threat, a defilement to be cut off," and what is death-bearing in man (106). The stress put on incest taboo and the archaic mother allows this conception of the tendency to murder to be seen in terms of the problematic of *the threat of non-differentiation*. Kristeva works to reveal incest prohibition as the unconscious foundation of Hebraic monotheism's logicizing movement, and so to emphasize its articulation and accommodation of the tendency to murder, that is to say of nonobjectal relationship, a deep economy of the speaking being. She finds in Judaic law the *recognition* of inescapable abjection. In prophetic discourse, establishing the rule of the life of Israel:

> The impure is neither banished nor cut off, it is thrust away but within—right there, working, constitutive. . . . Abjection—dietary, sanguine, and moral—is pushed back within the chosen people, not because they are worse than others, but because in the light of the contract that they alone have entered into, abjection appears as such. The existence and degree of abjection are thus predicated on the very position of the logic of separation. . . . We can interpret biblical abomination as the agency of a demoniacal reproduction of the speaking being, whom the contract with God points to, causes to exist, and banishes. (1980a, 106–107)

That is to say, the rules for the life of Israel provide a *precise* elaboration of abjection, which encompasses the production of abjection *by* symbolic Law. The elaboration comprises both a symbolization of the pervious border, necessary in order to accommodate and displace the threat of indifferentiation and the fear attending it, *and* the recognition that, here, abjection is brought into existence by the Law of the One. The abject is not autonomous, not an in itself (not one thing), but inherent in symbolic being, cast by it. "That order, that glance, that voice, that gesture, which enact the law for my frightened body, constitute and bring about an effect and not yet a sign" (1980a, 10). Biblical abomination therefore iterates primal repression, carrying it into the very constitution of symbolic Law and, at the same time, revealing that the latter produces abjection, without end. On Kristeva's account, the Hebraic symbolization of abjection amounts to an overcoming of repression and thereby goes beyond a sacrificial concept of the social and/or symbolic contract. The killed object is replaced by the *abject*. The abject, "if it guarantees a pure and holy law, turns me aside, cuts me off, and throws me out" (1980a, 111). On this view, a religion of abomination is the threshold that "marks the exit of religion and the unfolding of morals." It leads the subject of monotheism back "to the very device that it ushers in: logic, abstraction, rules of systems and judgments" (111). That is to say, Hebraic monotheism codes *itself* in its elaboration of abjection. Thus abjection appears *as such* in this symbolization.

This conclusion on the achievements of Hebraic monotheism provides a clue for understanding why Kristeva singles out Céline's writings to represent the literature of abjection in *Powers of Horror*. This literature runs a great risk, since what it figures (the semiotic) may absorb the figuring (the symbolic form-giving that the literature achieves). Then the literary domain presents a threat to the identity of self and society, for the abject is not thrust aside. Kristeva analyzes Céline's anti-Semitism as a defense in respect of this threat, one that turns the abject into an object of hatred. Far from being an arbitrary manifestation of abjection, his anti-Semitism turns on the fact that the Hebraic religion makes abjection appear as such. That is to say, Céline vents his drives on the moral and spiritual system where the alien thing appears as such. (See chapter 8, below.)

Spoken Sin

Before proceeding to the third moment in Kristeva's minor history of religion, let me underline the point that the latter presents, at each step, a different fate of abjection. In doing so it reveals, at each step, a new configuration of the connection between the subject and society. The discussion of Christianity makes this explicit. "What is happening is that a new arrangement of differences is being set up, an arrangement whose economy will regulate a wholly different system of meaning, hence a wholly different speaking subject" (1980a, 113). What is illuminated in the chapter on the Christian message is both the changing fate of abjection and, ultimately, a certain failing of the Christian treatment of abjection in contrast with its treatment in Judaism.

The most important point in Kristeva's attention to the salvation religion is the idea of the formation of a speaking being who is innerly divided on account of the interiorization of impurity. The fate of abjection in the Christian religion is its absorption into speech. The symbolization of abjection appears in the phenomenon of *spoken sin*. Kristeva's account of the formation and deformation of the subject that belongs to the Christian era unfolds a series of steps in Christianity's interiorization of impurity. The first step is a change in emphasis from the pure/impure distinction to an inside/outside boundary, placing the threat "within." This transformation of the site of abjection is unfolded in the Gospels, particularly of Matthew and Mark. "There is nothing from without a man, that entering into him can defile him: but things which come out of him, those are they that defile the man" (*Mark* 15). Kristeva remarks: "evil, thus displaced *into* the subject, will not cease tormenting him from within, no longer as a polluting and defiling substance, but as the ineradicable repulsion of his henceforth divided and contradictory being" (1980a, 116). At the same time, Kristeva's attention to miracles and parables, which suggest an agency of satisfying nourishment, proposes that the Christian message brings a reconciliation with, if not rehabilitation of, maternal principle. There is an attempt to control a fantasy tied to archaic relationship: not the phantasmatic archaic power brought to light in biblical abomination of the fecund feminine body, but *the fantasy of devouring*. "Through oral-dietary satisfaction, there emerges, beyond it, a lust for swallowing up the other, while the fear of impure nourishment is revealed as deathly drive to devour the other" (118). The Eucharist is comprehended as the catharsis of this fantasy. "Body and spirit, nature and speech, divine nourishment, the body of Christ, assuming the guise of a natural food (bread), signifies me both as divided (flesh and spirit) and infinitely lapsing. I am divided and lapsing with respect to my ideal, Christ, whose introjection by means of numerous communions sanctifies me while reminding me of my incompletion. Because it identified abjection as a fantasy of devouring, Christianity effects its abreaction. Henceforth reconciled with it, the Christian subject, completely absorbed into the symbolic, is no longer a being of abjection but a *lapsing subject*" (118–119, emphasis added).

Insofar as the body of Christ *remains,* through repeated communions, the foundation for the spiritualization of the impure, the Eucharist represents the relationship of the speaking being to *an "achieved" balance of heterogeneity,* a nondiscordant passage between body and spirit. The introduction of heterogeneity into the divinity sets up the ideal of a balanced heterogeneity: *heterogeneity held in place.*

The Eucharist, which enacts the communication with the ideal through divine nourishment in the guise of a natural food and drink, elaborates the fantasy of devouring. Thus considered, eating and drinking the flesh and blood of Christ accomplishes an introjection of the drive-quality attached to archaic objects. The Eucharist abreacts abjection. At the same time, reconciliation with abjection "by means of numerous communions" infinitizes the path of spiritualization, holding the impossible division to the infinite path, a "bad" infinity. In sum, the fate of abjection in the Christian message is the *lapsing subject,* the sinner. With Kristeva, "sin" accommodates the heterogeneous conflictual subject insofar as it "signifies me both as divided and infinitely lapsing." The promise of the remission of sins—reconciled heterogeneity—then instantiates the Christian time-design. Accomplished in receding future time, the remission of sins is the "vanishing point of all fantasies." The distance between man and God turns, not on the prohibition of murder, but on a path of spiritualization whose end is infinitely projected. Accordingly, sin is "the rock where one endures the human condition as separate: body and spirit, body jettisoned from the spirit; as a condition that is impossible, irreconcilable, and, by that very token, real" (1980a, 120). In sum, the separateness of the human condition is rooted in an impossible heterogeneity, one that cannot be held in place. Yet human incompleteness and incommensurability are recognized as such through communication to the sinner of achieved heterogeneity and the promise of the remission of sins.

On this view, the Eucharist manifests a confrontation with abjection that saves the subject from the alien thing that looms in the negotiation of irreconcilable heterogeneity. The abject encroaches on the boundary of subjectivity and threatens to convert the place of the subject into "no-place." Kristeva finds this insight into the Christian accomplishment in Hegel. "Between sin and its forgiveness there is as little place for an alien thing as there is between sin and punishment. Life has severed itself from itself and united itself again" (Hegel 1798–1799, 239; cited in Kristeva, 1980a, 162). However, she also tracks the way in which *Christianity does not pull off that placement of the abject* that is required if the subject, whose constitutive heterogeneity is incapable of settlement, is to find a place.

We recall the claim that what is taking place in the Christian message is the appearance of a wholly different system of meaning, hence a wholly different speaking being regulated by a new arrangement of differences. The Christian God-relation involves a change in status for the impure. Interiorized and spiritualized, it is no longer a substance that is cut off. "Sin is an action" (1980a, 119). That is to say, although the Eucharist sets up a division of the flesh—drive-related body/subdued and sublime (sublimated) body—that settles the *power* of sin in the flesh, the act of interiorizing and then spiritualizing the impure turns it into "an error in thought and speech." This act brings impurity "within man's jurisdiction, within the scope of his own responsibility" (121). "One could say, in fact, that sin is subjectified abjection . . . the created being, subordinated to God and at the same time separated from him by free will, can commit sin only through wilfull nonobservance of the rule. . . . Sin as action—as action stemming from will and judgment—is what definitively integrates abjection into logic and language" (128–129). Thus Kristeva finds that Christian sin "holds the keys that open the doors to Morality and Knowledge" (122), but this equally opens up a path to the Inquisition.

This claim relies on the link that is established between spoken sin and judgment. First, spoken sin makes discourse carry the burden of what departs from social order and identity. It also "absolves from sin" through "enunciation before the One." Second, the judgment that absolves in and through enunciation makes of the latter a *denunciation* of error in thought or speech: "sin guides one along the straightest paths of superego spirituality" (1980a, 122). This combination of judgment and speech allows for a judicial-verbal union that builds up into a persecuting apparatus. Kristeva understand this trajectory of spoken sin in terms of an *insufficient* placement of the abject in the Christian arrangement of differences. In contrast to the Judaic arrangement of abjection, which thrusts the abject aside, here abjection is interiorized and immediately set on the path of spiritualization. "Meant for remission, sin is what is absorbed—in and through speech. By the same token, abjection will not be designated as such, that is, as other, as something to be ejected, or separated, but as the most propitious place for communication—as the point where the scales are tipped toward pure spirituality" (127). Once abjection is made the very site of the path to reconciliation, the symbolic elaboration overreaches abjection. "The biblical conception remained closer to the concrete truth of the sexed and social being. The conception stemming from the New Testament resorbs the guilt of the previous one and, at the risk of cutting itself off from the course and intolerable truth of man that Judaism discloses, offers displacements of it that are perhaps elaborations—communital, logical, esthetic ones. On the one hand, we find the truth of the intolerable; on the other, displacement through denial for some, through sublimation for others" (1980a, 129).

Judaism achieves an elaboration of abjection by excluding the abject, thrusting it aside. Insofar as Christianity fails to thrust aside the abject, abjection is displaced rather than elaborated. Denial enters back in. Alternatively, with sublimation, where abjection is the very site of spiritualization and thereby immediately passed beyond, the abject abides within as a fearsome ineradicable evil, an "inexorable carnal remainder" (1980a, 120).

However, for Kristeva, the mystical deviations of Christianity, on the one hand, and art, on the other, open up another direction for spoken sin: a *felix culpa* that brings in the possibility of unfolding abjection in signs. Christianity therefore brings us to the threshold of the literature of abjection. "This marginal potentiality of spoken sin as fortunate sin provides an anchorage for the art that will be found, resplendent, under all cupolas. Even during the most odious times of the Inquisition, art provided sinners with the opportunity to live, openly and inwardly apart, the joy of their dissipation set into signs: painting, music, words. 'And these signs shall follow them that believe: in my name shall they cast out devils; they shall speak with new tongues'" (Mark 16:17) (1980a, 131).

The rehearsal of Kristeva's minor history of the religious codifications of abjection, undertaken here, has been made in order to underline her proposal that each precise social organization, or social symbolic "system," corresponds to a specific articulation of the speaking subject in the symbolic order, so that the codings of abjection present, in each case, the emergence of a new speaking subject. Let me stress, at this point, that my reading of Kristeva's thought on religion therefore differs from another one. Reineke's *Sacrificed Lives* (1997) attempts a synthesis of Kristeva and Girard for a theory of sacrifice that would explain the insistence of violence against women in modern culture. Although the seriousness of the question is acknowledged, and the attempt applauded, a danger attends this interpretation of Kristeva's writings as a theory of sacrifice. The danger is *dehistoricization,* so that the equation of violent outbreaks and the woman as victim becomes *a structural truth*. Kristeva shows clearly that the destiny of the archaic maternal is not simply that of the substance that is killed in the emergence of the symbolic. She does acknowledge this sacrificial logic in her attention to the meaning of the symbolic function, and it is a logic that might explicate how violence escalates in relation to women when identities are threatened (as Reineke supposes). However, Kristeva's 1980s trilogy is a sustained effort to show that the destiny of the maternal cannot be reduced to the logic of sacrifice. Her minor history of religion in *Powers of Horror* turns precisely on the necessity of separation from the mother's body. However, its major focus is the social and symbolic variants of elaborations of maternal authority that go beyond sacrifice. She certainly points to the phantasm of maternal power that *might* suggest why women remain victims of violence. But if the mother is *all*-powerful, where does the conception of the feminine that can make women a target for control and abuse come from?

Another way of explaining the phenomenon that Reineke investigates can be found in Benjamin (1998). In *Shadow of the Other* Benjamin suggests that the notion of the feminine as passive, weak, seductive, and so on might arise in the following way. Fathers project on to *daughters* all of men's anxiety about the all-powerful mother (1998, 57), and this is a source of child abuse. The father creates the daughter in the image of the passive in order to cope with the mother—her authority and the exclusivity of her generative power. The father gets all his drives out on the daughter as the available feminine. An added advantage of this view is that it breaks open the Oedipus complex by adding a fourth to the mother-father-son triangle. Indeed, given the all-powerful mother of early life, the child's turn to the father would be going for the soft option. What is needed is feminized fathers, but they are not available *because* they project the passive on to the daughter. This explanation also shows why motherhood can be acknowledged as a moment of empowerment in patriarchal society. The threat to men is resolved, Benjamin suggests, by their aggressing themselves on the daughter. In the discussion of Kristeva's "Stabat Mater" in chapter 8, below, I will consider Kristeva's confrontation with the symbolic-social acknowledgment of motherhood and the limitations of that acknowledgment.

In *Powers of Horror* the minor history of religion is precisely what shows that the phantasmatics of maternity (baleful power, devouring being) does not necessarily decide the meaning of "woman" in social and symbolic life. The minor history then provokes the question, what coding/s of abjection shape and support collective existence once the worlds of religions are "dead and buried," since "we are too aware of their techniques to yield to them"? (1980a, 133). In other words, *who is the speaking subject today?* It is clear that Kristeva's sustained attention to religious discourse points up the absence of a social symbolic arrangement of abjection in modern secular discourses. The real focus of her investigation in *Powers of Horror* is the secular aftermath of religion. This also implies that psychoanalysis arises as a discourse in these conditions. Psychoanalysis not only develops the conception of the "speaking subject," heterogeneous being of drives, desire, and language, but implies a failing of late modern societies to provide sites of representation for the limit moments of the ties between the individual and the social. The heterogeneous being and the social order are not connected but at odds in ways that leaves Narcissus—the corporeal, affective, and mimetic features of separateness and bonding—abandoned. It is as though the "discovery" of the heterogeneous speaking subject appears to go together with a certain blurring of it. Thus, once again, we find that the nihilism problematic informs Kristeva's view of the appearance and significance of psychoanalysis. In psychoanalysis abjection comes into view with the narcissistic crisis, and shows up as the lining of narcissism. Abjection indicates an exposure to the objective frailty of social organization where the social symbolic system fails to code that frailty by coding its own limits. Psychoanalysis comes upon this as the social failure to accompany the speaking being on its journey into nonobjectal relationship. In these conditions, the recourse to religion, now highly differentiated, is inadequate, since it cannot provide the needed coding of the limits of the social symbolic system, given secularization. In other words, the recourse to religion in response to the limits of the modern social symbolic is itself thoroughly inscribed within the problem of modern nihilism.

This problem equally informs Kristeva's turn to artworks in *Powers of Horror,* for she finds in certain instances of contemporary literature (selected European authors from Dostoyevsky to Céline) a "literature of abjection." Once the demise of world religions, as *historical* religions, and the failings of secular discourses and institutions leave the site of engagement of the semiotic and symbolic neglected, artworks confront the semiotic as a set of variants on nonobjectal relationship. The artistic accommodation of what is incomplete, incommensurable, and irreconcilable provides a marginal, transitory, and fragile place for the subject. On this view, the question "who is the speaking subject today?" cannot be approached if the artwork is neglected. That is to say, literary writing may provide us with some insight into the fate of the modern subject, to the extent that it performs the task of warding off the abject. The literature of abjection "maintains a distance where the abject is concerned. The writer, fascinated by the abject, imagines its logic, projects himself into it, introjects it, and as a consequence perverts language—style and content" (1980a, 16). Nonetheless, this perversion of language is far from constituting a social symbolic elaboration of abjection. Contemporary literature does not and cannot fulfill this requirement. What the perversion of language does is bring out the impossibility, that is to say, the "power play," the "necessary and absurd seeming" of religion, morality, and law as systems of representation (16). In other words, art *reveals* nihilism. The de-composition of the ideal that it accomplishes transgresses all the oppositions deployed to hem in the abject: pure and impure, prohibition and sin, morality and immorality. It appears, then, that the literature of abjection fully brings out the modern, secular failure in respect of the formation of a new speaking subject. The fate of the abject that Hegel discerned in Christianity is reversed. There is so much space for the alien thing that the literature of abjection itself becomes the site of abjection. Kristeva remarks that, just as "the sense of abjection is both the abject's judge and accomplice, *this is also true of the literature that confronts it*" (16). The danger that this poses is discussed in chapter 8, below, where the social and political meaning of Kristeva's thought on abjection is discussed further.

The point at which we now stand is the insight into the failure of religion that appears in the 1980s trilogy. The logical and spiritual elaborations of abjection in Western monotheism *overreach* the semiotic that they attempt to symbolize. Religious discourses provide no clue as to what a secular symbolization of the semiotic would look like at the everyday level. Thus Kristeva's attention to religion implies no nostalgia. Rather, the minor history of the sacred and religion works to illuminate the claim that art steps into the gap where modern, secular institutions and discourses fail to come up with sites for the transition from the semiotic (neglected by the symbolic) to the imaginary (the semiotic inscribed in the symbolic). As we will see in the following chapter, the question of art is the question of how the semiotic takes on symbolic form in conditions of the surrounding limitations of modern institutions and discourses.

CHAPTER 6

The Kristevan Aesthetic

Introduction

This chapter is dedicated to elucidating the meaning of the aesthetic in Kristeva's 1980s trilogy. As will become clear, the meaning of the Kristevan aesthetic must be garnered from her concrete and fine-grained analyses of artworks themselves. The discussion, here, is restricted to her analyses of Holbein and Duras in *Black Sun,* for reasons of time and space. However, there is another important reason for abiding with two moments in the minor history of art that appears there. Kristeva's selection of Holbein and Duras to begin and end this minor history allows me to lay the basis for my emphasis, developed in later chapters, on the import of her thought on the loss of loss in conditions of late modernity. Moreover, I return to her thought on the literature of abjection and discourses of love in chapter 8. This chapter describes an arc from Kristeva's discussion of Holbein's painting to her thought on Duras's *oeuvre.* Holbein stands as an artistic representation at the threshold of modernity. In the discussion of Duras, we find the challenges met by Holbein in the sixteenth century reappearing in the twentieth century in a form that sets grave difficulties for the aesthetic task. This permits me to bring into clearer view the significance of Kristeva's determination to tie her minor histories of modernity to sites of suffering and its overcoming.

The following discussion of Kristeva's thought on art develops from the previous chapter, insofar as she sees modern artworks taking over from religion the task of providing an articulation of the semiotic. However, it also picks up from Part 1 on the psychoanalytic chapters of the trilogy. For Kristeva's analysis of art, like her reading of religion, does not leave the psychoanalytic standpoint behind. I intend to show how, for her, the historical features of the minor history of artworks are bound to sites of suffering and its overcoming, and that they are so because, for her, unacknowledged suffering is the remnant of freedom in modern Western societies. To recall the conclusion to chapter 4, above, on primal loss and melancholy, it is clear that Kristeva turns directly to the analyses of artworks in *Black Sun,* without intermediate chapters on religion as such (unlike *Tales of Love* and *Powers of Horror*), because the works she discusses stand as a confrontation with two symptoms that turned up in her psychoanalytic thought on melancholy. For she does not find that nihilistic modernity is a wholesale loss of transcendence. Rather, she understands Western metaphysics as a belief in the possibility that its other—"the other of language"—can be conveyed, and she proposes that this belief has led to strong individuality and multiple styles in Western cultures. However, this belief and its consequences appear to have declined. As a result, two alternatives are thrown up: either the nihilistic attitude of despair over meaning and values or a belief in mere stylistic performance, one that forecloses the underlying moments of the text or artwork. This foreclosure leads to a fetishization of mere artifice, a development that lines up with the tendency of modern institutions and discourses to promote a merely linguistic universe. The two symptoms of the decline of metaphysics in question at this point in her writings are further evidence for the tendential severance of the semiotic and symbolic, or modern nihilism. When she shows that artworks, in specific instances, are a *counterindication* in respect of this tendency, she binds her analyses of them to the modern Narcissus, the figure of subjectivity in which the neglected semiotic shows up.

Narcissus is not only a figure of modernity, however. He or she takes on different guises—multiple ones—in the history of Western culture. One dimension of Narcissus is the confrontation with pain, loss, and death at the limit of the ties between the individual and the social, the specific topic of *Black Sun.* Each work of art Kristeva addresses in that book is a conveyance of a depressive moment in relation to social deformation or upheaval. For this reason, artistic sublimation (form-giving) is not uniform, but multiple and difficult. From Holbein's painterly confrontation with anguish at the death of God, to the aesthetic whose stake is love and death (Duras), the threefold question that is pressed in *Black Sun* is: *What is loss? What is lost? And what might mourning be?* Artworks are works of mourning only in specific instances, for loss and death have a history. That is why the meaning of the Kristevan aesthetic can only be accessed in and through the fine-grained analyses of the works themselves. Kristeva's minor history culminates with the analysis of an *oeuvre* reflecting and confronting the deepest moments of collapse of modern secular institutions and discourses in the twentieth century, a collapse that she reads in terms of symbolic collapse. In this way she stresses and tarries with the question of what mourning might be *for our time*.

Holbein: "God is Dead"

I have noted that *Black Sun,* unlike *Tales of Love* and *Powers of Horror,* moves directly from the psychoanalytic chapters to the discussion of art, without a middle portion dedicated to religion. However, the first moment of artistic representation she turns to in *Black Sun* is a representation on the threshold between religion and secular modernity. In other words, the question of religion turns up within the artwork she discusses first. Moreover, she chooses this *oeuvre* because its conveyance of loss, death, and melancholy is an exemplar of the artistic confrontation with an unsettling of the Christian world, one that does not go as far as atheism, however. I focus on one work in Holbein's *oeuvre,* the one she gives special attention to, because it is her exemplar of the artistic counterindication to nihilistic despair in these conditions. Holbein's depiction of the dead Christ in his painting *The Body of the Dead Christ in the Tomb* (1521–1522) confronts the threat to what Nietzsche called the "highest ideal" by discovering a change in the meaning of God at the threshold of secular modernity. Moreover, Kristeva does not simply set Holbein's painting into a historical background. Rather, her attention to various aspects of his painting develops an argument that certain artworks reveal and negotiate the deep features of modernity's divisions. She begins with the Holbein because of its status as a threshold. This, too, reveals that she avoids a metanarrative of the collapse of transcendence.

Holbein's *Dead Christ* is a work standing on the threshold of atheism, not crossing it, but occupying the point of the crisis of religious representation. Kristeva expressly connects the significance of the painting with Hegel's affirmation of Christianity as a form of religious representation in his own philosophy of modernity: "a supreme alienation of the divine Idea. . . . 'God is dead, God himself is dead' is a marvelous, fearsome representation, *which offers to representation the deepest abyss of severance*" (cited in Kristeva 1987, 136). Hegel makes explicit the severance of representation that inhabits the representation of severance once death is interiorized in the divine Idea: "*God* is dead, God himself *is dead.*" It will become apparent that Kristeva's analysis of Holbein's *Dead Christ* doubles the distance from the Heideggerian reading of Nietzsche's thought, "God is dead," first discussed in my introduction, above. She does not only avoid positing a wholesale loss of transcendence in the experience of the demise of religion. She also binds the historical features of her analysis of the artwork to the sites of suffering and its overcoming. She allows transcendence to have a history.

What interests her about the Holbein painting is the way in which it encounters the threat to transcendence when the God-relationship is unsettled at the opening of a new political world. This threat is also a test of the aesthetic: how does the aesthetic respond when what it means to *be* artistic representation is itself unsettled as part of a surrounding symbolic and political upheaval? Her analysis of the *Dead Christ* turns on the ways in which *this* image of severance—"God is dead"—renders the severance of representation (the challenge to the aesthetic) in artistic form. At the same time, Holbein's achievement with respect to the aesthetic test cannot be divorced from the way in which *this* work conveys—presents and passes through—the sites of suffering, or latent loss.

Four aspects of Holbein's painting are particularly emphasized. The first is the special impact that this image of Christ's death has on the viewer. The feeling of permanent death takes over from the Christian narrative of life, death, and resurrection. The second is the resulting isolation of the deeper workings represented by the cross—"caesura, discontinuity, depression"—in respect of which Kristeva's psychoanalytic thought becomes prominent. The third is the new vision of mankind that the image transmits. Finally, what makes the painting unique, an exemplar of works of mourning, must embrace the painterly moment itself ("new style, new technique"). Kristeva emphasizes Holbein's minimalism. She does not analyze the artwork as a moral quest for truth, nor does she find in it the adoption of one of the intellectual or spiritual currents of the time, even though Holbein is closest to the new humanism in his intimacy with death. Rather, *The Body of the Dead Christ in the Tomb* is a response, not to, but *of* melancholia, which also proposes a painterly idea. The key to her minor history of artworks, then, is exemplarity. Artworks are works of mourning only in specific instances. The achievement of the Holbein is to respond to the test of the standpoint of artistic form in a manner that negotiates the depressive moment when existing symbolic connections are in a process of deformation. Melancholia, the impact of loss registered in affect and mood, is the extreme manifestation of the fragility of the symbolic. The artwork that confronts the need to give form to melancholia survives the aesthetic test in and through a new painterly vision that imparts a new vision of mankind in respect, precisely, of loss and death. That is the achievement of the Holbein.

The return undertaken here to these dimensions of Kristeva's analysis of the *Dead Christ* brings out the twofold import of the work in her minor history of works of mourning. The analysis first shows how this image of Christ's death brings out the full significance of a dead God at the threshold of atheism. Second, the analysis both underlines Holbein's masterly vanquishing of a depressive moment and indicates the residues of that mastery that will show up once the new vision of mankind comes under pressure in secular modernity.

Kristeva builds up her argument for the significance of the *Dead Christ* by intertwining several approaches to the painting that serve to embed it in a socio-historical and art historical context, only to have it ultimately stand out from that context. Initially the essay turns on the disturbing effect of a painting that goes beyond presentation of Christ's suffering to an unsparing depiction of nature's dominion in death. The disturbing effect finds expression in the words of a character in Dostoyevsky's *The Idiot* (Prince Myshkin). "[Looking] At that picture! Why, some people may *lose their faith* by looking at that picture!" (cited in 1987, 107). This device for opening the analysis links Holbein's conveyance of melancholy—"an unbearable anguish before the death of God"—with the Dostoyevskyan moment of Kristeva's minor history. In the Dostoyevsky chapter it comes to light that Prince Myshkin's expression is an almost literal rendering of Dostoyevsky's own words on encountering the work in Basel's city museum, where he stood "as if stunned," with the facial expression recognized by his wife as one that preceded an epileptic seizure.[1] Kristeva specifies at the outset of the Holbein essay that the disturbing effect is drawn out in *The Idiot* in the words of a minor character, Ippolit, "who nevertheless seems in many respects to be the narrator's and Myshkin's double" (107).

> Here one cannot help being struck by the idea that if death is so horrible and if the laws of nature are so powerful, then how can they be overcome? How can they be overcome when even He did not conquer them, He who overcame nature during His lifetime and whom nature obeyed, who said *Talitha cumi!* and the little girl arose, who cried *Lazarus come forth!* and the dead man came forth? Looking at that picture, you get the impression of nature as some enormous, implacable, and dumb beast, or, to put it more correctly, much more correctly, though it may seem strange, as some huge engine of the latest design, *which has senselessly seized, cut to pieces, and swallowed up—impassively and unfeelingly—a great and priceless Being,* a Being worth the whole of nature and all its laws, worth the entire earth, which was perhaps created solely for the coming of that Being! The pic-

> ture seems to give expression to the idea of a dark, insolent, and senseless eternal power, to which everything is subordinated, and which controls you in spite of yourself. (1987, 108–109)

All the natural evidence, including that of God, is of nature as a death machine. If man is free from nature, then nature is free from God, even He is subject to its implacable power.

> The people surrounding the dead man, none of whom is shown in the picture, must have been overwhelmed by a feeling of terrible anguish and dismay on that evening *which had shattered all their hopes and almost all their beliefs in one fell blow.* They must have parted in a state of the most dreadful terror, though each of them carried away within him a mighty thought which would never be wrested from him. (109)

Ippolit's response brings out the isolation of the dead Christ, the desolation (What is the meaning of hope if God is a corpse?), and the question of what it is to have belief before such evidence, the "mighty thought" of God's absence. The image of flesh caught between a wounded body and decomposition transmits a feeling of permanent death. The effect is compounded by other features of the painting, for Holbein has voided it of any representation of transcendence. No vista stretches out behind the dead Christ to link him to the beyond, and no mourners tie him to the human realm. There are no spectators in the scene to guide the viewer in what attitude to take up to it. Over and above these features, Kristeva finds the feeling of permanent death in the details of style and composition. The isolation of the dead Christ is itself given in an act of composition, in the compression of space and an economy of delineation. "Hans Holbein has given up all architectural or compositional fancy. The tombstone weighs down on the upper portion of the painting, which is merely twelve inches high, and intensifies the feeling of permanent death: this corpse shall never rise again. The very pall, limited to a minimum of folds, emphasizes, through that economy of motion, the feeling of stiffness and stone-felt cold" (1987, 110). The conveyance of melancholic despair in these stylistic aspects of the work— "Everything is dying, God is dying, I am dying"—fulfills the first achievement of this painting.

Kristeva advances her psychoanalytic thought most pointedly in respect of the second aspect of Holbein's aesthetic activity. The deeper workings represented by the cross appear or are localized in one "prospect" introduced into the closed-in sepulchre: the protrusion of hand and hair over the pall that serves to frame the painting. Grief and compassion arise only through "the invisible appeal to our all-too-human identification with the dead Son" (1987, 117). If the psychic need to confront separateness, emptiness, and death is filled in an act of composition, Kristeva also finds here "a means of countervailing the loss of other and of meaning" (129). She presses the psychoanalytic thought.

> The break, brief as it might have been, in the bond linking Christ to his Father and to life introduces into the mythical representation of the Subject, a fundamental and psychically necessary discontinuity. Such a caesura, which some have called a "hiatus," provides an image, at the same time as a narrative, for many separations that build up the psychic life of individuals. It provides image and narrative for some psychic cataclysms that more or less frequently threaten the assumed balance of individuals. Thus, psychoanalysis identifies and relates as an indispensable condition for autonomy a series of splittings (Hegel spoke of a "work of the negative"); birth, weaning, separation, frustration, castration. Real, imaginary, or symbolic, those processes necessarily structure our individuation. (1987, 132).

The psychoanalytic conception of identification finds something more in the individual's implication in Christ's suffering and death than the infinite destructive guilt to which Nietzsche fixed it. The image provides an imaginary support for the subject, "an echo of its unbearable moments when meaning was lost, when the meaning of life was lost" (133). The subject, heterogeneous *because* she is separate and confronted with otherness, and therefore both a subject of symbolic and social capacities and subject to drives, and death, cannot as an individual alone find a balance for that constitutive heterogeneity. In the previous chapter, I stressed Kristeva's view of the powers and limitations of the Christian notion of sin—the lapsing subject. There she showed both how this conception acknowledges the destabilizing heterogeneity of the subject and sets it, too quickly, on the spiritualizing path that would overreach its abjection. We are on slightly different terrain in *Black Sun*. For here the subject is not set in relation to the ideal, to God as the achieved balance of word and flesh where "no alien thing" (abject) can intervene. Rather, here the psychoanalytic position tarries with the breaking of Christ's bond with God and life. It discovers a tentative hold over the destabilization that undermines the balance of individuals in the (appeal to) identification with the dead Son. Holbein's "composition in loneliness" is an act of mercy for our death, giving form to depression, and so to the psychic imprint of the fragile and unstable exposure to separateness, loss, and death. The psychoanalytic conception of imaginary identification thus points to *actual effects* of the image of the dead Christ. The image is "a powerful symbolic device that allows him [man] to experience death and resurrection even in his physical body" (134).

As much as Kristeva's vision and project in *Black Sun* emphasizes the psychoanalytic position, her art criticism is not exhausted by the precision it arrives at on the therapeutic dimension of art, however, especially if therapy is understood to be the healing of a merely private suffering. Holbein's *Body of the Dead Christ in the Tomb* is not simply selected as a prominent example of the therapeutic capacity of the artwork within and for a Christian world. The essay also discovers in Holbein's style and technique a new vision of mankind. This is the reason for the extent of Kristeva's inquiry into both the historical context of Holbein's *oeuvre* and the painting's departure from surrounding artistic styles. Holbein's aesthetic activity belongs to the moment of perhaps the most profound papal instability, the rise of Protestant iconoclasm and desire for gold, and the blood-soaked carving out of a powerful political realm. Kristeva notes the artist's lack of commitment to any of the spiritual currents of the time. Neither Catholicism nor Protestantism nor humanism claimed his aesthetic production. Holbein remained court painter to Henry VIII even after the tyrannical, murderous king ended the lives of those he had painted—not only the king's wives but his friend Thomas More, a fact that "shocked" Erasmus. The stern composure of both More and Erasmus, and, no less, the imposing authority of the English king, are themselves handed down by a Holbein painting. Kristeva finds in this *oeuvre* not only an aloofness that perhaps betrays "the coldness and emotional paralysis of the melancholy person," but an absorption of the spirit of the time, an artistic energy and project summoned up by a melancholy moment (1987, 125).

The analysis also considers the art historical context of the painting, comparing the direction Holbein gives to the *Dead Christ* with the one taken in Grünewald's *Isenheim Altarpiece* (1512–1515). In the *Altarpiece* the image of Christ taken down from the cross appears on the predella beneath the central *Crucifixion* panel. The human connection is sustained in each portion, both in the intensification of Christ's suffering and in the paroxysm of grief shown by the mourners. Holbein's image contrasts strongly with the Gothic expressionist one. By comparison with the eroticization of mental and physical pain in Grünewald's work, Holbein's derelict corpse is "commonplace." It conveys disenchantment, taking on the wager that disenchantment itself can be made beautiful. "Nothing seems desirable any more, values collapse, you are morose? Well, that state can be made beautiful, one can give desirability to the very withdrawal of desire, and as a consequence what might have appeared an abdication or a deadly dejection will henceforth be perceived as harmonious dignity" (1987, 122).

Here there is neither a world infused with God's presence nor a world devalued in opposition to future deliverance, but a vision that overcomes the depressive moment without crossing the threshold of atheism: "the continuous vision of a mankind always already entombed" (128). In sum, the third major aspect of the painting is its configuration of nonmeaning *become significant,* "the limit inherent in life." The work imparts a new morality of dignity in separateness. "Because he acknowledges his folly and looks death in the face—but perhaps also because he faces his mental risks, the risks of psychic death—man achieves a new dimension. Not necessarily that of atheism but definitely that of a disillusioned, serene, and dignified stance. Like a picture by Holbein" (119). Thus Holbein's image of Christ's death is not only considered for its benefit to the subject, as though Kristeva were making a move utterly tangential to Hegel's philosophical reconstruction of the representation "God is dead." In Hegel the latter appears as the self-consciousness of discontinuity in the realm of spirit: "death lives a human life." A direct clash between the psychoanalytic position and the Hegelian philosophy of modernity is held off by Kristeva's stress on the painting's symbolic feat in presenting a new vision of a humankind that, in and through disillusionment, is able to take on death's human life. It is a vision incorporated in a new social symbolic system: Church "and" State, religion *and* politics.

The intricacy of her psychoanalytic, art historical, and sociohistorical interpretation of Holbein's *Dead Christ* is conducted, throughout, in relation to Kristeva's attention to the meaning of the aesthetic standpoint. This is where we find the key to her selection of this work for an account of possibilities for mourning and melancholia. When she finds that Holbein's *Dead Christ* transposes the loss of the other and of meaning into art, that is to say, into the very execution of the work, she finds that the artistic illusion—a knowing artifice—can and does itself encompass and convey disillusionment. It therefore accompanies the viewer right up to the point of the loss of reality—the loss of a world imbued with God's presence—and, in its singularity, stands poised with the viewer at that point. Her concrete and fine-grained analysis of the Holbein painting therefore contains a reflection on the execution of the work.

First, from the psychoanalytic position, "the possibility of unfolding primary processes, spontaneously and under control, artfully, appears, however, as the most efficacious way of overcoming the latent loss" (1987, 129). The transposition of semiotic imprints into symbolic form triumphs over the depressive position. Such a view might only link the artistic achievement to the melancholia of the artist, if Holbein's aesthetic activity were not situated within a test of the painterly standpoint. "The problem is to give form and color to the nonrepresentable—conceived not as erotic luxuriance (as it appears in Italian art even and most particularly in the representation of Christ's Passion); rather, it is the nonrepresentable conceived of as the dissipation of means of representation on the threshold of their extinction in death. Holbein's chromatic and compositional asceticism renders such a competition between form and death that is neither dodged nor embellished but set forth in its minimal visibility, in its extreme manifestations constituted by pain and melancholia" (122–123). In this passage, Kristeva marks the connection between psychic risk and "the dissipation of means of representation," that is to say, the fate of the symbolic. The connection is itself made, or given, in the work. Moreover, only insofar as the Holbein submits artistic form to the competition between form and death does artistic form render the confrontation between form and death. That is to say, the artwork is bound to the effects of the thought that "God is dead," the *latent loss,* which is another way of saying that it is bound to sites of suffering. Insofar as this artwork is a movement of overcoming, it is so only by standing at and not crossing the threshold of atheism. The latter is sustained in a specifically artistic tension: Holbein's minimalism. "Redemption would simply be the discipline of a rigorous technique" (135). In sum, the *Dead Christ* binds the significance of the image—death as the essential sign of humanity, psychic risk as indispensable to psychic and symbolic life—to the execution of the work. Kristeva points to the insertion of date and signature next to Christ's feet. "The painter's name is not lower than Christ's body—they are both at the same level, jammed into the recess, united in man's death, in death as the essential sign of humanity, *of which the only surviving evidence is the ephemeral creation of a picture drawn here and now in 1521 and 1522!"* (114, emphasis added).

In *Black Sun* Holbein's *Dead Christ* is the first exemplar of the artwork as indicator of and counterindication to nihilism, the one that stands at the threshold of the modern world and seems, on Kristeva's analysis, to exhibit the ethic that would support the separation of Church and State. The choice of Holbein as the starting-point for her minor history of works of mourning reveals that Kristeva is not writing a general history of art and melancholia but tackling the problem of modern nihilism. She presses the question of mourning and melancholia *because* the interrogation of loss is the most deep-reaching interrogation of the life and death of symbolic representation. We have seen her tie the historical features of her analysis of the artwork to the sites of suffering and its overcoming. What we come across in the *oeuvre* that closes her minor history of works of mourning in *Black Sun* are the residues of loss and melancholy once Holbein's masterly vanquishing of a depressive moment is no longer one that can easily stand up to the experience of loss and death in the twentieth century. The difficult question, here, is that of what the aesthetic might be in a world in which loss is not a discernible feature of the world that has lost. Kristeva's minor history of artworks is bound to sites of suffering precisely because it is a struggle even to bring out the threefold question: What is loss? What is lost? What might mourning be? Here the aesthetic standpoint finds the latent loss—the exposure to pain, loss, and death—in suffering subjectivity "alone." This is why Kristeva turns to an aesthetic whose stakes are *desire and death*.

Duras: A New Suffering World

It might still seem surprising that Kristeva chooses Marguerite Duras for the endpoint of her account of the possibilities for mourning and melancholia, given her commitment elsewhere to high modernism (Joyce and Beckett, for example). However, if she had taken that line we would perhaps be inclined to look for the continuity between Holbein's minimalist technique and artistic modernism. For example, there is the way in which the depiction of the *Dead Christ* has the hand and hair slip over the pall that serves to frame the painting, bringing the viewer's attention to its very surface, to the paint itself, and so to the way in which the artifice of art is figured in the work. That would allow us to further the discussion of artistic representation in a particular direction. However, it would also lead us to overemphasize a certain continuity—a certain story of art—at the expense of Kristeva's stress on discontinuity, which is to say, her stress on how the aesthetic achievement is tied to what underlies it: the latent loss, or unacknowledged suffering. We can only elucidate her choice of Duras, then, if we let Kristeva's focus on the explosion of death and eroticized suffering stay in the foreground.

The analysis of Duras opens with a discussion of the individual and collective encounter with death in the conditions of the twentieth century. This ties the analyses to the Holbein discussion, thematically, but also emphasizes the important discontinuity with respect to the test of the aesthetic. For here the individual and collective encounter with death is not as such an encounter with nature, a discovery of mortality. Nor is it, at worst, an encounter with the recoil of the natural forces that were exploited and developed in order to serve the ethic of human goodness—or at least to tame nature—once the mastery of those forces returns as the atomic explosion. We do not only know that we are mortal. We are not only further exposed to mortality in and through the very project of protection against the irrational, that is to say, the unfolding of the enlightenment project: "we also know that we can inflict death upon ourselves. Auschwitz and Hiroshima have revealed that the 'malady of death,' as Marguerite Duras might say, informs our most concealed inner recesses. If military and economic realms, as well as political and social bonds, are governed by passion for death, the latter has been revealed to rule even the once noble kingdom of the spirit" (1987, 221). This was the vision that Freud brought before the eyes of a humankind that remained able to think and speak whether it tarried or turned away. Kristeva now links the discovery of death "within" to the military and political cataclysms of the twentieth century and this, in turn, to the poverty of symbolic means for taking up a relationship to death. Different genres of postwar art share a concern with the explosion of death, which is to say, not simply its eruption, but the explosion of its very significance.

Kristeva recalls the difficulty as it appears in Valéry's recourse to a physicist's observation: "in a kiln heated to incandescence: if our eyes endured they would see *nothing*. No luminous disparity would remain, nothing would distinguish one point in space from another. This tremendous, trapped energy would end up in invisibility, in *imperceptible equality*. An equality of that sort is nothing else than *a perfect state of disorder*" (1987, 222). Recognizing that modern secular discourses are unable to investigate the deepest moments of their collapse, Kristeva notes the various trends in artistic representation whose work confronts the "monstrous" nothing, as well as the moments of critical reflection on, for example, poetic production. She acknowledges Blanchot's work on "the invisible," for example, but also relocates his project in a separation of word and image that marks postwar apocalyptic rhetoric: "etymologically, *apocalypso* means de-monstration, dis-covering through sight, and contrasts with *aletheia*, the philosophical disclosure of truth" (223). On the one hand, a wealth of images gives a raw display of monstrosity ("images have us walk in fear," Augustine). On the other hand, there is a "holding back of words" in a literature become internalized, "working toward the origin of the work" (Blanchot). Literature voids itself of representation in order to seek the internal conditions of its practice—the minimal conditions of what it is for something to be a novel, a poem or a play. If, with Kristeva, word and image are but "seeming opposites" in divergent attempts to provide a vision of the "monstrous" nothing, they nonetheless impose a choice between mass communication arts and high modernist literature.

The divergence of word and image illuminates the choice of Duras. The awkward combination of high intellectual expression and hackneyed phrases that shows up in this *oeuvre* is far removed from the high modernism of Joyce or Beckett. It dissolves the high/low art distinction. The hollow gesture of popular romance resounds in the intense erotism. An inturned narrative device prevails. Another moment in the critical reception of Duras's *oeuvre* has closely analysed the various aspects of this device. In *Marguerite Duras: Apocalyptic Desire,* Hill demonstrates how the Durassian novel is often circular in structure, characters are each others' doubles, triangulation inserts further doubles, narration reduplicates content, and, as Duras comes to double the texts with another version of themselves, repetition "exceeds the confines of the single text" (1993, 45, 50, 85–86). For Hill, narrative replication of content produces the insight into apocalyptic desire, and, in his view, the same inturned device is maintained in the transition from novel to film, the genre exploring the relationship of word and image. "And desire in Duras's films becomes a quest that has as its goal the dissolution of the spectator into an affirmation of the pure, ecstatic difference that exists in the unrepresentable gap between word and image" (1993, 113).

However, Kristeva turns to Duras, neither to press the claim that this aesthetic surpasses the high/low art opposition, nor to affirm the tie between apocalyptic desire and the gap between word and image, but for Duras's confrontation with a shared problematic of word and image: "the silence of horror in oneself and in the world" (1987, 225). It is that confrontation that leads Duras "to an aesthetics of *awkwardness* on the one hand, to a *noncathartic literature* on the other" (225). For Kristeva, the inturned narrative device preempts the possibility of taking up any distance from or relation to eroticized suffering. The novels are deemed a noncathartic literature owing to their *levelling* of form and malady, leaving the reader immersed in the malady of grief. As a result, Kristeva's analysis of Duras's novels focuses on eroticized suffering rather than pure ecstatic difference. For, once again, her minor history of art binds the works to the sites of suffering.

Kristeva also sets the ambiguity of the inturned narrative device in relation to a political question. A passage that returns to Arendt's distinction between the public as the site of politics and the private as the realm of domesticity and affective relations reiterates a current thesis that the Arendtian opposition has become inverted. "Politics is not, as it was for Hannah Arendt, the field where human freedom is unfurled. The modern world, the world of world wars, the Third World, the underground world of death that acts upon us, do not have the civilized splendor of the Greek city state. The modern political domain is massively, in totalitarian fashion, social, leveling, exhausting. Hence madness is a space of antisocial, apolitical, and paradoxically free individuation" (1987, 235). This passage on Arendt might appear to exhaust the account of the changed relation to politics that surrounds Duras's artistic production. However, the Holbein analysis acts as a reminder of what is present but never made fully explicit in Kristeva's trilogy.The power of Holbein's aesthetic lies in its unfolding of a changed sensibility in the relation to God. The conveyance of melancholy through a minimalist technique is at the same time an aesthetic of severance (His absence rather than His presence). Holbein's art is one incorporated in the objective bearer of the relation of separateness and connectedness: Church "and" State. If this objective bearing of the relation has moved to the secular, one might have expected from Kristeva an account of its dynamic moment *as* secular—the moment that all of modern political thought wanted to think by interrogating the individual and the collective, assuming the state to be the site of collectivity. Brief references do suggest that Kristeva reads Hegel as allowing the relationship of state and civil society to be one of the bearers of the Church–State collapse, and so an objective site for our experiencing ourselves as separate and connected, for the entanglement of private need and social and political awareness. But Kristeva's question is what is the fate of the Holbein? How is our situation different from his?

All of Kristeva's work underlines the importance that an objective bearer of the relation of separateness and connectedness can't just be coded as experiential but must actually be so. The Hegelian recognition is presumed in her reference to Arendt. It is no longer an unproblematic societal accomplishment for state and civil society to be sites where we comprehend ourselves as separate and connected. The economy is a coda of mutual imposition, not individuation. The state is not a substantive universal or domain of connectedness. This is a reasonable claim given widespread recourse to nationalism for a discourse of collectivity. (Kristeva takes up the problem of nationalism in a later work, discussed in chapter 7, below.) State and civil society are experienced as detached and oppressive forces. The possibility of an assertion of transgression over a public domain devalued to a realm of housekeeping on the macrolevel comes to be harbored in the private realm ("madness is a space of antisocial, apolitical, and paradoxically free individuation"). Such is the power of Durassian desire. Nonetheless, the passage on Arendt immediately acknowledges the desperate nature of the inverted scenario and the pitfalls of a subversion played out in the private/public opposition. Confronting these acts of paradoxically free individuation, "political events, outrageous and monstrous as they might be—the Nazi invasion, the atomic explosion—are assimilated to the extent of being measured only by the human suffering they cause" (1987, 235). Suffering is acknowledged suffering then? No, the reverse is the case. What is missing is public response in the wake of the political events. Political events are not interrogated but assimilated to a vague, unthought indication of suffering (sentimentalism on the one hand, mere statistics on the other, perhaps). The interrogation of meaning and nonmeaning is abandoned to the private realm, but merely private suffering brings with it a weakening of the interrogation.

The passage on Arendt highlights the presence of the problem of modern nihilism in the analysis of Duras's works. Kristeva has clearly moved from the experience of the absence of God (Holbein) to the disintegrated experience of the absence of the political, and to the sites of representation of that disintegration. The real stakes of *Black Sun* lie in the menace that the inverted Arendtian scenario harbors. The absence of the political is also the suffering of a narcissistic constriction. Rather than passing over it, Kristeva explores an aesthetic dedicated to the "spectrum of suffering" where symbolic collapse spreads out. Where Holbein's art presided over the threshold of the extinction of symbolic means in death, turning melancholia, the extreme manifestation of the fragility of the symbolic, into harmonious dignity, the protagonists in Duras's novels presume the demise of the modern heroes she refuses to dream up. Characters and text fold in on a "sickly secret." Although most of the final chapter of *Black Sun* discusses Duras's novels, they are deemed to leave the confrontation with the malady at the point of complicity. Noteworthy, then, is Kristeva's proposal that Duras's entire work is contained in the text setting the plot of Resnais's film *Hiroshima Mon Amour* (1959), a film that puts Duras's "x ray on distress" in a historical and political setting. The analysis of the film is the centerpiece of Kristeva's conclusion to *Black Sun*.

Hiroshima Mon Amour opens with moving bodies, "preys either to love or to the pangs of death—successively covered with ashes, dew, atomic death—and the sweat of love fulfilled" (Duras, cited in Kristeva 1987, 231). It is an encounter of lovers who turn out to be a Frenchwoman in suspended mourning for the German lover of her youth, shot by partisans in the town of Nevers in occupied France on the eve of Liberation, and a Japanese businessman of European bearing who was absent from the city on the occasion of the atomic attack, though his family was not. The woman's melancholia prolongs the event and aftermath of the final secret assignation with her German lover, when she discovers his wounded and slowly dying body, which she covers with her own. Confined with shorn head to the cellar of the family home, and thereby both punished and saved from reprisal, she undergoes a double living death, the one imposed symbolically by incarceration, as though in pretense that she is dead, and the one that began on the night that ended her affair, when she absorbed his death into her stricken body. Despite eventual release, love remains for her the love of a dead person. "Mourning becomes impossible," Kristeva concludes, "and changes the heroine into a crypt inhabited by a living corpse" (1987, 233). What brings the woman to Hiroshima is fascination with an event in which boundaries are destroyed, affording her a release from guilt.

The ambiguous images of moving body parts that open the film alternate with passing footage of the aftermath of the atomic explosion, and shots of the museum that stands as testimony to the disaster. The offscreen dialogue unfolds on one side the woman's personal testimonial to everything she has seen, on the other the negations that form his response, especially one repeated phrase. "You saw nothing in Hiroshima. Nothing." Her self-undermining objection to his response turns on remembrance. "Like you, I know what it is to forget. Like you, I am endowed with memory.... Each day I resisted with all my might against the horror of no longer understanding the reason for remembering. Like you, I did forget." She knowingly pledges herself to the illusion of artifice. "The reconstructions have been made as authentic as possible. The films, too, were perfectly authentic. The illusion is so perfect that the tourists cry." But the moving images of the victims could be moving images of famine victims at one moment, of other war zones at another. The suffering is indistinguishable, global, and indefinite. "No, what was there for you to weep over?" he replies. Hiroshima is invisible. Although the blunt rebuttal that provokes this thought would appear to leave their encounter destined to a swift end, what actually upholds the dialogue is a reverberation of melancholia between her incantatory speech and his deadness of tone. An exchange in melancholia is the mainstay of their love, its life and breath. Kristeva captures its ambiguity precisely. "A love crippled by death or a love of death? A love that was made impossible or a necrophilic passion for death? *My love is a Hiroshima*, or else, *I love Hiroshima for its suffering is my Eros?*" (1987, 232). The ambiguity of a love that is on the one hand itself death-bearing, on the other a captivation of eros by unimaginable destruction is, she proposes, perhaps the postwar version of love. The film is no love *story,* if it were its analysis would appear in *Tales of Love*. The love in Hiroshima is distinctive because it is an impossibility sustained by a melancholic madness in which love and death are compressed together. "Today's milestone is human madness" (235). The lovers' spasmodic narration of wartime and love is haunted by the awareness of this, until—at last—it comes to be articulated in a speech that conducts their parting. "Hi-ro-shi-ma. Hi-ro-shi-ma. That's your name." "That's my name. Yes. Your name is Nevers. Nevers-in France" (Duras 1960, 83).

Once Kristeva underlines the import of an artwork where grief and madness are set in relation to historical events, the question must be raised of where she now places the emphasis. Is the major emphasis on a deadly passion that may come to appear in military and political cataclysm, suggesting a primacy of psychoanalytic discoveries to underpin the affirmation of Duras's aesthetic? Or is it on a sheltered disaster and the spread of numbness because of what took place in history, sustaining the implicit reflection on the appearance and significance of psychoanalysis itself as a discourse? *Powers of Horror* banished the chicken-and-egg setup of the choice between social or subjective cause.

Nonetheless, Kristeva seems to find that reference to historical cause is itself a symptom of the inverted Arendtian scenario. A private realm opposes itself to that problem—out there—but its own transgression is secretly fueled by powers of destruction. She also tends to withdraw first, and ultimately, from any overemphasis on the sociohistorical setting. Chapter and book close with an insistence upon a distress that is "essential and transhistorical." From there, it is a short step to affirming an aesthetic act that makes that distress one moment in a narrative synthesis. In this way, Kristeva affirms art's capacity to convey, not the political events, but the sheltered disaster, the site of suffering. *Black Sun* articulates certain implications of the thought presented in *Tales of Love* that "psychoanalysis is the most internalized moment of Western historicality" (1983, 276). The analysis of *Hiroshima Mon Amour* contains a thesis on the internalization of political horror, and it is this that best illuminates the choice of Duras, keeping this aesthetic negotiation of the "monstrous nothing" fundamentally linked to the inverted Arendtian scenario, and so to the sites of suffering, the unacknowledged or latent pain and loss.

Duras's aesthetic domain is one of political horror conducting a life of strangled, suspended, and intensely alluring love. The aesthetic whose stake is love and death assumes powers of destruction in the individual and society that have never "appeared as unquestionable and unavoidable as now," but which cannot be approached directly (1987, 221). Moral suffering dissolves in a political horror that "knows neither place nor party, but can rage absolutely" (232). This is perhaps the source of the disappearance, both from the film and from Kristeva's analysis of it, of a major protagonist in the atomic explosion: America. Nor do they make it a question of the relationship of France and Japan. Duras's script insists that the Japanese man be Western-looking in order "to minimize the differences between the two protagonists. If the audience never forgets that this is the story of a Japanese man and a Frenchwoman, the profound implications of the film are lost. If the audience does forget it, these profound implications become apparent" (Duras 1960, 109). Kristeva's commentary underlines the intention. "Up to a point, considering moral suffering, there is no common ground between a shorn lover in France and a Japanese woman scorched by the atom" (1987, 235). The common ground that melds the protagonists is the eclipse of uncommon ground—of geographical place and political party—in the transcendence of horror. As political events are absorbed into horror, moral suffering dissolves into political horror. No public negotiation of this situation is forthcoming. Artistic representation then confronts the powers of destruction in the domain of passion. Love, without the effect of renewal and rebirth proposed in *Tales of Love,* is an intimate repercussion of death in love, rendering it captivating.

"The nuclear explosion therefore permeates love itself, and its devastating violence makes love both impossible and gorgeously erotic, condemned and magically alluring" (231). In sum, *Hiroshima Mon Amour* turns on a love borne by a melancholic madness that appears in conditions in which modern secular discourses and institutions cannot negotiate their deepest moments of collapse. First, the inverted Arendtian scenario: "In the view of an ethic and an aesthetic concerned with suffering, the mocked private domain gains a solemn dignity that depreciates the public domain while allocating to history the imposing responsibility for having triggered the malady of death. As a result, public life becomes seriously severed from reality whereas private life, on the other hand, is emphasized to the point of filling the whole of the real and invalidating any other concern. The new world, necessarily political, is unreal. We are living the reality of a new suffering world" (235). Nietzsche the moral psychologist introduced the thought that to suffer from reality is to *be* a piece of the reality that has come to grief (1895, 137–138). Kristeva the psychoanalytic thinker finds that suffering subectivity, alone or almost alone, is the site of the uninterrogated significance of the deepest moments of collapse of modern institutions and discourses. So, second, there is the development that upholds the inverted Arendtian scenario: *"Private suffering absorbs political horror into the subject's psychic microcosm"* (234).

Social and political discourses neglect the individual and collective encounter with the explosion of death. If Adorno condemned the investigation of the psychic microcosm abstracted from the social dialectic, Kristeva's attention to the psychic microcosm points to its status as the remainder of a social and political world where individual and collective confrontation with death is cancelled. If the cancellation is upheld by the removal of the confrontation with death to private suffering, then this is where the psychoanalytic thinker goes for an analysis of the remainder, irrespective of whether or not this looks like a weakening of attention to the social dialectic. For an implication of the explosion of death—of its significance—is that death is caught up in a narcissistic constriction where the latent loss remains, unacknowledged. Yet again, this explains Kristeva's choice of Duras to close her minor history of works of mourning. For once the death-bearing event shuts out the powers of artifice—"our symbolic means find themselves hollowed out, nearly wiped out, paralyzed" (1987, 223)—what summons the aesthetic is the suffering where loss and mourning are locked in. This film does not open with the spectacle of the explosion of death, for the nuclear mushroom's easy entry into the circulation and exchange of images reflects the undermined aesthetic powers. Nor does Duras's aesthetic commit itself to the repercussions of atomic explosion, whose spectacle intensifies the assimilation of public events to the general human suffering they cause. Tragical, pacifist, or rhetorical artifice protracts the cancelation and suspension of the individual and collective encounter with death. "The knowledge of Hiroshima is something that must be set down, a priori, as being an exemplary delusion of the mind" (Duras, cited in Kristeva 1987, 231). Kristeva chooses this aesthetic because it is a commitment to the problem of the damage to systems of perception and representation, to *symbolic collapse.* "As if overtaxed or destroyed by too powerful a breaker, our symbolic means find themselves hollowed out, nearly wiped out, paralyzed" (223). "All one can do is speak of the impossibility of speaking of Hiroshima" (Duras, cited in Kristeva 1987, 231). True to that commitment, the film lays out the sheltered disaster, the melancholia that is *also* like an explosion in history.

Kristeva seems to claim that *Hiroshima Mon Amour* surpasses the novels, overcoming their complicity with the malady, by furthering the confrontation between form and death. First, there is the conveyance of the weight of human pain by making "the horror rise from its ashes by having it inscribed into a love that will inevitably be distinctive and 'wonder-filling'" (Duras, cited in Kristeva 1987, 231). Second, the novelistic leveling of text and malady is overcome in the dimensions brought to the unfurling of melancholia by cinematic technique, paramount from the opening of the film. The camera is prevented from setting up a privileged perspective on to a homogeneous space. Off-screen dialogue puts words where sight would be. The dialogue is uncannily divorced from the uncertainty of the image of moving bodies ("preys either to love or to the pangs of death"). The intensity of spectacle then reintroduces an excess of fascination to collapse the detachment of words. Where Hill finds in the detachment of voice from any supporting image the mysterious and surprising capacity of words "to envision the invisible" (1993, 95), Kristeva stresses the whole cinematic deployment of the gap between word and image for its undercutting of the effects they have as extremes (detachment/engulfment) and for its capacity to make artifice appear *as* convention, alien to its content. "If Duras uses the screen in order to burn out its spectacular strength down to the glare of the invisible by engulfing it in elliptical words and allusive sounds, she also uses it for its excess of fascination, which compensates for verbal constriction. As the characters' seductive power is thus increased, their invisible malady becomes less infectious on the screen because it can be performed: filmed depression appears to be an alien artifice" (1987, 227). Once text joins film, the aesthetic of love and death overcomes the complicity of artifice with the malady. It is an aesthetic that does not fetishize mere artifice, but, rather, preserves the underlying moments of the artwork. Artifice as "alienation" in Kristeva means the transformation of aesthetic complicity with the sickly secret into the conveyance of unacknowledged suffering—presenting it, revealing its significance, passing through it.

A New Amatory World

We have seen that, for Kristeva, the import of a certain highpoint of the Durassian aesthetic lies in its contribution to recovering and responding to the threefold question, *What is loss? What is lost? And what might mourning be, for our time?* The aesthetic counters the public neglect of the explosion of death in the economic, political, and spiritual world of the twentieth century. It bears within itself and conveys the loss of the significance of death in these conditions, and their aftermath, as well as the correlative damage to perception and representation (symbolic collapse). It goes to the sites of suffering that carry the latent loss of meaning and symbolic resources, and so sets suffering subjectivity in relation to the wide implications of this suffering. This aesthetic passes beyond complicity with the malady in and through the minimal resources of an alienating technique (artifice). There is no masterly vanquishing of a depressive moment, as with Holbein. That is to say, there is no claim comparable to the one that an illusion—art—achieves the symbolic feat of turning disillusionment into a new ethic. Yet it looks as though, from the aesthetic standpoint, the accomplishments set out above *are* what mourning might be for our time.

The nature and significance of the artwork as work of mourning can be specified further by considering the different aspects of psychoanalytic attention to suffering subjectivity that appear in *Tales of Love* and *Black Sun*. The first book turns on the question of what love is and can be. For Freud discovered the narcissistic investment that can lie at the heart of the love relationship. This led him to present two alternatives in the path that love might take, ones that are manifested in object-choice: either seeking oneself as a love object or, and *better,* object love, "the development of a true object-choice," as he says in the essay on narcissism (1914, 80–81). With Kristeva, however, narcissistic investment, and so love traumatism, is ineradicable. She passes beyond the morally evaluated distinction in object-choice that is to be found in Freud. For her, "Narcissus" already embraces a transcendent moment: primary idealization, or the transference on to a fleeting ideal that sets the living and loving other up at the core of the ego. In *Tales of Love* Kristeva calls the prototype of this ideal the imaginary father. Her thought on primary idealization leads her to propose that love always encompasses the projection of oneself through an ideal instance, and identifying with it (see Kristeva 1984). She therefore does not seek the fate of Narcissus in matters of object-*choice*. Rather, she finds that the narcissistic constriction—the loss of others—reflects the loss of the ideal. Where there is no secular variant of the loving father to support idealizing constructions, these are weak or missing. *Tales of Love* suggests what the recovery of others might mean. *Nations Without Nationalism* considers the importance of the topic of *Tales of Love* for the social bond (see chapter 7, below). With *Black Sun,* we discover an especially troublesome fate of Narcissus, one that reveals the need of the recovery of loss.

At the same time, Kristeva has joined voice with others in her tradition in commending the psychoanalytic model of the individual to the humanities and sciences. *Tales of Love* underlines the point that this model challenges any assumed balance of the individual. "Man as a fixed, valorized entity finds himself abandoned in favor of a search, less for his truth . . . than for his innovative capacities" (1983, 15). In the technical terms of that book, the individual is a stabilizing-destabilizing "open system" made up of and opened up to its heterogeneous components (drive, affect, desire, language), but also—and only because—it is connected to *other* open systems. The term *destabilizing* captures the significance of the semiotic: the continuity of traces of nonsymbolized exposure to loss, separateness, and otherness, and the possibility that drives and affects may hold sway over the subject. The term "stabilizing," and its typographically marked connection to the threat of the collapse of selfhood and the "other" (stabilizing-destabilizing), refers to signifying representations. The latter encompass the transition of semiotic imprints into symbolic form, and *require* an other as the condition for the production of meaning. Kristeva therefore speaks of this model of the individual in terms of "the image of man amenable to transference love" (1983, 15). The model is drawn from what is operating in the transference within the analytic setting, and assumes Kristeva's own reaccommodation of love in that setting. She finds that "the effect of love is one of renewal, our rebirth" (15). The dynamic of projection-identification underlies and supports the passage to meaning and connections with others.

The subject matter of *Black Sun* implies the failure to sustain the formation and deformation of meaning and the subject by means of transference love. The process illuminated by the theory of primary idealization—the capacity to project oneself through an ideal instance, and identify with it—has been overwhelmed. Let us say, more simply, that love, understood in this way, has run into difficulty. The dominion of melancholia outreaches or fails to accede to idealization, and so a certain path of mourning cannot be assumed, for we recall from *Tales of Love* that the imaginary father acts as consolation for loss. The protection against emptiness that this consolation provides is a support for the life of signs. Narcissistic melancholia, on the other hand—the subject of *Black*

Sun—is marked by the denial of signifiers identified with life and meaning. The access to signifying representations is cut off. Above all, the final book of the trilogy reveals how subjectivity can be the site of suffering in a very expansive sense. It may be—or bear—the trace of a whole reality that has come to grief. In this case, suffering is the prison where loss and mourning are locked in. Kristeva calls this an "impossible mourning," "entirely made up of sensations and *autosensations*," a mourning that is "inalienable, inseparable, and for that very reason, unnameable" (1987, 240).

The question of what mourning might be, in conditions where idealization is lacking, has received a surprising answer in *Black Sun,* now that we look at it again from the psychoanalytic standpoint. For mourning does not differ in *structure* from melancholia. It is no more than the transposition of mood into another material than the material which constitutes mood: the transposition from sensation to signs, rhythms, and forms. Once again, we see Kristeva turn to art because it *can* give symbolic form to the semiotic in conditions of their tendential severance. Narcissistic melancholy/depression is the signal and most intangible manifestation of that tendency. Thus literary and artistic creation are "that adventure of body and signs that bear witness to the affect" (1987, 22). Nihilism is countered in art wherever the artistic performance includes the communicable imprint of an affective reality, perceptible to the reader: "I like this book because it conveys sadness, anguish, or joy" (22). The affective reality is perceptible and, on this condition, the malady can be set aside. The challenge to the artistic standpoint lies, then, in the need of conducting a release from the reality of that "new suffering world" of which *Black Sun* speaks (235) by drawing up a distance from or perspective on the distress. Kristeva finds such an aesthetic in *Hiroshima Mon Amour* because the artifice that unfurls melancholia is itself made perceptible.

The question that arises next is this. Given that *Black Sun* provides us with no particular pointers in respect of the possibilities for modern institutions and discourses being able to negotiate their own deepest moments of collapse, what does the unfurling of and release from melancholia open on to? The answer comes in a further step in Kristeva's affirmation of the aesthetic. Art's capacity to make our "essential and transhistorical" distress one moment in a narrative synthesis sets aside the new suffering world. Aesthetic synthesis that elaborates the intangible melancholy may also revoke the demise of idealization. On Kristeva's view, this recovery of idealization is necessary for adequate separateness and connectedness, and a condition for innovative capacities. This itself implies that aesthetic synthesis, in unique instances, presents exemplars of possibilities for separateness and mutual recognition. Artistic and literary experience may offer a transition from the new suffering world to "a new amatory world," as Kristeva suggests on the final page of *Black Sun* (259). The distinction between the two worlds is quite in line with the one she presents about selfhood. On the one hand, there is the psychic prison: the worldless self where loss and mourning are locked in. As Kristeva expresses it in one moment of her writings, the subject "dwells in an untenable place, threatened by madness beneath the emptiness of heaven" (1984, xi). On the other hand, there is the "open system," or the image of man amenable to transference love. Art provides the link between the two. It reconnects the semiotic and symbolic by turning distress—unacknowledged suffering, the remnant of freedom—into one moment in a narrative synthesis. The dynamic of idealization can be brought into signs, once again, on condition that the sickly secret is elaborated. "The point now is to see in 'the malady of grief' only one moment of the *narrative synthesis* capable of sweeping along in its complex whirlwind philosophical meditations as well as erotic protections or entertaining pleasures" (1987, 258).

Nonetheless, if *Black Sun* closes with an endorsement of narrative synthesis, viewed as the adventure of body-and-signs, a problem remains. What disappears from the endpoint of *Black Sun* is the underlying problem of the depreciation of the public domain. The notion that modern secular discourses fail to cover the ground that needs to be covered in thinking through intersubjectivity, and so also the connection of self and society, is borne in every sentence in *Black Sun*. It also appears in the way in which each book in the trilogy moves directly from interpretation of the functions and failings of religions to a discussion of literary and artistic works, seemingly foreclosing the moment of modern social and political thought. This implies the failings of modern secular discourses and institutions, yet the notion of secular failure is never fully brought into the foreground. As a result a certain dogmatic semiotization colors Kristeva's thought. Faithfulness to the literary position does not allow the full stakes of her thought to be the stakes. There is in Kristeva the adventure of body and signs. But the problematic that makes psychoanalysis and art what they are in her vision and project is not fully approached. For the domain of the communicable imprint of affective reality—the artwork—also reveals the depths of our difficulties. We live in a melancholic age, which does not mean that everyone suffers the whole narcissistic cost. Some do achieve mourning, and this is neither private work nor generalizable. It is exemplary—neither universal nor particular. The technical achievement of *Hiroshima Mon Amour* is to show what mourning is now, just as Holbein's minimalism was for his time. However, the difference is that Duras's is not an art incorporated in a social-symbolic system, capturing its ethic. Here, the autonomy of artifice is fulfilled. Autonomous art provides a response to the question of what mourning might be only insofar as it shows that it *is* artifice, not solution. Thus the stake of the aesthetic at this endpoint is also the one of their being an objective moment of the felt absence of the political to counter the disintegration of the experience of its absence.

Although Kristeva emphasizes the technical achievement of *Hiroshima Mon Amour,* she does not draw out all the implications of autonomous art. As a result, narrative synthesis is presented as a new amatory "world." However, the narrative reconstruction of the loss of meaning and the other may be too weak to sustain the promise that it signifies in the trilogy as the recovery of love and loss. Moreover, not all witnessing and countering of nihilism is narrative synthesis. Modern artworks include instances that confront the weakening of one form of artistic practice, and seek out other means to give form to love and loss. This suggests that the trilogy does not adequately develop the conception of form, even though Kristeva has pressed the need, and analysed exemplars, of form-giving. Her concrete analyses of artworks themselves compose her thought on the problem of modern nihilism, and the possibilities for making love and loss intelligible. Yet no critical reflection on the meaning and achievements of artistic representation follows.

The absence of critical reflection in Kristeva's thought reveals her fear of falling into metanarrative, some identity-thinking that would close off the realm of imaginary discourses once again. It would seem that, for her, to introduce extended critical reflection on the meaning and possibilities of aesthetic form would be to presuppose that critical self-consciousness could "mend" what psychoanalysis reveals to be broken in its analysis of symbolically fragmented subjectivity. Since she knows that critical self-consciousness cannot "mend," she confines her thought to performing and showing: to artworks and the fine-grained analyses of them. Something—philosophy?—is disowned. However, this is a pretense because the performance does imply, and bear, reflectiveness. The refusal of critical reflectiveness is actually a grasp at innocence, and this is symptomatic of the fact that there is no theory without violence. The most important consequence of this refusal is that the commitment to semanalysis appears to blind Kristeva to the notions of form which, even in her own analyses of artworks, do the work of mediation. The analysis of the film *Hiroshima Mon Amour,* in particular, is a moment in which a certain collapse of narrative synthesis in its novelistic shape is confronted. Here, other means of artistic representation—cinematic ones—mediate the impact of separateness and otherness, giving form to love and loss. This shows that the concept of form could be further developed.

PART III

The Social and Political Implications of Kristeva's Thought

CHAPTER 7

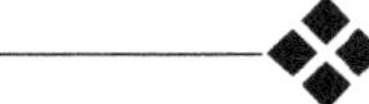

Ethics and Politics

Introduction

Given the presence in the trilogy of the problem of modern nihilism, it is surprising when Kristeva proceeds directly to draw out the social and political implications of her thought in terms of models that psychoanalysis provides for ethical and political relations. This has led many to mine her project for a Kristevan ethics or politics, without going through the problem of mediation that the psychoanalytic and aesthetic thought dwell on. There are many discussions in the literature of Kristeva's texts *Strangers to Ourselves* (1988) and *Nations Without Nationalism* (1993). This development in her writings can tend to dominate their reception in the anglophone world, a tendency which belies the problems that the trilogy presses, both overtly and covertly. The objective of my own reading of these texts is to foreground and critically assess the way in which the ethical and political writings develop out of the concerns of the 1980s trilogy. For the problem of mediation is set by the two correlative ways in which nihilism shows up in Kristeva's writings. First, the tendential severance of the semiotic and symbolic is indicated, as we have seen, by a dominion of the abstract sign, which does not accommodate the semiotic: the tendency to promote a merely linguistic universe. This might also be called the abstractedness of modernity, that is to say, the abstractedness of modern institutions, discourses, and experience. Second, there is the narcissistic constriction, which Kristeva analyses as the dominion in subjectivity of the semiotic deprived of symbolic form. Her "borderline subject" is one under the sway of affects and drives that are cut off from any symbolic life encompassing and supported by connections with others.

Let us first recall the suggestion that Kristeva's distinction between the semiotic and symbolic is a psychoanalytic version of the Kantian one between intuition and concept (for Kant, concepts without intuitions are empty and intuitions without concepts are blind). The difficulties she attends to in the 1980s trilogy are the emptiness of signifying representations and the blindness of semiotic traces. The work of mediation, undertaken by psychoanalysis and the aesthetic, is the work of reconnecting the semiotic and the symbolic. The psychoanalytic and aesthetic standpoints show how therapy and art are able to negotiate the depth of the ambiguities of self and society in these conditions. Yet *Strangers to Ourselves* and *Nations Without Nationalism* appear to overstep these ambiguities insofar as each text proceeds directly to present a psychoanalytically based model for ethical and social relations. What I am underlining, here, is the following. Psychoanalysis, as we have seen, is the method of Kristeva's thought because it is an adequate means of approach to a problem of which it forms a part. How can the discourse that discloses nihilism and responds to its symptoms then be introduced as the one from which models for ethical and social relations are to be drawn? The previous chapter showed how the aesthetic can link the broken moments of self and world that Kristeva attends to. The aesthetic can offer a transition from the new suffering world or psychic prison (narcissistic constriction) to the new amatory world or the psyche as "open system:" formation, deformation, and transformation of the subject and meaning. Does Kristeva think that psychoanalysis, too, in and of itself, can be a solution to the problems it exposes? At moments she appears to think so.

The question is whether or not this hope oversteps the ambiguity of world and subject that psychoanalysis is, precisely, poised to tackle in the therapeutic setting. In other words, can the positive aspects of what is encountered in psychoanalytic experience simply be drawn off from the latter and shaped into models for ethical and political subjects? Kristeva does attend to how the abstractedness of the symbolic and the blind fate of the semiotic show up in some of the foremost social and political ills of Western cultures: xenophobia, racism, nationalism, mysogeny, and sexism. In other words, she draws out the good *and* bad news that psychoanalysis brings to social and political thought. Does this prevent psychoanalysis from overreaching itself on this terrain? These questions are crucial if we are to grasp the scope and significance of Kristeva's ethical and political thinking. It may be that she shows both how psychoanalysis can be developed into an ethics and how its work brings us important insights into social and political phenomena, insights from which some solutions can be drawn. However, it is important to consider how far these solutions go. This is a criterion in the following reading of *Strangers to Ourselves* and *Nations Without Nationalism*.

The chapter develops in two parts, attending in turn to the book on ethics and the collection of her interventions into political debate on nationhood in France. The argument made here is that the two works presuppose the trilogy, and can be read as contenders to the title of providing an ethics and politics that accommodate the subject of psychoanalysis, which is to say, the Freudian unconscious. In other words, the ethical and political writings present a claim, from the psychoanalytic standpoint, about how modern secular institutions and discourses can make good on some of their failings in respect of the connections of self and society.

Strangers to Ourselves in fact develops the claim that psychoanalysis itself provides a basis for an ethics that has political implications. The ethics appears in the thought that the foreigner/stranger—"*l'étranger*"—is *the* exemplary figure on social and political terrain for the experience of otherness known to psychoanalysis. For Kristeva, then, the foreigner/stranger becomes the ground for working out a guarantor for nonreified identity and difference in social and political relations. It is a conception that has received much attention in the literature on her thought (for example, Oliver 1993a, Elliott 1992, McAfee 2000). The current discussion of her ethics of psychoanalysis looks closely at what leads her to the thought of *l'étranger,* asking what psychoanalysis contributes to comprehending the structure of being with others. So there is a long discussion in this chapter of her return to and extension of Freud's notion of the "uncanny," and the work it is doing in the presentation of her own conception of the "strange."[1]

Strangers to Ourselves also claims that the ethics of psychoanalysis implies a politics. *Nations Without Nationalism* develops this thought in its proposal of a "new" cosmopolitanism adjusted to the contemporary shape of Western nation states. The multinational society today is one in which mounting immigration brings together ever more diverse peoples. The traditional national project of assimilation to the host culture and language is surpassed by the strongly asserted particularities of immigrant peoples. Kristeva's emphasis on this development arises from how it has impressed itself on the inhabitants of France, her "host" country, but the demand it makes on rethinking the nation applies more widely. *Nations Without Nationalism* then faces the challenge of articulating what can ensure the transcending of particularities in multinational societies.

Kristeva presents the social body as a transitional dynamic, a view that offsets the need for an abstractly universal foundation for social bonds, and seeks to undermine the reflex that posits such a foundation in order to overcome the tendency of particulars—individuals and groups—either to pose as universal or to close in on themselves. The social body as a transitional dynamic is supported by the process of idealization known from *Tales of Love* and the mechanisms of identification set out in *Strangers to Ourselves*. It steers a path between the problem of intolerance for social others and the recourse to an abstract universal that means, and fails, to deal with this problem. The failure lies in overreaching the particularities rather than binding them in to the collective, so that bonding is failed. The conception of political binding that Kristeva introduces makes identification with an "ideal instance" central to the transcendence of particularities. The book can therefore be read as bringing the new amatory world known from *Black Sun* on to social and political terrain. In other words, it appears that a social symbolic form of the dynamic of idealization known from *Tales of Love* might be the symbolic value that would uphold social and political life in contemporary nation-states.

The analysis of Kristeva's ethical and political thought undertaken here comes to show that its psychoanalytic dimension is larger than is usually recognized. This also means, as we will see, that it is more restricting in respect of the hope of developing a Kristevan ethics as part of the search for an ethics responsive to the sociohistorical particularities of social and political experience, such as gender, race, and class. It cannot, therefore, respond to the desire for real otherness and futurity that supports and propels such projects. This limitation of her ethics of psychoanalysis is demonstrated, below, by means of a *reductio ad absurdum* argument. The argument begins as an attempt to restore what is missing from the psychoanalytic viewpoint without, however, departing from it, but the attempt fails. This strategy brings to light the scope and limitations of Kristeva's ethical and political thought. First, however, it needs to be shown just how Kristeva seeks to establish the role of psychoanalysis on this terrain.

The Ethics of Psychoanalysis

The apparent justification for writing a book on ethics despite the ambiguities of the trilogy lies in Kristeva's discovery of a specific locus that links psychoanalytic and contemporary social experience: the experience of the "foreigner/stranger." The latter is presented as a dynamic of return into the innermost recesses of the self-as-other, provoked by, and, it is claimed, sustaining the utmost confrontation with the other as other. Initially, the foreigner/stranger is the exemplar for this dynamic owing to immediate peculiarities that point beyond themselves: "those eyes, those lips, those cheek bones, that skin unlike others, all that distinguishes him and reminds one that there is *someone* there" (Kristeva 1988, 3). Although this suggests that the experience of the foreigner/stranger instantiates the moment of transcendence in intersubjectivity, it is crucial to Kristeva's thought that this experience encompasses, rather than foreclosing, the negative aspects of the confrontation with the strangeness of self and other. The negative aspects turn on the "perturbed logic" of the heterogeneous subject, in which the drive features largely. *Strangers to Ourselves* argues that the dynamic of transcendence that can encompass that negative feature is the ultimate foundation for *being with others.*

Since Kristeva constructs this argument in a very particular way, it is useful briefly to outline the structure of the book. The first chapter of *Strangers to Ourselves* presents an unsparing, and undaunted, review of the contemporary experience of foreigners in modern nation-states, a phenomenology of variants of both the recoil from the foreigner, on the one hand, and the foreigner's shield against that recoil and its origins, including their own "origins," on the other. Further on, Kristeva asserts the foreigner's tendency to adopt an antinomial attitude in the host country, which she puts down to an exclusion from and refusal of the symbolics of the law. The antinomial attitude draws the unconscious sympathy of contemporary citizens in nation states on account of the fact that national borders specify in such a clear-cut manner who does and who does not have rights. In sum, the foreigner is both a psychological and a political symptom. This standing of the foreigner/stranger is central to the final working out of the book's ethical and political thought. However, the approach to that thought also requires a temporary suspension of the legal category of the foreigner dominant in the world of nation-states, since the latter tends to obscure the substantial aspects of foreignness. The strategy of suspending what is today the dominant category of the foreigner permits Kristeva to unfold an archaeology of the notion of the foreigner from Greek through Hellenistic, Jewish, early Christian, Medieval, and Renaissance worlds. This allows her to draw out moments when a cosmopolitan thought arose in relation to these variants on the experience and negotiation of the foreigner/stranger: classical stoic cosmopolitanism, ethical cosmopolitanism in the Pauline Church, and the "inner cosmopolitanism" built up in the Renaissance literary genre of the voyage. The variants on the foreigner/stranger are ultimately sublated in a conception of the stranger derived from psychoanalysis, and this, in turn, leads to Kristeva's argument for a "new cosmopolitanism" in the world of modern nation-states.

Her argument requires, of course, that the legal category central to contemporary experience be readmitted, and its readmission forms the pivot of the text at the point where the archaeology of solutions to the reception of foreigners in historical worlds gives way to a genealogy of contemporary thought on "strangeness." The genealogy begins with the moment at which the modern legal category first comes into clear view: the emergence of Enlightenment thought and the specific working out of its ideology of equality in the French *Declaration of the Rights of Man and Citizen* (1789). That is the point at which we enter Kristeva's text here. Her emphasis on the import of the *Declaration* takes cognizance of political reflection on how its principles failed to ensure what they were meant to promise. Especially important here is Arendt's analysis of the drawbacks of the *Declaration* as they played themselves out in history, and her rejection of the conception of the rights of man. The reference to Arendt provides the way into Kristeva's translation of the distinction between rights of man and rights of citizen into a "splitting." This move, rooted of course in psychoanalytic discoveries, is to be the basis for working out the ethical and political role of "strangeness" in modern democratic societies.

The structure of *Strangers to Ourselves* therefore presents us with another fragmentary minor history of modernity, turning this time on the notion of the foreigner in Western history and on concepts of strangeness that appear in the unfolding of secular modernity. Once again, Kristeva is not generating an all-encompassing philosophy of history. She is focused on the significance of culture: "our predecessors do not only make up a history; they constitute a cultural distance that is to be preserved and developed, a distance on the basis of which one might temper and modify the simplistic attitudes of rejection or indifference, as well as the arbitrary or utilitarian decisions that today regulate relationships between foreigners" (1988, 104). *Strangers to Ourselves* therefore seeks out resources for preserving and developing a "cultural distance" in the face of the brutality of the commonplace response to the problem of belonging and not belonging bequeathed by the modern form of political institutions in which the scope of rights is coextensive with national boundaries. It appears that her rejection of philosophy of history is tied to a deep suspicion of the conception of *Volksgeist* (spirit of the people) in post-Kantian German thought. One might also conjecture that, owing to the tie in German thought between the *Volk* as she interprets it and philosophy of history, she finds the latter atavistic in contemporary conditions where "we are all in the process of becoming foreigners" (104). The very choice of the foreigner/stranger as the subject matter for her social and political thought points up her rejection of philosophy of history in its most familiar, "Hegelian" form. The objective here is to show that *Strangers to Ourselves* presents a point of convergence of the social and political, psychoanalytic, and aesthetic levels of her thought, and therefore contains in and of itself a fruitful nexus for evaluating the social and political implications of the *oeuvre*. Once her genealogy of thought on strangeness in the modern world is in place, Kristeva returns to the psychoanalytic conception of the "uncanny" for her demonstration of the linkage between the psychoanalytic, aesthetic, social, and political levels of her writings. This chapter follows that order of presentation before turning to an inquiry into the limitations of the ethics developed in *Strangers to Ourselves*.

The Declaration of the Rights of Man and Citizen: A "Splitting"

Strangers to Ourselves makes a point of emphasizing our contemporary inheritance from the French *Declaration of the Rights of Man and Citizen*—composed by "heirs to the Enlightenment, and to the philosophers' reflections on natural and political man." Kristeva claims for the *Declaration* the status of being the "unsurpassed touchstone for those freedoms to be enjoyed by any human being on our planet" (1988, 148). Yet its failure to ensure those freedoms is nothing external to the thought it contains on natural and political man. Kristeva's argument for the need to translate the rights-of-man/rights-of-citizen distinction into a "splitting" first points to the slippage that occurs from Article I to Article III of the *Declaration*. The universal notion "rights of man" gives way to a guarantee of freedom and equality of rights by political association. "Far from proclaiming a natural egalitarianism, the *Declaration* at once inserts equality in the grid of 'political' and 'natural' human institutions and more precisely within the scope of the *nation*. The national political body must act for all. The progressive and democratic aspect of that principle strikes the commentator and yet questions him. In fact, it is within the once constituted national grouping that all persons can remain free and equal of right. Thus the free and equal man is, *de facto,* the citizen" (149).

The *Declaration* both posits and collapses the distinction between rights of man and rights of citizen. One outcome of this collapse is the national legacy that "served as guarantee for Nazi criminality, at the beginning at least" (151). Kristeva returns to Arendt for the recognition that the notion of the rights of man fails both to ensure the detection of crimes against humanity and to answer the question of what rights the stateless could have. The "rights of man" has no resilience in the world of Nazism and its aftermath. As Arendt put it in *The Origins of Totalitarianism:* "The world found nothing sacred in the abstract nakedness of being human [. . .]. It seems that a man who is nothing but a man has lost the very qualities which make it possible for other people to treat him as a fellow man" (Arendt 1979, 299–300; cited in Kristeva 1988, 151–152). In contrast with the French *Declaration*, which links the rights of man to nature, the American *Declaration* relates them to God. Notwithstanding the possibility that a transcendental, divine guarantee may be more resilient in times of danger, Kristeva remains with the distinction made by the French *Declaration* in order to interrogate its advantages and the prospects it holds out for a secular support for social bonding. Accepting that the conception of the rights of man is an abstraction, she nonetheless views it as a recognition of universal human dignity, and sets out to substantiate this universality with the resources of psychoanalysis. Her opening strategy is to separate principle and content "in the spirit of eighteenth-century humanism" (1988, 152). The principle must be retained because it postulates universality as immanent *in* the speaking being and because it can not only be centered in but also goes beyond the reality of political institutions. Moreover, preserving the principle of universal human dignity is a condition for modifying its content. On her view, the abstract content "natural man" must be replaced with a content that reflects how humanity *actually* manifests itself. Psychoanalysis is far from eighteenth-century optimism. "One would notice, in addition to the social propensity for association and life, murderous surges, jouissance of death, pleasures of parting and narcissism, carrier waves of the social fabric's fragmentation but also that of the very identity of the individuals' body and their psychic space. The destructive tendencies of society come together with those that destroy human nature as well as human biology and the individual's identity" (152–153). We hear an echo in this statement of the thought in *Black Sun* that humankind in the twentieth century has had to face the explosion of death in the realm of spirit (see chapter 6, above).

Given this confrontation with how humanity manifests itself, the content of the universality of humanity can only be modified by making it more complex. This means that there is a demand, and not merely a justification, to go beyond rights (and so law courts) to desires and symbolic values. Finally, Kristeva contends that the task of modifying the content of universal human dignity "falls within the province of ethics and psychoanalysis" (1988, 153). Ethics and psychoanalysis are not two spheres with different functions in this task. Psychoanalysis is one component required for the fulfillment of an ethics that "should reveal, discuss and spread a concept of human dignity, wrested from the euphoria of classic humanists, and laden with the alienations, dramas, and dead ends of our condition as human beings" (154). Kristeva's psychoanalytic thought comes out here as a transhistorical conception of the human condition, and this is of course what impels her argument for modifying the concept of universal human dignity in a manner that will have it embrace "strangeness." The second component of this ethics is "education," a new, or newly formulated, facet of her writings. Its meaning must be sought in the way in which the Freudian notion of the unconscious, itself, turns up in Kristeva's minor history of the foreigner/stranger, and so in the context of Kristeva's attention to the social and political struggles of the modern world, and the irrationalities they display.

First of all, Kristeva's genealogy includes an analysis of a notion of education handed down from the development of German thought from Kant to Hegel. *Die Bildung* combines the meanings of education, cultivation, self-formation, and culture. On her account, this expansive conception of education as *Bildung* gains a certain stability as "German national culture," anchored, with Herder, in "the genius of the language." Herder's "national genius" initially binds the conception of *Volksgeist* (spirit of the people) to that of *Bildung* in the sense of process of formation. *Volksgeist* is rooted in a language "seen as a constant process of alteration and surpassing of itself" (1988, 179). As a moral conception detached from any biological, scientific, or political value, *Volksgeist* is attached to "culture" as an *autonomous* sphere. Kristeva evidently wishes to press the need of recognizing this autonomy owing to what she views as the resubmission of "culture" in German to a particular historicopolitical trajectory. For, once *Bildung* is removed from the notion of *Volksgeist,* the national genius has another fate. *Volksgeist* "becomes a conservative, reactional concept," "exalted of its original purity or consigned to the ineffable" (179). Although the notion of *Volksgeist* is the real target here, Kristeva does not attempt to recover *Bildung* as "process of formation," a notion that, it seems, cannot be extricated from the positing of German national language and culture. In Kristeva's view, then, the complex of education and culture in currents of post-Kantian German thought becomes invested in the national-political struggle in Germany, and shares in the irrationalities of that struggle. We will see, in chapter 8 below, the deep reasons for Kristeva's insistence on the autonomy of culture. Whether or not she is justified in collapsing the different appearances of the conception of *Volksgeist* in German thought into the reactional concept that does develop is in question in this chapter, however. Kristeva's endorsement of the French conception of culture (*la culture*) might show us what fills the role of education in *Strangers to Ourselves*. Whether this is so can only be decided by considering the place of *la culture* in her genealogy. The meaning of *la culture* emerges through an analysis of problems intrinsic to the birth of nationalism in the French Revolution.

It is helpful, first, to recall the phenomenological treatment of the foreigner in the opening pages of *Strangers to Ourselves,* where Kristeva stresses the otherness of the foreigner as one without permanent structure—as transient. "An otherness barely touched upon and that already moves away." The question becomes what path of education can lend itself to such impermanence? Perhaps education turns on achieving "the *harmonious* repetition of the differences that it [transient otherness] implies and spreads" (1988, 3). Kristeva's survey of the treatment of foreigners in the French Revolution sets the scene for her return to this thought. On her analysis, the fate of foreigners in the period of the French Revolution displays a transition from a cosmopolitan program, tied to the principle of human rights, to a rejection of foreigners. The transition does not simply provide a historical image of the oscillation between, in her words, a welcome that becomes assimilation and a rejection up to the point of persecution. Rather, the trajectory of the stance toward foreigners in the French Revolution reflects the birth of nationalism itself. The oscillation between assimilation and rejection is henceforth characteristic of nation-states.

The beginning of the French Revolution is marked by the welcoming stance that includes foreigners in the principle of human rights. "For the first time in the history of mankind, a statute of (honorary) integration was voted, which, in the name of human universality, recognized as *French* those who had done the most for mankind. . . . A decree was approved on August 26 [1792], as proposed by Chénier, conferring the title of French Citizen to those foreign writers and learned men who, 'in various areas of the world, have caused human reason to ripen and blazed the trails of liberty'" (1988, 156). Nonetheless, the French welcome collapses and is ultimately inverted under the pressure of the Revolutionary Wars. Foreigners become "foreign agents," suspicious; their clubs are disbanded; a law of 1794 excludes them from public service and rights. Kristeva finds that this is the birth of the restrictive and potentially totalitarian nationalist thought. "The scaffold took care of the cosmopolitan's lot" (160). Now, although the universal spirit of the time is located in its cosmopolitan trend, the latter is paradoxical by virtue of being tied to the project of spreading revolutionary ideas, for others cannot be included in the principle of human rights before those ideas are spread, and their being spread through military expansion induces the circumstances of the rejection of foreigners. Thus assimilation and rejection are not two poles that the revolutionary ideas of the time may fall into, as though a middle way could be recovered from the cosmopolitan trends of the time. Rather, the rejection of foreigners is an outcome of the paradox internal to spreading revolutionary ideas. Thus Kristeva's question: "Does not cosmopolitanism, eccentric by definition, tend toward extremism?" (160). In sum, the cosmopolitan project is not something that can be recovered from the events and ideas which form the precursors to the birth of nationalism.

It may seem obvious that the cosmopolitan ideal is undermined by the tie between the spread of revolutionary ideas and military expansion. After all, we have the textual history of German philosophical support (even in the midst of French military expansion) for the significance of the revolutionary upheavals in France, a support that turned to focus on revolutionary *reason* (see, especially, Fichte 1793). Kristeva herself devotes the final paragraphs of her discussion of the Revolution to the dedication to revolutionary reason reflected in Thomas Paine's opposition to the execution of the French king. Her review of Paine's fate is repeated here in order to illuminate the link she makes between French "culture" and a certain cosmopolitan ideal. For Paine, the king is subject to punishment as an enemy but, once deposed, he is not excluded from the rights of man. He may lose his liberty but not his life. The plea is quashed by Marat's declaration that it is based on religious principle. Paine himself is later arrested, eluding the guillotine only to live unlauded in America, and to die, in Kristeva's words, "deprived of rest." The recognition of the complexity of Paine's fate leads Kristeva to refine the meaning of cosmopolitanism. "Of what place could he be, if not the place where a crisis brewed, an explosion or a revolution took place? Deprived of rest, without conclusion, 'cosmopolitan'—in the sense of a permanent shattering . . ." (1988, 167). The figure of Paine as representative of a cosmopolitan ideal saturated with impermanence represents the point of transition between Kristeva's recovery of the meaning of the French *Declaration*—"political and natural man"—and the chapter in which she homes in on the conception of universality that is to embrace "strangeness." This is what turns the rights-of-man/rights-of-citizen distinction into a "splitting." What is crucial is that Paine's cosmopolitanism recalls the conception of negativity that Kristeva promotes as *la culture,* and which appears throughout her *oeuvre* in repeated returns to Diderot's text, *Rameau's Nephew*. Paine is the spectral bearer of such a negativity carried into the French Revolution, and it is Kristeva's view that Diderot and Paine provide us with the negativity that is intrinsic to *modern* cosmopolitanism. In a remarkable section entitled "Might Culture Be French?" she affirms *la culture*—a polymorphic culture—insofar as it maintains this negativity beyond xenophobic and assimilating trends.

> [Such a culture] does not always withstand the dogmatic attempts of those—economically or ideologically disappointed—who restore their "ownness" and "identity" by rejecting others. The fact remains nonetheless that in France such attempts are immediately and more than elsewhere seen as a betrayal of *culture,* as a loss of spirit. And even if, at certain times in history, such a healthy cultural reaction tends to be forgotten, one feels like counting on it so as to maintain France as a land of asylum. Not as a

> house of welcome but as a ground for adventure. There are foreigners who wish to be lost as such in the perverseness of French culture in order to be reborn not with a new identity but within the enigmatic dimension of human experience that, with and beyond belonging, is called freedom. In French: culture. (1988, 147–148)

Thus, on the one hand, education in German, *Bildung,* apparently narrows in meaning, losing the conception of process of formation in order to stand for *German national* culture, so that there can be no doubt about where the foreigner arises and what this figure means: the disruption of national culture. On the other hand, Kristeva claims that in French culture "the 'foreigner as such' becomes neutralized" (147). *La culture* is the fount of and sustains resistance to fixed national identity because the disruption of identities is internal to it, as Diderot's drama of the "self-perversion" of values lays out. Thus *la culture* lends itself to the impermanent—transient—otherness disclosed in Kristeva's phenomenological treatment of the foreigner. This does not mean, however, that *la culture* fills out the conception of education necessary for Kristeva's ethics. For *la culture* is not only a permanent resistance but the permanently volatile element of formation.

The penultimate chapter of *Strangers to Ourselves,* turning to German post-Enlightenment philosophy, establishes the historicophilosophical context required for an illumination of the import of the Freudian unconscious in Kristeva's ethics. Kant is introduced as universal pacifist, presumably as the one who grasped the full significance of the military expansion of revolutionary ideas. Hegel is acknowledged and criticized for his thinking through of strangeness in "the Hegelian Negativity—which at the same time restored and systematized, unleashed and bound the power of the Other, against and within the consciousness of the Same" (1988, 169). Kristeva signals that her debt to Hegel will be limited to one moment of his project in the *Phenomenology of Spirit,* the moment where *Bildung,* apparently the path of identity-formation, is superseded by *Kultur,* which captures the volatile element of formation. Only the moment in which the philosopher presents the world of spirit become foreign to itself (*der sich entfremdete Geist*), that is to say, only the recognition of the dynamic of the self-perversion of values, will be retained from Hegel's phenomenology of spirit. It is Hegel's merit to have discovered and unfolded the consciousness of absolute inversion in *Rameau's Nephew.* He is commended, then, for his reading of Diderot. This, for Kristeva, is the highpoint of the system in which the philosopher accedes to polyphony (146). All else—all beyond that moment in the *Phenomenology of Spirit* and the system more widely—is thought-identity. "Indeed, Culture in Hegel's sense, in its scission and essential strangeness, proceeds by way of *disunion* and *contradiction,* which it unifies in its wrenching discourse; but the latter merely judges 'by reducing everything to the self in its aridity' and cannot grasp the substantial content of thought" (146). Thought-identity judges culture to be unable to grasp the substantial content of thought. For Kristeva, *Kultur* is to be recovered from this judgment, a standpoint thoroughly consistent with her turn to art. Nonetheless, the question remains, how can "I" in Kristeva's version of "the I that is We" and "the We that is I" go beyond a psychoanalytic insight into the self-as-other, which is to say, beyond recognition of the subject's full share of destructiveness and other tendencies requiring modulation?[2] How can "I" encompass the ethical? Through what education, what leading out?

The worry is that the ethics unfolded from the conception of the foreigner/stranger who is "without permanent structure," on the one hand, and the intrinsic foreignness in "culture," on the other, settles a generalization of strangeness at the heart of social and political experience, so that the desire for real otherness and futurity is dispelled for the sake of pressing the need of a recognition of the radical nature of Freud's thought. Kant and Hegel are introduced as "stages on the way to the 'Copernican revolution' that the discovery of the Freudian unconscious amounted to" (1988, 169). It appears that Kristeva's view of the radical nature of the Freudian discovery, a view she holds without anxiety, posits an epistemic and ontological event that is to bear all the weight of questions about otherness, and in fact leads to a mere generalization of strangeness. The question that needs to be pursued is whether her return to the Freudian "uncanny" actually mitigates this impression. Or, as one might put it, does the Freudian notion of the uncanny lead to a conception of education that opens this text up to those who cannot enjoy *la culture?* What this conception of education is cannot be clarified until Kristeva's treatment of the uncanny has been thoroughly explored. But *Strangers to Ourselves* now announces its approach to the outer borders of its own attempt to orient its thought in respect of the country in which Kristeva writes. It draws a "tentative line" from Kant to Herder and Freud, "so as better to point out the political and ethical impact of the Freudian breakthrough, or rather to outline an area where that impact might be thought out by others, by those who are foreign to the present book" (169).

The chapter which draws that tentative line, and which leads up to an interpretation of Freud on the uncanny, bears the title: *"Might not universality be. . . our own foreignness?"* The title might provoke the immediate suspicion that Kristeva will propose an essential strangeness of the self that remains forever above and beyond the specific challenges of social and political experience and struggle, one abstracted, then, from the arena in which the need of real otherness and futurity is felt. Alternatively, everything may depend upon what crossing the ellipsis might be, and what might be crossing the ellipsis, in reading Kristeva's text.

First, however, Kristeva's genealogy tracks the different ways in which the emergent idea of the nation is related to a conception of the foreigner or strangeness in postrevolutionary German thought. Kant's place in this genealogy is that of a practical cosmopolitanism that posed the union of mankind while respecting the right of separateness on the domain of foreignness. His is a cosmopolitanism "understood as coexistence of the differences that are imposed by the technique of international relations on the one hand and political morality on the other" (1988, 173). In contrast with Kant's political morality, and even more strongly with the Rousseauan contractual concept underpinning the modern nation-state, another conception of nationalism develops on the basis of a *mystical idea* that develops most fully in Germany. The notion of national community (*Gemeinschaft*) is, she says, "not a political one but organic, evolutionary, at the same time vital and metaphysical—the expression of a nearly irrational and indiscernible spirit that is summed up by the word *Gemeinsinn*. A supreme value, such a national spirit, *Volksgeist*, is not, with Herder, biological, 'scientific,' or even political, but essentially moral. It is only after 1806 that this *cultural* concept of 'nation' became *political* and became invested in the national-political struggle" (176–177).[3]

The cultural, "essentially moral" idea of the nation is mystical because it is the expression of an indiscernible spirit. The Romantic perception that the Enlightenment is "hollow," and its consequent withdrawal from universalist abstraction, are carried forth into the political idea of the nation emergent in Germany. Kristeva's objective in taking up the meaning of *Volksgeist* as national genius (Herder) and the meaning of *Bildung* as German national culture is not, however, simply to have *la culture* triumph over *Bildung*. Rather, the objective is to reiterate Freud's Romantic filiation. For the notion of *Volksgeist* at first exhibits a restoration of the particular which encompasses strangeness. The indiscernible spirit is "rooted in a language that is seen as a constant process of alteration and surpassing of itself" (1988, 179). Freud's project is now approached in terms of its connections with that development. "The localization of foreignness thus recognized and even positivized in national language and culture will be repeated within the Freudian unconscious, concerning which Freud specified that it followed the logic of each national language." Romantic occupation with "the supernatural, parapsychology, madness, dreams, the obscure forces of the *fatum*" reveals to Kristeva the relation of their integration of strangeness to the desire to grasp and domesticate the strange (180). The integration finds its reversal in various forms of a heterogeneous notion of the unconscious (Carus, Schubert, Schopenhauer, Hartmann). Finally, Freud takes up both the integration and its reversal, removing the domestication of the former and the externality of the latter. "With the Freudian notion of the unconscious the involution of the strange in the psyche loses its pathological aspect and integrates within the assumed unity of human beings an *otherness* that is both biological *and* symbolic and becomes an integral part of the *same*. Henceforth the foreigner is neither a race nor a nation. The foreigner is neither glorified as a secret *Volksgeist* nor banished as disruptive of rationalist urbanity. Uncanny, foreignness is within us; we are our own foreigners, we are divided" (181).

Unsurprisingly, the drive, understood as first inscription of an otherness that is both biological and symbolic, comes to guide Kristeva's interpretation of the nuances of Freud's recognition of the "other scene." Indeed the wider reception of her conception of *strangers to ourselves,* and the hope that it can be adopted as a resource for social and political thought on otherness, may not have given sufficient consideration to her interpretation of those nuances. For, Kristeva reminds us, among Freud's commitments was "his concern to face the other's discontent as ill-ease in the continuous presence of the 'other scene' within us" (181). With Kristeva, "my discontent in living with the other—my strangeness, his strangeness—rests on the perturbed logic that governs this strange bundle of drive and language, of nature and symbol, constituted by the unconscious, always already shaped by the other" (181–182). It already appears that, on a Freudian view, the fate of the confrontation with otherness is guided by the dynamics of the self-as-other, so that the negotiation of the unexpected "outside element" in the experience of the foreigner/stranger might only be, at best, an integration in the "same."

Yet, there is a moment in *Strangers to Ourselves* where Kristeva seems to indicate another possibility. For, with Freud, the unfolding of psychoanalysis, the most internalized moment of Western historicality, has a dimension set apart from the Romanticist filiation of his thought: "such an intimist restoring of the foreigner's good name [neither glorified nor banished] undoubtedly bears the biblical tones of a foreign God or of a Foreigner apt to reveal God" (1988, 181).[4] There follows Kristeva's reference to Freud's personal life—"a Jew wandering from Galicia to Vienna and London, with stopovers in Paris, Rome and New York (to mention only a few of the key stages of his encounters with political and cultural foreignness)" (181). These remarks refer not only to Freud's personal encounters with political and cultural foreignness, but to "the tones of a foreign God" that are carried into the project. It is unclear, however, what Kristeva means to indicate by this, since she does not pursue what the tones of a foreign God come to mean to Freud at the end of his life's work, in *Moses and Monotheism* (1939). This question is approached further on, within the discussion of the nature of the limitations of Kristeva's ethics of psychoanalysis. Kristeva herself presses the thought that this personal aspect of Freud's life affords him a disposition to embrace the ill-ease of living with the "other scene." Her eye is on the ethical impact of psychoanalysis that *Strangers to Ourselves* might bequeath to those foreign to the book, for its working out "elsewhere." "It is through unraveling transference—the major dynamics of otherness, of love/hatred for the other, of the foreign component of our psyche—that, *on the basis of the other,* I become reconciled with *my own otherness-foreignness,* that I play on it and live by it. Psychoanalysis is then experienced as a journey into the strangeness of the other and of oneself, toward *an ethics of respect for the irreconcilable*" (1988, 182, emphasis added).

The transference—occasion and setting of the dynamic informing her new model of the individual in *Tales of Love*—is here the key to the role of psychoanalysis in her ethics. In the transference (and countertransference) there can be a coming to terms with the "other scene" only because an other, negotiating "their" strangeness, *is there.* It is not, then, simply as an *insight* into the self-as-other that psychoanalysis has a role in ethics. This would restrict its role to the theoretical one it had in *Revolution in Poetic Language* (see chapter 1, above). Rather, psychoanalysis is itself ethical as a journey which, in discovery of and reconciliation with one's own strangeness, renders the content of universal human dignity more complex. "One" might tolerate a foreigner on these grounds. The question Kristeva raises is, will this enlightenment, this "small truth" of subjectivity, allow the people of our time "to put up with one another as irreducible, because they are desiring, desirable, mortal, and death-bearing?" (1988, 182). Her implicit dismissal of any attempt to generate an ethic of toleration from abstract universal principles does not only locate the ethical in a concrete moment of transcendence. It has this transcendence rest on the negative aspects of the confrontation with otherness/strangeness: discontent, ill-ease. The ethic of toleration is generated from the concrete individual precisely on the grounds of what rationalist urbanity finds disruptive. It is ultimately respect for the irreconcilable, and what makes this possible is the journey that the transference enables, provoking the recognition "we are divided."

It turns out that Kristeva's translation of the rights-of-man/rights-of-citizen distinction into a "splitting" has modified the content of universal human dignity by replacing the assumed balance of the individual necessary to the moral and legal concept of the person with inner strangeness. That "we are divided" is the source of our discontent and ill-ease in sociation. Yet to discover and be reconciled with ourselves as "shaped by the other" is to carry forth the awareness, not that the other is irreducible to me, but that their strangeness is not coincidental with mine. The foreigner/stranger is the trigger but not the origin of my ill-ease. That thought expresses the only common irreducibility of strangeness. A conception of universality like this one entails an emphasis in ethics on particularities understood as *singularities* rather than determinations of social and political life that are shared in such a way that they become the site of social and political struggle. The stress on singularities remains a stumbling-block for attempts to develop Kristeva's ethical standpoint into a resource for working through the complexities of the ethics or politics of difference within, for example, feminist thought. Kristeva's thought posits difference, *qua* the inner strangeness whose irreducibility is what is shared, as the ground for "the I that is We" and the "We that is I." All the same, the oft-quoted passages from *Strangers to Ourselves* such as the one above, portraying psychoanalysis as a journey toward an ethic of respect for the irreconcilable, do not decidedly express the contribution of psychoanalysis to an ethics/politics of difference, precisely because it is *discontent, ill-ease* which leads into the ethics of respect for difference.[5]

There is a tendency to sidestep the weight of Kristeva's insistence upon the need of accommodating "the negative" in ethics. That is to say, her psychoanalytic thought of inner strangeness cannot be used in the attempt to work out an ethics or politics of difference without considering the implications of the desideratum that the intolerability of the "other scene" *must be crossed.* And this is failed if the dynamics of the unconscious are bypassed. The chapter title of *Strangers to Ourselves* which poses the question "might not universality be... our own foreignness?" therefore suggests that no universality can be reached except through the experience of crossing a difference marked by *in*tolerance, a double and reciprocal intolerance whose two sides are irreducible to one another. The pattern for this intolerance is, as we will see, set by Freud's unconscious/conscious opposition. In brief, the question of what it might be for the ethical impact of the Freudian breakthrough to be thought out elsewhere is not really approached if Kristeva's return to Freud's thought on the uncanny is neglected.

The Uncanny

This section returns to the details of Kristeva's attention to Freud's essay on "The Uncanny" (1919). For her, the essay goes beyond the psychological phenomenon of uncanny strangeness in order to "acknowledge itself as an investigation into *anguish* [*Angst*] generally speaking and, in a fashion that is even more universal, into the *dynamics of the unconscious*" (1988, 182). Her reminder that the significance of psychic functioning appears in Freud's essay is examined first, here, for the sake of stressing how the intolerability of the "other scene" is central to her ethics. We will find, however, that the idea that the self and other are irreducible because they are desiring, desirable, mortal, and death-bearing cannot accommodate much less respond to the felt desire for real otherness and futurity in current social and political debates. The discussion therefore goes on to readdress Kristeva's view of Freud's thought on anxiety (*Angst*) in order to consider whether a certain limitation in her reception of that thought might be redressed in a way that could open her ethics of psychoanalysis up to that desire. As will be seen, however, the attempt forms a *reductio ad absurdum* argument which in fact works to reveal that her ethics of psychoanalysis has an intrinsic limitation which undermines attempts to use her thought as a resource in the search for an ethics or politics of difference that retains a conception of particularities irreducible to Kristevan singularities: the history of differences that are shared in the sociohistorical shaping of groups.

Kristeva's detailed attention to "The Uncanny" first notes, following the course of that essay, that Freud restores to the term *das Unheimliche* its intimacy with the familiar (*das Heimliche*). *Das Un-heimliche* contains the "known of old and long familiar" that is "concealed and kept out of sight" (1919, 224–225). The long *familiar* is "not known." As Freud puts it, "the prefix '*un*' [un-] is the token of repression" (245). In sum, what shows up in the uncanny is repression, for the uncanny instantiates the return of the repressed. The idea of the return of the repressed expresses an unusual temporal tension of past, present, and future. The following discussion of Kristeva's view of the uncanny seeks to evaluate her ethics by examining just where the emphasis lies in her own consideration of that temporal tension.

Focusing initially on the mode of the past, we find that what is disturbing in the uncanny is the reemergence of something long familiar that is "not known." Kristeva calls it the *improper past* of identity. To stop here would be to say that the uncanny *just is* the occasion of a resurfacing of the foreign component of the psyche that is "mine." As Kristeva puts it in a section heading, "the other is my ('own and proper') unconscious" (1988, 183). Starting at the point where the past is apparently isolated, the guiding question becomes "what 'familiar'? what 'past'?" The question draws Freud's thought on the archaic, narcissistic self into the study of the uncanny. This is most evident in considering one of the propitiating circumstances for the experience of uncanniness, "the double," for the double is related to the archaic dominion of the pleasure principle. In *Civilization and Its Discontents* (1930) Freud's inquiry into the emergence of the adult sense of self leads him to propose that the nucleus of the ego is formed in a phantasmatic resolution of the threat of destructive elements. The first form of the ego, "the pure pleasure ego," arises in and through a psychic arrangement of the sources of pleasure and unpleasure: all pleasure within and all unpleasure without. Under pressure from reality such a program of pure pleasure comes to be repressed and to exert its force unseen, remaining a mechanism that the ego may deploy unconsciously in order to shore up its organization against a threat (1930, chapter 1). What is disturbing in "the double," that is to say, the reason why it is a pretext for uncanny strangeness, does not lie in the pressure of an unfulfilled wish under the dominion of the pleasure principle. It lies, rather, in the "malevolent double" that is built up in the archaic narcissistic self's projection outward of *its* intolerable share of destruction.

The factor of malevolence connects the double with the second psychoanalytic notion that Freud introduces into the essay: repetition. The uncanny exhibits the compulsion to repeat. We recall that Freud's recognition of repetition-compulsion contributed to what led him to speculate on a thanatic drive, or the primacy of the destructive wave of the drive, in *Beyond the Pleasure Principle* (1920). The uncanny involves the operation of drive impulses "beyond" and overruling the pleasure principle. Finally, overlooking the import of anxiety for the moment, the last psychoanalytic notion that Freud introduces into his essay is that of the unconscious. Kristeva presses the point that the uncanny manifests the very dynamic of psychic functioning: repression and its perviousness. What is in play in the uncanny is neither only the return of the repressed, related to the pleasure principle, nor only drive-compulsion that overrules it, but repression itself, that is to say, the very dynamic that builds up the estranged and keeps it out of sight, and the perviousness of that barrier. Uncanny strangeness emerges in "going through repression"—not through the barrier to the repressed content but through the dynamic of repression *itself.*

Freud's recognition that *das Unheimliche* contains the "known of old and long familiar" does not lead to the revelation of any specific content or the recovery of a past moment. Rather, what shows up in the experience of the uncanny is psychic functioning itself. What Freud's thought subtly turns on, in Kristeva's interpretation, is death, the feminine, and drives as pretexts for going through repression and generating uncanny strangeness. Taking the confrontation with the image of death first, Kristeva reintroduces Freud's observation that religions promise immortality. The promise and the faith that takes it up ("I survive") would be indicators of the unconscious refusal of fatality. At the same time the *fear* of death that attends the confrontation with the image of death reveals that survival is conjoined with its enemy. The form that the uncanny takes in the confrontation with death—apparitions and ghosts—*composes* this ambiguity. The uncanny, then, is the composition of an "impossible end," which enacts the dynamic of repression and its perviousness.

Turning to a further, and connected, pretext for uncanniness, Kristeva considers the feminine, and especially the female genital organs, as source of the strange. Citing Freud: "It often happens that neurotic men declare that they feel there is something uncanny about the female genital organs. This *unheimlisch* place, however, is the entrance to the former *Heim* [home] of all human beings, to the place where each one of us lived once upon a time and in the beginning" (1919, 245). Here the uncanny composes the "impossible beginning" that fascinates and repels (holds off). In Kristeva's summary, where death and the feminine are the sources of uncanniness, what is breaking through is "the end and the beginning that engross and compose us" (1988, 185). The subject is composed in a beginning in which it has no part and an unimaginable end. The constitution of the subject in what is other than it settles the "other than" it at the heart of the subject as its "own" impossibility. In sum, the experience of uncanny strangeness is a resurfacing of the foreign component of the psyche that is "mine" only insofar as "I" cannot consciously frame it. Uncanniness therefore involves a depersonalization of the self. What is more, the dynamic of repression bears not only on the intolerance that builds up the strange (the "other scene") but equally on the intolerance on the part of the other scene for what is in sight. *Das Unheimliche* therefore stages a double intolerability in which the two intolerances are intimately connected but irreducible to one another. Kristeva proceeds from here to the third occasion of the uncanny: the destabilizing drive. Malevolent powers ascribed to another person "would amount to a weaving together of the symbolic and the organic—perhaps *drive* itself, on the border of psyche and biology, overriding the breaking imposed by organic homeostasis" (185). Thus the uncanny composes repression and its perviousness in ghosts and apparitions, in the threatening "place" of entrance to our former *Heim,* and in the malevolent powers of others.

In sum, the various pretexts for uncanniness reveal that the uncanny involves both going through repression (going through the defense) *and* defense. This is why Kristeva calls the uncanny "a paroxystic metaphor of the psychic functioning itself" (1988, 184). That is to say, the double intolerability pertaining to repression is neither made visible nor eclipsed, but *composed.* Intolerance here does not only mean that on one side are ideas inimical to the ego and on the other ideas, above all the idea of death, with no representation in the unconscious. It means that the unconscious *is* the foundation and refusal of the subject, and that the finite signifying subject, having the idea of death, is the break that banishes this refusal and sets up the "other scene." *Strangers to Ourselves*, then, presents a redescription of the heterogeneity of the semiotic and symbolic in and through the concept of uncanny strangeness. What is more, it is only in respect of that double intolerability that the improper past is the "improper" of the proper self. This presentation of the universality of inner strangeness in *Strangers to Ourselves* therefore aims to show how the split subject of psychoanalysis (semiotic and symbolic), and so the other scene, is active in the social and political sphere, where unconscious processes are "carrier waves of the social fabric's fragmentation but also that of the very identity of the individuals' body and their psychic space" (1988, 152).

What Kristeva means to accomplish, then, in her translation of the distinction between the rights of man and the rights of citizen into a splitting, is a demonstration of the need neither to discount nor to give only passing recognition to the double outcome of human finitude. First, human finitude—rooted in birth *and* death—requires recognition of the finite signifying subject, a recognition central to the modern concept of right, and so of the legal person and private property, embodied in secular institutions. This aspect of human finitude, then, is expressed in the conception "rights of citizen." The indispensability of this concept of the individual in the modern world notwithstanding, human finitude—rooted in the impossible beginning *and* the impossible end—equally determines the "improper" facet of the proper self. The self-as-other known to psychoanalysis is disruptive of rational urbanity and encompasses unconscious processes that are carrier waves of the social fabric's fragmentation. The notion "rights of man" is not only inappropriate here. It settles a permanent and prospectless division at the heart of the individual, one that can only be overcome on the ground of this misconceived conflict by subsuming man under citizen, thereby leaving the subject no terrain on which to negotiate the conflict. "Rights of man" is therefore translated into the need of social symbolic resources for working out the destabilizing factor of being *with* others. Freud's conception of the uncanny is a central feature of *Strangers to Ourselves* because it captures the splitting, which is irreducible but not prospectless. We now have a fuller picture of Kristeva's understanding of the self-as-other—the inner strangeness—that modifies the content of universal human dignity. The conception of the uncanny is a key component of the picture.

Thus far, Kristeva's discussion of the uncanny underlines the primacy of *the past* in the experience of uncanniness. The uncanny is a resurgence of the self-as-other—of the foreign component of the psyche that is "mine." The next step, however, is her consideration of the possibility of including the foreigner in the pretexts for the uncanny. It is therefore oriented to the dimension of the present moment in the temporal tension of the return of the repressed. To include the foreigner/stranger as a propitiating circumstance for uncanny strangeness is to stress what the latter repeats in all its variations: "the difficulty I have in situating myself with respect to the other" (1988, 187). Thus Kristeva's focus is on the difficulty the finite, signifying subject has in "being" refused (intolerable), for she is concerned here with the overtaxed self. This concern is fully commensurate with her thought in the trilogy on how the burden of responsibility for the connection of the semiotic and symbolic falls on the individual in the absence of social symbolic resources for making such a connection.

The thought introduced at this point in her book on ethics undermines the impression given thus far that her modification of the rights of man only urges attention to the fully human share of destructiveness in the social realm. For *Strangers to Ourselves* now recalls the subject matter of *Tales of Love*. In her words, the variations of the uncanny "keep going over the course of identification-projection that lies at the foundation of my reaching autonomy" (1988, 187). That is to say, Kristeva here reiterates the course of identification which, in the trilogy, is the binding moment in the semiotic processes giving access to the symbolic. In *Strangers to Ourselves*, whose focus is our contemporary social domain, the connection between the semiotic and symbolic appears as a connection established between the *outside foreign element*, on the one hand (a second foreign component perceived "by means of sight, hearing, smell" and not framed by consciousness), and the proper (finite, signifying) self, on the other. The connection is made in *going over* the course of identification-projection. It is the path of identification-projection, then, which supports Kristeva's inscription of the uncanny in an ethical possibility. It forms the initial passage, for the overtaxed self, in the path of working out the impact of the strange.

The argument for an ethics of psychoanalysis is therefore the argument that the confrontation with the foreigner/stranger triggers the return of the self-as-other (the improper past of identity), which may be deadly but may set off identification-projection, a psychic act that makes the foreign component an integral part of the same as a condition for *tolerating* its *irreconcilability*. In Kristeva's view, the dynamic of return into the innermost recesses of the self-as-other (the improper past of the proper self) is not only provoked by but sustains the utmost confrontation with the other as other (the irreconcilable), and so the irreducibility of otherness. Yet it needs to be asked whether this is ultimately unsatisfying, since it offers nothing to the desire for real otherness and futurity. For the return of the self-as-other is less an encounter with real otherness than *the return of the same*—the known of old and long familiar. That the improper past of the proper self is a universal of the human condition, grounded in human finitude—birth and death, the impossible beginning and the impossible end—is quite consistent with its mineness, even as it puts being-from-birth on a level with being-toward-death (Heidegger) in individuation. Moreover, going over the course of identification-projection makes any "new" foreign component an integral part of the same. Without a concern, from the beginning and throughout, for actual otherness and futurity in this process, the primacy of the past, and so the return of the same, remains paramount.

The following section considers whether an attempt to substantiate the second foreign component in the experience of uncanny strangeness—the unexpected outside element—can modify this outcome by filling out more of the present dimension of the return of the repressed. The attempt is justified by the circumstance that Kristeva's concept of singularities may guarantee nonreified difference in the field of social and political relations, but it does little for the search for an ethics responsive to the sociohistorical particularities of social and political experience. We therefore turn to the fourth psychoanalytic notion that Freud introduced into his essay on the uncanny, along with the double, repetition, and the unconscious: anxiety. It may be that redressing the limitations of Kristeva's interpretation of anxiety in Freud will give more substance to the outside foreign element in the experience of uncanny strangeness, since the latter is crucial for the ethical moment in Kristeva's thought.

Anxiety

What is lacking in Kristeva's treatment of the uncanny is an explicit consideration of Freud's later revision of the psychoanalytic concept of anxiety, a revision consequent on his introduction of the second topography and the radical alteration of his theory of the instincts. These changes led Freud to consider anxiety as the source of repression, and not consequent on it, as he had thought earlier. It is the earlier view which informs the essay on the uncanny. On reading it, we find the assertion of two considerations that contain the gist of the study, one of which pertains to anxiety. "In the first place, if psychoanalytic theory is correct in maintaining that every affect belonging to an emotional impulse, whatever its kind, is transformed, if it is repressed, into anxiety, then among instances of frightening things there must be one class in which the frightening element can be shown to be something repressed that *recurs*. This class of frightening things would then constitute the uncanny; and it must be a matter of indifference whether what is uncanny was itself originally frightening or whether it carried some *other* affect" (1919, 241). This view of the significance of anxiety deploys the economic model of the mind. Anxiety is a conversion of repressed affect—of any kind. Such a notion underlines the view that there is a primacy of the past in the uncanny. The uncanny is *this* class of frightening things in which something repressed recurs. That is why (the second consideration) linguistic usage itself reflects that the uncanny "is nothing new or alien but something long familiar and old established in the mind." The two considerations give a certain slant to Freud's liking for Schelling's formulation of the uncanny, and Kristeva's reiteration of it. With Schelling the uncanny "is the name for everything that ought to have remained . . . secret and hidden but has come to light" (cited in Freud 1919, 224; Kristeva 1988, 183). We have seen that this bringing to light is not a bringing into sight but a new defense that exhibits repression and its perviousness.

With Kristeva, the uncanny is a clue to our psychic latencies and the fragility of repression: "at the same time it is an indication of the weakness of language as symbolic barrier that, in the final analysis, structures the repressed" (1988, 187). Yet, however much anxiety is linked to uncanny strangeness, it disappears in Kristeva's account from what is crucial to the deep significance of *das Unheimliche.* This is because, for her, anxiety or anguish (*l'angoisse*) "revolves around an object." Anxiety is too much tied up with the object to take us as far as what is essential to uncanniness, a *destructuration* of the self. Shock and unease are central to the latter, but not anxiety. In sum, on Freud's first thesis, anxiety belongs ultimately to the familiar repressed. It therefore falls out of the moment in which Kristeva exhibits the present-future tension in the notion of the return of the repressed. "While it surely manifests the return of a familiar repressed, the *Unheimliche* requires just the same the impetus of a new encounter with an unexpected outside element: arousing images of death, automatons, doubles, or the female sex" (188).

It is important to note that, just as the content of the past dimension of the uncanny is not made explicit beyond the expansive phrase "infantile fears and desires"—expansive since their close determination is unique in each case—so the pretexts for going through repression (death, automatons, doubles, or the female sex) are aspects of the present dimension of the experience but not its present foreign outside element.[6] They are the images aroused by a new encounter with an outside element, which Kristeva calls the "strange." The impossible beginning and impossible end that compose the subject may be a general key to the destructuration of the self that the uncanny points to, but they are not the determinants of depersonalization. Nor are infantile fears and desires. There is the unexpected outside element. The clash with the "strange," which crumbles conscious defences, involves not only fear but *identification* on the part of the self-in-destructuration *with* the source of its uncertainty—with "what" has transgressed its boundaries. Kristeva emphasizes the two prospects opened up by the link Freud establishes between the impact of the strange and *Kulturarbeit,* "the task of civilization."

Those two prospects are what provides the answer to the question of what education is in Kristeva's ethics. "On the one hand the sense of strangeness is a mainspring for identification with the other, by working out its depersonalizing impact by means of astonishment. On the other hand, analysis can throw light on such an affect but, far from insisting on breaking it down, it should make way for esthetics (some might add philosophy), with which to saturate its phantasmal progression and insure its cathartic eternal return" (1988, 189–190). This passage exhibits the share of the future in the temporal tension of the return of the repressed that uncanny strangeness instantiates. The two components of Kristeva's ethics have fully emerged. Psychoanalysis throws light on the uncanny and the process of *identification* with the other—working out the destructuration of the subject—that enables tolerance for the irreconcilable, and so the ethic of respect for the irreducible. On the other hand, once Freud has proposed that the uncanny is a psychic law allowing us to confront the unknown and work it out in the process of *Kulturarbeit,* we find psychoanalysis giving way to "esthetics (some might add philosophy)." Aesthetics, and perhaps philosophy, would comprise the education component of Kristeva's ethics. (So much is gestured to and so little said on philosophy here.) The artworks analyzed in the trilogy, and those analyses themselves, can now be seen as the kind of work that fulfils Kristevan "education." For example, and perhaps ultimately, artistic configuration of the dynamic of idealization can be seen as a working out of the impact of depersonalization. Indeed, *Tales of Love* shows that the task of saturating the phantasmal progression of affect and having it return for catharsis is a notable feature in Kristeva's analysis of artworks. Love itself involves the wrenching, the depersonalization. The amatory field of depersonalization appears in a different connection in *Black Sun,* where the aesthetic descent into melancholy is one moment in a narrative synthesis, opening up "a new amatory world." In *Strangers to Ourselves* Kristeva makes this world a part of her ethics. Equally important for the ethics is the fact that the source of depersonalization, mainspring for identification, remains *indefinite.* There is no external element, no source of depersonalization "itself." This is what allows for the universality that "might be . . . our own foreignness," and so an ethics founded in strangeness.

A review of where we are in the unfolding of Kristeva's ethics is required at this point, for we are approaching the moment where she claims that the ethics of psychoanalysis implies a politics. Psychoanalysis clearly has a large share in Kristeva's ethics, which is, first, a working out of depersonalization toward reconciliation with inner strangeness, and so respect for the irreducible that arises across the process of identification. This is why the *symptom* "foreigner" is sustained. The foreigner/stranger is a provocation for the reactivation of the test of working out depersonalization: "we simply must come back to it [the symptom that the foreigner provokes], clear it up, give it the resources our own essential depersonalizations provide, and only thus soothe it" (1988, 190). There is a suggestion here that the test of the ethical standpoint turns on a depersonalization where what does not come into sight is *as such* the improper past of identity. Everything depends on how one interprets passages such as this one: "In the fascinated rejection that the foreigner arouses in us, there is a share of uncanny strangeness in the sense of the depersonalization that Freud discovered in it, and which takes up again [*renoue avec*] our infantile desires and fears of the other—the other of death, the other of woman, the other of uncontrollable drive. The foreigner is within us. And when we flee from or struggle against the foreigner, we are fighting our unconscious—that 'improper' facet of our impossible 'own and proper' [*cet 'impropre' de notre 'propre' impossible*]" (191).

The passage can, for example, be read as what is ultimately an individualizing stance, in line with the thought that the other is my (own and proper) unconscious. In this case, infantile fears and desires become the stopping point of "our own ghosts." Alternatively, it can be read as bringing the "improper" facet of the individual as far as our infantile fears and desires of the other, where the other/strange is not death, the feminine threat, or drive as such, but their others, what aroused the images of them: "the impetus of a new encounter with an unexpected outside element" (1988, 188). One wonders how far Kristeva's introduction of the biological-and-symbolic of an other may guide us in comprehending this constitutive outside element. If Freud "does not speak of foreigners" because "he teaches us how to detect foreignness in ourselves," does this teaching really culminate in the invitation to have "the courage to call ourselves disintegrated in order not to integrate foreigners and even less so to hunt them down, but rather to welcome them to that uncanny strangeness, which is as much theirs as it is ours"? (191–192).

Before developing the question it is worth noting that Kristeva's syntax in this passage ("to welcome them") may well reflect the concerns of *Nations Without Nationalism* in which she acknowledges the unsurpassed actuality of the nation. In *Strangers to Ourselves,* as we have seen, Kristeva unfolds a transition from the oscillation between welcome (as assimilation) and rejection (up to the point of persecution) to uncanny strangeness, "theirs and ours," which appears to be like in degree but otherwise irreducible. The persistence of the notion of welcome in the above passage seems to reflect the particular address that Kristeva is making in this book, in which she speaks as a foreigner in France ("nowhere is one *more* a foreigner," "nowhere is one *better* as a foreigner"), to a linguistic and cultural community in which she includes herself ("the courage to call ourselves disintegrated") (1993b, 30–31; 1988, 191–192). In doing this she attributes the splitting "theirs and ours" to all members of the multinational society. In which case, self-analysis *is* the analysis of foreignness. The position leads swiftly to an assertion of the politics that such an ethics of psychoanalysis implies. "By recognizing *our* uncanny strangeness we shall neither suffer from it nor enjoy it from the outside. The foreigner is within me, hence we are all foreigners. If I am a foreigner, then there are no foreigners. Therefore Freud does not talk about them. The ethics of psychoanalysis implies a politics: it would involve a cosmopolitanism of a new sort that, cutting across [*transversal à*] governments, economies, and markets, might work for a mankind whose solidarity is founded in the consciousness of its unconscious—desiring, destructive, fearful, empty, impossible" (1988, 192).

If Kristeva's work can be read as a repeated, and undeterred, introduction of the death drive into various domains—aesthetics, ethics, politics—one wonders whether at this point, where uncanny strangeness is called "a projection as well as first working out of the death drive," the symbolic-and-organic heterogeneity of the subject, which is the *primary* instance on which Kristeva's project opens up, may become a dead end. The symbolic-and-organic heterogeneity is perhaps the general form of strangeness, but how is the encounter with the strange to have any specificity in actual social and political experience? Before pursuing the question further, let me recap the central points in the discussion hitherto.

First, the discussion has attempted to show that Kristeva's treatment of *das Unheimliche* is a point of convergence of the social and political, psychoanalytic, and aesthetic levels of her thought. The dynamics in play in the experience of uncanny strangeness are those in play in the transference. A journey into strangeness is upheld and worked out in and through identification with the other as disturbing external element. In the terms of Freud's *Beyond the Pleasure Principle,* this would be the path of *eros,* the binding facet in the *charnière* (articulation, orientation) which the drive is, working against its dominant destructive wave. The aesthetic then takes over from psychoanalysis in the task of returning one to the course of identification-projection insofar as it not only reactivates depersonalization but works it out in a shared domain. Finally, Kristeva's ethics is rooted in the test of strangeness, and her new cosmopolitan politics opens up on the basis of such a test. With Kristeva, we find that what ethics is required to undergo is an *imprecise test* of its standpoint, not just because it is asked to encompass strangeness (for this is nothing new) but because the strange is a doubled tension of the known and unknown—"theirs and ours." What is important for Kristeva is the openness of the test that this doubled tension expresses.

Perhaps, by analogy with the stakes of the aesthetic in the 1980s trilogy, this test contains some prospect for exemplarity, too. We will now see whether the revision of Freud's concept of anxiety in his later writings can provide the right theoretical conceptions to substantiate this prospect. The precise points of change need to be brought into view. The three essays which explicitly reveal the change in the significance of anxiety for Freud are "Anxiety" (1917), "Inhibitions, Symptoms and Anxiety" (1926), and "Anxiety and Instinctual Life" (1933).

The first essay claims that anxiety is in the beginning and remains throughout "a nodal point at which the most various and important questions converge, a riddle whose solution would be bound to throw a flood of light on our whole mental existence" (1917b, 393). It makes an important and consequential distinction between neurotic and realistic anxiety (*Realangst*) that is only relaxed in his later thought. We follow through that distinction first. Realistic anxiety, the anticipation of injury from an external danger, is connected with a flight reflex, and so is a manifestation of the instinct for self-preservation. Its expedient element is preparedness for danger, or anxiety limited to a signal, "a mere abortive beginning." The inexpedient element is the generation of anxiety that "paralyzes all action." Freud then breaks neurotic anxiety down into various types and sets forth clinical observations that lead him to conclude that anxiety is the transformation of an affective impulse whose ideational content is subjected to repression owing to the danger that the instinctual impulse represents to the ego. The idea is repressed (dynamic factor) and the libido is discharged in the form of anxiety (economic factor). In phobias, for example, "unemployable libido is being constantly transformed into an apparently realistic anxiety and thus a tiny external danger is introduced to represent the claims of the libido" (1917b, 409). In sum, anxiety corresponds to the discharge of the libido attached to the repressed impulse. Hence, on the early view, repression is the "cause" or creation of anxiety. The distinction between realistic and neurotic anxiety supporting this position restricts the significance of anxiety to an economic process consequent on repression. Anxiety is not an ingredient of the psychic functioning which shows up in the uncanny as the return of the repressed. It would therefore be of little import in the ethics of psychoanalysis, and Kristeva would be right not to give it the same attention that she gives the other psychoanalytic notions in Freud's essay.

However, Freud's revisions of the theory of the instincts and the systematic model of the mind force a change in the theory of anxiety, and the change makes anxiety a central ingredient of psychic functioning. The following outline of the revision draws mainly from the 1933 essay, "Anxiety and Instinctual Life," where the implications are stated most explicitly. First, the ego is the sole seat of anxiety. This means that dynamic factors now replace economic factors in the investigation into the relation of anxiety and repression. It is therefore a matter of "introducing the right abstract ideas" into that investigation, a matter of getting hold of the right conception of anxiety rather than the material of which it is made (1933, 81). Second, it is not repression that creates anxiety but anxiety that makes the repression (86). Third, what is at issue is realistic anxiety and not neurotic anxiety. Anxiety is no longer the process of discharge, a *general* factor in repression. Instead, *Realangst,* related to a threatening external danger, has particular determinants. The point of following this through is that we are in search of the possibility of more specific determinants in the triggering of Kristeva's identification-projection in the field of social and political experience. Freud outlines those pertaining to stages in the maturation of the subject: "a particular determinant of anxiety (that is, situation of danger) is allotted to every age of development as being appropriate to it. The danger of psychical helplessness fits the stage of the ego's early immaturity; the danger of loss of an object (or loss of love) fits the lack of self-sufficiency in the first years of childhood; the danger of being castrated fits the phallic phase; and, finally, fear of the super-ego, which assumes a special position, fits the period of latency" (1933, 88).

In each of the later essays Freud pursues the significance of castration anxiety and fear of the superego and tracks both forms to the danger of loss of an object (the beloved mother). The thought fits with Kristeva's view (1980a, 33) that if object-relation is constituted by a "whole gradation in modalities of separation" (pre-objects, transitional objects), that gradation is always "a means of masking, of parrying the fundamental fund of anguish" (Lacan). Anxiety revolves on the object in separation. Yet this is to ignore the first determinant of anxiety in Freud's outline, which bears on the archaic narcissistic self and therefore, in Kristeva's thought, on nonobjectal relationship. With Freud, the anxiety of the archaic narcissistic self is owed to psychic helplessness, which remains the paradigmatic determinant of anxiety. The attempt to substantiate the unexpected outside element in the experience of uncanny strangeness, by this route, requires that anxiety not be restricted to being an effect of repression, and that it bear on the whole tension of past, present, and future in the return of the repressed. It is true that Freud's texts do not immediately encourage such a view, since the essays focus initially on the factor of reminiscences in the new relation of anxiety and repression, and this would confine the significance of anxiety to the recurrence of past experience. However, both "Anxiety and Instinctual Life" and "Inhibitions, Symptoms and Anxiety" come to argue that the particular determinants of anxiety belong, equally, to the present dimension of the temporal tension that composes the return of the repressed. Anxiety is then a defense in which something concealed *shows up* in respect of an external disturbing element that is present, and can thereby be connected to the significance of the uncanny. We will see how Freud arrives at the conclusion that anxiety itself is a defense.

The dominant factor in anxiety is that the ego feels weak. Anxiety then turns out to be a technique of the ego in respect to an instinctual threat that calls up a real danger. Freud first acknowledges that "we were not prepared to find that internal instinctual danger would turn out to be a determinant and preparation for an external, real situation of danger" (1933, 86). He then specifies the technique the ego deploys in relation to the instinctual impulse as *the method* for negotiating the situation that threatens. "The ego notices that the satisfaction of an instinctual demand would conjure up one of the well-remembered situations of danger . . . the ego anticipates the satisfaction of the impulse and permits it to bring about the reproduction of the unpleasurable feelings at the beginning of the feared situation of danger. With this the automatism of the pleasure-unpleasure principle goes into operation and now carries out the repression of the dangerous instinctual impulse" (1933 89–90). The technique works as follows: (1) An experimental cathexis of the impulse sets off (2) the anxiety *signal* that comprises unpleasurable feelings, which themselves (3) bring into operation the pleasure principle that rules repression. The expedient factor in anxiety—preparedness for danger—is highlighted, and this is what produces repression. Anxiety, then, is a technique of defense.

For Freud, the defense is a psychical binding of dangerous impulses that call up past situations of danger. As a technique producing repression, anxiety reveals that the repressed instinctual impulses have remained outside the organization of the ego. The latter has not succeeded in binding the instinct in such a way that its rebellion is held off. Freud specifies at the end of his essay that the unwelcome demands on the ego may involve the individual's aggressiveness as much as erotic components. In sum, as a technique to bring the pleasure principle into operation once again, anxiety reveals that the particular determinants are beyond the pleasure principle. The efforts of the latter have broken down. This factor leads Freud to introduce the conceptions that bring anxiety into the center of the significance that the uncanny has for Kristeva as depersonalization-and-identification. First, Freud poses the question, *What is actually* dangerous, and feared as a danger, in such situations? The feared danger is not a danger to a subject "viewed objectively." What is feared as dangerous is, rather, a state of highly tense excitation in mental experience, "the emergence of a traumatic moment, which cannot be dealt with by the normal rules of the pleasure principle" (1933, 94). Anxiety therefore presupposes the overruling of the pleasure principle by a traumatic moment. That is to say, it presupposes the breach of the ego's defenses that Kristeva calls depersonalization or the destructuration of the self. What provokes the defense whose technique is anxiety is an impression that puts the subject beyond its defenses or, in Kristevan language, which sends the subject to its very boundaries.

Freud's extension of this thought on the traumatic moment introduces what is useful for our inquiry into the possibility of developing Kristeva's ethics of psychoanalysis in what, for many, is a desirable direction, introducing real otherness and futurity into it. Freud speaks in terms of economic factors.

> It is only the magnitude of the sum of excitation that turns an impression into a traumatic moment, paralyses the function of the pleasure principle, and gives the situation of danger its significance. And if that is how things are . . . why should it not be possible for similar traumatic moments to arise in mental life without reference to hypothetical situations of danger—traumatic moments, then, in which anxiety is not aroused as a signal but is generated anew for a fresh reason. Clinical experience declares decidedly that such is in fact the case. It is only the *later* repressions that exhibit the mechanism we have described, in which anxiety is awakened as a signal of earlier situations of danger. The first and original repressions arise directly from the traumatic moments, when the ego meets with excessively great libidinal demand. . . . I can see no objection to there being a twofold origin of anxiety—one as a direct consequence of the traumatic moment and the other as a signal threatening a repetition of such a moment. (1933, 94–95)

The passage contains the thoughts that are helpful in working out the significance of anxiety in the uncanny. First, there is a twofold origin of anxiety. It is not limited to a technique involving reminiscences linked to hypothetical dangers revolving around object-loss. It may be generated anew, *for a fresh reason*. Anxiety's twofold origin brings in the tension of past and present elements in the generation of the uncanny. It therefore brings an unexpected encounter with a new, external element into the center of the meaning of the uncanny. The uncanny configures both the foreign component in the psyche (my [own and proper] unconscious) *and* the other foreign component. In sum, and this is the central objective of the current diversion through Freud on anxiety, we can find the real significance of the question "might not universality be . . . our own foreignness?" in the thought that universality is *available* only on the condition of a particular that crosses the ellipsis. Thus the test of the ethical standpoint is neither a universal as such nor a given particular as such. It is exemplary.

This is what becomes explicit in Freud's late essay *Moses and Monotheism* (1939). The essay links the whole work on repression and the infantile factors inherent to it to an exemplar of the "strange," for Freud's study of the Jewish religion finds that "the tones of a foreign God" *are* the external disturbing element. What Freud is concerned with is the very mechanisms that make up the tradition of Hebraic monotheism. With Freud, Moses introduces those who go into exile to a foreign God. That is the key point of his assertion that Moses was an Egyptian. To summarize the text in an oversimplistic fashion, the interpretation of the foundation of Hebraic monotheism in *Moses and Monotheism* has the following steps.[7] The encounter with the foreign God is *intolerable* to Moses' followers. The outcome of this intolerability is the (intolerable) act of the murder of Moses. The twofold intolerable—the Mosaic religion and the murder—is repressed. There follows a period in which another God, Yahwe, is adopted and appears to triumph over the forgotten Mosaic religion. The volcanic God sustains its rule in a constant struggle against the repressed. Although the Mosaic religion is unrepresented in the explicit and recognized religion, it persists in and through the oral tradition, and finally reasserts itself. Thus the foundation of Hebraic monotheism is dependent on latency. The thesis is that the foundation of this religion, this traditional *authority,* turns on the working out of a traumatic moment through repression and the return of the repressed. The improper past in the trauma is the radically intimate and unanticipated exposure to a foreign God, or *being chosen.*[8] Moreover, "latency" is Freud's term for the hiatus through which, in this essay, the monotheistic Mosaic God becomes tradition, foundational for culture. My intention here is to show that Freud's *Kulturarbeit* and Kristeva's "education," which connects with Freud's thought, might carry within them not only the notion of infantile fears and desires—an expression that can become so familiar that the "not known" of the familiar is passed over—but "the strange" as something *exemplary.* It now seems as though we have the basis for introducing real otherness and futurity into the ethics of psychoanalysis. The example of Freud's Moses—the (intolerable) tones of a foreign God opening up the Hebraic tradition through their impact on Moses' followers, and the consequences of that impact—displays both real otherness and a certain future in the phenomenon of the return of the repressed.

Trauma and the Ethical

However, it must be asked whether it is fruitful to remain with this thought, which makes trauma the key productive element of the ethical test. Indeed, what has transpired in this attempt to substantiate the outside foreign element in the experience of uncanny strangeness is that we have reached a familiar point in the effort to seek out an ethics that encompasses the historicophilosophical dimensions of modernity. Indeed, we have reached the point where we are today. For there is no little support, currently, for the linkage of trauma and futurity (for example, Caruth 1996) or trauma and the ethical (for example, Levinas 1996 and Critchley 1999). Yet there are many factors in the temporality and character of trauma that should give pause for thought in the project of tying ethics into that temporality. Not least, Freud's discussion of the absence of anxiety in the situation of danger (the traumatogenic event), and its later appearance, must mean that the connections that need to be made in respect of the *symptom* are out of step with what triggers the need to make them: the present situation which, with Freud, involves the effort to generate anxiety. The ethical relation is forced to consist in turning to the past in order to soothe the current disturbance, and cannot consist in the connection with the present disturbing factor. As Horowitz states in *Sustaining Loss: Art and Mournful Life,* the need of anxiety in order "to become prepared for an event that has already happened" lies in the need of the binding of past, present, and future. For the traumatogenic event "is properly characterized not as remembered but as relived, repeated again and again in an endless present, in an effort to make it recede into a past that only then will have been bound tight by a proper present that at long last it gives rise to" (2001, 123–124). Indeed, there is no present disturbing factor, *qua other*, and no futurity in traumatic suffering.

It should also be noted that Freud does not himself make the link between trauma and the ethical as real otherness and futurity. He avers, rather, that the tones of a foreign God (intolerable otherness) is what opens up a future in the sense of being foundational for the tradition of Hebraic monotheism. The future is opened up only because the traumatogenic event is *lost* as origin through the dynamic that turns on latency—the preserving hiatus—so that "tradition" itself takes on the mantle of foundation. Excessive otherness, here, is the condition of a certain destiny. The traumatogenic event of being chosen is transformed into a past inserted, on condition of being forgotten, into the tradition of Hebraic monotheism. In this way *tradition* establishes itself as the binding of past, present, and future. Put otherwise, the authority of tradition is predicated on the absolute loss of the outside other, a loss that is never recalled within the tradition but is, rather, as Caruth discerns, translated into "liberation." On her reading, this "return" is "more truly, a departure" (1996, 13). This is not where we are today, where traditional authority is dislocated and the prospect of returning to it, away from the modern value of self-determination, both impossible and undesirable. Moreover, the current linkage of trauma and the ethical seeks to establish the possibility of real otherness and futurity together. Psychoanalytic thought on trauma reveals to us some severe obstacles lying in the path, not a resource for taking that path. With Horowitz, the structure of traumatic suffering, understood as intolerance for any extant representations that would seek to mediate trauma, and the demand for a new idiom of representation, contributes to our understanding of form-giving and its relationship to subjectivity (2001, 123–125). The intolerance for extant representations in traumatic suffering is the demand for a way, but does not—cannot—come up with any. This is precisely expressed in *Sustaining Loss: Art and Mournful Life*: "traumatic neurosis is history's inexhaustible fury directed against the power of form. The dead press their claim against the living (in the light of which the living reveal that 'the living' is an alias for 'the survivors').... Trauma, in this sense, is the nonattained future of the past bursting through form and making the present derelict" (124–125).

Freud's account of Hebraic monotheism in *Moses and Monotheism* reveals, on the one hand, the violent outcome of trauma (the murder of Moses) and, on the other, the constitutive role of latency, form-giving, and absolute loss in the establishment of traditional authority. Caruth argues that Freud's *Moses and Monotheism* shows the import in trauma, not only of the endless present, "an unending confrontation with the returning violence of the past," but of the *unexperienced departure* into a future, which is the structure of survival: "the incomprehensible fact of *being chosen for* a future that remains, in its promise, yet to be understood" (1996, 69, 71). Caruth therefore articulates the resemblance that Freud draws out between the structure of trauma and the structure of historical futurity, here the future of Hebraic monotheism and Jewish historical experience. However, *Moses and Monotheism* equally reveals that there is no real future without the overcoming of the "endless present" of trauma through the transformation of the traumatogenic event into an absolute loss. But it is only on the basis of a forgetting of the loss of the outside other that traditional authority shores itself up, making the value of this "future" highly questionable.

This diversion through Freud's revision of the psychoanalytic concept of anxiety has been an effort to make good on the failure of Kristeva's ethics of psychoanalysis to respond to the desire for real otherness and futurity, by seeking to substantiate the foreign component that triggers the return into the innermost recesses of the self-as-other. For, as I have stressed, this is the return of the same. The hope was that this diversion through Freud would establish the status of the strange—the unexpected outside element in the experience of the uncanny—as exemplary. Instead, the passage through Freud's later writings on anxiety actually functions as a *reductio ad absurdum* argument, for it leads to the identification of a real *otherness* that would bring *futurity* into the ethical relation with trauma. In other words, unless we turn a blind eye to our intuitions about trauma, and to the efforts of traumatized sufferers to convey what is so inarticulable about the suffering and *how* it is so inarticulable—unless, that is to say, we thoroughly weaken the meaning of trauma—the position would be that the cycle of damage opens up real otherness and futurity, which is absurd. Traumatized suffering does not itself have futurity or real otherness. (Compare Oliver 2001 for a different way of pursuing this thought.) It is, following Horowitz, an endless present that marks intolerability for any extant forms of representation that would seek to mediate it. The *reductio ad absurdum* argument works to reveal the depth of the problem of Kristeva's ethics of psychoanalysis. She does not inscribe the structure of trauma in her ethics of psychoanalysis, a structure that others have brought into ethics in order to articulate the impact on the self which takes it beyond ego-narcissism. It has been argued here, however, that traumatized suffering is precisely what preempts the temporality of the ethical. Indeed, on these grounds, Kristeva's ethics *must* turn on "going over the course of projection-identification," which makes the other an integral part of the same, if it is to be an *ethics* of psychoanalysis, and so must remain without real otherness and futurity.

Kristeva herself avoids the passage through anxiety that would make trauma the basis of the ethical. The structure of trauma does not even tally with the experience of the foreigner/stranger in her thought, since the traumatogenic event does not "crumble conscious defenses" as Kristeva's clash with the strange does, and so could not be the trigger for going over the course of identification-projection. At the time of the traumatogenic event the conscious subject is not involved in any breach of consciousness. Critchley attempts to unify the Levinasian ethical relation with the Freudian view of trauma, introducing the term *Trauma-Arbeit* into his discussion (1999, 193). It is notable, however, that Levinas's position on ethics is far from deploying the temporality of trauma in Freud. "The receptivity of finite knowledge is an assembling of a dispersed given in the simultaneity of presence, in immanence. The passivity 'more passive still than any passivity' consisted in undergoing—or more exactly in having already undergone, in a nonrepresentable past which was never present—a trauma that could not be assumed: it consisted in being struck by the '*in*' of infinity which devastates presence and awakens subjectivity to the proximity of the other (*autrui*). The noncontained, which breaks the container or the forms of consciousness, thus *transcends* the inter*estedness* and simultaneity of a representable or historically reconstitutable temporality; it transcends immanence" (Levinas 1996, 142).

As Critchley specifies (1999, 183), for Levinas trauma is an affectivity—"thought thinking more than it thinks"—which appears to root the ethical in "an affective disposition towards alterity within the subject," where the subject is not the subject of consciousness but the subject of the unconscious, beyond the noetic-noematic relation or, as we would say, the ego-object correlation, and so beyond the order of representation or Kristeva's symbolic. With Critchley, that the subject is constituted in a transferential relation to an original trauma is the condition of possibility of the disposition toward alterity, and so of any ethics of phenomenology or ethics of psychoanalysis (1999, 184–185, 190, 195; see also Levinas 1996, 142). But note how Levinas presents the ethical's central feature of responsibility within the passages deploying the term trauma in "God and Philosophy." "This trauma, which cannot be assumed, inflicted by the Infinite on presence, or this affecting of presence by the Infinite—this affectivity—takes shape as a subjection to the neighbor. It is thought thinking more than it thinks, desire, the reference to the neighbor, the responsibility for another. This abstraction is nevertheless familiar to us in the empirical event of obligation to the other (*autrui*), as the impossibility of indifference—impossible without fail—before the misfortunes and faults of a neighbor, the unexceptionable responsibility for him. It is impossible to fix limits or measure the extreme urgency of this responsibility" (1996, 142).

There is, indeed, some commonality between problems of representation in traumatized suffering and going beyond finite knowledge in Levinas's notion of infinity. For there is a similarity *in structure* between trauma, on the one hand, and, on the other, the excess over representation that is fundamental to the ethical in Levinas (and others). This is what has led many to the misidentification of the traumatic and the ethical. The meaning of trauma in Levinas is too weak to have Freud's sense of trauma superimposed on it. Levinas's conception of the "relation" to an original traumatism has more in common with the Kristevan encounter with the foreigner/stranger than Critchley's *Trauma-Arbeit,* for the following reasons. It is concerned with how there can be "being with others"—on the very grounds of the destabilizing core of being *with* others—*in the present.* It links the obligation to the other to an immemorial past (a "nonpresent" in Levinas) without making the latter a traumatogenic event, which would inscribe the encounter with the other within a temporality that preempts relation and obligation, unless the endless present is cleared up in some way. The Levinasian conception of the relation to an original traumatism that takes shape as the relation to the neighbor may be comparable with Kristeva's identification-projection as the initial passage of the "ethical" relation, rooted in the shock of the other. However, Levinas's notorious rejection of psychoanalysis may well be a rejection of the concept of *Kulturarbeit* if the latter means, as it does in Kristeva, the negotiation of the shock of the other through the *working out* of depersonalization in and through integration in the same. What is more, Levinas's ethics contains a much weightier obligation for the subject than Kristeva's does.

> Upon reflection it ["this trauma," "this abstraction"] is something completely astonishing, a responsibility that even extends to the obligation to answer for another's freedom, to be responsible for his responsibility, whereas the freedom which would demand an eventual commitment or even the assuming of an imposed necessity cannot find a present that includes the possibilities which belong to the other (*autrui*). The Other's freedom can neither constitute a structure along with my freedom, nor enter into a synthesis with it. Responsibility for the neighbor is precisely what goes beyond the legal and obliges beyond contracts; it comes to me from what is prior to my freedom, from a nonpresent, an immemorial. (Levinas 1996, 142)

However, the central point in the discussion of trauma undertaken here is that Freud does not present trauma as a psychic law allowing us to confront the unknown and work it out in the process of *Kulturarbeit*. Given that this would be the "ethical" thought arrived at through the effort to make Kristeva's encounter with an outside foreign element *exemplary,* Kristeva is perhaps sanguine in confining her emphasis to the task of working out disturbances that represent one's own "foreign component" in order better to transcend them in the face of the other. The whole weight of this ethical implication of psychoanalysis lies in offsetting the tendency to bend outer foreigners to the *norms* of our own repression. Her project here is to present the "simple truth" that psychoanalysis brings to social and political phenomena, a truth that cannot be had otherwise, and not, in fact, to present an answer to the search for an ethics that would respond to the desire for real otherness and futurity. As she puts it in *Nations Without Nationalism*: "let us know ourselves as unconscious, altered, other in order better to approach the universal otherness of the strangers that we are—for only strangeness is universal and such might be the post-Freudian expression of stoicism" (1993b, 21).

The difference between these concerns and those of Freud's essay on Moses needs to be underlined. In *Moses and Monotheism* the traumatic moment is tightly linked to the formation of traditional authority. That is to say, tradition is a form-giving in respect of trauma and not only founded in it. Although the current exploration of trauma in ethics acts as a reminder of the import of the immemorial in futurity, it has not attended to the need of form-giving, without which there is no real otherness, only survival. Kristeva knows that ethics is not doing the work that tradition was recognized by Freud to have done. We may *know* more of tradition than tradition does, but this is a merely theoretical accomplishment not one that has a practical outcome. With Kristeva, depersonalization-identification informs the intrapsychic dimension of the social and political phenomena she points up. The attempt made here to supplement Kristeva's conception of singularities with a notion of exemplarity in the ethical test shows that the limitations of Kristeva's ethics cannot be overcome. There is an intrinsic restrictedness to the kind of contribution that psychoanalysis can make in ethics and politics, and this should not surprise us given the lessons of the 1980s trilogy. Psychoanalytic experience does suggest a new model of the subject to replace the classical modern one that must assume the balance of individuals, and Kristeva does endorse the analysis of singularities and anomaly as a way out of the problems set by the conception of the rights of man. Yet the subject of modernity is sedimented and deracinated, still tied to a past that no longer supports it. We can recognize this without positing a utopian resolution of the ambiguities of self and world discovered in the 1980s trilogy.

Nations Without Nationalism

It comes as no surprise that Kristeva's recommendation of a "new cosmopolitanism" in *Nations Without Nationalism* asserts "a transnational or international position situated at the crossing of boundaries" (1993b, 16). This is commensurate with her effort to find a social-symbolic representation of the dynamic of destabilization-stabilization whose ethical significance is laid out in *Strangers to Ourselves*. The principle of political binding that she offers in *Nations Without Nationalism* may appear flimsy from the viewpoint of much of the ethical and political thought which does not tarry with Freud, but we now have the right framework with which to approach the project of the essays on the national idea. When Kristeva adopts and modifies Montesquieu's conception of *esprit générale* in order to introduce the optimal national idea for late modern nation-states, what she is doing is seeking out a way of having a social-symbolic articulation of the dynamic of idealization that has been lacking in modern secular discourses and institutions. The primary significance of her *esprit générale* lies in its forming a response to the requirement that there be a social symbolic "ideal instance" that would work as a secular guarantor for the binding of members of today's multinational societies. *Esprit générale* is not merely of intrapsychic benefit. As a rehabilitation of Narcissus, *esprit générale* is also a moment in the *inter*psychic dimension of human relations, an idea Kristeva promotes in response to the need of working out the destabilizing feature of being with others.

The essay that introduces the anthology *Nations Without Nationalism* to anglophone readers sounds a cautionary note on the nature of its thought: "the book you are holding speaks to the anxiety of our compatriots, bringing together political and cultural items published in France as new events occurred" (1993b, 15). The arguments of the essays, published in France in 1990, are being conducted in a dialogue with *SOS Racisme,* an organization dedicated to the rejection of racism, xenophobia, and anti-Semitism in France, and seeking the right to vote for immigrants. This would explain their emphasis on the history and concept of the French nation, and on seeking resources in French thought for rethinking the meaning of the nation today. The situation is one in which the flux of immigration into France and its increasingly multinational character troubles the meaning of the nation. The essays therefore continue the project of *Strangers to Ourselves* insofar as the two books share a concern with the multinational society. Kristeva's thought develops on the premise that the nation will long remain a persistent entity. The crucial question is how it is a *modifiable* one. Standing back from French citizens' deprecation of the French national idea in the face of the troubled meaning of the French nation, Kristeva asserts that national pride is comparable to the narcissistic image or ego ideal whose suppression opens the doors to depression. What is learned from the function of the ego ideal is that "there is no way for an identity to go beyond itself without first asserting itself in satisfactory fashion" (59). That is why Kristeva's interventions into political debate focus on the national idea. The following discussion of *Nations Without Nationalism* draws on the two essays "What of Tomorrow's Nation?," written for the English-language publication, and "Open Letter to Harlem Désir," the title essay of the French publication (Harlem Désir being active in and spokesperson for *SOS Racisme* at the time).

As said earlier, *Nations Without Nationalism* expands the project of *Strangers to Ourselves* through an inquiry into what can support the transcendence of particularities in multinational societies. Given the persistence of the national entity this inquiry must interrogate what national identity can mean, especially since its repressive aspects are particularly evident in current times. The endeavor Kristeva undertakes is to seek out resources for modifying the less repressive aspects of the conception of national identity. "What of Tomorrow's Nation?" rests on the thought that human beings wage a transhistorical identity struggle. What is noticeable in Europe, and more widely, is that the struggle "has henceforth lost its ideological masks and is being carried out protected only by the shield of origins" (1993b, 1–2). The demise of ideologies such as Communism, without substitutes that would work to support the identity struggle, leads to responses that range from anxiety to the cult of origins and the attacks it incurs. The interrogation of the possibility of modifying the less repressive aspects of national identity therefore seeks out resources that would mitigate the fall into regressive "common denominators" (3). Kristeva's discussion of the nation and nationalism is therefore sensitive to the foremost social and political ills of modern Western societies.

However, given the actuality of the nation, the search must relate to possibilities that reside in specific national traditions. France, Germany, America, and Britain (the ones the book mentions) have different histories and concepts of the nation. Kristeva herself seeks out a support for the transcendence of particularities within the tradition of modern French thought, but not before indicating her understanding of what is peculiar to the American and British traditions, and why they do not present, to her mind, a model for rethinking national identity. The position is somewhat ambiguous, then, since it is unclear whether the resources of national traditions other than France cannot provide a model for rethinking national identity in respect of the members of the French nation only, or whether the failing is general: other national traditions simply have nothing like the resources that the French tradition has. This ambiguity about the depth of the failings of histories and concepts other than those of a French tradition haunts the book. For at one moment Kristeva asserts that "there exists a French national idea that can make up the *optimal rendition* of the nation in the contemporary world" (1993b, 39). The statement does not claim that such an idea exists only in France, only that there is a French national idea with features that do provide its optimal rendition. A statement in the letter to Harlem Désir appears to withdraw from this assertion. "Far be it from me to suggest *a* model, much less so *the* optimal national model" (53). The distinction between rendition in the first statement and model in the second remains obscure. Finally, at the end of the same essay she speculates that the features of the national idea she proposes, favored by the French tradition, could, if it triumphs over the *Volksgeist,* "be named Europe" (63).

Kristeva's reflections on the national idea in other nations don't do much to undermine the apparent bias toward France. Considering America to be "a country of immigrants," Kristeva finds nonetheless that "neither the American ethnic polyvalence nor the advantage of a federalism that links independent states resulted in a polyphony resistant to racism and xenophobia" (1993b, 8). Nor did they result in resistance to hierarchies. There is legal confusion over the status of immigrants, echoing similar problems in France. Finally, the inadequacy for her purposes of the American model lies in the following circumstance: "the cohesion of the American nation centered in the Dollar and God keeps troubling those for whom the future of men and women is centered in other values. The fierce struggle for profits, a war as *holy* in Washington as it is in Baghdad but in the name of another god and with incomparable humanitarian precautions (since the *Rights of Man* imposes certain duties): are those truly 'national values' the entire world, other 'nations,' 'ethnicities,' and 'origins' must submit to?" (11).

When Kristeva turns to consider the notion of the British national, she finds that it is complicated by the history of the Commonwealth. Manifest tolerance is accompanied by caution over defining the British national, a situation that runs the risk that particularities may be preserved but will not also be *mobilized* into their transcendence. This provides the clue to the project of *Nations Without Nationalism*. Its task is to consider how, in multinational societies, the mobilization of particularities into their transcendence may occur, a mobilization that would at the same time modify the less repressive aspects of national identity. Kristeva acknowledges that the very concreteness of the problem justifies that she be asked to explain where she is coming from. Her answer is a cosmopolitanism situated "at the crossing of boundaries," so long as this is understood to mean, not the abstraction that collapses differences, but *choosing* one's set: "the democratic capability of a nation and social group is revealed by the right it affords individuals to exercise that choice" (1993b, 16). She finds that cosmopolitanism in this sense is favored by a certain history and concept of the nation, the French one.

The essay "What of Tomorrow's Nation?" first reendorses the distinction between human being and citizen made in the French *Declaration*. It argues the need to bring the ancient and Christian cosmopolitanisms up to date. The Freudian component is, once more, central in achieving this task. The universal spirit expressed in the conception of the rights of man is reasserted, with a reminder of the proviso known from *Strangers to Ourselves*: "such upholding of a universality, of a symbolic dignity for the whole of humankind, appears to me as a rampart against a nationalist, regionalist, and religious fragmentation whose integrative contractions are only too visible today. Yes, let us have universality for the rights of man, provided we integrate in that universality not only the smug principle according to which 'all men are brothers' but also that portion of conflict, hatred, violence, and destructiveness that for two centuries since the *Declaration* has ceaselessly been unloaded on the realities of wars and fratricidal closeness and that the Freudian discovery of the unconscious tells us is a surely modifiable but yet constituent portion of the human psyche" (1993b, 27).

This combination of requirements contributes to the justification of her choice of certain resources in the effort to modify national identity: Montesquieu (1689–1755) and, once again, Diderot (1713–1784). It is noteworthy that Kristeva's failure fully to negotiate the inverted Arendtian scenario in *Black Sun*, that is to say, the failure to draw any conclusions there about the future of this inversion—a problematic that equally haunts *Strangers to Ourselves*—is now remedied in a particular direction. This is not a question of attempting to reverse the depreciation of the public realm within the private/public opposition. It is a matter of expanding the workings of the "private," understood not as restricted to the family cell but as the domain covered in the conception of civic rights, that is to say, the "social body." Notably, Kristeva is concerned with the domain—that of the social—which is traditionally, and continues to be, left with the task of mediating the incompatibilities and mutual resistances of the individual and collective instances in modern societies, once the state is assumed to be the site of collectivity, so that the collective has come to revolve on the concept of the legal person (rights of citizens). A quotation from Montesquieu, inserted into the book on ethics and now reiterated two or three times in the book on the nation, forms the platform on which Kristeva works out what is required to transcend particularities in today's nation-state, without imposing their erasure, always keeping in mind that the suggestions presuppose how humanity actually manifests itself to psychoanalysis.

> If I knew something useful to myself and detrimental to my family, I would reject it from my mind. If I knew something useful to my family but not to my homeland, I would try to forget it. If I knew something useful to my homeland and detrimental to Europe, or else useful to Europe and detrimental to Mankind, I would consider it a crime. (cited in 1993b, 28)

This forms the platform for Kristeva's project because, in the first place, it does not only claim respect for difference. The passage equally hints at what is required to unfold a new cosmopolitan politics from the ethics of psychoanalysis, which accommodates strangeness. For Montesquieu's thought accommodates the right of recognition of otherness that Kristeva derives as a political duty from the Freudian discovery. What is owed to Montesquieu is his "thinking of the social body as a guaranteed hierarchy of *private rights,* which he called *esprit générale.* Give a place to foreigners in the 'nation' understood as *esprit générale*—such is, as I see it, the optimal version of integration and of the nation today" (1993b, 31). When Kristeva brings the Freudian inflection into Montesquieu's idea, she introduces into the social body the process that makes *esprit générale* a mobile space of social and political bonds rather than a hierarchy. Conversely, *esprit générale* provides a social symbolic form of the movement of idealization set out in *Tales of Love*. We recall that the "imaginary father" inscribes a beneficial component within the structure of primary narcissism, establishing the most fundamental moment of the ego's mobility. We have seen, equally, that the process of identification-projection, which forms the initial channel for working out the intolerable and destabilizing confrontation with the strange, is what takes an identity beyond itself without passing through its collapse.

Notwithstanding these indications in Kristeva's social and political thought of the psychoanalytic background that generates it, *Nations Without Nationalism* sets out what delimits the contribution of psychoanalysis to social and political thought. "The complex relationships between cause and effect that govern social groups obviously do not coincide with the laws of the unconscious regarding a subject, but these unconscious determinations remain a constituent part, an essential one, of social and therefore national dynamics" (1993b, 50). The disclaimer is, perhaps, meant to meet the concern of those for whom psychoanalysis distracts from urgent questions about the relationships between cause and effect that govern social groups. The central question, here, is how illuminating Kristeva's reflections on the nation are as a way of introducing psychoanalytic thought into contemporary social and political concerns, where they are appropriate. Indeed, the essays remain focused on the foreigner/stranger because this figure introduces into the nation a symbolic value and function that *esprit générale* fulfills. *Esprit générale* is a national idea which allows for a space of freedom. This is the space of the social body, a space which is nonetheless also "dissolved in its own identity, eventually appearing as a texture of many singularities—confessional, linguistic, behavioral, sexual, and so forth" (32). The point expresses Kristeva's commitment, beyond all else, to singularities and "more singular truths," a commitment that has probably rendered her thought accessible and palatable to many in the USA.

"What of Tomorrow's Nation?" summarizes the French national idea she is offering on the basis of Montesquieu. The idea has three features: it is *contractual,* "a legal and political pact between free and equal individuals," it is *transitional,* and it is *cultural* (1993b, 40). The contractual element is the inheritance of the mature development of Enlightenment thought. Early Enlightenment thought bequeaths the transitional and cultural dimensions of the national idea, as can be seen from the components Montesquieu attributes to it, classified as follows in the letter to Harlem Désir (55–56).

- A historical identity with relative steadiness and subject to evolution
- A *layering* of concrete and diverse causalities
- The conception of *esprit générale*

The first item expresses the debt to Diderot, and so *Nations Without Nationalism* returns here to the affirmation of "self-alienated culture," now reinforcing it with a concrete history that is itself a symbolic identity. In Kristeva's view, there is in France a common, and not only elite, identification with art and literature, one that lends the national idea both stability and plasticity. First, this "has the advantage of stimulating the *shaping* and *ideating* of identification instincts, with the result that a distance (that is a sublimation) is set up from their dominating and persecuting aspects," underpinned as identification is by the drive. Second, the cultural feature encompasses the capacity to open up to "other sensitivities, other experiences, and strangenesses," presumably because of the workings of self-alienated culture (44–45).

The second item in the list refers to the range of causalities in the development of peoples, recognized by Montesquieu. The causalities go from climate to the past to customs, manners, and laws. As Montesquieu puts it in *The Spirit of the Laws*: "Human beings are ruled by several things: climate, religion, laws, principles of government, examples of things past, customs, manners; as a result, an *esprit générale* is constituted" (cited in Kristeva 1993b, 54). The third and crowning item provides the transitional logic which animates the transcendence of particularities, also going beyond political groups into higher entities supported, Kristeva asserts, by a spirit of concord *and* economic development. The transitional feature, echoing Kristeva's thought on the working out of destabilization, is the one that is exhibited in Montesquieu's words cited above on the self, family, homeland, Europe, and mankind. Montesquieu posits the integration of particular entities into higher ones that preserve them, so that—from a contemporary viewpoint—the spectrum of behavioural, sexual, familial, and ethnic rights, that is to say, for Kristeva, the *singularities* into which the social space dissolves, do not themselves collapse that space, which is the space of "the general interest": from the nation to Europe to the world. *Esprit générale* betokens "the general interest." In sum, in the connections of individual, particular, social, and political realms the transitive is *absolute*. Kristeva calls the rationality that Montesquieu's statement helps to yield "the serial logic of concord." The logic supports the securing of rights and duties between members and the state as well as in the relationships of the members. Her contractual, transitional, and cultural national idea may be "fragile," but she asks for consideration of it as a resource even in the face of, perhaps also on account of, the long trajectory of securing differences and freedoms that now faces peoples without the maturity or longevity that lends solidity to the French nation.

Kristeva's commitment to singularities reasserts itself in the radical opposition she sets up between *esprit générale*, on the one hand, and the German national idea on the other. For, in her view, the latter has only proffered a conception of the social body defined by language, but also soil, which collapses the possibility of the dynamic of social space afforded by the tendency of social space to *dissolve* itself into singularities. *Volksgeist* may have had a positive moment when it reintroduced the particular in the face of the abstractedness of Enlightenment universality, but today we know too well the threat it harbors: "the secret notion of *Volksgeist,* one that is intimate and indeed mystical (in the sense of *Gemüt* and *Einfühlung*), appears to me as favoring hegemonic claims (be they German, Hungarian, or Romanian) and is a product of the same disease, with differences that are simply quantitative and, one would hope, consequences less catastrophic than those of the Third Reich, wherever that ideology turns up. I would thus assert that nationalism is neither 'good' nor 'bad,' but that within the reality of national identities, which cannot be transcended today or in a long time, I would choose Montesquieu's *esprit générale* over Herder's *Volksgeist*" (1993b, 33). From the standpoint of the trilogy we ascertain that the intimate and mystical *Volksgeist* fails to give symbolic form to the process of idealization that ensures the ego's *mobility.* The contrast between the value of French intellectual resources and that of German ones is made more than once in *Nations Without Nationalism.* It represents the discomforts with respect to European history that are borne in these essays.

Perhaps one cannot fault Kristeva for letting it seem as though the German national idea she recovers for criticism would be the *only* resource for thinking through the social space in German, for she has made it clear that the thought she presents here belongs to an intervention in a debate on national and religious conflicts, immigration and racism in France, with a wider audience than the academic one. Even so, the failure to point to the language in which Freud wrote, other than in terms of his Romanticist filiation, is troubling. The reason for the rejection of German resources is the following. "I am among those who dread and reject the notion of *Volksgeist,* 'spirit of the people,' which stems from a line of thinkers that include Herder and Hegel . . . the romantic interpretation and the Nazi implementation of the *Volksgeist* cause me to be perplexed by the nationalist boom among East European peoples today" (1993b, 53–54). Fair enough. It needs to be recalled, however, that Hegel is wrongly assimilated to the notion she dreads and rejects. The "layering" of concrete and diverse causalities that make up one component of Kristeva's national idea, thanks to Montesquieu, are well attested to in his philosophical project.[9] Moreover, the whole question of the mediation of particular and universal is at the center of his philosophy of modernity, for example in the conceptions of *Sittlichkeit* and *Moralität,* and in the thought of objective spirit, where civil society is closely analyzed for the moments in it which work to mediate the opposition of the family and the state.[10] Hegel's thought continues to draw attention and be elaborated on precisely because he x rayed the problem of mediation in modern secular discourses and institutions. Kristeva's thought can appear slight in comparison with these efforts. However, her psychoanalytic standpoint leads her to join wider suspicion of Hegelian philosophy of history as totalizing. That said, not everyone shares her outright dread and rejection of Hegel, a position that leaves the resources in his thought for thinking through modern social and political experience preemptively suppressed. Kristeva does not flinch from hinting at the past that informs her dread. "Is history about to resume its gruesome course, one that, after Napoleon's conquests, changed the surge of French-inspired revolutionary universalism on the continent into a nationalism that was revivalist at first but nevertheless ended up in Balkanizing the cultural, political, and economic forces of European peoples, who were thus exposed to the dominance of the strongest hegemonist?" (1993b, 54).[11]

The question of the differences between Hegel's philosophy of modernity and Kristeva's psychoanalytic of modernity is a complex one. What can be said here is that when she ties Hegel to the Romantic conception of the *Volk* that he criticized she commits the offense she otherwise hunts down. The German culture and language are sent back to a homogeneous origin. Both prior to and after Fichte's introduction of the word "nation" into German (*Reden an die Deutsche Nation*, 1808), German philosophical reflection on what makes for the unity of a people is enlivened by the interrogation of the formation, deformation, and transformation of peoples (*Völker*), without rooting their formation in a mystical idea. Kristeva's treatment of the conception of *Volk* commits the offense she otherwise hunts down because, here, the cosmopolitanism situated at the crossing of boundaries comes to redraw the limit at the Rhine. Her reasons for doing so are, we assume, ones of personal and cultural history.

The problem does not, however, detract from the otherwise careful outline of what psychoanalytic insights into social and political phenomena can bring to bear in the domain of multinational societies. Kristeva is quite specific on where this insight does and does not lead. Psychoanalytic references must be abandoned if the thought is to unfold where it must, in political sociology (1993b, 53). Her contribution has been the one of bringing the psychoanalytic insights to bear, and drawing attention to the need of a new model of the individual as member of contemporary political society, especially after the lessons learned from the twentieth century.

Nonetheless, as we have seen, the ethics of psychoanalysis that Kristeva's political thought on a new cosmopolitanism proposes does little to forward the search for an ethics or politics responsive to the desire for real otherness and futurity. By locating her politics at "the crossing of boundaries" the confrontation with otherness appears to be generalized once again. There is a serious question, too, about what scope the borders of nation-states and the foreigner/stranger have as, respectively, the exemplary site and exemplary figure of the confrontation with otherness. The first is truly unilluminating for race theory in the USA, or anywhere with a history of internal racial borders. It does not ring true for many questions drawn out in feminist thought. On the ground of feminist thought, we need to see whether there are other resources in Kristeva's writings for working out an ethics responsive to the desire for real otherness and futurity. We therefore turn, in this book's final chapter, to her explicitly feminist writings.

CHAPTER 8

Kristeva's Feminism

> So let us again listen to the *Stabat Mater,* and the music, all the music . . . it swallows up the goddesses and removes their necessity.
>
> —Kristeva, "Stabat Mater"

Introduction

What is Kristeva's feminist thought? There is no book on feminism like the one on ethics, nor any collection of feminist writings like that on the contemporary nation. Insofar as Moi's *Kristeva Reader* (Kristeva 1986) remedies this situation it then seems unrepresentative of the *oeuvre* as a whole. There are, of course, writings that take an explicitly feminist turn, of which "Stabat Mater" (1977) and "Women's Time" (1979)—both returned to in this chapter—are notable. Each was first published as a self-standing piece before reappearing as a chapter of a later book, *Tales of Love* and *New Maladies of the Soul,* respectively, whose main project, however, is not dedicated to developing the feminist content.[1] Taking her book-length publications, Kristeva's feminism may be an ingredient of but does not appear to form a distinct part of the project, unlike the ethical and political writings on the foreigner/stranger and cosmopolitanism.

The ingredient is pervasive, and in a certain way fundamental, but it is never posited as the key note of Kristeva's vision. Yet in the anglophone world Kristeva is primarily known as an important if not principal member of "French feminism," featuring centrally in Marks and de Courtivron's much cited anthology *New French Feminisms* (1981), and more generally ranked with Irigaray and Cixous in the "holy Trinity" of French feminism, even if as "the 'odd man out,' so to speak" (Oliver 1993a, 176). Grosz includes her with Irigaray and Le Doeuff in *Sexual Subversions: Three French Feminists* (1989), negotiating both Kristeva's critical attitude toward feminism and her concentration on male writers hitherto. Finally, Kristeva's *oeuvre* has been quarried for its usefulness for the project of articulating a feminist ethics and politics, as well as criticized for its shortcomings in this light (see, for example, the anthology on her thought, *Ethics, Politics, and Difference*, Oliver (ed.) 1993b).

Oliver's own lengthy study, *Reading Kristeva: Unraveling the Double-Bind*, importantly shows how the feminist reception of Kristeva's thought tends to fall into opposing camps (1993a, 1–2). Oliver sets out to avoid those extremes and show that Kristeva's theories are useful in a feminist context. *Reading Kristeva* acknowledges the commitments to psychoanalysis and art in a culture whose "empty signature" is a crisis in values, but equally discerns the moments in Kristeva where diversely "feminine" or "maternal" experience also presents models for possibilities of change in this context. Certainly a new, secular discourse of maternity is attempted and, Oliver stresses, offered as the basis for a "reconceived ethics" (1993a, 8, 159). This chapter returns to the question of the relationship between maternity and ethics in Kristeva's writings. It reads that relationship in terms of the connections in her thought between the "feminine," phantasmatics, lost nature, and form-giving. The discussion develops in three parts. It begins, in section 1, with an initial consideration of Kristeva's association of "woman" and "nature." This part of the discussion addresses Kristeva's diagnosis of the limitations of Freud's thought on the feminine, and addresses the question whether an essentialism haunts Kristeva's association of woman and nature. Section 2 stages an encounter between Kristeva's and Butler's respective projects, focusing on how their differences on the subject of abjection illuminate the divergences in their thought, but also drawing out a point of contact between them on the subject of abjection. Section 3 then returns to Kristeva's association of "woman" and "nature" in order to follow through her connection of maternity and the ethical in the essay "Stabat Mater." This part of the discussion draws Kristeva's thought into relationship with some moments in early Frankfurt School critical theory, in order to support the different approach taken here to the thorny questions of the maternal, the feminine, and the connections between them in her writings.

"Woman" and "Nature"

If Kristeva's feminist thought is to be clarified in its own light, this means emphasizing rather than seeking to weaken its largely unwelcome aspects, especially the moments in her thought that have drawn and continue to draw the criticisms of essentialism and heterosexualism. (See for example, Coward's questioning in Kristeva 1984, and Butler in Oliver 1993b.) Kristeva's feminism lies precisely in those moments where she refuses to strengthen the project of dissociating woman from nature, most conspicuously in her thought on the maternal as pregnant and childbearing woman, a thought which underlines irreconcilable alterity at the level of the maternal body. Kristeva's notion of the maternal body has caused some anxiety in the feminist reception of her thought, for she appears to repeat the identification of woman and nature that has been a prominent object of criticism. We may recall, here, de Beauvoir's statement that "one is not born a woman, but rather, becomes one" (1949). The statement belongs to a critique of the process in which women became the Other of men. This is the historical process in which autonomy came to be seen as requiring a denial of embodiment. Women became other to men when men projected onto women all their embodiment and conceived of women, generally, as enacting embodiment (birth and death), and so nature, for them.

The worry that Kristeva's notion of the maternal body is essentialist is the worry that she treats its "naturalness" as a fact. But Kristeva is well aware that the fact of the maternal body as a stand-in for nature is a *social* fact. Her attention to the maternal body simply takes the historical projection of nature onto woman at its word. The projection de-forms both nature and the feminine. Many feminist thinkers have stressed that the meaning of the "feminine" nevertheless remains open and contestable, some citing an early essay of Kristeva's to support this view: "Woman Can Never Be Defined" (*La femme ce n'est jamais ça*) (1974, republished in Marks and de Courtivron 1981). The emphasis put, in this chapter, on Kristeva's conception of the *maternal* feminine will appear to some as though I am withdrawing from that recognition. However, I mean to follow through Kristeva's tracking of the historical fate of "woman" and "nature" as a central feature of modern nihilism. That is to say, I argue that these two terms in Kristeva are to be understood in respect of the perennial historical crisis that we call modernity. However, I will return to the questions about maternity "and" femininity at the close of the chapter. For the present, I intend to set up the claim that Kristeva goes to the maternal body for the claim of "lost nature," a lost past that Freud called the *dark continent,* leaving it in the shadows.

Since the claim of lost nature is the claim of a lost past, it will not appear in prevailing public discourses. What prevails and what is public is the social fact of the process in which women became other to men. Once this is understood, psychoanalytic attention to phantasmatics becomes more intelligible. For it is here that psychoanalysis first discovers the claim of *lost* nature. With Kristeva, the maternal body is the site of this phantasmatics. The phantasmatics both contains the claim of lost nature and distorts it in the direction of the historical deformation of nature and the feminine. Here we find Kristeva's thought on the "myth of woman." However, the maternal body is more than the site of this distortion. It is also where the projection of embodiment onto women is *actually undergone* rather than being routinely repeated. The experience of the weight of the projection is an experience, however slight, of something else. In other words, the maternal body is a specific level of female experience where the claim of the lost past is made. Women cannot be dissociated from the projection of embodiment onto women without losing this experience. So it is inevitable that one will find the problem of woman's identification with nature in Kristeva's thought on the maternal body. At the same time, Kristeva herself does not repeat that identification. She goes to the maternal body to eke out the claim of lost nature. Nonetheless, she cannot proceed immediately to the level of female experience she is interested in, since it is deprived of any discourse. Her pathway must be a traversal of phantasmatics, for the claim of lost nature appears in *some* form in phantasmatics, albeit, and inevitably, a distorted form.

The import of the phantasmatic is the reason why the essay "Stabat Mater" begins with the assertion that the maternal is the only "consecrated" representation of femininity in Western civilization, and why it proceeds carefully to recapitulate the discourse that has developed the major variants on this image: the Marianite discourse of the Catholic Church. Kristeva is fully aware of the outcome of the Marian image concisely stated in Horkheimer and Adorno's comment on *Mater Dolorosa* in *Dialectic of Enlightenment.* "The image of the Mother of Sorrows was a concession to matriarchal residues. Yet the church used the very image that was supposed to redeem women from her inferiority to sanction it" (1969, 206). But Kristeva's purpose is to explore what, and how, the image intended to redeem. She finds in it a subtle accommodation of the feminine and the unconscious. The virginal maternal salvages what is heterogeneous to the Word.

> Milk and tears became the privileged signs of the *Mater Dolorosa* who invaded the West beginning with the eleventh century, reaching the peak of its influx in the fourteenth. But it never ceased to fill the Marian visions of those, men or women (often children), who were racked by the anguish of a maternal frustration. Even though orality—threshold of infantile regression—is displayed in the area of the breast, while the spasm at the slipping away of eroticism is translated into tears, this should not conceal what milk and tears have in common: they are the metaphors of non-speech, of a "semiotics" that linguistic communication does not account for. (1977, 249)

The analysis clearly situates the meaning of *Mater Dolorosa* within the heterogeneity of the semiotic and symbolic. The Marian image in painting calls on and restores the representations close to primary processes, turning on loss, anguish and extinguished eroticism, which are suppressed in the organization of the "subject" in relation to divine Law.[2] "Stabat Mater" equally explores the seal of the Church's authority. On the one hand, the essay recognizes the ingenuity of the Trinity, whose mediations develop the relationship of the sinner—he or she who cannot alone achieve a balance of the heterogeneity of word and flesh—with divine Law. On the other hand, the introduction of the maternal feminine, representing a predominance of the flesh, threatens that spiritualization. Doctrine struggles with the difficulty of eliminating sin from the feminine, and so the son. The effort to void the Marian image of mortality partly resolves this difficulty, but it haunts the theological accommodation of the maternal feminine nonetheless.

"Stabat Mater" turns on Kristeva's insistence that feminist rejection of the image of motherhood "circumvents the real experience that fantasy overshadows" (1977, 234). Her consideration of the only consecrated representation of "the other sex" underlines the significance of fantasy as a return of the repressed. She knows all the while that the image is impossible (alone of her sex, sexless, deathless) with respect to a woman's speech or desire. Her verdict on this image of woman might be less adamant than others' but she takes the adamancy very seriously, and her diagnosis of it might be the most forceful yet: "When women speak out today it is in matters of conception and motherhood that their annoyance is basically centered. Beyond social and political demands, this takes the well-known "discontents" of our civilization to a level where Freud would not follow—the discontents of the species" (236). This is clearly a point at which criticisms of essentialism might be brought to bear, since the allusion to the species would appear to assume a piece of human nature that is fixed and immutable. Yet her attention to discontent surrounding motherhood, especially the formulation of this strange phrase "the discontents of the species"—its plural needs to be noted—might equally suggest the reverse.[3] We know that Kristeva's is a forcibly faithful return to Freud by comparison with many recent feminist approaches to his thought, notably Irigaray's.[4] For Kristeva, psychoanalysis goes to meet the struggle of the two heterogeneities, semiotic and symbolic. "Analytic discourse, by holding to it, is perhaps the only one capable of addressing this untenable place where our speaking species resides, threatened by madness beneath the emptiness of heaven" (1980b, xi). Again, the reference to the species would seem not only to make the struggle transhistorical but to keep nature, in its furthest recesses, given and immutable. However, as the final phrase of the statement on analytic discourse indicates, "this untenable place" would appear to be ours—late modern. We recall that the concluding chapter of *Black Sun* suggests an intensification of the crisis of meaning and values in contemporary Western societies, and a correspondingly heightened challenge to aesthetic capacities to respond to it. This is also the setting for Kristeva's interrogation of sexual difference.

The concern that Kristeva appears to leave woman as a species being—some fixed and eternal human nature—in fact involves a misrecognition of the philosophical meaning of species being, which must bring Marx to mind, even though Kristeva's later writings are noted for their abandonment of the Marxian thought that contributed to *Revolution in Poetic Language*. Rose reminds us of the meaning it has in his thought. "Marx's notion of man as a 'species being' was intended precisely to avoid the presupposition of a fixed, eternal human nature. Marx presents the view that men make and remake their own nature and the societies in which they live through their productive activities and relations" (1978, 28). Kristeva has been a strong critic of what she sees as a one-sided emphasis in Marxist culture on the objective process of changes in modes of production as fulfilling the "making and remaking" of human nature and societies and, hence, a failure to consider the process of the subject (especially in *Revolution in Poetic Language*). She considers species being in terms of the relations of reproduction, rather than productive activities and relations, and does so in a manner which is *also* directed against the presupposition of a fixed, eternal human nature. Above all, attending to "our species," to *where it resides,* does not leave the fate of nature uninterrogated. With Kristeva, psychoanalysis is the most far-reaching theoretical discourse in this effort—"perhaps the only one capable of addressing this untenable space where our speaking species resides." She joins those who take psychoanalysis to be a—for some *the*—limit discourse of modernity. From Freud onward, psychoanalysis opens up the question of what nature undergoes in civilization.

I have stressed that in the 1980s Kristeva's attention to the semiotic became an interrogation into how the less visible features of selfhood and connections with others take on, or fail to take on, symbolic form. In the context of her thought on the feminine this is equally an investigation of the fate of "lost nature," a lost past. Thus, while the fate of the semiotic is traced in artworks that convey unacknowledged suffering, it is also vital to pay attention to fantasy as the return of the repressed, in an effort to work out the significance of what nature undergoes in civilization. In sum, Kristeva's "nature" is not a given and immutable dimension of human being but *a historical past.* The destruction of this past—"lost nature"—constructs the "archaic" that is signaled in fantasy. Fantasy is a mode of form-giving with respect to a lost past, where this is otherwise lacking. It reveals and recovers *loss* in a form that distorts both what is lost and loss.

What, then, does Kristeva's avowal of Freud's limitations—"a level where Freud does not follow"—imply? Freud's attention to phantasmatics discovered the feminine as the content of fantasy, but his focus on the father left the investigation of the maternal feminine neglected. This leaves a skewed picture of "nature," of what it undergoes in civilization. It leaves something unexamined about how the historical past juts into the present in fantasy. Kristeva insists that psychoanalytic confrontation with the fate of nature is not sustained without the attempt to draw the feminine out from the shadows, from Freud's "dark continent."

> When Freud analyzes the advent and transformations of monotheism, he emphasizes that Christianity comes closer to pagan myths by integrating, through and against Judaic rigor, a preconscious acknowledgment of a maternal feminine. And yet, among the patients analyzed by Freud, one seeks in vain for mothers and their problems. One might be led to think that motherhood was a solution to neurosis and, by its very nature, ruled out psychoanalysis as a possible other solution. Or might psychoanalysis, at this point, make way for religion? In simplified fashion, the only thing Freud tells us concerning motherhood is that the desire for a child is a transformation of either penis envy or anal drive, and this allows her to discover the neurotic equation child-penis-feces. We are thus enlightened concerning an essential aspect of male phantasmatics with respect to childbirth, and female phantasmatics as well, to the extent that it embraces, in large part and in its hysterical labyrinths, the male one. The fact remains, as far as the complexities and pitfalls of maternal experience are involved, that Freud offers only a massive *nothing,* which, for those who might care to analyze it, is punctuated with this or that remark on the part of Freud's mother, proving to him in the kitchen that his own body is anything but immortal and will crumble away like dough; or the sour photograph of

> Marthe Freud, the wife, a whole mute story... There thus remained for his followers an entire continent to explore, a black one indeed. (1977, 254–255).

The maternal feminine is present in Freud's thought on religion, but mothers and their problems are not found among Freud's patients. Motherhood might seem to be an alternative to psychoanalysis but it is primarily known as the discovery of a "neurotic equation," child-penis-feces that belongs, first, to the male phantasmatics on childbirth, and then to female phantasmatics insofar as it embraces the male one. Freud bequeaths for further exploration no case history with a mother as patient, only the dark continent—in its entirety.

Kristeva's focus on the mother, complementing and countering Freud's on the father, does not of course simply intend to balance the books on the role of the familial in history and society. Her investigation of fantasy that contains the maternal feminine represents a sustained effort to bring out, name, and articulate an authority other than paternal law. Her circumvention of the feminist strategy of declaiming against the "myth of woman" therefore belongs to an attempt to articulate the maternal feminine where psychoanalysis finds it: in fantasy. This is not to lose sight of the problem of woman's confinement in fantasy. The thought is that "lost nature" reasserts itself in fantasy, but phantasmatics *distorts* what is lost—for example, in the fantasy of original fulfillment in unity with nature—and so distorts loss. A comparison with Kristeva's earlier thought is useful here. The notion of the "subject-in-process" in *Revolution in Poetic Language* can be read as an emphatic argument for the return of nature against the nature/culture dichotomy. In Kristeva's later writing, on the other hand, the recovery of the "feminine" is the recovery of *loss*. As we have seen, the 1980s trilogy explores, among other things, various figures of distortion that belong to a phantasmatics turning on the archaic mother. Indeed, Kristeva's conception of the psychic prison, counterposed to her new model of the individual as an "open system," also invokes the problem of woman's confinement with lost nature in fantasy. The phantasmatic stands in the way of the formation *and* deformation of the subject. The problem of the phantasmatic also looms large in Kristeva's reminder, in *The Sense and Non-Sense of Revolt* (1996), of the precise way in which the centrality of Oedipus (Freud) installs the primacy of the phallus or "phallic monism."

> Freud makes a clear distinction here that his later readers have had a tendency to neglect: he emphasizes the fact that it is a matter of a phallic organization localized at a certain moment in the subject's history, which endures as an unconscious fantasy but is not at all the optimal outcome of adult human sexuality. The optimal outcome would be the recognition of

> both sexes and relations between them. When one speaks of the primacy of the phallus, therefore, one must not lose sight of the fact that it is, I repeat, a matter of a *fantasy* linked to *infantile* genital sexuality. If some remain fixed there, it is their structure, but it is not the path Freud envisages in the development of the human psyche. This stage, these fantasmatic unconscious contents, are repressed in the adult, and Freud does not in any way identify phallic monism thus defined with completed adult sexuality, the advent of which he assumes and that is perhaps somewhat of a utopia. Perhaps none of us ever really accedes to this supposed genitality where we recognize our sexual difference and can have relations with beings of different sexes (*des relations entre êtres ayant des sexes différents*). Perhaps this is another utopic fantasy, indispensable to psychoanalytical theory this time, but rarely if ever attained by real subjects. (1996, 74)

Freud does not mean adult sexuality, then, when he speaks of the primacy of the phallus, since adult sexuality would recognize both sexes and relations between them. Yet the endurance of phallic organization as an unconscious fantasy in adult sexuality speaks against that recognition. On the one hand, phallic monism is a fantasy linked to infantile genital sexuality. On the other hand, the phantasmatics turning on the primacy of the phallus is not only *not* absent from adult sexuality. It is all over the place! Freud's later readers have a tendency to neglect a distinction which perhaps constitutes a utopic fantasy, and does not reflect actuality.[5] What prospect, then, does Kristeva's reminder hold out? Would the "chance" of adult sexuality be given or improved if the confinement of woman in fantasy were confronted? At any rate, the attempt to develop such a confrontation is a central feature of her focus on the early mother-child relationship, and more widely of the conception of the semiotic in Kristeva's investigation of sexual difference. The question hovering over this return to her feminist thought is, then, the extent to which she thinks it is possible to give the traces of immemorial semiotic authority, a lost past, a form other than the phantasmatic ones by which it is known. This is an important stake in her theorizing of the imaginary, as we will see. Section 3, below, returns to this issue, and attempts to substantiate the claim that Kristeva's feminist thought needs to be clearly grasped and expressed as a confrontation with the confinement of the maternal feminine in fantasy. The endeavor obviously covers textual ground that has been covered in other readings of Kristeva. However, it gives the texts a different slant by bringing to bear a body of thought that is not usually associated with Kristeva's writings on sexual difference. Moments from Frankfurt School critical theory are introduced in order to elucidate and consider further her association of woman and nature.

Section 2, which follows, stages an encounter between Kristeva and Butler, drawing especially on moments from Butler's *Bodies That Matter* (1993) and *The Psychic Life of Power* (1997). The aim is to have the startlingly different deployments of psychoanalysis in their respective projects further clarify Kristeva's psychoanalytic standpoint. The section heading below reflects the sense of facing a choice between those deployments, and more generally between more or less faithful, more or less critical, feminist deployments of Freud. Butler's project is of course no easier to summarize in any straightforward way than Kristeva's is. What they share is the attention they give to the question of the borders of the individual and society. Despite this similarity, Butler does not take a psychoanalytic standpoint on her subject matter. Her thought is introduced, then, for its implicit—and sometimes explicit—challenge to Kristeva's psychoanalytic position on subjectivity and sexual difference. There is an oft-reiterated impression that Kristeva's investigation of sexual difference has no immediate ethical and political payoff. Butler herself has charged Kristeva with a conservative standpoint on gender identities, if not a relegitimation of the status quo. The encounter between the two thinkers is made in order to reinvestigate this question about the limitations of Kristeva's thought with respect to ethics and politics.

Kristeva or Butler?

> Although one is tempted to claim that social regulation is simply internalized, taken from the outside and brought into the psyche, the problem is more complicated and, indeed, more insidious. For the boundary that divides the outside from the inside is in the process of being installed, precisely through the regulation of the subject.
>
> —Butler, *The Psychic Life of Power*

For those confronting and disputing the binarism of sexed positions ("masculine"/"feminine"), and critiquing its social and political implications, Kristeva's thought on sexual difference does not only harbor serious pitfalls. It may itself reproduce the mechanisms of legitimation of those positions. Although Butler puts as much emphasis as Kristeva does on the role of the familial, her theory of subjectification (*assoujetissement*), with its debt to Foucault's thought on power, is very much at odds with Kristeva's thought in the evaluation of that role. As is widely known, Butler's thought attempts to fill a lacuna in the Foucauldian theory of power. Foucault supplemented the critique of relations of domination between persons with a theory of the operations of power that cannot be referred to a subject and object of domination. This is a loose reference to Foucault's thought on power, but the point is that, for Butler, Foucault's thought indicates a more fundamental subjection than subjection "from outside": "if, following Foucault, we understand power as *forming* the subject as well, as providing the very condition of its existence and the trajectory of its desire, then power is not simply what we oppose but also, in a strong sense, what we depend on for our existence and what we harbor and preserve in the beings that we are" (Butler 1997, 2). Foucault did not, however, elucidate how power is harbored and preserved in the subject it regulates. Butler's theory of subjectification does exactly that. What is important, here, is that her theory of subjectification draws on precisely the psychoanalytic categories that are central to Kristeva's thought: identification and idealization, loss and melancholy, and abjection. For Butler, the articulation of these subjective dynamics—discovered at the pre-oedipal level in psychoanalysis—reveals both the deep mechanisms by which a certain social organization is upheld and the actual possibilities of resistance to it. Her idea of "performativity" captures both the mechanisms and the possibilities of resistance. Yet, however much Butler stresses the familial and psychic organization, and however much she aims at a theory of social and political transgression located in the instability and ambiguity of these profound aspects of psychic formation, she insists that the social has primary causality. That is the key to the meaning of subjectification.

Butler's thought equally responds to debates on sex and sexuality that turn on an opposition between the determinist account of the assumption of sex, an essentialist view, and the notion that sex and sexuality are "constructed," with its implication of voluntarism. Butler's theory of subjectification aims to avoid both fatalism and naïve optimism. However, of her book-length responses to the sex/gender debates, the first, *Gender Trouble* (1990), presented a theory of the performativity of "sex" which led readers to assume that her own arguments on the refusal to comply with sexed positions implied voluntarism. *Bodies That Matter* (1993) and *The Psychic Life of Power* (1997) both work to undermine this impression. For example, she insists that "constructivism needs to take account of the domain of constraints without which a certain living and desiring being cannot make its way" (1993, 94). Butler is equally concerned to overcome the pitfalls of a Lacanian feminism, which holds to a stability and discreteness between the imaginary and the symbolic that keeps resistance restricted to the imaginary, and thereby correlates perfectly with the power of the symbolic to organize dissent within an enclosure (1993, 106). Kristeva's emphasis on the need of imaginary discourses can easily look like a prominent example of Butler's target. Yet, with Kristeva, the question must be whether putting emphasis on the need of imaginary discourses does, indeed, correlate perfectly with the power of the symbolic. A full negotiation of this question requires a discussion of the meaning of the philosophy of culture in her thought. This is developed below. The point, for now, is that Butler's sights are set on the symbolic "itself."

Butler fully accepts the psychoanalytic recognition that loss, identification, and desire are central to the maturational processes of subject-formation, a recognition that implies the constitution of the subject is inseparable from the assumption of "sex." She argues, nonetheless, against both essentialism and the undeveloped thought of constructivism, that there are constitutive constraints in the conditions of the assumption of "sex," and that they need to be thought of as the operations of a symbolic demand that cannot be thrown off, but is not fully determinant. Thus far, this is quite consistent with Lacanian feminism. But, for Butler, the subject is constituted in a social organization that entrenches what is imaginable and what is not imaginable—more precisely, what is "radically unthinkable" and correspondingly *unviable*—as desire or loss, and what paths identification may take. The manner in which the symbolic demand organizes *these* processes must be the object of investigation if the power of the symbolic is to be thought through, if it is not to have the first and final word. With Butler, then, the (constitutive) constraints that generate sexed positions are a symbolic entrenchment of what is imaginable or thinkable as identification, loss, and desire. Constitutive constraints are constraints which make certain identities appear, or more precisely be experienced, as possible, and divergence from them as fundamentally impossible, so that Kristeva's "relations with beings of different sexes" have a domain of cultural viability. There is a force of prohibition on divergence from that domain: "Every such [living and desiring] being is constrained by not only what is difficult to imagine, but what remains radically unthinkable: in the domain of sexuality these constraints include the radical unthinkability of desiring otherwise, the radical unendurability of desiring otherwise, the absence of certain desires, the repetitive compulsion of others, the abiding repudiation of some sexual possibilities, panic, obsessional pull, and the nexus of sexuality and pain" (1993, 94).

Butler specifies two mechanisms for what is constitutive amongst the constraints that apply to the paths of identification in the constitution of the subject. The first, "repudiation," operates in the field of *desire* and identification. It refers to an attachment that is subsequently disavowed. The second, "foreclosure," operates in respect of *loss* and identification. It structures the forms that any attachment may assume. Foreclosure has the force of prohibition bear on what can be recognized *as* loss and what forms of love are possible. This thought fulfills Butler's diagnosis of the melancholia that afflicts a society or sociality: "What happens when a certain foreclosure of love becomes the condition of possibility for social existence? Does this not produce a society afflicted by melancholia, a sociality in which loss cannot be grieved because it cannot be recognized as loss, because what is lost never had any entitlement to existence?" (1997, 24). With Butler, the "loss of loss" *just is* the carving out of the legitimate domain of losses, griefs, and attachments.

Foreclosure and repudiation therefore correspond in such a way that the objective force of prohibition and its subjective fulfillment are inseparable. In her view, then, subjectivity is formed as such through constitutive constraints that determine the paths of identification, and so the identity of "sex." The constraints on "sex" implement a certain social and symbolic existence, which in turn upholds the social organization. That is Butler's account of the very establishment of social organization, an ongoing process which embraces a reference to a foundational moment. In sum, constraints in the constitution of sexed identity must be thought in terms of *repetition* not *ground*. This thought is the basis of Butler's conception of performativity. The apparent fixity of the constraints does not derive from the Law as an original authority or ground, but resides in the reiteration of the law. "The 'performative' dimension of construction is precisely the forced reiteration of norms" (1993, 94). Butler calls on the figure of the judge in legal process to illuminate this thought. "The performative speaking of the law, an 'utterance' that is most often within legal discourse inscribed in a book of laws, works only by reworking a set of already operative conventions. And these conventions are grounded in no other legitimating authority than the echo-chain of their own reinvocation" (107). In the social regulation of subjects the reiteration of norms takes place through foreclosures of identifications that "must remain as refuse, as abjected, in order for that intensified identification [of the subject] to exist" (116). The thought could, she suggests, be illuminating for theories of race, gender, or class, but her focal problem is the "heterosexual regime." I shall call it a regime of truth since the account bears on norms and values characterizing the construction and imposition of reality. The regime of truth represents and conceals real domination.

Butler unflaggingly points up the illusory character of this regime of truth—her "domain of cultural viability"—by revealing the instability of the processes drawn into it: identification and idealization, loss and melancholy. Indeed, the very marking of *impossibilities* for sex and sexuality both constitutes the domain of viability and lets what is excluded appear in the form of threatening phantasmatic figures which uphold the "impossible." These are Butler's "abjects."

> In the oedipal scenario, the symbolic demand that institutes "sex" is accompanied by the threat of punishment. Castration is the figure for punishment, the fear of castration motivating the assumption of the masculine sex, the fear of not being castrated motivating the assumption of

> the feminine. Implicit in the figure of castration, which operates differentially to constitute the constraining force of gendered punishment, are at least two inarticulate figures of abject homosexuality, the feminized fag and the phallicized dyke; the Lacanian scheme presumes that the terror over occupying either of these positions is what compels the assumption of a sexed position within language, a sexed position that is sexed by virtue of its heterosexual positioning, and that is assumed through a move that excludes and abjects gay and lesbian possibilities. (1993, 96)

Butler's figures of abjection—the feminized fag and the phallicized dyke—are the *mark* of prohibition in the domain of culturally viable existence. The refusal to comply with sexed positions or to concur with the figures of abjection, in other words with the forbidding and brutal binarism of heterosexuality/homosexuality itself, might, she conjectures, "necessitate a critical rethinking of the psychoanalytic economy of sex" (97). Only thus, perhaps, will it be possible to offset the foreclosure of "the kind of complex crossings of identification and desire which might exceed the binary frame itself" (103). A critical rethinking of the psychoanalytic economy of sex cannot simply construct an alternative schema, however, without reverting to voluntarism. Thus Butler's objective is to investigate "what sexual (im)possibilities have served as the constitutive constraints of sexed positionality, and what possibilities of reworking those constraints arise from within its own terms" (96). It is clear that, whereas Kristeva abides by the psychoanalytic and artistic standpoint, Butler's thought is committed to the urgent need of the political standpoint and so to discovering the connections between psychic formation and the workings of social power. One might ask, then, why attempt to bring the two projects into an encounter rather than leave each endeavor to yield its fruits? The reason is that there is a profound divergence between them on the very significance of subjectivity, and this demands attention.

There is one conception common to both projects that can be examined for the immediate parting of the ways in their respective deployments of psychoanalysis, and attentive readers will already have noticed it. My intention here is to illuminate the differences between Butler and Kristeva on abjection in order to see what light those differences throw on the fundamental divergence of their thought on the import of subjectivity, but also with a view to clarifying the emergence of a particular usage of "abjection" that now pervades wider debate. It is vital to note that abjection has a very different significance in the two projects. That is to say, Butler and Kristeva are especially at odds on what is of import in what gathers at the inside/outside boundary in psychic formation. For Butler, the important thing is the regulation that imposes itself at this site of ambiguity: "the boundary that divides the outside from the inside is in the process of *being installed*, precisely through the regulation of the subject" (1997, 66–67, emphasis added). For Kristeva, contemporary psychoanalysis witnesses the calling up of that very ambiguity and ambivalence, a borderline position of the subject. Butler sees the loss of viable identity as the threat regulating the subject. Kristeva discovers in contemporary subjects an intensification of a phantasmatics which turns on the fear of loss of one's being, and this corresponds to a weakening of the regulation or authority that bears on the inside/outside boundary, a power vacuum, as she puts it in *The Sense and Non-Sense of Revolt,* which is indicated by a weakness of responsibility in contemporary social being (1996, 25).

Both projects contain the thought of the intrinsic instability of the symbolic function. Yet, for Butler, the fear of loss of a viable identity is how the law *prepares* the subject for the inscription of sexual identity. "There must be a trembling before the law, a body whose fear can be compelled by the law, a law that produces the trembling body prepared for its inscription, a law that marks the body *first* with fear only then to mark it again with the symbolic stamp of sex" (1993, 101). For Kristeva, in contrast, "the law's frightened body" presupposes a prohibition—the demarcating imperative—at a level of psychic formation where the prohibition and what it triggers do *not* in and of themselves work to install subject (and so sexed) positions, nor do they necessarily lend themselves to the process of installing them. The demarcating imperative remains deeply entangled with what and whom it prohibits, since it belongs to the bodily exchange of mother and child or, more properly, the drive-based *chora.* Only with triangulation does the prohibition move to a "place" (the paternal apex) other than the dual relationship that makes primary repression so opaque in its bearing. Neither the demarcating imperative nor abjection that corresponds to it are a force of stabilization. The looming of abjection indicates *de*stabilization—subjective and social.

What is more, abjection reveals to Kristeva the functioning of another authority, found at the site of inaugural loss, a "semiotic" authority directed to repulsion in relation to another in order to become autonomous. Here, the force of repulsion is the destructive wave of the drive. Recalling that the drive is a strange entanglement of biology and otherness heterogeneous to the sign, primary autonomization is thoroughly rooted in the otherness through which prohibition arises. That primary autonomization is "borrowed from" the prohibition would be quite consistent with the object of Butler's critique, were it not for the fact that, here, psychic representation—the "abject"—composes the entanglement of the demarcating imperative (semiotic authority), the target of abjection (the mother's body, which is also the life support), and the drive force triggered by the prohibition, which Kristeva calls ab-jection of the mother's body. That is to say, the concept of the drive marks the thoroughgoing entanglement of the prohibition and the field of its operation. This means that abjection can only be a "territorialization" of the shared terrain so that a place for the ego *can* come into being. Kristeva's "abject" is, then, the psychic representation of this "dual war" where no boundary is established. For this reason her notion of the abject does not share in but precisely works against the binary logic that installs sexed positions. Furthermore, the operation of the drive, here, is one where the primacy of its destructive wave is paramount. In other words, the death drive is not bound up with eros, the sexual drive, so that, with Kristeva, abjection does not and cannot turn on desire. The abject is not an impossible object of desire but the impossible object that collapses the space of the desiring subject.

From this point of view, even though Butler's "abjection" does not figure domination between persons, it does express subjection "from outside." This externality is crucial to Butler, corresponding as it does to the causal primacy of the social. This means that, for her, Kristeva's maternal body still figures as the nurturing vessel in continuity with the infantile dependant. Having missed the meaning of drive re-jection as a logic of primary autonomization in *Revolution in Poetic Language,* Butler's examination of Kristeva in *Gender Trouble* takes the semiotic *chora* to be *one* "field of impulse," heterogeneous to symbolic law but homogeneous in itself (1990, 82). Kristeva then appears to be a leading member of Lacanian feminist thought on the discreteness and stability of the imaginary and symbolic that leaves dissent itself organized by the symbolic. The view recurs in Butler's essay on "The Body Politics of Julia Kristeva." "It is unclear that the subversive effects of such drives can serve, via the semiotic, as anything more than a temporary and futile disruption of the hegemony of paternal law" (in Oliver 1993b, 165). *Bodies That Matter* repeats the underlying problem. "Julia Kristeva *accepts* this collapse of the *chora* and the maternal/nurse figure" (1993, 41). But if the semiotic were *one* field there would be no fear attaching to this level. Thus, when Butler develops the thought of abjection, she can only have fear attaching to "castration." With Kristeva, fear of castration presumes the process of the body's territory being separated from the signifying chain, and it is this process that confers unity on the body. In contrast, the fear that corresponds to abjection attaches, not to the force of prohibition, but to nondifferentiation itself, where a body is not yet separated from another body. Nondifferentiation is what the demarcating imperative (primal repression) *brings out.* Fear of nondifferentiation, then, marks the primitive noncontinuity between mother and child. In sum, the "field of impulse" is neither one nor two.

For Butler, on the other hand, fear attaching to the nondifferentiation of the ego would still correspond to the force of prohibition, for much of that force turns on the need of self-preservation, where the ability of the subject to make its way is confined within the boundaries of livable being regulated by the symbolic demand that institutes "sex." Butler presses this aspect of the constitution of the subject by making it essential to the Lacanian view of the priority of the symbolic order.

> How is it that the subject is the kind of being who can be exploited, who is, by virtue of its own formation, vulnerable to subjugation? Bound to seek recognition of its own existence in categories, terms, and names that are not of its own making, the subject seeks the sign of its own existence outside itself, in a discourse that is at once dominant and indifferent. Social categories signify subordination and existence at once. In other words, within subjection the price of existence is subordination. Precisely at the moment in which choice is impossible, the subject pursues subordination as the promise of existence. This pursuit is not choice, but neither is it necessity. Subjection exploits the desire for existence, where existence is always conferred from elsewhere; it marks a primary vulnerability to the Other in order to be. (1997, 20–21)

In sum, the *force* of symbolic law depends upon the struggle for survival, so that the subject depends for its existence on the power which delimits that existence. Butler's political thought therefore puts a high value on courage in the face of such a threat to the conditions of existence. We see that Butler is analyzing abjection in the context of the concealed operation of symbolic law, and so in the context of the superego and, correlatively, the field of secondary identifications. In this context the operation of symbolic law turns abjection *into* a mechanism in the cultural supervision of gender identities. I return to this point below. For the present, let me draw out how, in a particular respect, Kristeva's thought on abjection turns on something quite different from the symbolic law's regulation of subjects. For her, the fear in question is the one that belongs to the presymbolic moment of nondifferentiation that reveals the workings of an authority *other* than that of symbolic, paternal law. Moreover, the task is to recognize the boundary between the two: semiotic/symbolic. It has already been shown that Kristeva's "semiotic" articulates an exposure to exteriority other than the confrontation with the symbolic function. Butler focusses on the exposure to exteriority that *is* the vulnerability to the Other *qua* discursive conditions of existence. Given that the focal problem, for her, is the vulnerability which *makes possible* subordination/subjection as an ineliminable dimension of subjectivity, she compacts abjection with the functioning of symbolic law. She does not discern, or accept perhaps, the qualitatively different exposure to exteriority and imperative that are introduced when Kristeva discerns a pre-oedipal translation of the "vital support" into the "maternal entity."

The difference between Butler and Kristeva on abjection is therefore a pivotal one for examining their divergence on the formation and significance of subjectivity more closely. In sum, the meaning of abjection in Butler is absorbed by a mechanism of exclusion that must be understood as the repudiation and foreclosure of identifications, installing the boundary that divides the inside from the outside. It is a mechanism that works as the bearer of the social imperative, a force of stabilization that presupposes the undecidability or indefiniteness of "sex" but deprives that presupposition of significance through a logic of noncontradiction. The subject corresponding to the assumption of sexed positions is constituted in that logic. The first meaning that abjection has in Kristeva's thought, on the other hand, is a kind of negativity other than the workings of repudiation, one which above all does not obey the logic of noncontradiction, for no identity or position is established. Butler's "abjection," then, is a political *category*. It belongs fully to the workings of symbolic power that structure the borders of identity, as a force brought to bear on primary autonomization, entrenching what is imaginable or thinkable as desire. Moreover, it is a threat deployed in response to any reassertion in the social field of the complexities of primary autonomization.

Butler's thought on abjection therefore contributes to articulating what *structures* society and social being. We have already seen the two figures of abjection—fags and dykes—that reveal and repeat the enforcement of a certain trajectory for desire in *Bodies That Matter*. Butler carefully acknowledges that these are only two amongst a number of possible figures. Thus, in line with her usage, current deployments of the idea of abjection that examine its bearing on social and political terrain speak of other figures "being abjected." This phrase could not appear in Kristeva's treatment of abjection since it presupposes a subject-object relationship that is missing where there is an upsurge of abjection in the primary sense this has at the level where separation is established. Here abjection is a response to the threat of symbolic collapse. The abjection of "self" or an "other," which does appear in *Powers of Horror,* is a defense against that threat. Although the Kristevan thought on the abjection of an "other" may work in the same way as it does in current political critique of "being abjected," her analysis of this phenomenon carries all the weight of the looming of abjection corresponding to subjective and social deformation. This standpoint reveals her sensitivity to the problem of modern nihilism. Where abjection appears in the sense of a defense against social and symbolic collapse, it is grasped by Kristeva as the process of turning the *abject* into an *object,* or taking an object *for* the abject. The abject is a figure, not of the inside/outside division, but of the permeable boundary of the subject where fear of nondifferentiation looms. Thus abjection corresponds to inside/outside ambiguity and perviousness. This may, indeed, serve as a site for the inscription of symbolic law, and Kristeva has followed through the priority that this inscription has in monotheism (see chapter 5, above). But abjection itself only shows up *as abjection* insofar as symbolic authority is weak or missing. Abjection does not instantiate the advent of symbolic power but presupposes the weakness of bonds upheld by symbolic, "paternal" law and the absence of anything to substitute for that support. Like narcissistic melancholy, then, abjection belongs to a battle with symbolic collapse.

But if this does not simply imply once again the difference between Butler's and Kristeva's commitments, where does it lead us? Abjection is a nodal point for the difference between Butler and Kristeva but it does not in and of itself constitute the divergence in their respective deployments of psychoanalysis to articulate subjectivity. To discover what does, we need, first, to pursue the issue of primary causality, recalling that Butler's theory of subjectification endows the social with primary causality in the constitution of the subject. Kristeva, in contrast, refuses to specify a primacy for determination of the social by the subjective or the other way around. Where a tendency to prioritize an economy of the subject in early psychic formation shows up, this is meant to declare a preferred object-domain for her thought: "a deep psycho-symbolic economy," she says of abjection, "that analytic listening and semanalytic deciphering discover in our contemporaries" (1980a, 68). Even though an order of priority creeps in wherever Kristeva asserts the universality of the subjective economy she analyzes, the thought that the semiotic must take on symbolic form does not imply that subjective economy determines that form. Furthermore, this focus on subjective economy is continuous with the theory of *signifiance,* which ultimately proposes a mode of transformation of the subject and meaning transversal to or even substituting for (dialectical) political transgression. The Kristevan imaginary covers, among other things, such transformations. For her, then, this dimension of the imaginary is to be recognized and sustained in conditions where dialectical political transgression is unavailable or, she avows, "dated," given the weakness of responsibility in contemporary social being and the power vacuum it indicates. *The Sense and Non-Sense of Revolt* stresses that this is not a lack of social responsibility in any conservative sense, but the demise of dialectical political struggle—"prohibition/transgression"—reflecting a power vacuum, in Kristeva's view (1996, 29).

In sum, Kristeva's structurations of the speaking being in the symbolic order—primary identification, abjection, and primal loss—may *correspond to* but are not caused by a (social) symbolic system. They have some independence from it. The 1980s writings are committed to the thought of a "change" from culture to nature, and nature to culture, marked by the three modalities of the semiotic understood in terms of nonobjectal relationship. Since identification, loss, and abjection are prior to secondary repression's force of prohibition, they reach into a nature that is not subjugated. This is an important reason for Kristeva's staying close to the psychoanalytic standpoint in her analyses of cultural artifacts. Artworks that configure the crossroads of nature and culture encompass subjective "processes" because melancholy, primary idealization, and abjection all compose the reassertion of "lost" nature in subjectivity that fantasy recovers in distorted ways. We know, then, that artworks for Kristeva are works in which the reassertion of lost nature enters into form-giving other than the phantasmatics where psychoanalysis finds it. Art can reveal and avert the ways in which fantasy distorts the claim of the lost past in a direction that exhibits but shores up the historical deformation of nature and the feminine.

With Butler, in contrast, these pre-oedipal dynamics of psychic life may illuminate the flexible margins of social and symbolic existence—a certain instability in the symbolic order—but they share the latter's full implication in *social* processes. They are what power puts to work, and are only significant as part of the workings of power. In Kristeva, too, identification, the impact of loss, and abjection have forms that belong to the workings of power. We have seen some of the forms they take in monotheism. Kristeva is cognizant also of the fascist manipulation of the vulnerabilities pertaining to the narcissistic structure. (See also Ziarek 2001, chapter 4, for further discussion of this aspect of her thought.) What is crucial, however, is that in Butler what corresponds to the dynamics of Kristeva's primary narcissism has no special status as "presymbolic." More precisely, Butler does not make the distinction between primal and secondary repression. She considers instead a specific pre-oedipal mechanism of the *force* of the prohibition pertaining to symbolic law. Kristeva's elucidation of primal repression appears, significantly, in *Powers of Horror* as the imperative which sets off ab-jection, the re-jection of an other who is not fully parted from: "Our earliest attempts to release the hold of *maternal* entity even before ex-isting outside of her" (1980a, 13). To press the point, these attempts do not set off the process of establishing *separation* or, then, installing the boundary that sets up sexed positions.

Consistent with these differences between Butler and Kristeva, in the former there is no imaginary realm that is otherwise than the symbolic. In her thought the "imaginary" as currently discussed in feminist thought is the domain of symbolic power's operation in psychic formation, and the enclosure within which power organizes dissent, which is therefore "a subordinate rebellion with no power to rearticulate the terms of the governing law" (Butler, 1993, 111). Kristeva was an explicit target for this criticism in *Gender Trouble,* having failed to "seriously challenge the structuralist assumption that the prohibitive paternal law is foundational to culture itself" (Butler, 1990, 86). From a certain perspective Kristeva's distinction between the imaginary and the symbolic can seem naive, as though she meant to claim that the imaginary is a realm set quite apart from the workings of power. It is widely remarked that her distinction leaves the symbolic both theoretically unaltered and, in the final instance, practically untransformable. The force of Butler's thought lies in her insistence that a radical alteration of the symbolic *itself* is a condition for actual resistance to the regulation of desire (1993, 110–111). Her conception of constitutive constraints setting up the culturally unviable or unthinkable—focally, "the repudiation and abjection of homosexuality"—implies that the symbolic itself must be the target if the vision of a differently legitimated sexual future is not to be preemptively set aside (110). Moreover, she has specified a problem that Kristeva, perhaps, leaves too much in the shadows. For Butler's analysis of abjection in the context of the superego suggests that the regulation of subjectivity by the symbolic law is central to the current fate of abjection. Kristeva does draw up the connection between the superego and abjection ("to each ego its object, to each superego its abject," 1980a, 2), but she never states the connection in quite the way that Butler does, despite the fact that the whole of *Powers of Horror* is attentive, precisely, to the question of the fate of abjection.

Having acknowledged the manifest differences between Kristeva and Butler on the significance of abjection, the question now is how the profound divergence between the two thinkers can be illuminated, and whether a point of contact between them can be made. A way into this, ultimately the crux of the matter, is the different conceptions of culture in their thought. In Butler's *Bodies That Matter* culture is the domain of the culturally viable and the attempts to contest it. In her terms, it is the domain of the (im)possible and of the possibilities of reworking the constraints constituting the (im)possible. "Phantasmatic Identifications and the Assumption of Sex" concludes with the thought that the crossroads at which the culturally viable is installed, through foreclosure and repudiation of other identifications, itself illuminates the complex crossings of identification and desire, and that identity in the social realm needs to be *seen as* a site of crossings. Butler therefore contests the psychoanalytic schema that has sexed positions instituted through the mutual exclusion of desire and identification. There is a much discussed moment in Freud's *The Ego and the Id* where he proposes that paternal law—prohibition and the fear of castration—apportions *identification* to one pole of oedipal triangulation and *desire* to substitutions for the other pole. In the case of the boy—the only comprehensible case—identification is with the father and desire is for substitutions for the mother. On this view, the whole oedipal scenario, predicated on loss of the primary object (a lost love), exhibits how the pre-oedipal attachments to both parents (affection and hostility) are *destined* to reorganization. Oedipal destiny is the destiny of the subject of civilization—the "speaking subject" in Lacanian parlance. Butler attacks the psychoanalytic schema which distributes desire and identification across the divide that marks heterosexual positions. She suggests, instead, that identifications are multiple and contestatory. "It may be that we desire most strongly those individuals who reflect in a dense and saturated way the possibilities of multiple and simultaneous substitutions, where a substitution engages a fantasy of recovering a primary object of a love lost—and produced—through prohibition. Insofar as a number of such fantasies can come to constitute and saturate a site of desire, it follows that we are not in the position of *either* identifying with a given sex *or* desiring someone else of that sex; indeed, we are not, more generally, in a position of finding identification and desire to be mutually exclusive phenomena" (1993, 99). The complex crossings of identification and desire, which are the crossroads at which the culturally viable is installed, therefore form the point of focus for the vision of a differently legitimated sexual future. They are also what Butler draws attention to for the debate on the politics of difference.

> The contemporary political demand on thinking is to map out the interrelationships that connect, without simplistically uniting, a variety of dynamic and relational positionalities within the political field. Further, it will be crucial to find a way both to occupy such sites and to subject them to a democratizing contestation in which the exclusionary conditions of their production are perpetually reworked (even though they can never be fully overcome) in the direction of a more complex coalitional frame. It seems important, then, to question, whether a political insistence on coherent identities can ever be the basis on which a crossing over into political alliance with other subordinated groups can take place, especially when such a conception of alliance fails to understand *that the very subject-positions in question are themselves a kind of "crossing," are themselves the lived scene of coalition's difficulty.* The insistence on coherent identity as a point of departure presumes that what a "subject" is is already known, already fixed, and that that ready-made subject might enter the world to renegotiate its place. But if that very subject produces its coherence at the cost of its

> own complexity, *the crossings of identifications of which it is itself composed,* then that subject forecloses the kinds of contestatory connections that might democratize the field of its own operation. (1993, 114–115, emphasis added)

Butler claims that the point is not "to prescribe the taking on of new and different identifications" that have been disavowed (115). Moreover, what normative constraint could unify the proliferation of identities this would be part of, without coercion? Continuity between the political field that requires alliance between subordinated groups, on the one hand, and the cultural domain of viable identities and their contestation on the other, is gained only if the political field is opened up to the workings of subjectivity. Only thus may the hazards of an identity politics that rests on the need of coherent identities be offset.

Kristeva, too, has underlined her distance from identity politics (see, for example, the interview in Riding 2001). However, in her case, the distance correlates with a conception of culture that is designed to demonstrate what transformations of subjectivity and meaning there have been, or might be, in conditions of the tendential severance of the semiotic and symbolic. She therefore draws attention to the kinds of "cultural distance" from the dominion of the prohibitive, paternal function that are evident in the Western cultural heritage. There are also the modern moments of culture that embrace literary and artistic experience, for which the political field cannot provide the map, and that cannot easily remap the political field. That this is so suggests that Butler is both right and wrong about the imaginary. The subordinate rebellion may have no power to rearticulate the terms of the governing law, but *imaginary discourses giving form to the semiotic are no less futile than the narrow space of freedom that "performativity" permits.* Butler's suspicion that they are futile rests on her failure to grasp Kristeva's transition from the standpoint of rebellion to her thought on what presents counterindications with respect to the nihilism problematic. I have already remarked on the peculiarity that Kristeva does not recapitulate this insight of the trilogy when she turns to draw out the ethical and political implications of psychoanalysis in her posttrilogy thought (*Strangers to Ourselves* and *Nations Without Nationalism*). The insight is there somewhat covertly, and perhaps explains why the interconnections between Kristeva's "psyche" and the social and political field are drawn so thinly in those texts. The constraints on passing from the cultural to the political field, and vice versa, are set by the extensive and intensive problem of the tendential severance of the semiotic and symbolic.

The meaning of culture in Kristeva's thought therefore needs further clarification. Her usage of the term is manifold, but the central meanings are as follows. *First,* there is the "nature and culture" distinction, corresponding to that between the semiotic and the symbolic, according to which the symbolic designates the social and symbolic order. This sense corresponds most closely with Butler's social "regime" because it encompasses the mark of the social symbolic system in the inevitable suppression of unstable aspects of subjective formation, a suppression that has classically been seen as the condition for autonomization and social bonds. In Butler that suppression is the very site of the workings of power. But Kristeva's "nature and culture" adds to this thought the problem of the neglect of the semiotic in modern secular discourses. *Second,* there is artistic production that counters the failure of modern discourses and institutions to give the semiotic symbolic form. *Third,* there is culture as the general—and autonomous—field of modern artistic production. *Fourth,* and, for Kristeva, continuous with the last two, there is the assertion made in *The Sense and Non-Sense of Revolt* that "Europeans are cultured in the sense that culture is their critical conscience" (1996, 6). The second and third meanings are particularly important here. Much of Kristeva's writing of the 1980s and 1990s is devoted to demonstrating transformations of meaning and the subject in cultural artifacts. One implication of this is that art steps into the gap left by the failure of modern discourses and institutions to give the semiotic symbolic form. But a further implication is that this failure is the failure of a social-symbolic system to negotiate symbolically what social regulation does *not* cover. Put otherwise, if society fully regulated its members there would be no subjectivity. In exemplary instances artistic production absorbs and configures what is not reached by social and political regulation. To suggest that modern social and political institutions have neglected the less visible features of selfhood and connections with others—what religion attempted to negotiate—does not mean that they need to regulate them. For these are, we recall, the features of the *limit* of the ties between the individual and the social. Thus, when Kristeva speaks of culture, she is interested in it as the site where the cultural and the social, *qua* society's organization of its members, do not overlap. This is why she asserts the fourth sense when she develops her thought on revolt (a thought returned to in the conclusion to this book).

My objective here is to seek a point of contact between Butler and Kristeva on the basis of the recognition that there would be no subjectivity if society fully regulated its members. The aim is to show that the meaning abjection has in Butler's thought can be supplemented with a Kristevan meaning without abandoning Butler's commitment to the social symbolic field. Butler's own conception of performativity permits this. First, to recap, abjection in Butler is a mechanism that upholds the foreclosure and repudiation of identifications that "remain as refuse" in order to shore up the institution of the subject that corresponds to sexed positions. Abjection is a fundamental mechanism within the performative dimension of the construction of sexed identity—"the forced reiteration of norms" (1993, 94). Her term *performativity* expresses the thought that the institution of identity and sexed positions is not an origin but a mode of repetition. Thus "performativity" equally indicates how there can be actual resistance to the regime of cultural viability. "If the figures of homosexualized abjection *must* be repudiated for sexed positions to be assumed, then the return of those figures as sites of erotic cathexis will refigure the domain of contested positionalities within the symbolic. Insofar as any *position* is secured through differentiation, none of these positions would exist in simple opposition to normative heterosexuality. On the contrary, they would refigure, redistribute, and resignify the constituents of that symbolic and, in this sense, constitute a subversive rearticulation of that symbolic" (109).

Now, if we recollect that for Kristeva the modern failure to give abjection social symbolic form is the failure of society to represent its *own* limits and thereby accompany the subject on its journey to the unstable boundary of subject and society, Butler's project can be viewed as an attempt to make up for this absence. It is a social symbolic articulation of abjection in Kristeva's sense. Performativity in Butler is, on the one hand, the *ritual* of the repetition of norms and, on the other, the practice that undermines the power of ritual over the subject by turning ritual into irony and parody. Returning to Kristeva's analysis of the symbolizations or codings of abjection in religion, we recall that the ritual symbolization of abjection is not a symbol of subjective dynamics but a social act. *Powers of Horror* pursues the variants of this act in the field of the sacred and religion in order to argue that, in symbolizing the instability of subjective boundary and of fundamental symbolic bonds themselves, the purification rites surrounding "defilement," for example, *ward off the abject.* Having acknowledged the pitfalls and ultimate deformation of the religious codings of abjection, in which the symbolic overreaches the semiotic, Kristeva suggests—again, assuming the conditions of modern nihilism—that something *like* ritual is needed if abjection is to take on symbolic form in the secular aftermath of religion. This need corresponds to the need to forestall the forms of abjection which come, through a twist that is a defense against the looming of the abject, to bear on persons. Thus, from a Kristevan point of view, the critique of the heterosexual regime presupposes and *exhibits* the failure of a society to code its own limits, with the consequence that abjection recoils on the subject and society. Performativity in Butler's wider sense, which undermines the power of ritual over the subject, can also be understood as something "like" ritual in the sense of Kristeva's desideratum.

To be *like* ritual, to recall Kristeva's argument, is to accomplish the warding off of the abject without tying the logic of abjection to a founding instance: the Law. It is clear that Butler's critique of sexed positions undoes that tie when she argues that subjectivity is constituted iteratively, not on the basis of a foundational law, and that reference to a foundation is a major element in iterability. For example, "it is precisely through the infinite deferral of authority to an irrecoverable past that authority is constituted. That deferral is the repeated act by which legitimation occurs. The pointing to a ground which is never recovered becomes authority's groundless ground" (1993, 108). The repeated act by which legitimation occurs correlates with the power of ritual over the subject.

It must now be asked whether Butler's "performativity" encompasses a warding off of the abject in Kristeva's sense. Kristeva's analysis of the variants of the logic of abjection in the history of religions argues that symbolizations of abjection displace the abject onto the realm of things: neither persons nor objects but borderline elements. Butler's indication of how irony and parody, undermining the power of ritual over the subject, *actually* take place suggests such a displacement of the abject. Note, first, her insistence that performativity is "neither free play nor theatrical self-presentation; nor can it be simply equated with performance" (1993, 95). This assertion does not only confront the problem of voluntarism. It argues that performativity is certainly not impersonation, which preserves the lines of normative heterosexuality. What can be added here to trends in current thinking that challenge the assumption that practices refusing to comply with sexed positions reinscribe them through impersonation, is the thought that such practices are *like* ritual insofar as they displace the abject onto the realm of "things." Performativity turns on boundary elements: hair, clothes, skin, which do not impersonate "a sex" but present the indefiniteness of sex. The *presentation* of the indefiniteness of sex, displacing the instability of subjective boundary onto things, is what wards off the abject, and so the threat of nondifferentiation as well as the phantasmatics turning on it.

More needs to be said, however, in order to show what is widely at stake in the thought of a social-symbolic elaboration of abjection. The meaning of abjection takes many forms in Kristeva's writings, and there is no consistent typographical distinction to help clarify what, at any one point in the discussion, is at issue. There is the hypothesis of presymbolic abjection (sometimes ab-jection) of the mother's body, corresponding to primal repression. There is what supports this hypothesis in contemporary psychoanalytic listening: the looming of abjection in symbolic collapse, known through a phantasmatics turning on the fear of nondifferentiation. There is the abjection of "self" in response to an encroachment on the borders of self and world. There is taking an other for the abject as a defense against symbolic collapse. There is also abjection as the primer of culture, and the gladly hailed literature of abjection, despite what it displays at its highpoint (Céline). It is not surprising to read in *Powers of Horror* that abjection is above all ambiguity, but this claim also provides the clue to the proliferation of the meanings of abjection.

First, abjection is not a category, political or otherwise, if categories articulate what fundamentally structures a society. Rather, *abjection* is a term that captures the *inarticulate, at the limits of society.* Abjection belongs to subjectivity because it is a journey into what is not organized—or regulated—by society. That is why Kristeva can read Sophoclean tragedy as a symbolization of abjection (1980a, 83–89). The proliferation of sites of abjection in current usage of the term is owed, not only to the fact that the range of the term corresponds to the field of the inarticulate, but to the fact that this is precisely what modern societies push out of sight: death, illness, old age . . . as well as the indefiniteness of sex. Abjection *shows up as* abjection—after tragedy, defilement, abomination, and sin—precisely because modern secular discourses neglect "messy stuff," what is loose and baggy with respect to the ties which relate the individual to society. To ward off the abject is to preempt the hazard of occupying the boundary subjectivity that Kristeva calls abjection. This is the hazard of being without existence outside of the abject: her "impossible" subjectivity. More lucidly, the need of symbolizations of the demarcating imperative and its correlate, the abject, corresponds to the need to negotiate the "inarticulate" symbolically.

Having suggested that, where *abjection* and desire are in question, Butler's concept of performativity provides a social-symbolic elaboration of abjection in the field of "sex," I must acknowledge the implication that, here, her thought does not belong to the political field in the sense of the domain that is regulated by society. Rather, it generates social values exactly where these are missing in a society that pushes the inarticulate out of sight. One gets a sense of this in Butler's own writing. "The temporal paradox of the subject is such that, of necessity, we must lose the perspective of a subject already formed in order to account for our own becoming. That 'becoming' is no simple or continuous affair, but an uneasy practice of repetition and its risks, compelled yet incomplete, wavering on the horizon of social being" (1997, 30). Subjectivity in Butler includes a practice which lies, not within the political field where social organization holds sway, but at its limits. It must be emphasized that this does not mean that the problem of abjection is not at all political. For Butler's "performativity" delivers social values of a particular kind: symbolic negotiations of the inarticulate which, if not negotiated symbolically, is ripe for an outbreak, rebounding within the political field as hatred. The analyses of the "abjection" of an other and "being abjected" that have entered into current cultural thought are analyses of *this mechanism* of hatred, oppression, and persecution. I am suggesting, then, that "performativity" forms the kind of secular response to the problem of abjection that Kristeva deems necessary.

If the attempt made here to connect Kristeva's and Butler's thought on abjection is to be persuasive, it needs to be shown that the defensive rebound of abjection within the political field is present and articulated in Kristeva's own writings. It appears in her lengthy analysis of Céline's writings in *Powers of Horror*.[6] There are three major moments in the analysis. *First,* there is the context and thematics of his writings.

> All of Céline's narratives converge on a scene of massacres or death—the *Journey* [*to the End of the Night*], beginning with the First World War, had pointed the way, *Rigadoon* and *North,* spread out over a Europe laid waste by the Second, deepen and sustain the fixation. It is true that contemporary times are conducive to such representations, rife with slaughter as they are, and Céline remains the greatest hyperrealist of the period's massacres. But we are far removed from news accounts of wars, even of the most horrible kind. Céline tracks down, flushes out, and displays an ingrained love for death, ecstasy before the corpse, the other that I am and will never reach, the horror with which I communicate no more than with the other sex during pleasure, but which dwells in me, spends me, and carries me to the point where my identity is turned into something undecidable. (1980a, 149–150)

Second, there is Céline's probing of the breakdown of religion, morality and legality, which goes to the limits of language and meaning in what Kristeva calls a journey into abjection. "It is as if Céline's scription could only be justified to the extent that it confronted the 'entirely other' of signifiance; as if it could only be by having this 'entirely other' exist as such, in order to draw back from it, but also in order to go to it as to a fountainhead . . . what is disconnected regains its coherence in the permanence of abjection" (1980a, 149). The journey into abjection is not only the outcome but also becomes the very source and point of return for Céline's unrelenting, wild probing of the collapse of values and authority.

Third, Kristeva highlights the misogyny, homophobia, and anti-Semitism compressed together in the anti-Semitic fantasy that pervades Céline's fiction. The following passage reveals that the collapse of symbolic authority can be attended by intense fantasies *of* symbolic power, drawing in images of the feminine. This phantasmatics converges on anti-Semitic fantasy because, in Kristeva's view, the logic of abjection in Hebraic monotheism is the most successful in quelling the untenable boundary position of the subject without pushing it out of sight. What is important is that the phantasmatics of anti-Semitic discourse, "which is frightened desire for the inheriting brother," exhibits and turns on the fear of nondifferentiation which looms just where paternal authority collapses. The subject protects itself against the collapse by relegating the phantasmatic object (the Father) to the place of the *abject.* "The Jew" figures, and so forestalls, the abjection of self in which the subject is put, literally, "beside itself."

> If he joys in being under the Law of the Other, if he submits to the Other and draws out of it his mastery as well as his jouissance, is not this dreaded Jew an object of the Father, a piece of waste, his wife as it were, an abjection? It is on account of being such an unbearable conjoining of the One and the Other, of the Law and Jouissance, of the one who Is and the one who Has that the Jew becomes threatening. So, in order to be protected, anti-Semitic fantasy relegates that object to the place of the ab-ject. . . . The Jew becomes the feminine exalted to the point of mastery, the impaired master, the ambivalent, the border where exact limits between same and other, subject and object, and even beyond these, between inside and outside, are disappearing—hence an Object of fear and fascination. *Abjection itself.* He is abject: dirty, rotten. And I who identify with him, who desire to share with him a brotherly, mortal embrace in which I lose my own limits, I find myself reduced to the same abjection, a fecalized, feminized, passivated rot: "the repulsive Céline." (1980a, 185)

Céline's anti-Semitic pamphlets, "his indefensible political stands," give form to the hatred that protects him against the anti-Semitic fantasy (133, 136). Both the fantasy and the hatred compose a defense against the journey into abjection that is accorded an absolute place in Céline's otherwise dichotomous universe (expressed in the capitalized antitheses above). This is "a journey without project, without faith, to the end of the night" (186). With Céline, in the aftermath of the highpoints of death's explosion in social and symbolic bonds, there is only an "impossible" boundary subjectivity. What taking an object for the abject does is set up a subject-object relationship through which the subject finds a border, and so a position, for itself. That relationship is hatred. With the object relegated to the place of the abject, the latter is absorbed into an object of hatred. Such a "defense" presumes the collapse or avoidance of any constraints that would settle the subject's borders otherwise.

Butler's crossings of identifications and desire, which challenge the fixed constraints of symbolic law, do not dispense with *constraint* in subjectivity: "constraint is not necessarily that which sets a limit to performativity; constraint is, rather, that which impels and sustains performativity" (1993, 95). The vision she holds out is that of a *differently legitimated sexual future.* On her own account, of course, such legitimation cannot be thought of as a foundational principle or even a groundless ground. However, she does not elucidate the nature of a constraint that could operate without as such installing normative heterosexuality. Perhaps the gap is filled by Kristeva's conception of the subject "assuming" the demarcating imperative, since this is how symbolizations of abjection may come about. In that case, Butler's "performativity" is a response to the trajectories that are laid out so clearly in the Célinian universe. We note, also, that Butler's project reflects the desire for real otherness and futurity that was found to be lacking in Kristeva's ethics of psychoanalysis in chapter 7.

To summarize the results of the encounter staged between Kristeva and Butler, we have found, first, that Butler's assertion that the subversive effects of the imaginary may be temporary or futile has undervalued Kristeva's thought. This is because she has missed the extent of Kristeva's departure from the revolutionary standpoint of her 1970s thought and therefore misrecognizes the claim of the 1980s trilogy. Imaginary discourses are not rebellions. They are temporary, but not futile, abilities to give the semiotic symbolic form, so that meaning may emerge at the limit of the ties between the individual and society, and this is of particular import where the ties are insubstantial. If we grasp the emergence of psychoanalysis in the light of the collapse of the symbolic, it becomes unsurprising that there is no immediate or direct ethical and political payoff—no rearticulation of the terms of the governing law. A psychoanalytic sensitivity to the problems of the tendential severance of the semiotic and symbolic cannot itself compensate for the lack of symbolic means. At times Kristeva appears to want it to, but at others—where the tension of the ambiguity in self and world is foregrounded—she is tentative on the question of the powers of psychoanalysis in relation to the deformed symbolic. Psychoanalysis always bears this ambiguity in its therapeutic commitments.[7]

The disparity between Kristeva and Butler can now be grasped in its broadest significance as follows. The depth of Kristeva's nihilism argument is precisely what appears to prohibit her thought from being immediately turned to ethical and political ends. Conversely, the social causality that allows Butler to view fags and dykes as abjects, thus giving her thought an immediate ethicopolitical weight, is what prohibits her framework from being sensitive to or capable of saying anything about modern nihilism. Although she displays the transformation of ritual into irony and parody, this is not a great space. In sum, depth and weakness—blindness and insight—go together for both thinkers. Kristeva's sensitivity to the nihilism problematic and Butler's focus on ethical and political ends are precisely what prohibits each project from being open to what the other delivers.

Despite the advantages in discovering a point of connection between Butler and Kristeva on abjection, the above discussion may have led us to overemphasize the issue of abjection and the prospect held out by symbolizations of it. Those symbolizations can be asked to do too much work, as though they could open up a differently legitimated sexual future, and resolve the problem that modern societies push the inarticulate out of sight. Indeed, in our view, abjection is asked to do too much work whenever cultural theory deploys it as a political category. The thought on primary idealization and loss must not be allowed to slip into the background. (Butler herself does not commit this error.) The hazards attending the appearance of abjection as abjection can be met otherwise, as Kristeva's trilogy shows. The alternative path appears in *Black Sun*'s notion that *sadness holds back hatred.* Yet that book also indicates what is probably the deeper problematic beneath abjection. Modern societies are afflicted by the loss of *losing*. This is more insidious even than the social melancholia where the loss of loss turns on specific loves, and so griefs, that are never entitled to existence. Kristeva is concerned with the loss of loss itself. That said, since I am going to make a lot of her thought on the need of the recovery of loss in the next, and final, section of this chapter, I must acknowledge a counterposition on the psychoanalytic value of mourning. In the debate between Butler and Phillips in Butler's *Psychic Life of Power* there is a counterargument to the standpoint that makes the loss of loss (inadequate mourning) the crux of failings in subject formation and connections with others. Butler and Phillips suggest that, when psychoanalysis makes mourning our deepest act, the one that constitutes human community, it turns repressed gender identities into ones that must be lost and mourned. This limits the scope of the maturational processes available for subject formation, since it limits the repertoire of gender identities (Butler 1997, chapter 5).

However, Kristeva's inquiry into the cultural loss of loss must be considered if her thought on sexual difference is to be intelligible, for it is central to her development of the meaning of the maternal body. Her feminism lies in her emphasis on the connection between woman and nature, where "woman" means the pregnant and childbearing mother, which she calls "the mother's body."[8] As we will see, the feminist critique of essentialism cannot be made to fit because Kristeva's association of the feminine and lost nature links the recovery of the "feminine" with the recovery of loss.

The Maternal Feminine

> Woman as an allegedly natural being is a product of history, which denatures her.
>
> —Horkheimer and Adorno, *Dialectic of Enlightenment*

The development here of Kristeva's thought on "woman" and "nature" passes through Horkheimer and Adorno's philosophy of modernity because, we contend, a focal issue in Kristeva's refusal to dissociate woman from nature lies in her confrontation with what the *Dialectic of Enlightenment* presents as nature "denatured" in enlightenment reason.[9] Horkheimer and Adorno's philosophy of modernity turns in part on a Marxian analysis of reification. What distinguishes modernity for them is how the commodity form—rendering equivalent what is qualitatively different—becomes an autonomous value. The production of value in exchange is misrecognized such that "exchange value" is taken to be a property of the commodity. This process is, in sum, "the formation of the commodity *qua* commodity" (Rose 1978, 21).[10] The supposedly autonomous value comes to have increasing dominion in modern societies. Reification is the term used in specific analyses of the invasion of the commodity form into the social realm, culture, and intimacy. The analysis of the overall tendency, called "the social process," is fulfilled in a critique of modern reason. *Dialectic of Enlightenment* therefore analyzes the significance and effects of the rationality that developed in the eighteenth century. Kant's essay on Enlightenment sets down its fundamental meaning as release from self-incurred tutelage, the courage to use one's own reason. When he poses the question, "Do we now live in an *enlightened age?,*" the answer is no, "but we do live in an *age of enlightenment,*" by which he meant an age of *criticism:* the free use of one's reason as a critical thinker (Kant 1963, 8, 5). Adorno and Horkheimer spell out the fate or "self-destruction" of Enlightenment, which turns on the apotheosis of the self-reflexive subject in all relationships between subject and object. (See Bernstein's introduction to Adorno 1991 for a fuller explications of this.) Given the ascendancy of the self-reflexive subject, the enlightenment idea of free human social life brings with it the project of controlling nature. More precisely, for Horkheimer and Adorno, enlightenment is solidified with reason's ability to recognize "no function other than that of working on the object as mere sense material in order to make it the material of subjugation" (1969, 65). Inner and outer nature are "denatured," translated into mere objectivity, which is to say, "dead" nature.

On this view, the feminist critique of woman "reduced to her reproductive capacities" presupposes that reproduction is already "reduced." The expression "reproductive capacities" itself exhibits the objectification of reproduction. Since the preeminence of the autonomous, self-reflexive subject brings with it the abstraction from whatever holds the subject in heteronomous relations—since it abstracts the subject from exposure to and contact with an outside—the complexities of reproduction as a process, and of the relations of reproduction, are lost. Abstraction returns what is lost to the subject in the form of a merely mechanical process. Thus the feminist critique presupposes the denaturing of nature in enlightened modernity. For Horkheimer and Adorno, "enlightened modernity" embraces the pervasion into all modes of life and representation of the translation of nature into "mere" nature, so adapting them to and co-opting them for the project of controlling nature. Furthermore, the social process permeates responses to it. In particular, efforts to bring nature to bear against the trends of society rest on what is already an effect of the social process: nature posited as *other than* society. "Nature, in being presented by society's control mechanism as the healing antithesis of society, is itself absorbed into that incurable society and sold off" (1969, 119). But subjectivity—and herein lies its importance—bears the trace of lost nature. "Thought arose in the course of liberation from terrible nature, which is finally subjugated utterly. Pleasure, so to speak, is nature's revenge" (82). *Dialectic of Enlightenment* is far from suggesting that pleasure is undistorted ("pleasure, so to speak"). "Nature's vengeance" captures the thought of the reassertion of lost nature in phantasmatics. This is where critical theory incorporates the psychoanalytic perspective. With Horkheimer and Adorno, the effort to keep nature confined in fantasy is part of what characterizes modernity. And woman as alleged natural being, confined with nature in fantasy, *belongs to this history*. Kristeva would view antiessentialist feminist standpoints as tending to leave nature to its occidental fate rather than giving it the attention it needs, which is to give *loss* the attention it needs.

The respective treatments of phantasmatics in Kristeva and critical theory do not, of course, neatly coincide. The difference can be referred to major developments in psychoanalytic thought on narcissism since the period of Horkheimer and Adorno's writing, including Kristeva's own extensions of primary narcissism. It also has a great deal to do with the difference between the Frankfurt School's analysis of the social process and Kristeva's turn to psychoanalysis itself to structure her thought, bringing her to investigate the phantasmatic in the historical religions as well as enlightened modernity.[11] Yet we are simply trying to articulate the space where the two projects intersect. Kristeva's conceptions of the semiotic and the imaginary have the double task of digging deeper into the phantasmatic, recognizing how it appears and functions in Western discourses, and so *showing* the reassertion and confinement of lost nature in fantasy, as well as invoking the need to bring the feminine out of her confinement, with nature, in fantasy.

Kristeva's close association of woman and nature can put feminist readers off, not least because she speaks of the biological when she makes this association. Moreover, her writings on the feminine are perplexing precisely because she so often turns to the feminine as the content of fantasy rather than critiquing the *myth* of woman. However, it is the connection between these two aspects of her thought—the biological and the phantasmatic—which illuminates her investigation into sexual difference. First, the significance of the biological here is—necessarily counterintuitively—central to the attempt to confront nature "denatured." Her conception of the biological always turns on the drive, which, as we have seen, is not a given and immutable piece of nature but a strange compact of the biological and *otherness* that is heterogeneous to the signifying field in which nature is posited as absent from culture. So the connection she makes between the recovery of the feminine and the biological is an attempt to turn the absence of nature into *loss* and not what is *ejected* from culture. The difference between the two is that the second pushes nature into the past, as though nature and the past could be conclusively left behind. The past then juts into the present in distorted ways, or haunts the present. The first restores a relationship to the past in an effort to settle the debt to the past. This is a crucial dimension of the Kristevan conception of the imaginary, and shows that if we lose its full significance, the scope of her thought on subjectivity and history drops out.

We recall that, at the level of her strictly psychoanalytic thought, Kristeva unfolds *three* modalities of a biological entwined with otherness. Abjection, primary identification, and primal loss are patterns of primary autonomization that illuminate the complex role that nature plays in love and loss, as well as the capacity for destruction that is so entangled with the need of separateness.[12] Kristeva's determined emphasis on the heterogeneity of the semiotic and symbolic is made in part in order to show the reassertion of lost nature in conditions that inflict and suffer the ejection of nature from culture, so that nature comes to mean the betrayal of culture. In this sense, too, unacknowledged suffering—notably, the semiotic content deprived of symbolic form that Kristeva discovers in the modern narcissistic constriction—is the remnant of freedom. When Kristeva associates woman and nature, then, nature is a historical past. Her three variants of nonobjectal relationship, primary idealization, abjection, and primal melancholy, are three variants of the return of lost nature. The return of lost nature in subjectivity may only be known from the phantasmatic structure of narcissistic struggle. However, the three kinds of nonobjectal relationship equally illuminate symbolic forms—imaginary discourses—that counter the nature/culture binarism of modern nihilism by giving nonphantasmatic form to the return of lost nature. They recover loss and so work to establish a relationship to the past. Thus Kristeva's confrontation with nature denatured is especially supported by the trilogy's articulation of *three* modalities of the semiotic, which is the archaic. These offset nature/culture binarism by drawing out the intertwinements of nature and culture, in accordance with how the semiotic takes on symbolic form in imaginary discourses—depending on whether it is abjection, love, or loss that is in view, and always recalling that each way in which they take on symbolic form is *another* fate of love, loss, or abjection. In that sense *Powers of Horror*, *Tales of Love*, and *Black Sun* are quite distinct books.

This means of course that Kristeva's thought on sexual difference does not absorb the project of confronting nature "denatured." There is, as Oliver and others aver, a feminist ethics in Kristeva without, for all that, a claim that sexual difference is fundamental to ethics.[13] It needs to be asked, however, fundamental to what ethics? For Kristeva does make sexual difference fundamental to an ethics, precisely at the point where the fate of lost nature, deemed to be crucial to the ethical, is tied up with the fate of the "feminine." Kristeva's discussion of the maternal body in "Stabat Mater" closes with the thought of an ethics drawn through it. The references made here to the philosophy of modernity in critical theory aim to clarify the meaning of this ethics.

Kristeva stresses the maternal precisely as childbearing woman because, here, real experience confronts representation abruptly. "Real" suggests "lived," *actually* undergone, marking this experience off to some extent from the artistic/literary experience she generally promotes. But there is no straightforward way of articulating real experience, abandoned as it is to the widespread effects of enlightened modernity. Real experience is not undamaged. This thought appears in Kristeva's *New Maladies of the Soul* as the threat to psychic life in a world of desire and power, once the formation of inner experience over 2000 years of Western history loses its foundations and leaves modern subjects with the "prison of the soul": a "suppressed space of psychological ill-being" (1993a, 28). However, as others have underlined, the maternal body in Kristeva presents a certain resistance to this fate. It is a way of traversing the threat. Her association of the maternal body with "the unspoken" both measures the extent of this resistance and demonstrates how embattled it is. Kristeva isolates and affirms a level of female subjectivity that "no signifier can uplift." This would imply that there is an experience that escapes the dominion of the Lacanian sign or the structure of language in which nature is ejected from culture. "Stabat Mater" immediately presents the other side. "Silence weighs heavily nonetheless on the corporeal and psychological suffering of childbirth" (1977, 260).

The confrontation between real experience and representation, as well as its difficulties, are absorbed into the very style of "Stabat Mater," which is written in two columns. The left-hand column, in bold type, presents a more embodied and poetic writing on the experience of pregnancy and childbirth. It embraces at least three aspects of the confrontation between maternal embodied experience and representation. In the first, everything turns on how the signifying ambition is both tied to the (enlightenment) project of control and reflects a necessity and need of the speaking being, bringing subjectivity under the law. Remoteness from the law therefore rebounds on the subject's symbolic capacities. The first aspect of the confrontation in the maternal body, then, pertains to the loss of the capacity to represent that accompanies the upsurge of the biological in pregnancy and childbirth. "Nothing reassures, for only the law sets anything down. Who calls such a suffering jouissance? It is the pleasure of the damned" (1977, 250). In contrast to this, second, there is the fierceness of the avowal of bonds unspoken: bonds in pregnancy with "this internal graft and fold," bonds with the cosmos, bonds with the mother or the upsurge of "forgotten body relationships" and finally, thereby, bonds with women. "The community of women is a community of dolphins" (257). The phrase easily sounds sentimental or just "off" to our ears. The essay "Women's Time" gives the sense more clearly insofar as it turns on the question of submerged temporalities that differ from the linear time that Kristeva calls the time of history. The clarification this offers will be addressed before returning to "Stabat Mater" for the third aspect of the confrontation between real experience and representation at the level of the maternal body.

Critical scholars of artistic modernism have found that modernity is characterized by the ascendancy and dominion of linear time, drawing all life and representation into the temporality of the "project." This temporality is well attested in Clark's bold definition of modernity in *Farewell to an Idea: Episodes in the History of Modernism*.

> "Modernity" means contingency. It points to a social order which has turned from the worship of ancestors and past authorities to the pursuit of a projected future—of goods, pleasures, freedoms, forms of control over nature, or infinities of information. This process goes along with a great emptying and sanitizing of the imagination. Without ancestor-worship, meaning is in short supply—"meaning" here meaning agreed-on and instituted forms of value and understanding, implicit orders, stories and images in which a culture crystallizes its sense of the struggle with the realm of

> necessity and the reality of pain and death. The phrase Max Weber borrowed from Schiller, "the disenchantment of the world," still seems to me to sum up this side of modernity best. (1999, 7)

The middle of Clark's statement resonates strongly with Kristeva's diagnosis of late modern life: the crisis in meaning and values, the impoverishment of the imaginary, the import of stories or narrative in respect of suffering, and the encounter with death. However, its first two sentences and the last one contain what is at issue here. The absorption of pleasures and freedoms into the pursuit of a projected future, known to Clark, is closely analyzed in Horkheimer and Adorno's *Dialectic of Enlightenment*. Horkheimer and Adorno's analysis reveals not only how the desirability of pleasures and freedoms is isomorphic with that of "goods," but that it is so because pleasures and freedoms are themselves infused with the commodity form. Although Kristeva no longer brings a theoretical Marxian dimension to her inquiries into subjectivity, the tradition briefly resonates at moments in her thought where she contextualizes her inquiries. In *The Sense and Non-Sense of Revolt* she writes, "the primacy of the market economy over the body is certainly something to worry about, perhaps even to get dramatic about, to protest before things are firmly established, before it is definitely too late" (1996, 6). The statement manages both to call up the tendential severance of the semiotic and symbolic as though it were a metanarrative of collapse and insinuate an indefinite distance from any such metanarrative.

Dialectic of Enlightenment itself draws connections between the commodity form's invasion of pleasures and freedoms and the modern project of controlling inner and outer nature. In turn, that project is tightly linked with what Adorno's *Negative Dialectics* (1966) calls identity-thinking: a mode of thought characteristic of classical modern philosophy, which cannot go beyond the self-reflexive subject to the *object*. What unifies the arguments is the analysis of Enlightenment ("reason") as an all-embracing ideology that fails to recognize itself as such. The ideology remains ascendant despite prevalent, conscious experience of its contradictions. In Horkheimer and Adorno's essay "The Concept of Enlightenment" the effort to reveal enlightenment ("reason") for what it is, importantly undermines its distinction from what it is not—myth and superstition—showing that Enlightenment is consistent with what it purports *not* to be by virtue of the very force with which it dissociates itself.[14] "Abstraction, the instrument of enlightenment, stands in the same relationship to its objects as fate, whose concept it eradicates: as liquidation. Under the leveling rule of abstraction, which makes everything in nature repeatable, and of industry, for which abstraction prepared the way, the liberated finally themselves become the 'herd' (*Trupp*), which Hegel identified as the outcome of enlightenment" (1969, 9). (The reference is to Hegel's *Phenomenology of Spirit,* where *Trupp* is translated as "group" [1806, 342].) The notion of enlightenment's reversion to myth implies neither a simple continuity between the two nor a simple persistence of the past. It suggests, rather, the force of *irrationality* of enlightened modernity that stems from the leveling domination of abstraction. Reversion to myth, like the return of the repressed, is not the return of the identical. It is not something unaltered by the ascendancy of the self-reflexive subject and the dominion of the commodity form as an autonomous value. Whereas myth has structure and significance, "reversion to myth" covers the trajectories of, first, unreason disowned, that is to say, the fate of what is beyond the self-reflexive subject, as disowned by it; as well as, second, the pervasive *irrationality* that ensues; and finally, third, the trajectories of irrationality disowned.

The complexity of the subject matter of *Dialectic of Enlightenment* means that drawing up the connections between identity-thinking, the (enlightenment) project of control, and the commodity form is far from straightforward, as Rose has elucidated (1978, chapters 1 and 2). The use here of quotation from the book therefore runs the risk of rendering the sentences too declamatory, or at least simply thetic, and so losing the principal aim of *Dialectic of Enlightenment,* which is to avoid turning processes into entities. However, the intention is merely to indicate the echoes of critical theory's philosophy of modernity in Kristeva's project, and then clarify her difference from it as a means of drawing up the specific import of her thought on sexual difference.

The echoes are somewhat mute. A statement appearing in *Powers of Horror* could even be taken for a strong declaration of Kristeva's intent to distance herself from that philosophy. "The subjective-symbolic dimension that I am introducing does not therefore reinstate some deep or primary causality in the social *symbolic system*" (1980a, 67). But "social symbolic system" does not capture the sense of "social process" in Horkheimer and Adorno, a phrase intended to grasp a *tendency* in the modern social-symbolic to turn processes into entities. If one avoids turning "the social process" itself into an entity, Kristeva's position on primary causality does not leave her opposed to the thought of critical theory. Moreover, there is a passage in "Women's Time" where an echo of Frankfurt School thought appears. The passage bears directly on the essay's subject-matter—time and the feminine—and differentiates three temporalities.[15] It includes a reference to the argument that premodern social orders *contain* the temporality characterizing modernity, an argument she finds abundantly demonstrated. This argument appears most forcefully, perhaps, in *Dialectic of Enlightenment,* whose guiding thought is that the beginnings of enlightenment are already in myth, undermining the alignment between myth/enlightenment and prehistory/history. Myth sets off the taboo on magical thinking, which sustains "manifold affinities between existing things" and "pursues them [its ends] through mimesis, not through an increasing distance from the object" (1969, 7). Myth begins the suppression of those multidinous affinities "by the single relationship between the subject who confers meaning and the meaningless object, between rational significance and its accidental bearer" (7). The awakening of the self that characterizes enlightenment is already realized in myth. "Oedipus's answer to the riddle of the Sphinx—'That being is man'—is repeated indiscriminately as enlightenment's stereotyped message, whether in response to a piece of objective meaning, a schematic order, a fear of evil powers, or a hope of salvation" (4). Enlightenment fulfills the ascendancy of the self-reflexive subject, cut off from and seeking mastery over the object. Finally, there is the famous phrase: "Just as myths already entail enlightenment, with every step enlightenment entangles itself more deeply in mythology" (8).[16]

Implicitly isolating the first phrase, "myths already entail enlightenment," Kristeva recognizes that the time of history "is inherent in the logical and ontological values of any given civilization." This is what has already been abundantly demonstrated. In "Women's Time" she herself characterizes the time of history as what "renders explicit a rupture, an expectation or an anguish which other temporalities work to conceal" (1979, 192). Thus linear time, the time of history, refers in fact to a break in the logic of historical succession—not a closing event with respect to a certain logic but the *rendering explicit* of a rupture, an expectation or an anguish. The description resonates with Clark's assertion that modernity denotes a social order that has turned away from past authorities and, more precisely, that *modernity means contingency.* Contingency, Clark stresses, is not "an absolute, quantitative increase in uncontrolled and unpredictable events" but "the turning from past to future, the acceptance of risk, the omnipresence of change, the malleability of time and space" (1999, 10). What distinguishes the modern from the premodern is not the realization of linear time but its systematic dominion over other temporalities.

For Horkheimer and Adorno, the ascendancy of the self-reflexive subject correlates with the disenchantment of the world, the thought that *Dialectic of Enlightenment* opens with. "Enlightenment's program was the disenchantment of the world. It wanted to dispel myths, to overthrow fantasy with knowledge" (1969, 1). Kristeva, too, has brought her thought to bear on the question of disenchantment. Recall *Black Sun*'s analysis of Holbein's *Body of the Dead Christ in the Tomb,* that "composition in loneliness" that conveys the affect of loss and sublimates it in a new vision of a morality of dignity in separateness. This vision is under pressure in secular modernity. Compare Clark on Corot. "His grey pastorals grapple head on (not even defiantly) with the disenchantment of the world. They aim to include the disenchantment in themselves, and thus make it bearable" (1999, 12). Clark's second sentence could come straight from *Black Sun.* Holbein's *Dead Christ* is a composition in disenchantment, and Kristeva has the painting pose the question, "Can disenchantment be beautiful?" (1987, 126). The question does not reinstate the classical association of art with beauty. Rather, it makes artistic modernism the starting point of her minor history of the fate of loss and mourning in cultural artifacts, and finds a moment of modernism in the painting of 1521–1522. Here, with the Holbein, the content, that is to say, the representation of severance—the Dead Christ—is inseparable from the style, the severance of representation. Severance as form is form responsive to the disenchantment of the world. It is the moment of materialism in modern art. As Horowitz (2001, chapter 1) has stressed, materialism is how what is lost to art constitutively, as artifice, not possessing natural life, configures what is lost to it contextually, as modern, autonomous: "nature." Kristeva's focus on Holbein's minimalist technique is made in order to underline that lost nature is transposed into the execution of the work, and this transposition counters the loss of the other and of meaning.

Nonetheless, Kristeva's discussion of disenchantment reveals her divergence from Clark's artistic modernism, as well as the philosophy of modernity presented in *Dialectic of Enlightenment.* For what appears to a critic of artistic modernism as the circumstances of the production of artistic modernism comes in Kristeva to be the very dynamic of the speaking subject as a destabilizing-stabilizing "open system." Compare Clark—"modernism is caught interminably between horror and elation at the forces driving it" (1999, 8)—with Kristeva's analysis of Holbein's minimalism as an intimate, slender response *of* our melancholia. With her, melancholia appears as a metaphor for (a conveyance and sublimation of) the unstable moments of the subject as a destabilizing-stabilizing "open system." When Kristeva turns the antithesis of horror and elation, or hope and despair, into a subjective process she underlines the reassertion of lost nature in subjectivity.

The whole issue is reviewed in terms of temporalities in "Women's Time." The essay diverges from the philosophy of modernity to be found in critical theory, and from the kind of analysis of artistic modernism Clark delivers, because Kristeva's emphasis on the temporality characterizing modernity gives it its *subjective* meaning. The linear time of the project assumes the recognition of finitude. Subjectively, then, it is the time of rupture, anguish. "Women's Time" pursues the question of the presence in modern life of temporalities other than the linear one in order to consider their link with the reassertion of lost nature in subjectivity. Kristeva focuses on two other temporalities—for her, cyclical and monumental time—and interprets them in terms of "women's time." That is to say, she finds the submerged temporalities, precisely, at a certain level of female subjectivity. "As for time, female subjectivity [*la subjectivité féminine*] would seem to provide a specific measure that essentially retains *repetition* and *eternity* from among the multiple modalities of time known through the history of civilizations" (1979, 191). On the one hand, repetition (cyclical), on the other eternity (monumental). First, female subjectivity involves "cycles, gestation, the eternal recurrence of a biological rhythm which conforms to that of nature and imposes a temporality whose stereotyping may shock, but whose regularity and unison with what is experienced as extra-subjective time, cosmic time, occasion vertiginous visions and unnameable *jouissance*" (1979, 191). It is important to see that the experience of cyclical time is not some pure reemergence of a temporality other than the time of history, for it is a rhythm that conforms to *what is experienced as* extra-subjective time. Cyclical time *is* no more than its subjective register, or—recalling the discussion of Butler and Kristeva above, which stressed that there is only subjectivity if society does not fully regulate its members—subjectivity *is* the register of cyclical time. Put otherwise, *jouissance can only be modern.*

Of the second submerged temporality, Kristeva says: "There is the massive presence of a monumental temporality, without cleavage or escape, which has so little to do with linear time (which passes) that the very word 'temporality' hardly fits: all-encompassing and infinite like imaginary space, this temporality reminds one of Kronos in Hesiod's mythology, the incestuous son whose massive presence covered all of Gea in order to separate her from Ouranos, the father" (1979, 191). The mythological reference reveals both the overlapping of monumental time and the time of history ("in order to separate her") and how the realization of rupture is already revoked ("the incestuous son whose massive presence covered all of Gea").

I do not mean to suggest that Kristeva's thought simply aims to reveal the presence in modern life of temporalities that linear time works to suppress. The point, rather, is that the reasserted temporalities can be taken to signal unreason *disowned.* Kristeva constantly underlines the connection of those temporalities with the phantasmatic as a reassertion of lost nature *and* a figure of distortion. Nor do the particularities of female subjectivity she returns us to mark off a sphere of experience unaffected by the processes which led Horkheimer and

Adorno to see intimacy overtaken as well.[17] Kristeva's attention to the real experience of a certain level of female subjectivity does not carve out a realm of undistorted intimate reactions. Thus the relatively overt or implicit question of much of her feminist reception might be how far Kristeva succeeds in seeking out the intertwinement of nature and culture that female subjectivity provides a measure of without re-presenting the myth of woman that the modern project of the control of nature sustains and deploys. For the myth offsets the reduction of reproduction to reproductive capacities without challenging that reduction. It is hardly an easy task to assess the degree of Kristeva's success. This is not least because if one attributes to her the desire to bring woman out of her confinement with nature in fantasy, just at this point where she develops the thought of semiotic "authority," one might be attributing to her the desire that content *be* form. For, if phantasmatics is all that has met the demand that the traces of semiotic authority—something archaic that juts into the present—be given form, how can the feminine be brought out of confinement in fantasy without simply basing one's hope on a formless content, ripe for an outbreak? Kristeva's 1980s trilogy turns constantly on this problem of the semiotic, and it would place a blunt contradiction at the heart of her thought if one attributed to her the desire that content, the semiotic, *be form*. Let us recall, once again, on the analogy with Kant, that the symbolic without the semiotic is empty, and semiotic traces deprived of symbolic form are blind. The ethical thought of "Stabat Mater" turns on the connection between the feminine, nature "denatured," and the need of form-giving. As I am consistently underlining, this includes, especially, the need of imaginary discourses to give form to loss.

We can now complete the outline of the three dimensions of the confrontation between real experience and representation that appear in the left-hand column of "Stabat Mater." The first was the threat to symbolic capacities, owing to remoteness from the law in the upsurge of the biological in pregnancy and childbirth. The second was the fierce avowal of bonds unspoken. In the third, the maternal body involves an uneasy confrontation with the world that has receded, most poignant in and ultimately resolved into a clash with the self-assertion of "the other woman."

> When the other woman posits herself as such, that is, as singular and inevitably in opposition, "I" am startled, so much that "I" no longer know what is going on. There are then two paths left open to the rejection that bespeaks the recognition of the other woman as such. Either, not wanting to experience her, I ignore her and, "alone of my sex," I turn my back on her in friendly fashion. It is a hatred that, lacking a recipient worthy enough of its power, changes to unconcerned complacency. Or else, out-

> raged by her own stubbornness, by that other's belief that she is singular, I unrelentingly let go at her claim to address me and find respite only in the eternal return of power strokes, bursts of hatred—blind and dull but obstinate. I do not see her as herself but beyond her I aim at the claim to singularity, the unacceptable ambition to be something other than a child or a fold in the plasma that constitutes us, an echo of the cosmos that unifies us. (1977, 257–258)

In summarizing one aspect of what is at issue here, Kristeva proposes that transverbal communication between bodies makes up an unnameable community of women (258). This does not of course fulfill the meaning of the maternal feminine, for the experience of the unnameable community of women is streaked by "the other woman," rejection of whom bespeaks recognition of her. This calls to mind the reciprocal but mutually irreducible intolerances, and intolerabilities, of the finite, signifying subject and the "other scene" that came out in the discussion in chapter 7, above, of Kristeva's return to the "uncanny" in *Strangers to Ourselves*. But now the double intolerance is complicated by sexual difference, showing, *contra* Oliver, that Kristeva does specifically address a crisis in relation to women.[18]

The main objective of "Stabat Mater" is to aim at the radical tension of the *feminine*. Following the need to work through how the feminine is marked or represented in the culture, this tension must be aimed at through a traversal of the effort to tame it. The attempt precedes and underlies modern abstractedness, which works to conceal recognition of that tension. Kristeva attends to the Christian confrontation with the feminine. "Did not Christianity attempt, among other things, to freeze that seesaw? To stop it, tear women away from its rhythm, settle them permanently in the spirit? Too permanently . . ." (1977, 259). At this point the right-hand column of "Stabat Mater," a more analytical writing, extends beneath the left-hand column to fill the entire width of the page, as if to bolster those words with the theoretical discourse turning on the distinction between the semiotic and symbolic.

> The unspoken doubtless weighs first on the maternal body: as no signifier can uplift it without leaving a remainder, for the signifier is always meaning, communication, or structure, whereas a woman as mother would be, instead, a strange fold that changes culture into nature, the speaking into biology. Although it concerns every woman's body, the heterogeneity that cannot be subsumed in the signifier nevertheless explodes violently with pregnancy (the threshold of culture and nature) and the child's arrival (which extracts woman out of her oneness and gives her the possibility—but not the certainty—of reaching out to the other, the ethical). Those particularities of the maternal body compose woman into a being of folds,

> a catastrophe of being that the dialectics of the trinity and its supplements would be unable to subsume. (1977, 259–260)

Since this passage distinguishes and articulates the particularities of the maternal body, it carries out the objectification that theoretical discourse brings about. The left-hand column offsets the objectification of the maternal body by having structure, law, and the sign felt, thereby invoking the *heterogeneity* of the semiotic and symbolic—of the return toward biology, on the one hand, and the separation from nature, on the other—more powerfully than the analytical writing can. Yet this is still no undistorted experience. Again, the phantasmatic is the path and stands in the path. Both the right-hand column and the more analytic moments of the left-hand one are a constant reminder of this. "Archaic maternal love would be an incorporation of my suffering that is unfailing" (1977, 252, left-hand column). Pursuing the theoretical path Kristeva takes, the objectification of "every woman's body" is intensified. "A mother is a continuous separation, a division of the very flesh. And consequently a division of language—and it has always been so" (254). The question here is not whether Kristeva reduces woman to her reproductive capacities but what division "has always been so" and what future of this past is envisaged.

"Stabat Mater" proposes that the maternal body verges on *the ethical.* Kristeva's maternal body is an encounter with unassimilable and unobjectifiable exteriority. "I confront the abyss between what was mine and is henceforth but irreparably alien. Trying to think through that abyss: staggering vertigo" (255). The experience of the maternal body is auspicious for "reaching out to the other" because, here, the impossibility of assimilating or objectifying the other is *actually undergone,* at close quarters, so to speak. Support for Kristeva as a contributor to the task of articulating a feminist ethics lays most emphasis on moments of her thought like this one. With Oliver, what is central to a Kristevan ethics is the move beyond the need of external law. "Her reformulation of ethics results in an ethics that is not based on restriction and repression. When sexuality is reconceived as grounded in pleasure and violence, *jouissance,* rather than the repression of *jouissance,* then the ethical imperative is reconceived as the necessity to articulate that *jouissance*" (Oliver 1993b, 16). In this way, maternity as well as poetry and psychoanalysis provides a "model" for ethics (17). With Ziarek, "the mark of alterity points to the subject's indebtedness to the other, to a forgotten maternal gift, which enables our ethical orientation in the world" (in Oliver 1993b, 74). Yet there is a difficulty in developing a reconceived ethics (Oliver) or working out our ethical orientation in the world (Ziarek) on the basis of the maternal body. First, both pleasure and violence merely abstracted from law, on the one hand, and the "forgotten maternal gift" as such, on the other, are *content without form*. Everything, then, depends on the *articulation,* whose necessity Oliver stresses. Second, the voice of the left-hand column of "Stabat Mater" cannot be abstracted from the maternal body and expanded into an ethics without the latter losing what makes it an actual ethics. Kristeva's tendency here is to reach "back" into the maternal feminine rather than "forward" into an expanded *theoretical* articulation of the ethical moment rooted in this component of sexual difference. She returns constantly to the moments at which the maternal feminine itself can be heard, or simply to where the need to hear and elaborate it resounds as loudly as possible. The ethical orientation always waits on further resonance. On the one hand, theory or even writing alone, cannot meet the need of the ethical, for it is in part a question of what women themselves bring to and from their experience, its stumbling-blocks and its intricacies. "Now, if a contemporary ethics is no longer seen as being the same as morality; if ethics amounts to not avoiding the embarrassing and inevitable problematics of the law but giving it flesh, language, and jouissance—in that case its reformulation demands the contribution of women. Of women who harbor the desire to reproduce (to have stability). Of women who are available so that our speaking species, which knows it is mortal, might withstand death. Of mothers" (1977, 262–263). On the other hand, there is psychoanalytic listening, as she underlines in *The Sense and Non-Sense of Revolt*: "beyond the uncomfortable feminine position that many of us are familiar with, the psychical bisexuality of the woman remains a promised land that we must attain, particularly in psychoanalysis, by curving the pleasure that our professional, clinical, theoretical, and clearly phallic accomplishments give us toward *the barely expressible and highly sensitive territory of our silent mothers*" (1996, 105, emphasis added).

In summation, the ethical orientation resting on the complexities of the maternal body can only be drawn *through* the experience of the maternal body. There is such orientation because, as we have seen, Kristeva's maternal body as a "natural history," a history of living nature, if you like, is discontinuous from the start. The natural history is already a lost past, for there is no maternal body without "the other woman": finite, signifying, positing herself as singular and so inevitably caught up in the problematics of the law. The maternal body is not only a *change* from culture to nature but invokes—and must repeat, for the mother and the child—the change from nature to culture. Indeed, the presence of "the other woman" reflects and reproduces the abstraction without which the maternal body could not *be* the basis for an ethical orientation—could not be normative. Put otherwise, without "the other woman," the maternal body could not underlie a modern ethics. Yet, since any modern experience is marked by abstractedness and leveling—tied to the effects of enlightened modernity—"real" experience in Kristeva must mean that the return of lost nature *binds experience to experience.* Modern experience, in its abstractedness, is only actually returned to a nature-culture crossroads if the experience turning on this crossroads is bound to itself, if it cannot be divorced from itself and turned into a mere abstraction once more.

It is consistent with the *difficulty* in modern ethical experience of binding experience to experience, that the feminist reception of Kristeva's "maternal body" suggests that it provides the possibility of an ethics, and then tends to stop short. For "possibility" is the wrong modality altogether for this situation. The conception of "*l'héréthique*"—"herethics" in the English translation—does not suggest that the maternal body is a site of possibility for ethics. "Nothing, however, suggests that a feminine ethics is possible" (1977, 262). The only modality of the maternal body is actuality. Oliver has underlined that this is not an ethics for persons. Put otherwise, the ethical that this actuality opens up in one way excludes men, and it embraces some women more than others. Oliver's emphasis on the distinction between a morality that organizes relations between persons and a Kristevan ethics that would expand on the side of *jouissance* is true to the spirit of Kristeva's thought (Oliver 1993b, 16–17). Her assertion that the ethical imperative is reconceived as the necessity to articulate *jouissance,* the pleasure and violence that grounds sexuality, recognizes that the only modality of the maternal body is actuality. But, again, it needs to be recognized that *jouissance* is *modern.* It presumes repression, and assumes a change from culture to nature, just as its articulation presumes a change from nature to culture. The articulations of *jouissance* must also contain some allusion to repression, and so to law and the effects of law. Nonetheless, that nature binds experience to experience suggests that there may be a binding of nature and culture to offset the nature/culture dichotomy. Kristeva speaks of the ethical implication of the maternal body because these are fundamental bonds. If this level of female subjectivity is equally the site of a phantasmatics that carries threats greater even than phallic monism, perhaps this is because nothing can offset the instability of those bonds given the extent to which the feminine is confined in fantasy. Where emphasis on the "need" of paternal law turns up, it is often predicated on cognizance of that instability. But Kristeva works to show the ethical implications of those bonds nonetheless. The final passage of the right-hand column of "Stabat Mater" suggests the place that *l'héréthique* has in modernity, considering now its widest reach in respect of whom it encompasses. "For an heretical ethics separated from morality, an *herethics,* is perhaps no more than that which in life makes bonds, thoughts, and therefore the thought of death, bearable: herethics is undeath [*a-mort*], love ... *Eia mater, fons amoris...* So let us listen to the *Stabat Mater,* and the music, all the music ... it swallows up the goddesses and removes their necessity" (1977, 263). The accompanying final words of the left-hand column suggest that herethics—as undeath, love—equally bears on the problem of the inarticulate that is captured, differently, in the term abjection.

> The other is inevitable, [the mother] seems to say, turn it into a God if you wish, it is nevertheless natural, for such an other has come out of myself, which is yet not myself but a flow of unending germinations, an eternal cosmos. The other goes much without saying and without my saying that, at the limit, it does not exist for itself. The "just the same" of motherly peace ... constitutes the basis of the social bond in its generality, in the sense of "resembling others and eventually the species." Such an attitude is frightening when one imagines that it can crush everything the other (the child) has that is specifically irreducible: rooted in that disposition of motherly love, besides, we find the leaden strap it can become, smothering any different individuality. But it is there, too, that the speaking being finds a refuge when his/her symbolic shell cracks and a crest emerges where speech causes biology to show through: I am thinking of the time of illness, of sexual-intellectual-physical passion, of death. (1977, 262–263)

What this shows is that, with Kristeva, there is a relationship between maternity and ethics only if the second step of form-giving shows up. *L'héréthique* is an *imaginary construct* that gives form to fundamental bonds. These are bonds of love—the essay, after all, appears as a chapter in *Tales of Love.* Yet the thought of herethics equally acknowledges that the immemorial past—semiotic authority—*is* immemorial, unrepresentable. Herethics gives form to the upsurge of forgotten body relationships, a past that was never present. The return of forgotten body relationships, of "fundamental bonds," in maternal experience therefore binds experience to experience only by binding experience to *loss.* That is to say, *l'héréthique* turns "lost nature" from its fate as *dead nature*—as nature ejected from culture—into loss. The transformation is captured in the expression "undeath, love" (*a-mort, amour*). The imaginary construct encourages us to take up a relationship to the past, in response to and countering the dismissal of nature that pushes it into the past. For that act of dismissal is fundamental to the projection of birth and death, and so nature, onto women. This is how Kristeva's investigation of the feminine undermines the generality of the "subject" in *Strangers to Ourselves* by introducing sexual difference into it. Yet introducing sexual difference into the subject *in this way* does not make good on the lack of real otherness and futurity in Kristeva's ethics of psychoanalysis. This is a convenient point at which to fulfill the promise made near the beginning of section 1, above, to thematize further the meaning or meanings of the "feminine" in Kristeva. I noted there the support in the literature for Kristeva's recognition that the meaning of the "feminine" is open and contestable ("woman can never be defined," *la femme ce n'est jamais ça*). This point is a crucial one for feminist debates on sexual difference. Nevertheless, I have given the whole discussion of the feminine in Kristeva over to a reinvestigation of the meaning of the *maternal* feminine in her thought. This requires some justification. The major objective has been to show that Kristeva's thought on the maternal is a place where we discover the importance of her conception of the *imaginary*. It needs to be set down clearly that this is a vital concept in her thinking on subjectivity and history. The imaginary covers not only the problematic of phantasmatics, where, I have argued, a lost past is reasserted in distorted forms. It also delivers her thought on the sites of possibility *for our time*. Kristeva's discussion of the maternal feminine shows clearly that the imaginary means the recovery of the semiotic, never as the presymbolic content (a past that was never present), but as re-formed in relation to and differently from previous forms that it has taken. Comparable to the exemplary works of mourning that appear in Kristeva's minor history of modernity in *Black Sun*, the imaginary construct formulated in "Stabat Mater"—the idea of *l'héréthique*—is a recurrence of symbolization of the semiotic. Comparable to those works of art, it is tied both to sites of suffering—the remnant of freedom—and to its own historicality. Like them, it is both linked to a certain past and open with respect to future instances of form-giving.

However, I must still respond to the question whether Kristeva's formulation of the "heretical ethics separated from morality" ties the feminine to the maternal. As others have shown, the question of the feminine in Kristeva is not collapsed into her revision of the discourse of maternity. For example, Ziarek underlines how "Women's Time" bears on other dimensions of sexuality and sexual difference, and stresses their significance for democratic politics (2001, 145–146). My own reading of "Stabat Mater" and "Women's Time" has worked to emphasize how the revision of the discourse of maternity is not simply a revision of the meaning of motherhood. For Kristeva's attention to what she calls "maternality" aims to undermine the opposition between maternity and femininity that can beset even feminist interrogations of sexual difference. This opposition is a feature of patriarchal culture, where the meaning of the maternal is so often confined to the naturalized body of the "nurse," so that the maternal is associated with enclosure or domesticity, as Smith remarks in *Julia Kristeva: Speaking the Unspeakable* (1998, 11). The meaning of the feminine, opposed to that of the maternal, then carries the other attributes projected on to women, such as passivity, seductiveness, and weakness. Obviously feminist thought contests and counters both images of woman. Even so, the worry about whether a critical thinker like Kristeva has the "maternal" subsume the "feminine" needs to be self-critical about whether a residue of the patriarchal opposition pervades its own thinking. Smith (1998) has issued a timely reminder of the danger of reading the meanings that accrue to the term *feminine* in the Anglo-American world into translations of the French term *le féminin* (10). As Ziarek (2001) has shown, Kristeva does keep open the meaning of the feminine. My discussion of Kristeva has stressed the meaning of the maternal in Kristeva as a level of female subjectivity where there is an experience that confronts extant representations of maternity—just *where* the projection of (denatured) nature onto women is pervasively upheld. Kristeva's analysis of that confrontation is equally a recovery of the maternal *feminine.* In the right-hand column of "Stabat Mater" Kristeva addresses the cult of Mary in part because it achieves a certain refeminization of the mother, and so a certain recovery of the tension of the feminine (that it also tames). The objective of "Stabat Mater" as a whole, and other of Kristeva's writings, is to bring out the maternal *feminine* in conditions that work to conceal recognition of the feminine at all, that is to say, in late modern societies. There may be a bias of interest on Kristeva's part when she repeatedly stresses the significance and fate of the maternal. At the same time, this bias of interest has unearthed what worries about the reduction of the feminine to the maternal pass over too quickly: that the maternal is not to be set off from the feminine, that it is an aspect of *all* subjectivity, which both men and women must negotiate, and that it is the theory of the unconscious (encompassing the semiotic *and* symbolic) that reveals this.

Finally, Kristeva's feminist essays return us to the whole question of the need of giving the semiotic symbolic form, and so to the moments in her writings that work to fulfill this need in and through an investigation of the imaginary. We recall that this is the category where Kristeva's thought on subjectivity and history is both most dense and most developed. I will now close the journey through Kristeva's most explicitly feminist writings with a brief summary of what it has shown, in order to recuperate my argument for the importance of Kristeva's thought on loss. Kristeva's writings on the feminine have worked to bring out, name, and articulate semiotic (maternal) authority, and thereby overcome Freud's focus on the father. Semiotic authority itself is immemorial, a lost past that is unrepresentable. Nonetheless, the lost past protrudes into the present in ways that distort what is lost and suppress the loss—that is to say, phantasmatically. Kristeva equally proposes that at a certain level of female subjectivity, the experience of the maternal body, there is a recovery of a lost past of a kind that draws the feminine and lost nature out of their confinement in fantasy. The return of lost nature turns up as nonsignifying—"unspoken"—memory. The memorialization of forgotten body experiences in pregnancy and childbirth does not, however, restore what is lost. It lets what is lost, and so the *loss,* figure and be figured. In this way, "maternality" binds experience *to* experience. That said, this memory of a lost past does not, in and of itself, provide any direction for form-giving to take. That is why "Stabat Mater" concludes with the transitory ideal of "undeath, love," an imaginary construct giving form to the lost past. It is the *two steps,* both the binding of experience to experience in the nonsignifying memory of forgotten body experiences, and the development of the imaginary construct giving form to love and loss, which make Kristeva's "maternality" normative: an ethics.

Kristeva's feminist thought acts as a reminder, then, of the danger highlighted earlier, that the thought of abjection is currently being asked to do too much work in the investigation of the boundaries of subject and society. So we emphasize, here, that there are resources in Kristeva that go beyond current discussions of abjection, but also trauma, in respect of recognizing the contributions psychoanalysis can make to the search for non-narcissistic relationship. Kristeva's thought on the "feminine" underlines the import of the topics of *Tales of Love* and *Black Sun*. That is to say, Kristeva's feminist thought contains the thought of primary idealization and exhibits the value, at the level of symbolic functioning, of transitory ideals to support limit experiences. It equally shows how these ideals are necessarily connected with the recovery of loss in a world afflicted by the *loss of loss*.

Kristeva's "herethics" does not, however, as I underline above, present us with some final say on what giving form to the semiotic may be. For, on the one hand, once we have the conception of the semiotic as the reminder of our being part of nature, and as the reminder of nature's living history, what turns up at the limit of the ties between the individual and the social is not fixed. On the other hand, what might give form to these less visible features of selfhood and connections with others remains an open question. Kristeva's *oeuvre* continues to discover and articulate further responses to the question of form-giving and the ethical. She has recently done so in a way that fills a certain lacuna in the major writings discussed in these chapters, as I will suggest in the conclusion, below. The conclusion is dedicated to drawing together and readdressing some major criticisms that circulate in the reception of her thought. It also begins a reflection on what is familiar and what is new in her most recent major publications.

CONCLUSION

Revolt Culture and Exemplary Lives

This book has stressed that Kristeva's thought on psychoanalysis, religion, and art, especially as it is developed in the 1980s trilogy, is vital for grasping the significance and scope of her project. It has also suggested that when she proceeds to draw out the social and political implications of the psychoanalytic standpoint, she appears to overstep the ambiguities in self and world that this standpoint exposes. For psychoanalysis does not only offer a new model of the individual to the humanities and sciences, a point that has been made in the above chapters, and that I recapitulate in the following sentences. The new model of the individual that Kristeva proposes on the basis of psychoanalytic experience carries the cost of losing eighteenth-century optimism about the assumed balance of individuals, but it also surpasses that faulty conception by proposing, not so much a theory of the "truth" of the subject, but a grasp of its innovative capacities—capacities for playing a part in a world qualified by the challenges of separateness and otherness. The conception of the heterogeneous subject stresses the destabilization of the subject in respect of pain, loss, and death, a destabilization of the identity of body and psychic space, which carries fragmentation into the social fabric. But it equally emphasizes repetitions and discontinuities given life, value, and meaning, which counterbalance destabilization, not as the alternative to it, but as what can arise in passing through it. With Kristeva, psychoanalysis does not only offer this new model of the individual, however. It also discovers the prison of the modern soul—"new maladies of the soul"—and a new suffering world. It may discern the remnant of freedom in unacknowledged suffering, but this remnant is, precisely, a broken-off piece of the reality that has come to grief. The upsurge of abjection, the weakness of resources to support idealizing constructions, and the loss of loss remain fundamental features of Western cultures, and leave the maturational processes typically available for subject-formation in those cultures inadequate. I have therefore underlined the need to take on the question of mediation foregrounded in the 1980s trilogy, which focuses on the achievements of therapy and artworks with respect to recovering the sites of suffering and creating other paths for the broken-off pieces of reality. Above all, I have argued that Kristeva's conception of the imaginary is a vital locus for her thinking on subjectivity and history. This thinking makes a strong commitment to revealing the hazards of being ordained to a merely linguistic universe, and so losing a world of nature, for this is also to lose a historical world.

On these grounds, a major commitment of this book has been to show that deployments of her more overtly social and political, including feminist, thought will be hampered if they miss the problem of mediation. This is the problem that reveals Kristeva's sensitivity to the perennial historical crisis we call modernity. Without cognizance of these central features of her project, the reception of her writings will continue to break off in puzzlement or impatience over her psychoanalytic standpoint, or, alternatively, will only turn to other thinkers to shore up the gaps in the ethical and political stakes of her thought. I will now attempt to localize the reasons for some stumbling blocks that continue to affect the reception of her thought, although I am not of course claiming to be able to clear them up entirely.

One of the major stumbling blocks in the appreciation of her writings relates to the awareness that both her categorial distinction between the semiotic and symbolic and her conception of the imaginary are introduced in a thought that fully inherits the Lacanian conception of the symbolic that turns on castration and lack. This has left the pervasive impression that Kristeva leaves the symbolic *qua* prohibiting, paternal law as the foundation of culture, that is to say, both theoretically unaltered and, in the final instance, practically untransformable. The debate with Butler in chapter 7 covered some ground in explicating this problem. It is true that Kristeva accepts the Lacanian story about language and lack. It is also true that her attention to the new maladies of the soul overcomes Lacan's antipsychological tendency, allowing attention to the pre-imaginary structures of subjectivity to sustain the commitment to sites of suffering and the possibilities of overcoming it. Kristeva has shown that it is only a fine-grained account of subjectivity—not one that is dedicated to the existential and the symbolic alone—that can get at the nature of suffering at a fundamental level, and so at its deepest significance and prospects. Nonetheless, because Kristeva accepts the story of language and lack as well, she forces everything else that is important psychologically—bar the imaginary father—into the pre-imaginary level of relationship to the archaic mother where the life of the drives is most emphatic. This does leave the impression, for example, that loss always reverts to the question of the mother in Kristeva. It also leaves some wanting to ask about moments in subject formation that might lie between the archaic and the emergence of symbolic functioning. There are other differences to be explored than that between semiotic authority and paternal law. Finally, on different terrain, this focus on the psychological importance of the archaic mother sometimes disbars her from an adequate engagement with cultural material on its own terms. This is a fundamental reason for the view that sees in her work a reduction of the significance of art and literature to the subjectivity of the artist. I have argued against this formulation of the objection, since Kristeva's attention to sites and modes of suffering has such a broad scope in her thought, but there is a basis for the objection. Drawbacks of her negotiation of the psychoanalytic and aesthetic standpoints such as these ones cannot be dealt with peremptorily. They require further elaboration and critical response that is beyond the reach of the current project. So I will focus on the more familiar problem of her relationship to the Lacanian symbolic.

Kristeva's notion of the imaginary, where much of her thought on subjectivity and history is to be found, underscores the need of discourses and imaginary constructions that give shape to the remnant of freedom discovered in suffering subjectivity. However, Butler's attention to the symbolic demand that organizes subjects into sexed positions highlights a problem that is not dispensed with by arguing for the imaginary. For it is not only a question of finding that traces of semiotic authority and pre-imaginary structures—that is to say, corporeal responsiveness, affective experience, and mimetic relations—are left unmoved if the task of giving them symbolic form is neglected. Nor is it just a question of showing how far that form-giving takes us from the vicissitudes of the neglected semiotic content and the phantasmatics turning on it. There are other authorities, revolving on paternal law—however deracinated, fragile, or empty this place of power is—that arise right beside the imaginary realm and have the power to overwhelm it. For, even if the untruth of paternal law's adequacy for guaranteeing social and symbolic being has neared the surface in modern Western societies, this has led to changes in its mode of operation, not to some other kind of social and symbolic authority. In other words the deformation of paternal law has not led to forms of social authority other than abstractly universal ones that leave the changed mode of operation of paternal law—Butler's concealed symbolic demand—to prevail in social and symbolic life. Kristeva is fully aware of this, and has developed a number of responses to it.

Before proceeding to those responses, let me suggest something about Kristeva's appreciation of the Lacanian story of language and lack, whose stroke of genius, as I have proposed, lies in its radical discovery of finitude at all points of the human adventure, as well as the need of accepting it and the infinite potential this acceptance implies, for Lacan. Kristeva's positive reception of this story means that she must inherit and endorse oedipal destiny, since Lacan hooks the symbolic on to the oedipal structure. She therefore misses an opportunity to underline moments in Freud that reveal his insight into the way in which the paternal law is the trace of a past, bad authority. Reading from *Totem and Taboo* (1912–1913), to *Civilization and Its Discontents* (1930), to *Moses and Monotheism* (1939), one can see the following discoveries in Freud's exploration of totemic societies, religion, and the superego. In *Totem and Taboo* he connects the father complex as one source of religion, social organization, and morality with the Oedipus complex discovered in the psyche of modern subjects, simply by analogy. In *Civilization and Its Discontents* he is attentive to the tyrannical disposition of the superego as the psychic instance of the Other that represents the assumption of the prohibiting, separating function of paternal law. Freud's attention to the superego finds that the psychic law of separation inhibits the carrying out of its own imperative, since it withdraws the ego from its surrounding world, locking it into a guilt structure of subjectivity, or better, shows that the oedipal structure of subjectivity corresponds to a guilt culture. Finally, *Moses and Monotheism* explicates the actual formation of traditional authority in monotheistic religion. *Totem and Taboo* had already proposed that paternal authority is at its height as a social authority in religion. Far from celebrating this, Freud finds it to be a harsh revenge taken against the transgression against or deposing of the father's power. This appears to him to be a feature of the tyrannical disposition of the superego, too. These moments of Freud's thought delineate a particular insight. Religion begat the psyche, that is to say, the oedipal structure that, for Freud, is the central character of the psyche. This means that the oedipal structure is the trace of a past form of authority. It is the trace of a bad form of authority because it leaves guidance for separateness, responsibility, and morality both in the taboo structure and magical. In sum, these moments in Freud show that oedipal destiny rests on an unnegotiable authority.

Kristeva accepts the Lacanian story of language and lack—and so the symbolic, paternal law—for its meaning as individuation and finitude. Symbolic lack remains at the center of her thought because she must press the need of a second moment of separateness, after the separating imperative that devolves on maternal authority, because the latter imperative remains tangled up with failure, even in its success. That is to say, the mother's power is so overbearing and overinclusive that a second moment of separateness is needed if the emergent ego is to find a place to come into being. Kristeva supports the oedipal structure because she wants to defend strong individuation. This explains her emphasis on the meaning of "crisis" as *kairos,* interpreted in *The Sense and Non-Sense of Revolt* as "cut" and "decisive encounter," which "henceforth seals the fate of the human being as desiring and speaking being" (1996, 97). This is a direct reference to the value of symbolic lack in Lacan, and appears to weld her approval of it as a decisive "splitting" to phallic primacy. Kristeva therefore misses the opportunity to relativize her support for lack and law as oedipal *destiny*, as many want her to do. This is something she could have done if she had not restricted the range of Freud's analysis of religion to his discovery of the forgotten past of totemic religion. Her ability to write fragmentary minor histories of religion perhaps carries the cost of weakening this Freudian insight. For Freud finds that what we have left behind—the taboo structure of authority—has not been left behind, and he clearly shows that the oedipal structure is what bears this fate. On a final note, Butler's recognition that the symbolic demand is the concealed functioning of a bad law might be illuminated further if that law were grasped as the trace of a past, bad form of authority. In sum, Kristeva's inheritance and endorsement of the Lacanian thought of lack and law can look as though she maintains the symbolic law as foundational for culture. However, let me stress again that she is fully aware that the pretensions of the symbolic, paternal law to be "all" are a problem. I now turn to some of the responses she has developed in respect of this.

One response, which she homes in on in *Black Sun*, is to suggest that the topic of *Tales of Love*, that is to say, the recovery of the value of the living and loving father of prehistory, can modify the stringency of the symbolic demand and, by implication, its effects. She argues in *Black Sun* that what is required is a blending of the imaginary father and the oedipal one. This would amend many of the problems of the narcissistic constriction explored in the 1980s trilogy. In her words, "it is imperative that this father in individual prehistory be capable of playing his part as oedipal father in symbolic Law, for it is on the basis of that harmonious blending of the two facets of fatherhood that the abstract and arbitrary signs of communication may be fortunate enough to be tied to the affective meaning of prehistorical identifications, and the dead language of the potentially depressive person can arrive at a live meaning in the bond with others" (1987, 23–24). The thought bears directly on the problem of being ordained to a merely linguistic universe, and the consequent vicissitudes of the disowned realm of corporeal responsiveness, affective meaning, and mimetic relations, whose full cost is not borne by everyone, but which pervade the social and political ills of Western cultures. Nonetheless, this imperative to blend the two facets of fatherhood is a moment of ideality in her thinking. There is little to suggest that it can root itself in a culture defined, rather extensively, by the lack of a secular variant of the loving father. Kristeva herself has shown that idealization cannot happen at one level (individual) if it is missing at the other (societal). Her support for the oedipal structure is intelligible insofar as, if it worked, it would synthesize the relationship between the ego ideal—whose core in Kristeva *is* the transcendent moment of the imaginary father—and the superego. The sense that the oedipal structure is historical, which comes out in some of Freud's writing, is that it just does not seem to be able to do that. Given what she says about the imaginary father and her agreement with Lacan—which is her support for strong individuation—Kristeva *has* to have the convergence. But it remains an ideal.

Another response to the problem of the pretensions of symbolic law has been foregrounded in her recent thought on "revolt culture" in *The Sense and Non-Sense of Revolt* (1996) and *Intimate Revolt* (1997), the two volumes of her latest interrogation of the powers and limits of psychoanalysis. This work is gaining increasing attention in the literature on her, but its central thought is familiar from the 1980s writings. On thing that is stressed in the thought on "revolt" is how women's position in relation to symbolic law endows them with a situation that encourages insight into the *illusory being* of phallic primacy. Put simply, women see through the lies of the culture. Kristeva has returned to the theme of illusion and disillusionment also known from *Black Sun*. There the connections she proposed between illusion and disillusionment took an aesthetic standpoint on the presentation of a new ethic of dignity in the face of mortality and the pain of loss (Holbein). We saw that this ethic could not stand up to the pressure put on the aesthetic when the latter confronted the challenge of responding to the explosion of death in the cataclysms of the twentieth century (Kristeva's analysis of Duras). The thought of revolt culture, then, does not especially draw out the question of the ethical. Yet the more recent discussion of illusion and disillusionment has drawn and will continue to draw the attention of feminist sympathizers because it stresses the connection between the feminine and the distance that can be taken from the pretensions of phallic primacy.

This notion of distance is a central feature of her idea of revolt culture, an idea, then, that links the sites of possibility strongly to the potentialities of women. It may seem to some as though this new thought on revolt recovers the kind of political standpoint apparently lost since *Revolution in Poetic Language*. However, I maintain that it is continuous with the changed view of the meaning of the semiotic and symbolic in the 1980s. For the thought of this distance, in and *as* culture, is known from *Strangers to Ourselves,* where cultural distance is a stance available for tempering and modifying the simplistic attitudes of rejection or indifference toward foreigners, as well as the arbitrary or utilitarian decisions regulating relationships between them. More pertinently, the connection between the feminine and the possibility of sustaining the insight into the illusory being of phallic primacy had a major role in *Tales of Love,* where Kristeva developed her thought on maternality. In the 1996 text her discussion of women's situation in relation to phallic primacy suggests that the transition out of the sway of phantasmatics, which was an issue in "Stabat Mater," can be accomplished by dis-illusionment, women's insight into the illusion of that primacy. Disillusionment, for her, is "a maintenance and an estrangement of illusion as illusion" (1996, 106). This is a variation on Freud's thought in *The Future of an Illusion* (1927). Despite her comment, "Freud the rationalist was right: everyone wants an illusion and insists on not knowing that it is one" (106), her own definition of disillusionment makes it clear that the question is how one can have illusions in the full knowledge that they are illusions. The affirmation of art has been one answer to this question. The imaginary construct of "undeath, love," which symbolically re-forms the lost past of the archaic mother, was another. Interestingly, the brief discussion of illusion in *The Sense and Non-Sense of Revolt* suggests that her own text—this text in which she is delineating the potentialities of women—might itself be an illusion. "And I admit that what I have said may only be an illusion as well" (106). Kristeva's thought that women have insight into the illusory being of phallic *primacy*, without their collapsing the acceptance of finitude, suggests that the tension of the feminine (semiotic-and-symbolic, or nature and culture) gives women a privilege in exploring the question and so sustaining the culture of revolt: "a woman is better placed than anyone to explore illusion" (106). Her thought is that women have insight into the illusion that sees in individuation an accomplished and unquestionable autonomy, as well as the ability knowingly to take up the illusions that the imaginary realm delivers. Kristeva's thought on revolt culture is therefore a further development of her historical category of the imaginary, one which links its entire significance to the destiny of women. This means that it is worthy of close attention, but it also needs to be acknowledged as a continuation and expansion of her 1980s thought.

The two volumes on the culture of revolt are also continuous with the 1980s trilogy in another way. Their general structure and composition is similar. For they combine psychoanalytic reflection on what is important psychologically for sites of possibility with analyses of modern literary adventures that compose and exhibit the revolt. This also means that they share a limitation of the earlier trilogy, one that I flagged at the end of chapter 8 as a lacuna in the major writings discussed thus far, and undertook to consider in this conclusion. For one of the disappointing things about the trilogy, finally, is that there's artwork and therapy, but, even though she has political claims, it's just not clear how people make lives. The power of her thought on imaginary discourses and revolt culture—psychoanalysis, literature, art—rests on the conviction that they provide us with the fragmentary but persistent reconnections of the severed moments of modern experience. But this doesn't illuminate how lives are made. What holds the subject together is semblance, not world.

This appears to have occurred to her, too, and her response to the problem develops the notion that women are especially well placed to see through the lies of the culture. For her most recent major work is a trilogy on three women of "genius": Hannah Arendt, Melanie Klein, and Colette. Kristeva's thought on these three figures is not only a reflection on their life works. It is *biography*. That is to say, it pays attention to their lives *as* the lives they forged. Kristeva has turned to writing biography in order to ask how there can be exemplary lives. This is how the later trilogy responds to the lacuna of the 1980s writings. For, if we assume the privilege of women—that they do not buy the lies of the culture—then it is no accident that the later trilogy comes through with the exemplary lives of women. If women have few resources for self-deception, then they are pressured into forging exemplary lives. The thought of "genius" interestingly compacts Kristeva's support for strong individuation—which underlies her acceptance of the Lacanian story of lack and law—with the notion of women's ability to see through the illusory being of phallic primacy. To speak of genius is to speak of exemplarity. This is not the time to go into detail on how each of these three lives is an exemplary one, for Kristeva. Suffice it to say, for now, that in choosing these three figures she shows the uniqueness of each life, and so the flexibility of possibilities for exemplary lives. For there are three forms of life undertaken and composed by women here: the intellectual life (Hannah Arendt), the life of healing (Melanie Klein), and the life of writing (Colette). These three styles of life are one dimension of her thought, and maybe it is no accident that these are all women. Moreover, as I will now suggest, these biographies show clearly how the thought of the feminine in terms of exemplarity is an ethical notion, showing that her investigation of the feminine is not confined to the maternal.

When Kristeva writes biography in this way, she does not simply give us a picture of the circumstances and events surrounding the respective life works of her subjects, or the influence of personal and intellectual relationships on those lives and works. Rather, in the same fragmentary way in which therapy and artistic practice works in the trilogy, the notion of exemplary lives is a modernist way of proceeding toward the concrete. It suggests that there is nothing more in the way of ethical and political guidance that a non-Platonic form of writing can offer except exemplification. Kristeva's later trilogy therefore persists with "an ethics separated from morality," to recall her phrase from "Stabat Mater." The notion of exemplary lives pushes forward with the thought that there *can* be an ethics separated from morality, that is to say, an ethics separated from criteria that are to guide responsibility and actions, given apart from and in advance of the situatedness of those responses and actions. This ethical thought has already been recognized, in this book and by others, as a major stake of her writings. One of the things this book has sought to highlight is that Kristeva has the modernist temperament of refusing totalizing, even of the critical perspective. That temperament, as well as the sensitivity to nihilistic modernity that informs it, is evident in her more recent publications as well as the earlier ones. She continues to write the kind of fragmentary minor histories—be it in relation to religion, art, the nation, the feminine, or living a life—that both remain attentive to unacknowledged suffering as the remnant of freedom *and* interrogate the possibility of ethical and political guidance for our time. It would be an interesting further step to consider what kind of notion of ethics can flow from her idea of exemplarity—what an ethics of exemplarity might be.

NOTES

Introduction

1. Kristeva's handling of the "semiotic" and "symbolic," the fundamental categorial distinction of her thought, can be conceived of as the psychoanalytic successor to Kant's notion of intuition and concept, that is to say, a continuation of it at the psychoanalytic level, as I will suggest later.

2. See especially the "The antinomy of pure reason" in Division 2 of the *Critique of Pure Reason* (1787). For Kant's practical philosophy, see the *Groundwork of the Metaphysic of Morals* (1969) and *Critique of Practical Reason* (1788).

3. Gillespie (1995) questions Nietzsche's thought on the origin and meaning of nihilism. He argues that nihilism has its roots in the very foundations of modernity, that is to say, in how "the late medieval conception of an omnipotent God inspired and informed a new conception of man and nature" (xiii).

4. Heidegger acknowledges that Dostoyevsky's writing on Pushkin condones the latter for his recognition of the appearance of nihilism in this sense among the Russian intelligentsia. He also notes that the term *nihilism* became fashionable through Turgeniev, where it actually means positivism: the negation of tradition, authority, or any other specific value for the exclusive acceptance of the evidence of the senses (1982, 3).

5. This is a thought that appears in Hegel's transition from the dialectic of lordship and bondage—the master-slave dialectic—to ancient stoicism and skepticism, in the *Phenonomenology of Spirit* (1806, chapter 4).

6. Hollingdale's translation reads, "to suffer from actuality means to be an abortive actuality."

7. For an excellent clarification of this argument, see J. M. Bernstein's introduction to the collection of Adorno's essays on *The Culture Industry* (1991).

8. Post-Maoist because, as we will see in chapter 1, Kristeva's doctoral thesis of 1974—*Revolution in Potic Language*—reflects her commitments to the idea of the Cultural Revolution at that time.

9. Smith's book, *Julia Kristeva: Speaking the Unspeakable,* is a valuable reminder of how misinterpretations of Kristeva's thought can arise in the Anglo-American context because of matters of translation. However, her analysis of key concepts in the *oeuvre* begins, *inter alia,* with the statement that *Revolution in Poetic Language* is "the text from which all others might be seen to emerge and to which they lead back" (1998, 12). This book strongly disagrees with this view because it veils the changed significance of the relationship between the semiotic and the symbolic in the later writings, and so also the ethical and political import of this change.

10. For documentation on Kristeva's involvement with the *Tel Quel* group, see Ffrench (1995).

11. For her experience with the Psy & Po movement after her trip to China in the mid-1970s, see *Revolt, She Said: An Interview by Philippe Petit* (2002, 29).

12. The attention given to Butler in chapter 8 returns to her references to Kristeva in *Gender Trouble* (1990), but focuses particularly on two of her more recent publications, *Bodies That Matter* (1993) and *The Psychic Life of Power* (1997).

Chapter 1

1. It is noteworthy that the English-language translation of *Revolution in Poetic Language* contains only the first part of Kristeva's lengthy, tripartite treatise of poetic language, the part titled *Préliminaires théoriques.* The French original contains a very technical second part, presenting her revision of linguistics through semanalysis (*Le Dispositif sémiotique du texte*), and a third part, turning on the relationship between what semanalysis reveals and the social and economic functioning of the bourgeois state (*L'État et le mystère*). See *La Révolution du langage poétique, l'avant-garde à la fin du seizième siecle: Lautréamont et Mallarmé,* Paris: Éditions du Seuil, 1974.

2. Both essays appear in the English-language translation of selections from *Écrits* (1966). Compiled under Lacan's direction, *Écrits* publishes his spoken lectures of two decades. The notorious degree of complexity of these essays, which is not equaled by the *Seminars,* stands in relation to their being intended to be heard, and not read, by an audience largely composed of members of the psychoanalytic community.

3. The order of discussion of the symbolic and the imaginary reverses the order of their appearance in subject formation. For the mirror stage (the appearance of lack) precedes, and proceeds to, the institution of the symbolic (the acceptance of lack). However, the order of discussion is appropriate for the transition to Kristeva's introduction of the *semiotic* and symbolic in *Revolution in Poetic Language.* Since her notion of the semiotic

turns on her view of the presymbolic life of the drives, it would seem necessary to have a section of this chapter dedicated to the difference between her conception of the drive and Lacan's. However, further discussion of the drive in Lacan is not going to shift the story of Kristeva's departure significantly, and reference to it can be made along the way.

4. For a discussion of the two phases see Dews 1987. Dews refers to Lacan's early thought as his "humanist phase" in which the philosophical position on the relations between historicity, subjectivity and truth are arrived at by a "largely Hegelian route" (60).

5. While this is one of the moments where it is clear that Lacan's thought is embedded in awareness of a social and historical problematic, it is Kristeva's later writings that turn on an interrogation of the modern isolation of the soul. Lacan's essays remain unflagging demonstrations of the "truth" of the subject disclosed in psychoanalytic experience.

6. Lacan's theory of the drives appears in Seminar XI (1973). *The Four Fundamental Concepts of Psychoanalysis*, ed. Jacques-Alain Miller. Trans. Alan Sheridan. Penguin Books. 1977.

7. At the strictly psychoanalytic level, this is a matter of significant differences in emphasis, in Lacan and Kristeva, when it comes to thinking through the relationship between the drive and desire in the structures of subjectivity. From the philosophicohistorical perspective, these differences have momentous implications in certain respects. As he would be the first to acknowledge, Shepherdson does not take on this perspective, apart from arguing that psychoanalysis draws us away from a dualism that blights contemporary debates on subjectivity, embodiment, and representation: the dualism of essentialism (the reduction of sexual and other differences to a biological substrate) and social constructionism (the idea that subjectivity is constructed by historically contingent representation, and by this alone). The psychoanalytic differences between Lacan and Kristeva bear on the whole significance of the relationship between love, loss, and lack. We will begin to see this in chapter 2 below, where Kristeva's conception of the imaginary father inscribes an "object-relation" that is certainly tied to the presymbolic exposure to otherness, a "splitting" that both call primal repression. However, the "imaginary father" is not *itself* a conception of lack in Kristeva. For this and other reasons, she makes a strong distinction between presymbolic *loss* and the thought of lack. In this book, the question of the relationship between love, loss, and lack in Western cultures stands as what elucidates, and might decide, the issue of what *counts as* an "excessively linguistic or disembodied" theory—or, better, culture.

8. This tendency appears, for example, in Butler 1993. "Kristeva *accepts* this collapse of the *chora* and the maternal/nurse figure" (41). But it is not as a *nurse* figure that the mother contributes to the formation of the semiotic *chora*. Nor is the *infans* passive in this formation. The point is discussed further in relation to Butler in chapter 8, below.

Chapter 2

1. Kristeva references many texts contributing to this body of thought in the trilogy, with Winnicott (1965), Klein (1952, 1957, and 1960), and Green (1973, 1979, and 1983) featuring prominently.

2. The later modifications are: the second topography of the unconscious, id–ego–superego, which replaces the earlier one, Unconscious–Preconscious–Conscious; the revised theory of the instincts; and the fundamental change in the psychoanalytic view of anxiety. Freud's revision to his theory of the instincts substitutes the opposition between the life and death instincts/drives (*eros* and *thanatos*) for the opposition between the sexual instincts and the ego instincts (the drive towards the other versus the drive to self-preservation). His later thought on anxiety inverts the causal relationship between repression and anxiety, asserting that his earlier view that anxiety was an economic phenomenon—the result of a conversion of repressed libido into anxiety—was mistaken. It is *anxiety* that leads to repression.

3. Freud (1914) drew out the connections between primary narcissism and the love relationship at a moment when he considered the idea that the *ego* was the source of libido, which was only later sent out to objects. Klein's analysis of children illuminated the function of aggression in pre-oedipal development, an illumination that Lacan drew on when he connected aggressivity and primary narcissism. Winnicott developed the notions of emptiness, "maternal holding," and transitional objects prior to oedipal triangulation. Green set out the thesis on a distinction between negative and positive narcissism, or the narcissism of death and the narcissism of life. (See note 1, above.)

4. For Lacan, Kristeva refers to *Écrits* (1966) and *Encore* (Seminar XX, 1975).

5. The "gaping hole" of the mirror stage and the "bar" resisting signification in the structure of the sign are, for Kristeva, both transfigurations of loss/emptiness (Kristeva 1983, 23–24).

6. The Kristevan imaginary is explicated in terms of experiences situated, not in the homeomorphism of the mirror stage—which is visual or specular—but in the bodily exchange of mother and child where touch and sound precede sight.

7. See Freud 1914. The distinction between a "narcissistic" and an "anaclitic" (attachment) object choice is a distinction between seeking *oneself* in an other or seeking *another* (paradigmatically the mother) as a love object. Kristeva is emphasizing and questioning Freud's notion that only the latter is a "true" object choice.

8. In *An Ethics of Dissensus* Ziarek stresses Kristeva's departure from the classical Freudian view of narcissism in this view. "If the ubiquity of narcissism in psychic life, from the formation of the ego Ideal to sexual relations, shows, according to Freud, the reduction of the Other to an imaginary reflection of an ideal image of the ego, Kristeva

argues that the aporetic structure of primary narcissism also reveals the opposite economy —namely, the fact that emergence of the archaic form of the ego is already an effect of the inscription of the void in the psyche and the presymbolic relations to alterity" (2001, 129–130).

9. On a different point, another and equally troubling effect of Shepherdson's restriction of the mother to the symbolic is that, when he comes to discuss *femininity* in Kristeva, he marks it off from *maternity,* so that the mother can be a symbolic mother and the feminine can be the site of an excess over the symbolic order. However, this seems to repeat the opposition of maternity and femininity that patriarchy imposes, one that Kristeva puts a great deal of effort into undermining.

10. Once again, because Shepherdson (2000, 71) finds only one effect in the exposure to maternal entity—the traditional one that the discovery of the mother's incompleteness has an overwhelming effect (Lacan calls it the *jouissance* of the Other)—he completely misses the presence of the third in Kristeva's discussion of archaic relationship. Once this is missed, her thought on the presymbolic structurations of the subject cannot be differentiated from Lacan's thought on pre- or protosymbolic modalities of lack, and her argument that loss is prior to lack would appear to presuppose a misreading of Lacan, one that identifies lack with symbolic lack. First, Kristeva herself credits Lacan with grasping the *series* of splittings of the subject. Second, her conception of the imaginary father is not a modality of lack. It tends in the reverse direction without being the opposite (fullness, plenitude, the phallus) for it is a "potential presence" that serves as a magnet for identification, and compensates for the anguish of primal loss. The mother's "gift" is not only her symbolic being, which prevents the child from sacrificing itself to the *jouissance* of the Other. It is the gift of an other that puts loving idealization at the heart of ego formation, a loving idealization, then, that *inscribes* the alterity of this nonobjectal other at the core of the self. Since this alterity is always potential alterity, it carries the subject toward the symbolic, and others, without compromising its autonomy in the journey.

11. Current discussions of *agape,* including Kristeva's, reference a central text in the discussion of the social meaning of the Christian notion of love: Nygren's *Agape and Eros* (1982).

Chapter 3

1. For Anna Freud's case study Kristeva refers to a contribution to the former's 1946 seminar. Anneliese Schnurmann: Observation of a Phobia. *Psychoanalytic Study of the Child* 3–4: 253–270.

2. "Dissolution" (*der Untergang*) does not imply the vanquishing of the conflicts making up the Oedipus complex. As Loewald stresses "dissolution" (*Untergang*) "means

a going under or going down," a submergence—repression—of the ideational contents attaching to the complex (1980, 385). Thus, the new psychical action introduced at this point—identification with parental authority through which the nucleus of the superego is formed—does not represent the successful socialization of the child. Instead it introduces a further set of conflicts involving the superego's surveillance over the pressure exerted on the ego by the "earlier" complex that persists, repressed, in the unconscious.

3. "I learnt nothing new from the analysis, nothing that I had not already been able to discover (though often less distinctly and more indirectly) from other patients analysed at a more advanced age. But the neuroses of these patients could in every instance be traced back to the same infantile complexes that were revealed behind Hans's phobia. I am therefore tempted to claim for this neurosis of childhood the significance of being a type and a model, and to suppose that the multiplicity of the phenomena of regression exhibited by neuroses and the abundance of their pathogenic material do not prevent their being derived from a very limited number of processes concerned with identical ideational complexes" (Freud 1909, 147). It is only on the basis of Freud's later view—that anxiety is the maker of repression, rather than being liberated on account of repressed libido—that phobia would be situated at the level where Kristeva now situates it, the level of primal and not secondary repression.

4. There is an echo here of Hegel's remarks in the *Phenomenology of Spirit* (1806) on the Terror of the French Revolution. Human death has no more significance than cutting off the head of a cabbage. The sunlit severed head conveys the absence of secular symbolic connections. Kristeva's trilogy also suggests such a breakdown of a world that has erased its borders.

Chapter 4

1. Readers should also see Kristeva's *New Maladies of the Soul* (1993), whose title announces so poignantly her historical thinking on the structures of subjectivity and their relationship to the conditions of late modernity.

2. With Freud, "an affect includes in the first place particular motor innervations or discharges and secondly certain feelings; the latter are of two kinds—perceptions of the motor actions that have occurred and the direct feelings of pleasure and unpleasure which, as we say, give the affect its keynote. But I do not think that with this enumeration we have arrived at the essence of affect. We seem to see deeper in the case of some affects and to recognize that the core which holds the combination together is the repetition of some particular significant experience" (1917a, 395–396).

3. Kristeva takes the phrase from Jean-Michel Petot (1932). *Melanie Klein, le moi et le bon objet.* Paris: Dunod.

Chapter 5

1. The reference to Bataille's *Essais de sociologie* gives no further publication details.

2. Thus the abject in Kristeva is not the impossible object of desire but the impossible object that collapses the space of the subject, a point that will be emphasized in the discussion of Butler's thought on abjection in chapter 8, below.

Chapter 6

1. As recalled in Anna Dostoyevksy's stenographic notes (Kristeva 1987, 276–277, n. 18).

Chapter 7

1. Ziarek recognizes the import of the thought on the uncanny in *Strangers to Ourselves*. She looks to the connections there between the psychoanalytic concept of the heterogeneous subject and the idea of the foreigner/stranger in order to argue that the Kristevan thought can modify and contribute to the radical democracy tradition. For her, the community implied in the theory of the foreigner/stranger might fail to produce "a common sense or identity," but it is "the only mode of solidarity with others that reflects the democratic ideas of pluralism, antagonism, and diversity" (2001, 144).

2. I acknowledge that for Kristeva the expression "the I that is We" and "the We that is I," taken from Hegel's *Phenomenology of Spirit* (1806, 110), is unmistakably idealist, and am merely emphasizing the links with German idealism present in *Strangers to Ourselves*.

3. Kristeva does not clarify her statement that the cultural concept "nation" became political in Germany in 1806. Nor does her interpretation of the trajectories of the concept of *Volk* make reference to the incorporation of the word "nation" into German philosophy in 1808 in Fichte's *Addresses to the German Nation*.

4. See also chapter 3 of *Strangers to Ourselves*, a moment in Kristeva's archaeology of premodern historical worlds titled "The Chosen People and the Choice of Foreignness."

5. Ziarek recognizes this in *An Ethics of Dissensus*. "In *Strangers to Ourselves* the task of ethics is to traverse the hatred and the fear experienced in the face of the Other by acknowledging the dis-ease with 'the other scene' within the subject" (2001, 126).

6. Evidently psychoanalytic conceptions posit general structures for infantile fears and desires, but Freud, of course, stressed that these general conceptions follow psychoanalytic experience and do not present the framework of that experience. See also Kristeva's assertion in *New Maladies of the Soul* that "analysts who do not discover a *new*

malady of the soul in each of their patients do not fully appreciate the uniqueness of each individual. Similarly, we can place ourselves at the heart of the analytic project by realizing that these new maladies of the soul go beyond traditional classification systems and their inevitable overhaul" (1993a, 9).

7. For an insightful reading of *Moses and Monotheism,* see Cathy Caruth's *Unclaimed Experience* (1996).

8. See Caruth (1996, 67–72). "Chosenness is thus not simply a fact of the past but the experience of being shot into a future that is not entirely one's own. The belated experience of trauma in Jewish monotheism suggests that history is not only the passing on of a crisis but also the passing on of a survival that can only be possessed within a history larger than any single individual or any single generation" (71).

9. See, for example, the preface to Hegel 1806. "Culture (*die Bildung*) and its laborious emergence from the immediacy of substantial life must always begin by getting acquainted with *general* principles and points of view, so as at first to work up to a *general conception* of the real issue, as well as learning to support and refute the general conception with reasons; then to apprehend the rich and concrete abundance [of life] by differential classification; and finally to give accurate instruction and pass serious judgment upon it. From its very beginning, culture must leave room for the earnestness of life in its concrete richness; this leads to an experience of the real issue" (3).

10. See Hegel 1806, and *Elements of the Philosophy of Right* (1821).

11. See Julia Kristeva 1985, for some reflections on her Bulgarian background. See also the interviews in Guberman 1996.

Chapter 8

1. The citations from "Stabat Mater" will be referenced parenthetically in the text by the date of first publication of the essay (1977). The page references are to the chapter in *Tales of Love* (1983) where it reappears. (The date 1976 that Kristeva inserts at the end of "Stabat Mater" when it is republished in *Tales of Love* would appear to refer to the year of writing the essay.) The citations from "Women's Time" will also be referenced by the date of its first publication (1979), and page references are to *The Kristeva Reader* (1986). See the latter for details of the publishing history of these essays (Kristeva 1986, 160, 187).

2. See also "Motherhood according to Bellini," in Kristeva 1980b.

3. The plural is explained by Kristeva's insistence on *individual* features of experience rather than group identity. The commitment is reiterated in the *New York Times* article responding to the publication of her trilogy on Arendt, Klein, and Colette. Her questions are: "How is each woman an individual? What can each woman contribute to other women

or to humanity?" "I'd like my readers to ask, 'How am I special?' 'What individual spark do I have in my life, in my sexuality, in my spirit?'" (See the interview in Riding 2001.)

4. A strategic critique of Freud takes up the first half of Irigaray's *Speculum of the Other Woman* (1974). See also Chanter's *Ethics of Eros* (1995) and Whitford's *Luce Irigaray* (1991).

5. The much debated essays of Freud on sexuality include his *Three Essays on the Theory of Sexuality* (1905). As is widely known, he returns to the enigma of the "feminine" in his late essay "Female Sexuality" (1931). Many readers will not be content with Kristeva's remark on Freud's utopia, since this essay seems to show that his so-called utopia is normative in a way that is quite in line with phallic monism.

6. See also Ziarek (2001, 122–123) for a discussion of Kristeva's thought on Céline in the context of an analysis of the racist fantasy that supports fascist ideology.

7. See Freud's renowned essay, "Analysis Terminable and Interminable" (1937).

8. I do not think that this emphasis needs to dismiss the social practices that are developing a rightly sought diversity for motherhood. *Tales of Love* is itself a text which turns on the question of "new codes of love" and, at one moment, acknowledges that these are "sought after in those marginal communities that dissent from official morality" (1983, 7).

9. The references made in the following section to Horkheimer and Adorno's *Dialectic of Enlightenment* draw heavily on Gillian Rose's explication of central concepts in Adorno's, thought, in *The Melancholy Science* (1978). However, the discussion cannot be completely faithful to the spirit of Rose's book, to which Kristeva's special focus on and treatment of subjectivity is inimical.

10. Rose argues that too much emphasis on this dimension of what distinguishes modernity for Horkheimer and Adorno, the debt to Marx, runs certain risks. Much of the deployment and criticism of Frankfurt School critical theory has isolated the concept of "reification" from the presence of non-Marxist influences, "Hegelian and post-Hegelian," especially on epistemological and methodological issues (1978, 3). In Adorno's writings these influences, and notably Nietzsche, inform above all the relationship between the object of analysis and the presentation of it: the relationship of "style" and content. This relationship presumes that "the relation of a thought or a concept to what it is intended to cover, its object, is problematic" (12). Classical philosophical methods cannot "see beyond" the subject to the object, and Adorno's focus on style is intended to wrench method away, for example, from the imposition of devices on material in order to organize and explain it (11–12). The relationship of style and content assumes "a split and antagonistic reality that cannot be adequately represented by any system which makes its goals unity and simplicity and clarity." Such a system does not achieve the "objective" or "scientific" style it aims at, but results "in a kind of distortion" (15).

11. Questioned in interview on the similarity between her diagnosis of cultural possibilities and the work of Adorno and Horkheimer, Kristeva replies: "in what concerns the 'cultural industry' they are absolutely right, although in the analysis of aesthetic products I use different terms, I stand closer to psychoanalysis and rhetoric." ("Avant-garde Practice" in Guberman 1996, 217).

12. For another interpretation of psychoanalysis deployed to similar ends, see Jonathan Lear (1991).

13. Compare this with the implication of one of Luce Irigaray's major texts that if we can sort out sexual difference all else will follow. *An Ethics of Sexual Difference* (1984).

14. For an excellent commentary on Adorno's thought, see Jarvis 1998.

15. Kristeva acknowledges Nietzsche's differentiation of three modes of time in his essay *On the Advantage and Disadvantage of History for Life*. However, she does not remain faithful to his distinction between critical, antiquarian, and monumental kinds of history, or to the meanings any of them have in the context of his arguments on German culture. Notably, her thought on linear (Nietzche's "critical") time does not develop the significance it has in Nietzsche's essay as the time which "belongs to the living man . . . so far as he suffers and is in need of liberation," nor take up his declamation against the "surfeit of history" in the German culture of his time (1980, 18–19, 28).

16. Rose elucidates the relationship between content and style in sentences like this one. The sentence is a chiasmus, "a grammatical figure by which the order of words in one clause is inverted in a second clause. . . . The use of chiasmus stresses the transmutation of processes into entities that is a fundamental theme of Adorno's work. He presents this theme in this way in order to avoid turning processes into entities himself" (1978, 13).

17. "The most intimate reactions of human beings have become so entirely reified even to themselves that the idea of anything peculiar to them survives only in extreme abstraction: personality means hardly more than dazzling white teeth and freedom from body odor and emotions" (Horkheimer and Adorno 1969, 136) Rose (1978) draws attention to the use of hyperbole in *Dialectic of Enlightenment* as a strategy for depicting the society it criticizes. This strategy is at work in this announcement on intimacy.

18. "In most of her latest work Kristeva addresses the crisis in the Western psyche or imaginary, but she does not specifically address any crisis in relation to women" (Oliver 1993a, 178).

BIBLIOGRAPHY

Adorno, Theodor W. 1966. *Negative dialectics*. Trans. E. B. Ashton. London: Routledge. 1990.

———. 1968. Sociology and psychology—II. *New Left Review* 47.

———. 1991. *The culture industry: Selected essays on mass culture,* ed. J. M. Bernstein. London: Routledge.

Allison, David B. (ed.). 1977. *The new Nietzsche: Contemporary styles of interpretation*. New York: Dell Publishing Co.

Arendt, Hannah. 1979. *The origins of totalitarianism*. New York: Harcourt, Brace, Jovanovich.

Beauvoir, Simone de. 1949. *The second sex*. Trans. E. M. Parshley. New York: Vintage. 1989.

Benjamin, Jessica. 1995. *Like subjects, love objects: Essays on recognition and sexual difference*. New Haven and London: Yale University Press.

———. 1998. *Shadow of the other: Intersubjectivity and gender in psychoanalysis*. New York and London: Routledge.

Bernstein, J. M. 1996. Confession and forgiveness: Hegel's poetics of action. In *Beyond representation: Philosophy and poetic imagination*, ed. Richard Eldridge. Cambridge: Cambridge University Press.

Butler, Judith. 1989. The body politics of Julia Kristeva. *Hypatia* 3, 3: 104–118. Republished in Kelly Oliver (ed.). 1993. *Ethics, politics, and difference: Julia Kristeva's writing*. London and New York: Routledge.

———. 1990. *Gender trouble: Feminism and the subversion of identity*. New York: Routledge.

———. 1993. *Bodies that matter: On the discursive limits of sex*. New York: Routledge.

———. 1997. *The psychic life of power: Theories in subjection*. Stanford: Stanford University Press.

Caruth, Cathy. 1995. *Trauma: Explorations in memory*. Baltimore: Johns Hopkins University Press.

———. 1996. *Unclaimed experience: Trauma, narrative and history*. Baltimore: Johns Hopkins University Press

Chanter, Tina. 1995. *Ethics of eros: Irigaray's rewriting of the philosophers*. New York: Routledge.

Chanter, Tina and Colman, Athena. 2001. Abjection, film, politics: Race, gender, class and nation in Neil Jordan's *The crying game*. *Glimpse*, 3, 2: 51–62.

Chasseguet-Smirgel, Janine. 1986. *Sexuality and mind: The role of the father and the mother in the psyche*. New York: New York University Press.

Cixous, Hélène and Clément, Catherine. 1975. *The newly born woman*. Manchester: Manchester University Press. 1986.

Clark, T. J. 1999. *Farewell to an idea: Episodes from artistic modernism*. New Haven and London: Yale University Press.

Clément, Catherine and Kristeva, Julia. 1998. *The feminine and the sacred*. Trans. Jane Marie Todd. New York: Columbia University Press. 2001.

Critchley, Simon. 1999. *Ethics–politics–subjectivity: Essays on Derrida, Levinas, and contemporary French thought*. London and New York: Verso.

Crownfield, David (ed.). 1992. *Body/text in Julia Kristeva: Religion, women, and psychoanalysis*. Albany: State University of New York Press.

Dews, Peter. 1987. *Logics of disintegration*. London: Verso.

Diderot, Denis. 1981. *Rameau's nephew, D'Alembert's dream*. Middlesex: Penguin Books.

Douglas, Mary. 1969. *Purity and danger*. London: Routledge & Kegan Paul.

Duras, Marguerite. 1960. *Hiroshima mon amour, Text by Marguerite Duras for the film by Alain Resnais*. Trans. Richard Seaver. New York: Grove Wiedenfeld, 1961.

Elliott, Anthony. 1992. *Social theory and psychoanalysis in transition: Self and society from Freud to Kristeva*. Oxford: Blackwell.

Ffrench, Patrick. 1995. *The time of theory: A history of* Tel Quel *1960-83*. Oxford: Oxford University Press.

Fichte, Johann Gottlieb. 1793. *Beitrag zur Berichtingung der Urteile des Publikums über die französische Revolution*. Hamburg: Felix Meiner Verlag.

———. 1797. *Science of knowledge*. Trans. Peter Heath and John Lachs. Cambridge: Cambridge University Press. 1982.

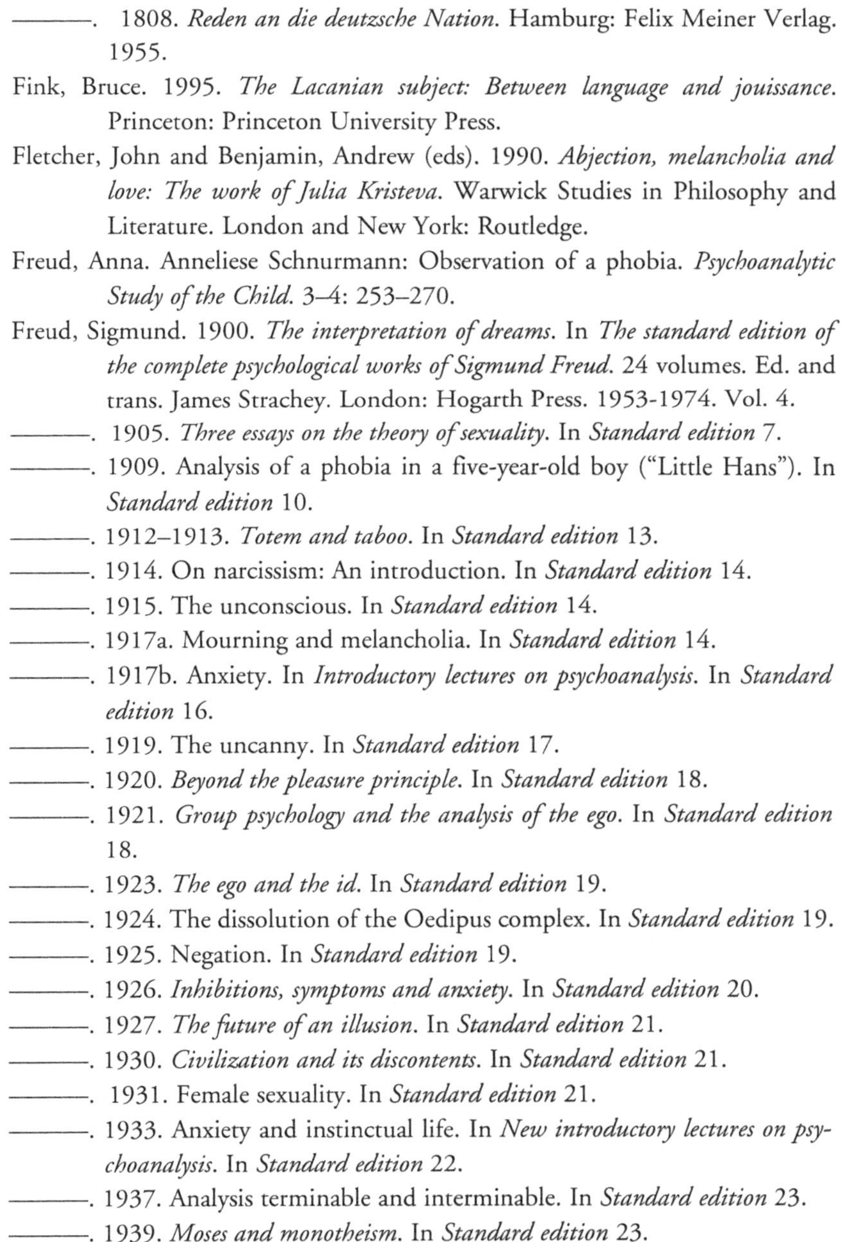

———. 1808. *Reden an die deutzsche Nation*. Hamburg: Felix Meiner Verlag. 1955.

Fink, Bruce. 1995. *The Lacanian subject: Between language and jouissance*. Princeton: Princeton University Press.

Fletcher, John and Benjamin, Andrew (eds). 1990. *Abjection, melancholia and love: The work of Julia Kristeva*. Warwick Studies in Philosophy and Literature. London and New York: Routledge.

Freud, Anna. Anneliese Schnurmann: Observation of a phobia. *Psychoanalytic Study of the Child*. 3–4: 253–270.

Freud, Sigmund. 1900. *The interpretation of dreams*. In *The standard edition of the complete psychological works of Sigmund Freud*. 24 volumes. Ed. and trans. James Strachey. London: Hogarth Press. 1953-1974. Vol. 4.

———. 1905. *Three essays on the theory of sexuality*. In *Standard edition* 7.

———. 1909. Analysis of a phobia in a five-year-old boy ("Little Hans"). In *Standard edition* 10.

———. 1912–1913. *Totem and taboo*. In *Standard edition* 13.

———. 1914. On narcissism: An introduction. In *Standard edition* 14.

———. 1915. The unconscious. In *Standard edition* 14.

———. 1917a. Mourning and melancholia. In *Standard edition* 14.

———. 1917b. Anxiety. In *Introductory lectures on psychoanalysis*. In *Standard edition* 16.

———. 1919. The uncanny. In *Standard edition* 17.

———. 1920. *Beyond the pleasure principle*. In *Standard edition* 18.

———. 1921. *Group psychology and the analysis of the ego*. In *Standard edition* 18.

———. 1923. *The ego and the id*. In *Standard edition* 19.

———. 1924. The dissolution of the Oedipus complex. In *Standard edition* 19.

———. 1925. Negation. In *Standard edition* 19.

———. 1926. *Inhibitions, symptoms and anxiety*. In *Standard edition* 20.

———. 1927. *The future of an illusion*. In *Standard edition* 21.

———. 1930. *Civilization and its discontents*. In *Standard edition* 21.

———. 1931. Female sexuality. In *Standard edition* 21.

———. 1933. Anxiety and instinctual life. In *New introductory lectures on psychoanalysis*. In *Standard edition* 22.

———. 1937. Analysis terminable and interminable. In *Standard edition* 23.

———. 1939. *Moses and monotheism*. In *Standard edition* 23.

Gillespie, Michael Allen. 1995. *Nihilism before Nietzsche*. Chicago: Chicago University Press.

Girard, René. 1977. *Violence and the sacred.* Trans. Patrick Gregory. Baltimore: Johns Hopkins University Press.

Green, André. 1973. *Le Discours vivant.* Paris: Presses Universitaires.

———. 1979. L'Angoisse et narcissisme. *Revue française de psychanalyse* 1.

———. 1983. *Narcissisme de vie, narcissisme de mort.* Paris: Minuit.

Grosz, Elizabeth. 1989. *Sexual subversions: Three French feminists.* Boston: Allen & Unwin.

———. 1994. *Volatile bodies: Toward a corporeal feminism.* Bloomington and Indianapolis: Indiana University Press.

Guberman, Ross (ed.). 1996. *Julia Kristeva: Interviews.* Columbia: Columbia University Press.

Hegel, G. W. F. 1798–1799. The spirit of Christianity and its fate. In *Early theological writings.* Trans. T. M. Knox. Chicago: Chicago University Press. 1984.

———. 1806. *Phenomenology of spirit.* Trans. A. V. Miller. Oxford: Clarendon Press. 1977.

———. 1821. *Elements of the philosophy of right,* ed. Allen Wood. Trans. H. B. Nisbet. Cambridge: Cambridge University Press. 1991.

Heidegger, Martin. 1982. *Nietzsche. Volume IV, nihilism,* ed. David Farrell Krell. Trans. Frank A. Capuzzi. San Francisco: Harper & Row. *Nietzsche II, Zweiter Band.* Verlag Günther Neske Pfullingen. Dritte Auflage. 1961.

Hewitt, Andrew. 1992. A feminine dialectic of enlightenment? Horkheimer and Adorno revisited. *New German Critique* 56: 143–170. Reprinted in Jay Bernstein (ed.). *The Frankfurt School critical assessments.* 6 volumes. Vol. 3. London: Routledge. 1994.

Hill, Leslie. 1993. *Marguerite Duras: Apocalyptic desires.* London and New York: Routledge.

Horkheimer, Max and Adorno, Theodor W. 1969. *Dialectic of Enlightenment: Philosophical fragments,* ed. Gunzel Schmid Noerr. Trans. Edmund Jephcott. Stanford: Stanford University Press. 2002.

Horowitz, Gregg. 2001. *Sustaining loss: Art and mournful life.* Stanford: Stanford University Press.

Irigaray, Luce. 1974. *Speculum of the other woman.* Trans. Gillian C. Gill. New York: Cornell University Press. 1985.

———. 1984. *An ethics of sexual difference.* Trans. Carolyn Burke. London: The Athlone Press. 1993.

Jacobi, Friedrich Heinrich. 1799. Open letter to Fichte. Trans. Diana I. Behler. In *Fichte, Jacobi, Schelling: Philosophy of German Idealism,* ed. Ernst Behler. New York: Continuum. 1987.

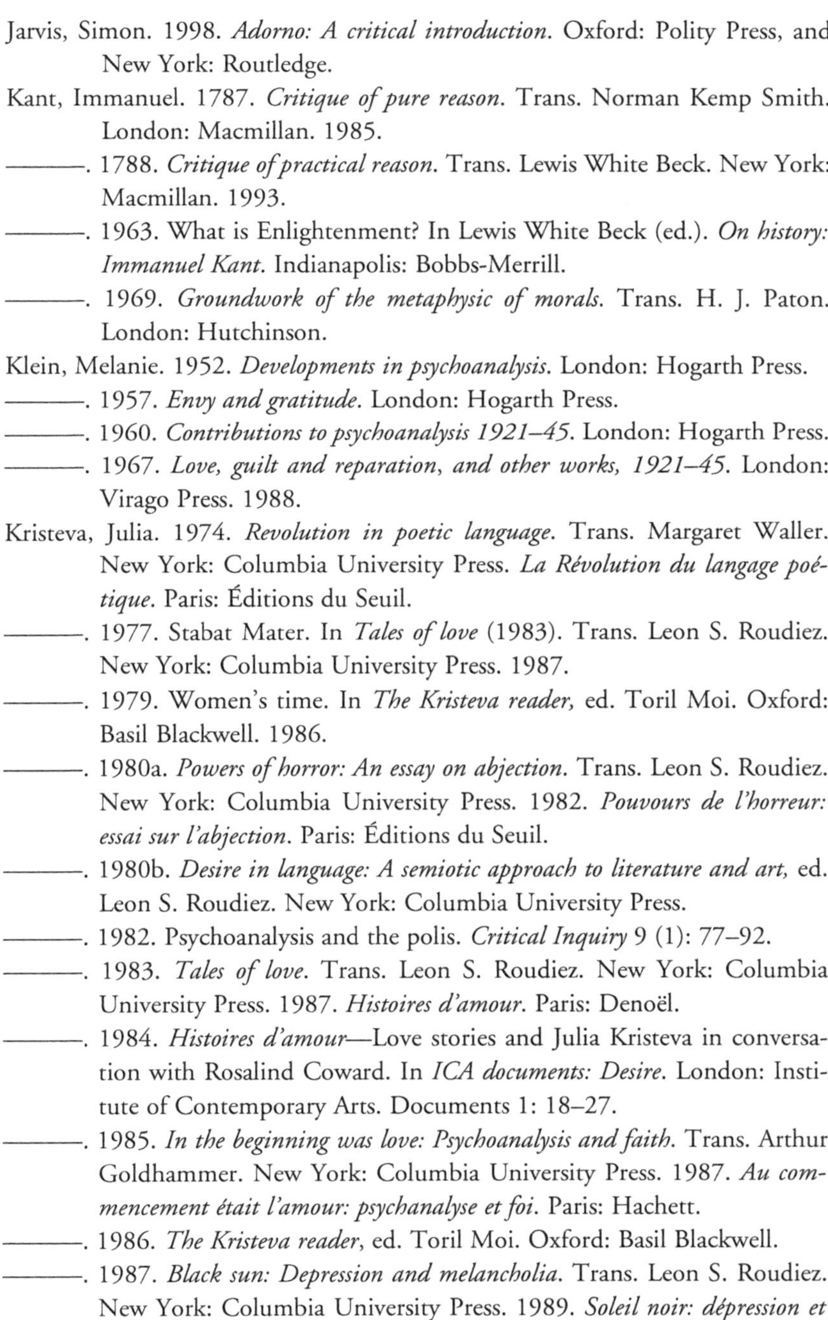

Jarvis, Simon. 1998. *Adorno: A critical introduction.* Oxford: Polity Press, and New York: Routledge.

Kant, Immanuel. 1787. *Critique of pure reason.* Trans. Norman Kemp Smith. London: Macmillan. 1985.

———. 1788. *Critique of practical reason.* Trans. Lewis White Beck. New York: Macmillan. 1993.

———. 1963. What is Enlightenment? In Lewis White Beck (ed.). *On history: Immanuel Kant.* Indianapolis: Bobbs-Merrill.

———. 1969. *Groundwork of the metaphysic of morals.* Trans. H. J. Paton. London: Hutchinson.

Klein, Melanie. 1952. *Developments in psychoanalysis.* London: Hogarth Press.

———. 1957. *Envy and gratitude.* London: Hogarth Press.

———. 1960. *Contributions to psychoanalysis 1921–45.* London: Hogarth Press.

———. 1967. *Love, guilt and reparation, and other works, 1921–45.* London: Virago Press. 1988.

Kristeva, Julia. 1974. *Revolution in poetic language.* Trans. Margaret Waller. New York: Columbia University Press. *La Révolution du langage poétique.* Paris: Éditions du Seuil.

———. 1977. Stabat Mater. In *Tales of love* (1983). Trans. Leon S. Roudiez. New York: Columbia University Press. 1987.

———. 1979. Women's time. In *The Kristeva reader,* ed. Toril Moi. Oxford: Basil Blackwell. 1986.

———. 1980a. *Powers of horror: An essay on abjection.* Trans. Leon S. Roudiez. New York: Columbia University Press. 1982. *Pouvours de l'horreur: essai sur l'abjection.* Paris: Éditions du Seuil.

———. 1980b. *Desire in language: A semiotic approach to literature and art,* ed. Leon S. Roudiez. New York: Columbia University Press.

———. 1982. Psychoanalysis and the polis. *Critical Inquiry* 9 (1): 77–92.

———. 1983. *Tales of love.* Trans. Leon S. Roudiez. New York: Columbia University Press. 1987. *Histoires d'amour.* Paris: Denoël.

———. 1984. *Histoires d'amour*—Love stories and Julia Kristeva in conversation with Rosalind Coward. In *ICA documents: Desire.* London: Institute of Contemporary Arts. Documents 1: 18–27.

———. 1985. *In the beginning was love: Psychoanalysis and faith.* Trans. Arthur Goldhammer. New York: Columbia University Press. 1987. *Au commencement était l'amour: psychanalyse et foi.* Paris: Hachett.

———. 1986. *The Kristeva reader,* ed. Toril Moi. Oxford: Basil Blackwell.

———. 1987. *Black sun: Depression and melancholia.* Trans. Leon S. Roudiez. New York: Columbia University Press. 1989. *Soleil noir: dépression et mélancholie.* Paris: Gallimard.

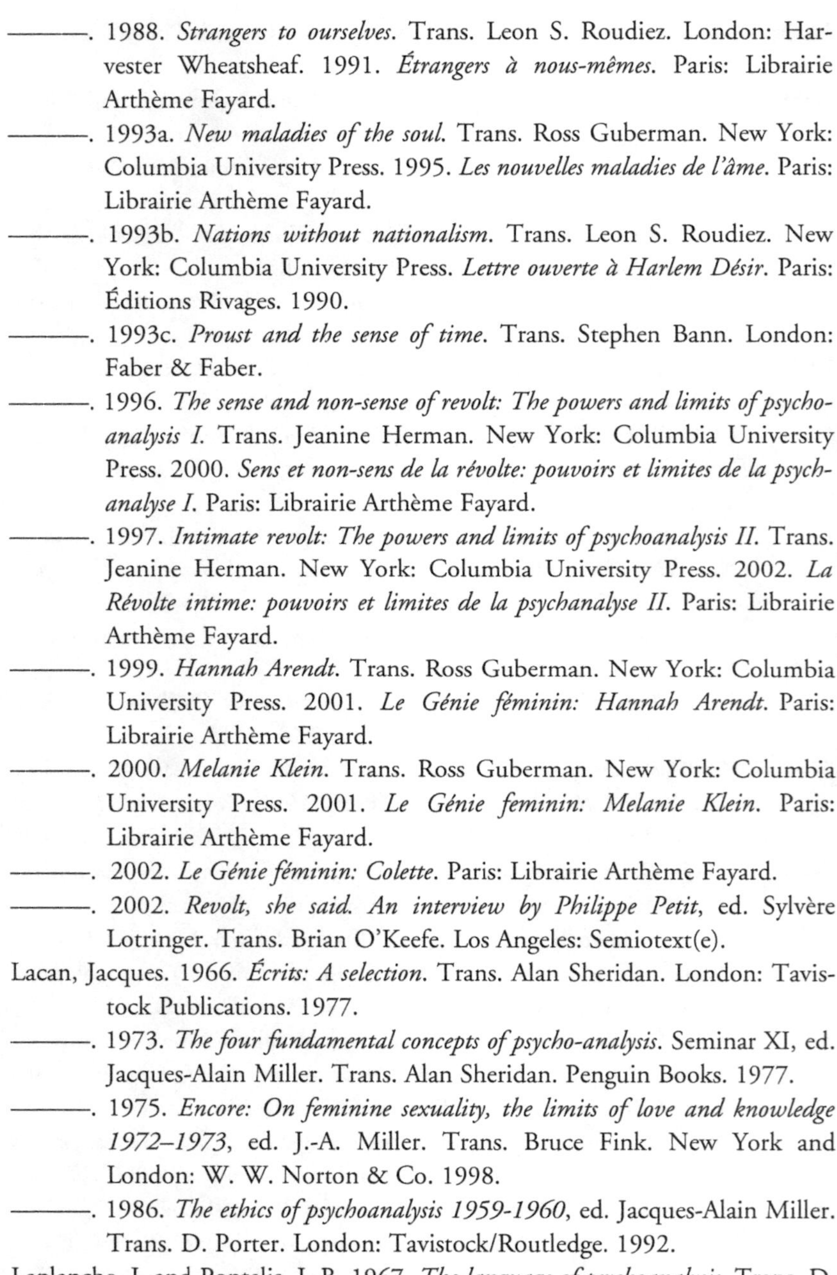

———. 1988. *Strangers to ourselves*. Trans. Leon S. Roudiez. London: Harvester Wheatsheaf. 1991. *Étrangers à nous-mêmes*. Paris: Librairie Arthème Fayard.

———. 1993a. *New maladies of the soul*. Trans. Ross Guberman. New York: Columbia University Press. 1995. *Les nouvelles maladies de l'âme*. Paris: Librairie Arthème Fayard.

———. 1993b. *Nations without nationalism*. Trans. Leon S. Roudiez. New York: Columbia University Press. *Lettre ouverte à Harlem Désir*. Paris: Éditions Rivages. 1990.

———. 1993c. *Proust and the sense of time*. Trans. Stephen Bann. London: Faber & Faber.

———. 1996. *The sense and non-sense of revolt: The powers and limits of psychoanalysis I*. Trans. Jeanine Herman. New York: Columbia University Press. 2000. *Sens et non-sens de la révolte: pouvoirs et limites de la psychanalyse I*. Paris: Librairie Arthème Fayard.

———. 1997. *Intimate revolt: The powers and limits of psychoanalysis II*. Trans. Jeanine Herman. New York: Columbia University Press. 2002. *La Révolte intime: pouvoirs et limites de la psychanalyse II*. Paris: Librairie Arthème Fayard.

———. 1999. *Hannah Arendt*. Trans. Ross Guberman. New York: Columbia University Press. 2001. *Le Génie féminin: Hannah Arendt*. Paris: Librairie Arthème Fayard.

———. 2000. *Melanie Klein*. Trans. Ross Guberman. New York: Columbia University Press. 2001. *Le Génie feminin: Melanie Klein*. Paris: Librairie Arthème Fayard.

———. 2002. *Le Génie féminin: Colette*. Paris: Librairie Arthème Fayard.

———. 2002. *Revolt, she said. An interview by Philippe Petit*, ed. Sylvère Lotringer. Trans. Brian O'Keefe. Los Angeles: Semiotext(e).

Lacan, Jacques. 1966. *Écrits: A selection*. Trans. Alan Sheridan. London: Tavistock Publications. 1977.

———. 1973. *The four fundamental concepts of psycho-analysis*. Seminar XI, ed. Jacques-Alain Miller. Trans. Alan Sheridan. Penguin Books. 1977.

———. 1975. *Encore: On feminine sexuality, the limits of love and knowledge 1972–1973*, ed. J.-A. Miller. Trans. Bruce Fink. New York and London: W. W. Norton & Co. 1998.

———. 1986. *The ethics of psychoanalysis 1959-1960*, ed. Jacques-Alain Miller. Trans. D. Porter. London: Tavistock/Routledge. 1992.

Laplanche, J. and Pontalis, J. B. 1967. *The language of psychoanalysis*. Trans. D. Nicholson-Smith. London: Karnac Books. 1973.

Lasch, Christopher. 1979. *The culture of narcissism: American life in an age of diminishing expectations.* New York and London: W. W. Norton & Co.

Lear, Jonathan. 1991. *Love and its place in nature: A philosophical interpretation of Freudian psychoanalysis.* New York: The Noonday Press.

Lechte, John. 1990. *Julia Kristeva.* London and New York: Routledge.

Levinas, Emmanuel. 1996. *Basic philosophical writings,* ed. Adriaan T. Peperzak, Simon Critchley and Robert Bernasconi. Bloomington and Indianapolis: Indiana University Press.

Loewald, Hans. 1980. The waning of the Oedipus complex. *Papers on psychoanalysis.* Yale University Press.

Marcuse, Herbert. 1955. *Eros and civilization: A philosophical inquiry into Freud.* Boston: The Beacon Press. 1967.

Marks, Elaine and de Courtivron, Elizabeth. 1981. *New French feminisms: An anthology.* New York: Schocken.

McAfee, Noelle. 2000. *Habermas, Kristeva, and citizenship.* Ithaca and London: Cornell University Press.

Nietzsche, Friedrich. 1886. *The gay science.* Trans. Walter Kaufmann. New York: Random House. 1974.

———. 1895. *Twilight of the idols/The Anti-Christ.* Trans. R. J. Hollingdale. London: Penguin Books. 1968.

———. 1967. *The will to power.* Trans. Walter Kaufmann and R. J. Hollingsdale. New York: Random House.

———. 1980. *On the advantage and disadvantage of history for life.* Hackett.

———. 1989. *The genealogy of morals.* Trans. Walter Kaufmann and R. J. Hollingdale. New York: Random House.

Nygren, Anders. 1982. *Agape and eros.* Trans. Philip S. Watson. London: SPCK.

Oliver, Kelly. 1991. Kristeva's imaginary father and the crisis in the paternal function. *Diacritics* 21: 46–93.

———. 1993a. *Reading Kristeva: Unraveling the double-bind.* Bloomington: Indiana University Press.

———. (ed.). 1993b. *Ethics, politics, and difference in Julia Kristeva's writings.* New York: Routledge.

———. 1998. *Subjectivity without subjects: From abject fathers to desiring mothers.* Lanham: Rowman & Littlefield.

———. 2001. *Witnessing: Beyond recognition.* London and Minneapolis: University of Minnesota Press.

Reineke, Martha. 1997. *Sacrificed lives: Kristeva on women and violence*. Bloomington and Indianapolis: Indiana University Press.

Riding, Alan. 2001. Correcting her idea of politically correct. *New York Times*. July 14.

Rose, Gillian. 1978. *The melancholy science: An introduction to the thought of Theodor W. Adorno*. Macmillan Press.

Segal, Hanna. 1964. *Introduction to the work of Melanie Klein*. London and New York: Karnac Books. 2002.

Shepherdson, Charles. 1998. The gift of love and the debt of desire. *Differences: A Journal of Feminist Cultural Studies*. 10, 1: 30–74.

———. 2000. *Vital signs: Nature, culture, psychoanalysis*. New York and London: Routledge.

Smith, Anne-Marie. 1998. *Julia Kristeva: Speaking the unspeakable*. London: Pluto Press.

Smith, Paul. 1988. *Discerning the subject*. Minneapolis: University of Minnesota Press.

Warren, Mark. 1988. *Nietzsche and political thought*. Cambridge and London: MIT Press.

Weber, Max. 1919. Science as a vocation. In *From Max Weber: Essays in sociology*. Trans. H. H. Gerth and C. Wright Mills. Oxford: Oxford University Press. 1946.

Weber, Samuel. 1978. *Return to Freud: Jacques Lacan's dislocation of psychoanalysis*. Trans. Michael Levine. Cambridge: Cambridge University Press. 1991.

Whitebook, Joel. 1995. *Perversion and utopia, A study in psychoanalysis and critical theory*. MIT Press.

Whitford, Margaret. 1991. *Luce Irigaray: Philosophy in the feminine*. London and New York: Routledge.

Wilden, Anthony. 1968 (ed.). *Jacques Lacan: The language of the self, the function of language in psychoanalysis*. Trans. A. Wilden. Johns Hopkins University Press.

Winnicott, D. W. 1965. *The maturational processes and the facilitating environment: Studies in the theory of emotional development*. New York: International Universities Press.

———. 1971. *Playing and reality*. New York: Basic Books.

Ziarek, Ewa Plonowska. 2001. *An ethics of dissensus: Postmodernity, feminism, and the politics of radical democracy*. Stanford: Stanford University Press.

INDEX

www.ingramcontent.com/pod-product-compliance
Lightning Source LLC
Chambersburg PA
CBHW030641270326
41929CB00007B/158
* 9 7 8 0 7 9 1 4 6 1 9 0 7 *